THE SBL COMMENTARY ON THE SEPTUAGINT

An Introduction

Septuagint and Cognate Studies

Wolfgang Kraus, General Editor

Number 67

THE SBL COMMENTARY ON THE SEPTUAGINT

An Introduction

Edited by

Dirk Büchner

SBL PRESS

 **PRESS**

Atlanta

Copyright © 2017 by SBL Press

Library of Congress Cataloging-in-Publication Data

Names: Büchner, Dirk, editor.
Title: The SBL commentary on the Septuagint : an introduction / edited by Dirk Büchner.
Description: Atlanta : SBL Press, [2017] | Series: Septuagint and cognate studies ; number 67 | Includes bibliographical references. | Description based on print version record and CIP data provided by publisher; resource not viewed.
Identifiers: LCCN 2017021413 (print) | LCCN 2017022025 (ebook) | ISBN 9780884142430 (ebook) | ISBN 9781628371871 (pbk. : alk. paper) | ISBN 9780884142447 (hardcover : alk. paper)
Subjects: LCSH: Bible. Old Testament. Greek—Versions—Septuagint—Criticism, Textual. | Bible. Old Testament—Translating.
Classification: LCC BS744 (ebook) | LCC BS744 .S25 2017 (print) | DDC 221.4/86—dc23
LC record available at https://lccn.loc.gov/2017021413

Printed on acid-free paper.

Contents

Preface

This volume is the fruit of a process begun with a special session of the Canadian Society of Biblical Studies Annual Meeting in May, 2013 in Victoria, British Columbia, as part of the greater Congress of the Humanities and Social Sciences. Victoria is a stone's throw away from Langley, the location of Trinity Western University and the John William Wevers Institute for Septuagint Studies. The location of the Congress that year enabled the Institute to hold one of its regular colloquia in a larger scholarly environment. The session was dedicated to the theoretical approach of the Society of Biblical Literature Commentary on the Septuagint and its application to a representative spread of translational approaches found in the LXX corpus. Seven contributors to the SBLCS presented a perspective or a chapter of commentary from their assigned books and in the months that followed, scrutinized one another's papers and engaged in further conversations. The chapters as they now appear are the culmination of this valuable process.

A commentary series needs to be clear about its presuppositions and approach, as well as how these are to be put into effect, which is why the volume begins with Albert Pietersma's chapter on what the LXX is and what should be found in the commentator's toolkit. The rest of the contributions present the reader with commentary samples that range from legal material and narrative to wisdom and poetry, as follows: Genesis 1 by Robert Hiebert, Exodus 2 by Larry Perkins, Leuitikon (Leviticus) 3 by Dirk Büchner, Numbers 22 by Spencer Jones, Esther 2 in the Old Greek and the Alpha Text, by Cameron Boyd-Taylor, Iob (Job) 34 by Claude Cox, and Psalm 57 by Jannes Smith.

In each case a careful effort is made to describe and explain the *process* of translation that was followed by each translator as they rendered their *Vorlage* into Greek for the benefit of, and according to the cultural norms of their immediate audiences. In an appendix is found the Preamble to the Guidelines for the Contributors to the Society of Biblical Literature

Commentary on the Septuagint. It is hoped that the volume will serve as a
handbook for commentators in the series, and open up a new perspective
on the delightful quest to discover how the translators went about their
work and what they intended by it.

Acknowledgments

Financial assistance toward the expenses of the conference attendees came from an Aid to Small Universities grant of the Social Sciences and Humanities Research Council of Canada, as well as from the Wevers Institute endowment fund. Thanks are due to Elsie Froment and Sue Funk in the Trinity Western University research office, and to Robert Hiebert as director of the Institute.

It is to Al Pietersma that we owe the conception of the commentary series, with its solid theoretical foundation. Over the past two years he put in a tremendous amount of time to minutely scrutinize each contribution and write copious comments. For his expertise, rigor, and watchful eye we are most grateful, as we are for every other member of the team and their congenial way of sharpening each other's work. Spencer Jones, who was responsible for the final formatting and uniformity of each paper, spent countless hours in conversation with contributors and has been an invaluable helper to us all.

Langley, February 2016

Abbreviations

Technical Abbreviations

*	Greek form is hypothetical
√	root form
1°, 2°, etc.	first occurrence, second occurrence, etc.
1x, 2x, etc.	once, twice, etc.
ca.	circa
esp.	especially
fem.	feminine
Heb.	Hebrew (language)
IO	indirect object
G	Old Greek translator
gen.	genitive
Gk.	Greek (language)
impv.	imperative
κτλ.	καὶ τὰ λοιπά ("and the remaining")
masc.	masculine
MS(S)	manuscript(s)
pers.	person
pers. comm.	personal communication
pl.	plural
PN	proper name
S	subject
sg.	singular
s.v.	*sub verba* ("under the word")
V	verb
Vpass	passive verb

Primary Texts

α′	recension attributed to Aquila
θ′	recension attributed to Theodotion

σ′	recension attributed to Symmachus
Ag.	Aeschylus, *Agamemnon*
A.J.	Josephus, *Antiquitates judaicae*
Anab.	Xenophon, *Anabasis*
Ant.	Sophocles, *Antigone*
Argon.	Apollonius Rhodius, *Argonautica*
Art.	Plutarch, *Artaxerxes*
Autol.	Theophilus of Antioch, *Ad Autolycum*
BdA	Harl, Marguerite, ed. *La Bible d'Alexandrie*. Paris: Cerf, 1986–.
BGU	*Aegyptische Urkunden aus den Königlichen (later Staatlichen) Museen zu Berlin, Griechische Urkunden*
BHK	*Biblia Hebraica*, ed. R. Kittel
BHS	*Biblia Hebraica Stuttgartensia*. Edited by Karl Elliger and Wilhelm Rudolph. Stuttgart: Deutsche Bibelgesellschaft, 1983.
*BHS*app	*Apparatus criticus* to *BHS*
Brenton	Brenton, Lancelot Charles Lee. *The Septuagint Version of the Old Testament: According to the Vatican Text, Translated into English*. London: Bagster, 1844.
Caes.	Plutarch, *Caesar*
Cat.	Aristotle, *Categoriae*
Conf.	Philo, *De confusione linguarum*
Cor.	Plutarch, *Marcius Coriolanus*
Crat.	Plato, *Cratylus*
Cyn.	Xenophon, *Cynegeticus*
Cyr.	Xenophon, *Cyropaedia*
Deipn.	Athenaeus, *Deipnosophistae*
Descr.	Pausanius, *Graeciae descriptio*
El.	Sophocles, *Elektra*
Eq.	Xenophon, *De equitande ratione*
Eth. nic.	Aristotle, *Ethica nicomachea*
Euthyd.	Plato, *Euthydemus*
FGH	*Die Fragmente der griechischen Historiker*. Edited by Felix Jacoby. Leiden: Brill, 1954–1964.
Frag.	*Fragmenta*
Gen. litt.	Augustine, *De Genesi ad litteram*
Geogr.	Strabo, *Geographica*
Haer.	Irenaeus, *Adversus haereses* (*Elenchos*)

Hell.	Xenophon, *Hellenica*
Herm.	Tertullian, *Adversus Hermogenem*
Hist.	*Historiae*
Hom. Phlm.	Chrysostom, *Homiliae in epistulam ad Philemonem*
IG	*Inscriptiones Graecae: Editio Minor.* Berlin: de Gruyter, 1924–.
Il.	Homer, *Iliad*
Leg.	Plato, *Leges*
LXX	Septuagint
LXX.D	Kraus, Wolfgang, and Martin Karrer, eds. *Septuaginta Deutsch: Das griechische Alte Testament in deutscher Übersetzung.* Stuttgart: Deutsche Bibelgesellschaft, 2009.
Mem.	Xenophon, *Memorabilia*
m. Menaḥ.	Mishna Menaḥot
Mos.	Philo, *De vita Mosis*
MT	Masoretic text
NETS	New English Translation of the Septuagint
NJB	New Jerusalem Bible
NRSV	New Revised Standard Version
Oed. tyr.	Sophocles, *Oedipus tyrannus*
Opif.	Philo, *De opificio mundi*
Or. Graec.	Tatian, *Oratio ad Graecos*
Pesh	Peshitta
Phaed.	Plato, *Phaedo*
Phileb.	Plato, *Philebus*
Phoc.	Plutarch, *Phocion*
Praep. ev.	Eusebius, *Praeparatio evangelica*
P.Rev Laws	Papyrus Revenue Laws
Prom.	Aeschylus, *Prometheus vinctus*
Ra	Rahlfs, Alfred. *Septuaginta: Id est Vetus Testamentum graece iuxta LXX interpretes.* Revised by Robert Hanhart. Stuttgart: Deutsche Bibelgesellschaft, 2006.
Rahlfs	Rahlfs, Alfred. *Psalmi cum Odis.* SVTG 10. Göttingen: Vandenhoeck & Ruprecht, 1967.
Rhet. Alex.	Pseudo-Aristotle, *Rhetorica ad Alexandrum*
Sam.	Menander, *Samia*
SamPent	Samaritan Pentateuch
Septim.	Hippocrates, *De septimestri partu*
Sib. Or.	Sibylline Oracles

Sik.	Menander, *Sicyonii fragmenta aliunde nota*
Sp. Laws	Philo, *Special Laws*
Superst.	Plutarch, *De superstitione*
Syh	Syro-hexapla, the Syriac version of Origen's Hexapla
Teb.	Tebtunis Papyrus
Tg. Job	Targum for Job
Tg. Neof.	Targum Neofiti
Tg. Onq.	Targum Onqelos
Tg. Ps.-J.	Targum Pseudo-Jonathan
Them.	Plutarch, *Themistocles*
Tim.	Plato, *Timaeus*; Aeschines, *In Timarchum*
T. Iss.	Testament of Issachar
T. Reu.	Testament of Reuben
Vesp.	Aristophanes, *Vespae*
We^ed	Wevers's Göttingen edition at the pertinent location
Zi	Joseph Ziegler's Göttingen edition at the pertinent location

Secondary Sources

ACCS	Ancient Christian Commentary on Scripture
ACW	Ancient Christian Writers
AASF	Annales Academiae Scientiarum Fennicae
AAU	Acta Universitatis Upsaliensis
AB	Anchor Bible
AnBib	Analecta Biblica
BCOTWP	Baker Commentary on the Old Testament Wisdom and Psalms
BDAG	Danker, Frederick W., Walter Bauer, William F. Arndt, and F. Wilbur Gingrich. *Greek-English Lexicon of the New Testament and Other Early Christian Literature*. 3rd ed. Chicago: University of Chicago Press, 2000.
BDB	Brown, Francis, S. R. Driver, and Charles A. Briggs. *A Hebrew and English Lexicon of the Old Testament*. Oxford: Clarendon, 1907.
BDR	Blass, Friedrich, Albert Debrunner, and Friedrich Rehkopf. *Grammatik des neutestamentlichen Griechisch*. Göttingen: Vandenhoeck & Ruprecht, 1976.
BETL	Bibliotheca Ephermeridum Theologicarum Lovaniensium

Bib	*Biblica*
BIOSCS	*Bulletin of the International Organization for Septuagint and Cognate Studies*
BKAT	Biblischer Kommentar Altes Testament
BSac	*Bibliotheca Sacra*
BTL	Benjamins Translation Library
BTS	Biblical Tools and Studies
BZAW	Beihefte zur Zeitschrift für die alttestamentliche Wissenschaft
CBSC	Cambridge Bible for Schools and Colleges
CGLC	Cambridge Greek and Latin Classics
COut	Commentaar op het Oude Testament
C-S	F. C. Conybeare and St. George Stock. *Grammar of Septuagint Greek*. Grand Rapids: Baker Books, 2010.
CTSRR	College Theology Society Resources in Religion
DCH	Clines, David J. A., ed. *Dictionary of Classical Hebrew*. 9 vols. Sheffield: Sheffield Phoenix, 1993–2016.
DJD	Discoveries in the Judean Desert
DK	Diels, Hermann, and Walther Kranz, eds. *Die Fragmente der Vorsokratiker, griechisch und deutsch*. Zurich: Weidmann, 2004.
ECC	Eerdmans Critical Commentary
EeC	Études et commentaires
EIr	*Encyclopaedia Iranica*. Edited by Ehsan Yarshater. London: Routledge & Kegan Paul, 1982–.
EnAC	Entretiens sur l'antiquite classique
GELS	Muraoka, Takamitsu. *A Greek-English Lexicon of the Septuagint*. Leuven: Peeters, 2009.
GKC	Gesenius, Wilhelm. *Gesenius' Hebrew Grammar*. Edited by Emil Kautzsch. Translated by Arthur E. Cowley. 2nd ed. Oxford: Clarendon, 1910.
GRBS	*Greek, Roman, and Byzantine Studies*
HALOT	Koehler, Ludwig, Walter Baumgartner, and Johann J. Stamm. *The Hebrew and Aramaic Lexicon of the Old Testament*. Translated and edited under the supervision of Mervyn E. J. Richardson. 2 vols. Leiden: Brill, 2001.
HBS	Herders biblische Studien
HCOT	Historical Commentary on the Old Testament
HCS	Hellenistic Culture and Society

HKAT   Handkommentar zum Alten Testament
HRCS   Hatch, Edwin, and Henry A. Redpath. *Concordance to the Septuagint and Other Greek Versions of the Old Testament.* 2 vols. Oxford: Clarendon, 1897. Repr., Grand Rapids: Baker, 1998.
HUCA   *Hebrew Union College Annual*
IBHS   Waltke, Bruce K., and Michael O'Connor. *An Introduction to Biblical Hebrew Syntax.* Winona Lake, IN: Eisenbrauns, 1990.
ICC   International Critical Commentary
JBL   *Journal of Biblical Literature*
JHS   *Journal of Hellenic Studies*
JJS   *Journal of Jewish Studies*
Joüon   Joüon, Paul. *A Grammar of Biblical Hebrew.* Translated and revised by T. Muraoka. 2 vols. Rome: Pontifical Biblical Institute, 1991.
JRitSt   *Journal of Ritual Studies*
JSCS   *Journal of Septuagint and Cognate Studies*
JSJSup   Supplements to the Journal for the Study of Judaism
JSOT   *Journal for the Study of the Old Testament*
JSOTSup   Journal for the Study of the Old Testament Supplement Series
JSS   *Journal of Semitic Studies*
JTS   *Journal of Theological Studies*
KAT   Kommentar zum Alten Testament
L&N   Louw, Johannes P., and Eugene A. Nida, eds. *Greek-English Lexicon of the New Testament: Based on Semantic Domains.* 2nd ed. New York: United Bible Societies, 1989.
LCL   Loeb Classical Library
LEH   Lust, Johan, Erik Eynikel, and Katrin Hauspie, eds. *Greek-English Lexicon of the Septuagint.* Rev. ed. Stuttgart: Deutsche Bibelgesellschaft, 2003.
LHBOTS   Library of Hebrew Bible/Old Testament Studies
LSJ   Liddell, Henry George, Robert Scott, and Henry Stuart Jones. *A Greek-English Lexicon.* 9th ed. with revised supplement. Oxford: Clarendon, 1996.
Mayser   Mayser, Edwin. *Grammatik der griechischen Papyri aus der Ptolemäerzeit.* 2 vols. Berlin: de Gruyter, 1906–1933.
MM   Moulton, James H., and George Milligan. *The Vocabulary*

	of the Greek Testament. London: Hodder and Stoughton, 1929. Repr., Peabody, MA: Hendrickson, 1997.
MSU	Mitteilungen des Septuaginta-Unternehmens
NIDOTTE	VanGemeren, Willem A., ed. *New International Dictionary of Old Testament Theology and Exegesis.* 5 vols. Grand Rapids: Zondervan, 1997.
NRSV	New Revised Standard Version
OBO	Orbis Biblicus et Orientalis
OLA	Orientalia Lovaniensia Analecta
OTL	Old Testament Library
RHR	*Revue de l'histoire des religions*
RVV	Religionsgeschichtliche Versuche und Vorarbeiten
SBLCS	Society of Biblical Literature Commentary on the Septuagint
SBLDS	Society of Biblical Literature Dissertation Series
SBLPS	Society of Biblical Literature Pseudepigrapha Series
SBLTT	Society of Biblical Literature Texts and Translations
SCS	Septuagint and Cognate Studies
Smyth	Smyth, Herbert W. *Greek Grammar for Colleges.* Revised by Gordon M. Messing. Cambridge: Harvard University Press, 1956.
Suppl.	Aeschylus *Supplices*
SVTG	Septuaginta: Vetus Testamentum Graecum
SVTP	Studia in Veteris Testamenti Pseudepigraphica
TAPA	*Transactions of the American Philological Association*
TDOT	*Theological Dictionary of the Old Testament.* Edited by G. Johannes Botterweck and Helmer Ringgren. Translated by John T. Willis et al. 16 vols. Grand Rapids: Eerdmans, 1974–2006.
THB	Text of the Hebrew Bible
Thackeray	Thackeray, Henry St. J. *A Grammar of the Old Testament in Greek according to the Septuagint.* Cambridge: Cambridge University Press, 1909.
TLG	*Thesaurus Linguae Graecae*
TLZ	*Theologische Literaturzeitung*
VT	*Vetus Testamentum*
VTSup	Supplements to Vetus Testamentum
WBC	Word Biblical Commentary

WMANT   Wissenschaftliche Monographien zum Alten und Neuen
             Testament
WUNT   Wissenschaftliche Untersuchungen zum Neuen Testa-
             ment
ZAW   *Zeitschrift für die alttestamentliche Wissenschaft*

The Society of Biblical Literature Commentary on the Septuagint: Basic Principles

Albert Pietersma

Introduction

After a long gestation period, the Guidelines for producing the Society of Biblical Literature Commentary on the Septuagint were finalized in 2013. Later that year a Septuagint section was organized within the congress of the Canadian Society of Biblical Studies (CSBS) for the purpose of discussing and demonstrating the application of the Guidelines to the writing of the commentary.

In this introductory paper I will limit myself to the Preamble of the Guidelines, which delineates a series of four principles, each with its own explanatory subsections (for the text of the Preamble, see the appendix at the end of this volume). But even here I will be selective.

A Backward Glance

The commentary series now labeled "SBLCS" was effectively conceived in 1995/1996 when a committee of the International Organization for Septuagint and Cognate Studies (IOSCS) was struck to create a prospectus for a commentary series on the anthology commonly known as the Septuagint (LXX) or the Old Greek (OG). The prospectus was published in 1998 (Pietersma 1998), and the commentary was formally sponsored by the IOSCS in 1999.[1] Like the SBLCS Guidelines, the preamble of the earlier prospectus delineates a series of principles, five in number (see

---

* My thanks to Cameron Boyd-Taylor for critiquing this paper. Any mistakes or infelicities that remain are mine alone.

1. The members of the planning Committee were Albert Pietersma (convener),

http://ccat.sas.upenn.edu/ioscs/commentary/). Although these principles were honed and reformulated for the current Guidelines, there is an obvious conceptual connection between the two sets of principles. Furthermore, an equally obvious link has, from the beginning, existed between NETS and the commentary series under whatever title. One might here speak of a continuum from NETS to SBLCS, or as two stages of a single interpretive effort (e.g., Pietersma 2004, 1008).

The Text-as-Produced and the Text-as-Received

I can think of no more important distinction in the NETS approach than the axiomatic distinction between, on the one hand, the text-as-produced and, on the other, the text-as-received (Pietersma 2005, 2008, 2010), and it is for this reason that the Preamble of the Guidelines begins with this distinction. I quote:

> The objective of the Society of Biblical Literature Commentary on the Septuagint (SBLCS) is to elucidate the meaning of the text-as-produced in distinction from the text-as-received. "Meaning," however, is neither to be presupposed nor to be superimposed from either the source text or the text-as-received.

The distinction may be called "axiomatic" because it is part and parcel of the historical study of literature and a starting point for diachronic inquiry, whether the literature be (original) composition or (derived) translation. As it applies to translation literature, it references, in a nutshell, the translated text as an entity *dependent* on its source text (Guidelines 1.1.1) in distinction from the translated text, cut loose from its historical moorings, and therefore a *free standing* text, or "the text in its own right," as it is sometimes called.

In the NETS approach the text-as-received or the text in its own right or the text as a freestanding entity alongside its source text is *never* in view—except as a text to be ignored or, perhaps, to be noted as a *curiosum* of what happened to the text-as-produced in reception history.[2] In fact, we

---

Claude Cox, Moises Silva, Benjamin Wright, David Aiken, and John W. Wevers (consultant); the publication of *BIOSCS* was a year behind schedule.

2. Broadly speaking the reception history of the Greek text may be divided into Jewish reception history in distinction from Christian reception history. Although the

can go one step farther and say that the text in its own right has no role to play in the study of the Old Greek *qua translation,* even though it is its logical and historical extension. Instead, as an independent text, standing alongside its erstwhile source, it belongs to the reception history of the Hebrew Bible as a literary document. While genealogically the Greek text remains perforce a translation forever, genetically it ceases to be one when it becomes a text in its own right.

This distinction needs to be stressed the more since, if my experience is any indication, a failure to distinguish between these quite different Greek texts or a failure to delineate them as clearly as possible typically leads to a schizophrenic approach to the LXX—treating it *now* as a translation and *then* as a text in its own right, both within a single study.[3]

Some of the reasons for this confusion are not far to seek. The first is probably the common interpreter's pitfall of trying to make a text say more than what is justified by its linguistic make-up, especially when one is dealing with a translation of formal correspondence. Another may well be inherent in the general act of writing a commentary, when the common assumption must surely be that the text on which one is about to write a commentary is a fully fledged text, a discourse in written form, which, qua discourse, may be expected to cohere as a unit. While it can scarcely be denied that such units exist in the translated corpus and can in fact be said to exist aplenty, even though many of these may be small or even *very* small in scope, in the light of the constitutive character or the verbal make-up of all the translated books and the *interlinear assumption* of the NETS approach, textual coherence cannot be *presupposed* to exist but must be *shown* to exist. It is clear, therefore, where the burden of proof must lie.[4]

Letter of Aristeas (ca. 130 BCE) looms large on the Jewish side, the oldest extant evidence hails from Demetrius the Chronographer in the late third century BCE. Christian reception history commences effectively with the earliest Christian writings. For the possible use of reception history see further Prospectus, Principle (2).

3. Needless to say, the distinction applies to *all* translations, whether that be an English translation of a novel by Dostoevky or a Dutch translation of one of Shakespeare's plays. One can either study them qua translation, in which case the translation is mapped onto its original and is studied for interference by the source text, or one can study them as freestanding texts in their own right, apart from or alongside of the text from which they were derived.

4. Cameron Boyd-Taylor (2015, 138) felicitously speaks of interlinearity as a theory of interference. If Toury is correct in arguing that the law of interference is the norm in translations, the question is not *whether* interference occurred but *how*

According to the NETS approach, the amount and kind of interference from the source text in the translated text warrants the interlinear paradigm. This does *not* mean that, de facto, all translated books or individual books in their entirety are characterized by interlinearity from beginning to end. Nor does it mean that it can be dismissed as an interpretive straitjacket or a theory of LXX origins. But what it *does* mean is that, since the text displays characteristics of interlinearity, in descriptive terms interlinearity forms its baseline, and that it is a powerful heuristic tool for the modern interpreter.

Now, if the assumption of textual cohesion and coherence is part and parcel of the writing of commentaries, it should occasion no surprise that a commentator on the text-as-produced is always in mortal danger of getting derailed or of "falling off the wagon" (so to speak), either on the side of the source text—with the result that the commentary turns out to be more about the Hebrew text than about the Greek text-as-produced, or on the side of the Greek text-as-received, that is to say, the text as an independent, free-standing entity, where, for example, items from a source at variance with MT are no longer so perceived; where the translator's mistakes and instances of ignorance of the source language no longer exist; where the unintelligible tends to become intelligible; where coincidental instances of alliteration and other potentially literary flourishes are happily ascribed to the translator's intent; where examples of reputed intertextuality tend to be pointed out in great number, even though they are nothing more than inadvert by-products of Greek-Hebrew defaults and thus instances of interference from the source text.[5] In short, interference from the source text does not exist in the text-as-received.[6]

---

much and *of what kind*. His formulation is: "in translation, phenomena pertaining to the make-up of the source text tend to be transferred to the target text." Toury further argues that between translational and nontranslational modes of text production and language use, there exists a basic functional opposition (Toury 1995, 275 and 216, respectively).

5. It bears underscoring that, in the text-as-produced, intertextuality can only occur (1) at the level of the translated (Greek) texts (2) and can only be demonstrated to exist when translated texts agree despite their respective source texts. Needless to say, thematic similarity or identity can seldom be considered intertextual, since it typically belongs to the source text.

6. To be distinguished from "linguistic strangeness," often thought of as a mark of Holy Writ or even the language of the Holy Spirit.

As it happens, I have recently had occasion to read Eric Zenger's Hermeneia commentary on the so-called Psalms of Ascent (Hossfeld and Zenger 2011).[7] At the end of each of the Psalms, Zenger has a few pages on the corresponding Greek psalm. His comments on the psalm in Greek are often of interest, despite being selective. The problem is that, although his vantage point is patently that of the text-as-received, he typically assigns what he finds to the text-as-produced. Thus, he repeatedly gets derailed or falls off the wagon, on the side of the Greek text "in its own right." Alternatively, one could say that he makes the mistake of superimposing the text-as-received on the text–as-produced or, to put it yet another way, he ascribes far more to the text-as-produced than it can linguistically bear.[8]

A commentary like Zenger's offers a good transition to my next point, namely, that, within the modern history of our discipline with its pronounced New Testament dimension, the LXX is regularly construed as the Old Testament of the New Testament, witness, for example, the titles of both Swete's (1909–1922) and Rahlfs's (2006) popular editions. From this perspective, it is scarcely surprising that the reigning paradigm in LXX studies tends to be that of a translation which has replaced its source text, rather than a text dependent upon it (Guidelines 1.1.1); hence a text *in its own righ*t, a text to be placed alongside of other texts in *their* own right qua documents, like the Hebrew Bible, the New Testament, the Peshitta or whatever text *in its own right* one might care to add. The reason for this paradigm is, no doubt, as Cameron Boyd-Taylor has aptly put it, that what is wanted from this perspective is a translator one can talk to, one with whom the modern reader can carry on a conversation (pers. comm., February 23, 2013).

Not without interest is the fact that this perspective is epitomized by the title of the Göttingen Septuagint, namely, *Septuaginta: Vetus Testamentum Graecum*, perpetuated from Alfred Rahlfs's 1931 edition of the Psalms and the Odes (Rahlfs 1931). Even more noteworthy is that it bears this title

---

7. In the Greek these psalms are called the Psalms of the Steps.

8. For a random example see Ps 125(126).1bc, which speak of return from exile and of being comforted (παρακαλέω). According to Zenger (2011, 378), G is here drawing on Esa 40.1–2; 51.12; 53.9 (*sic*) because these passages also speak of return and use of παρακαλέω. Strangely he makes no mention of the fact that παρακαλέω in Ps 125.1c renders חלם, as it does in Esa 38.16.

despite the fact that it offers a reconstructed original of a text that predated the early Church by several centuries.[9]

All of the above is *not* to say that, in principle, one cannot write a commentary on the Greek as a text in its own right (even though methodological problems loom large), but it *is* to say that doing so is an undertaking quite distinct from writing a commentary on the LXX qua translation, that is, qua text-as-produced. Similarly, the above does not deny that the Greek became the Old Testament of the New Testament, nor does it deny that it played a mediating role between the Hebrew Bible and the New Testament, but it *is* to question the *nature* of such mediation.

What has become patently obvious is that, for our commentator on the text-as-produced, it is far easier to fall off the wagon than to stay on it, to get derailed rather than to remain on track. Or, to use a different metaphor, to write a commentary on the text-as-produced is like sailing between Scylla and Charybdis. Whether one shipwrecks on the one or on the other is immaterial. A shipwreck is a shipwreck by any name.

The Text-as-Produced

But if, as the Guidelines state, it is the text-as-produced that is the object of the commentary, how then does one access it for commentary and what label might one attach to it? As I have already intimated, the text-as-produced can only be accessed by mapping the Greek text onto its Hebrew (or Aramaic) source text. As for a label—part of the answer is to point out what the text-as-produced is *not*. First, as noted, it is *not* the text-as-received, that is, it is not conceptualized as a text in its own right, but rather as a text that is *compositionally* dependent on its source text, as the Guidelines rightly insist (Guidelines §1.1.1). What that means essentially is that the translator does not undertake to compose his own discourse but renders, in some fashion or other, the discourse of his source text into his own linguistic medium. And this applies to *all* translations within the corpus, regardless of textual-linguistic make-up, that is to say, from Ecclesiastes to Greek Job (see n. 3, above).

Second, as noted, it is *not* Vetus Testamentum Graecum. In whatever form the pre-Christian LXX became the Holy Writ of the Christian

---

9. See as well *Septuaginta Deutsch: Das griechische Alte Testament*; *La Bible d'Alexandrie*; and *La Biblia Griega: Septuaginta*; *La Bibbia dei Settanta*.

Church, in terms of both text-form and text-semantics, it was *no doubt* distinct from its ancient forebear. Nor, for that matter, did the translation, upon inception, automatically become Jewish Scripture (see Guidelines §4.14). As Gideon Toury writes, "There is no way a translation could share the same systemic space with its original; not even when the two are physically side by side." (Toury 1995, 26; see also Honigman 2003, 95).

Third, it is *not*—until proven otherwise—a fully fledged, full-scale text, a discourse in written form. Rather, it is typically a fragmentary text, a text with all kinds of holes in it, despite interpretive nuggets among them. Time and again, for example, when the translator uses nothing but default equivalents and conveys nothing of local or general interest, the commentator is left with nothing to say—except perhaps just how many times Greek X translates Hebrew Y.[10] What this means is that a commentary on the text-as-produced cannot be expected to look like a commentary on the text in its own right. For that reason one might best think of the text-as-produced as *a text between texts,* the Semitic source text, on the one side, and the freestanding Greek text on the other.

The text-as-produced—the text *between* texts—may usefully be described as a two-dimensional text. On the horizontal plane morphemes are knit together into syntactic units to convey information; on the vertical plane the *parent* text forms the de facto context for meaning. As a result of excessive one-for-one dependence on the source text, the target text may be rendered disjointed or worse. À propos here is Northrop Frye's distinction between the literary genres of the modern novel and sentimental romance. Whereas in the novel as a realistic narrative the writer attempts to keep the action horizontal, using the technique of causality to keep the narrative moving from within, romance "moves from one discontinuous episode to another, describing things that happen to characters, for the most part, externally" (Frye 1976, 47; see also Pietersma 2013b, 158–60). The implication of the text's two-dimensionality for lexicography and grammaticography should be obvious.

Crucial for determining the linguistic make-up of the text-as-produced, or rather its *constitutive character*, is, on the one hand, to map the translated text onto its source text, in order to establish what sort of translation one is dealing with, and, on the other, to consult Greek composition

---

10. This is not to say, however, that such information is of no importance, since it falls, after all, into the category of interference from the source text and it is the study of such interference that is the primary focus of the study of the Greek text qua translation.

literature of the period in order to determine what sort of Greek document it is (Guidelines §1.3.2). With Boyd-Taylor we might here speak of the *text qua translation* in distinction from the *translation qua text* (Boyd-Taylor 2011, 432).[11] Put the results of these two analyses together and one has the foundation for formulating one's interpretive procedures (Guidelines §1.1.2).[12]

As the Preamble indicates in several places, compositional dependence is balanced by semantic autonomy (Guidelines Introduction; §§1.1.1; 1.2.1). It begins by noting that meaning cannot be presupposed. What does this statement mean? James Barr has shown long ago that, distributed throughout most of the translated LXX, are instances in which translators may be said to decode the source text but effectively do not recode it in the target language, as a result of which they can be said to *represent* the source text rather to *translate* it. Therefore—so Barr—the mantra that translation is always interpretation is a "highly misleading truism" (Barr 1979, 16).[13] Similarly, according to the NETS approach, the text-as-produced includes fragments that are unintelligible (Guidelines §1.3.3). Although certain elements of the source text are clearly *represented* and a given piece may even be grammatical, it cannot be said to communicate information. Although these pieces constitute a minority, they cannot for that reason be swept under the rug, any more than instances of negative transfer in grammaticography and lexicography. In a similar vein, Martin Flashar, a century ago, spoke of *Verlegenheitsübersetzungen*, translations of last resort (Flashar 1912, 113). Since all such items are in the text, they belong to the text and are part of its *constitutive character* and as such refuse to be ignored. In point of fact, any explanatory paradigm of the text that cannot accommodate them must be considered to have been found wanting.

At first blush, the statement that meaning cannot be *presupposed* and that it cannot be *superimposed* on the text-as-produced (from the source text or from the text-as-received) may seem at cross-purposes. In fact they point to the same principle the NETS approach insists upon, namely, that the Greek of the text-as-produced *must* be taken seriously *as Greek*, whether it be standard or stilted usage, literary nuggets or linguistic warts, instances of intelligibility or unintelligibility, it is all Greek!

---

11. He speaks of the two dialectically related concepts as axioms for exegesis.

12. For "levels of interpretation," see Pietersma 2013e, 212–27.

13. For an excellent exposition of Barr's typology in relation to interlinearity see Boyd-Taylor 2008b and 2015; see also Pietersma 2013a, 362–65.

There is no tolerant reader who can be counted upon to transform translationese Greek into living language. Accordingly, semantic autonomy indicates that the text means what it means "in terms of *conventional* linguistic usage (i.e., the grammar and lexicon of the target language) rather than in terms of what may be encountered in translation Greek" (Guidelines §§1.2; 1.2.1). Here we have what I see as the second most important implication of the NETS approach for the writing of the commentary.

Grammaticography and Lexicography

The key phrase in Guidelines §1.2 is "*conventional* linguistic usage," and it is *conventional* usage that is the domain of the disciplines of grammaticography and lexicography. In fact, the two stand or fall together. I begin with the former since, if there is ever going to be a Grammar of the LXX worthy of the title, it has not as yet been written, and that for a very good reason. No doubt as commentators on the LXX, we are all familiar with peculiar grammatical constructions that arise not from straightforward, creative, use of language but rather from a mimicking of the Semitic source text. Since these, like instances of lexical unintelligibility, are an integral part of the text-as-produced, they belong to its constitutive character. Toury refers to them as instances of negative transfer, that is, usage that violates Greek linguistic code (Toury 1995, 274–79).[14] By definition, negative transfer does not constitute conventional usage but rather the opposite. To the extent that such instances of negative transfer can be reflected in English translation, NETS has attempted to do so. In any case, they are grist for the commentary mill, since use of language is a clear component of writing a commentary. When one adds to the phenomenon of negative transfer in grammar the factors of positive transfer, that is, overuse of viable Greek constructions because they mimic the source language, as well as the less than straightforward use of language we typically find in the target text, it is scarcely a surprise that a grammar of the LXX has been so long in coming. To put it another way, a *separate* grammar for an anthology of texts presupposes creative use of language, but it is precisely creative use of language that is in rather short supply in our anthology of

---

14. To be noted further is that whereas in composition literature unintelligibility is routinely attributed to the vicissitudes of transmission history, in translation literature, especially in the LXX, it may well be original, as suggested by the text-critical principle, *lectio difficilior preferenda est.*

translated texts. Thus the question is whether a distinctive grammar for such an anthology makes sense or is even viable.

As intimated above, from LXX grammaticography it is a very small step to LXX lexicography. In this area, however, the discipline now not only has LEH (before LEH we of course had Schleusner 1820–1821), but also and more importantly, *GELS*. Ostensibly, therefore, our discipline is well served. While the two lexica espouse different methods in lexicography, from the perspective of the NETS approach they fall nevertheless in the same category.[15] I will therefore focus only on *GELS*. As in grammaticography so in lexicography, *separate* treatment of the subject presupposes straightforward and creative use of language.

John Lee in his recent review of Muraoka's lexicon rightly notes that *GELS* is not a lexicon of the LXX *as-produced* (Lee 2010). But if that is correct—and I hold that it is—one may well ask, What *is* it a lexicon of, if not of the LXX as produced, that is to say, the LXX *as a translation*? Unfortunately, Lee, despite his seminal article in *Glotta* over forty years ago (1969), does not ask this question and thus fails to apply his earlier insight to the lexicography of the LXX.[16] Instead, he simply cites Muraoka to the effect that the lexicon caters to the reader of circa "250 B.C.–100 A.D. who was ignorant of Hebrew or Aramaic" (Lee 2010, 118). Consequently, instead of being a lexicon of the LXX *qua translation*, it is patently a lexicon of the LXX *qua text*, namely, the translation cut loose from its historical moorings and, therefore, the text in its own right. But if, as I noted earlier, the LXX as a freestanding text, standing alongside the Hebrew Bible and the New Testament, is irrelevant to the study of the LXX *qua translation*, must not the same be concluded about a *lexicon* of that very same text?

Consider the following. If it be true that both grammaticography and lexicography record *conventional* usage—and if that is controversial, I am not aware of it—it can only mean that in the process of writing a lexicon (or a grammar) on the *text-as-received*, namely, the text *in its own right*, the latter is summarily declared to constitute *conventional* usage. But how can such a declaration be justified, any more than it can be justified in the case of LSJ's typical entries on the LXX? While *GELS* is not LSJ and *GELS* has taken important steps to distance itself from LSJ, the distance is, from the NETS perspective, one of degree rather than of kind, since the

---

15. For an interesting discussion involving both, see Büchner 2009.
16. For an exposé of this article with Lee's public endorsement, see Pietersma 2012.

same lexicographical principle remains in full force, namely, that context (*any* context) determines meaning. Furthermore, *GELS* blurs the distinction between the text-as-produced and the text-as-received by inventing the tolerant reader who magically transforms nonconventional usage to conventional usage.[17] I use *magically* advisedly because to assume that an individual reader can bring about such a transformation and can thus institutionalize language use on the fly is nothing short of magical (see Boyd-Taylor 2001, 53, 55, 73–74).[18]

Thus our commentator in the areas of both grammar and lexicon is apparently faced with a dilemma: either, by personal fiat, one declares *nonconventional* usage to be *conventional* usage and thus blatantly transgresses the law of conventionality, or one contests the rule of the law of conventionality as it applies to translation literature of the kind we have in the Old Greek. There is, however, a perfectly principled solution to the problem.

In his *Glotta* article of 1969, referenced above, Lee argues that certain semantic components in the 1968 *Supplement* to the Liddell-Scott-Jones Lexicon fail to stand up to methodological scrutiny (Liddell, Scott, and Jones 1968). To show the seminal nature of Lee's article I can do no better than to cite the example with which he begins his argumentation, namely, ψυχή in Gen 12.5, which on the strength of that verse (and a reputed example from 1 Makk 10.33) is assigned the added semantic component of "slave."[19] While it happens to be true that the reference of ψυχή in this verse is to a bought individual, rather than being determined by contextual considerations, it is triggered instead by the occurrence of נפש in the source text.[20] The problem here is that, as Lee points out, the *Supplement*

---

17. For the same concept, see Troxel 2008, 57, 61. For an assessment of this book see, Pietersma 2013c. To introduce the tolerant reader into the LXX qua translation is like introducing, by the back door, Henry S. Gehman's notion of the LXX having been written in Jewish Alexandrian Greek. At least Charles Thomson, when translating the LXX (1808), was up front about his working assumption that the LXX was a composition in Greek rather than a translation from Semitic (see Muses 1954, xi–xii).

18. Boyd-Taylor questions the viability of *any* lexicon of the LXX. On the one hand, the text-as-produced lacks a creatively conventional dimension that might warrant separate treatment and, on the other hand, the usage of the text-as-received that might warrant separate treatment turns out to be patently nonconventional.

19. The *Supplement* includes 1 Makk 10.33, but there we lack a source text.

20. As a result, the de facto context is the Hebrew. Differently put, the *Supplement* superimposes the sense of the Hebrew onto the Greek. While ψυχή, in time, might have developed the sense of "slave," we have no evidence that it ever did.

violates a standard principle in lexicography, namely, the distinction
between sense (a word's conventional meaning, to be recorded in a dic-
tionary) and reference (the referent it has in a specific context). More
importantly, in terms of the NETS approach, ψυχή in Gen 12.5 belongs
to the Greek text's *vertical* dimension, not to its *horizontal* dimension.[21]
Thus what we are dealing with here is not simply a failure to distinguish
between "sense" and "reference" but, more importantly, a failure to reckon
with the fact that, throughout the LXX, Greek ψυχή is a stereotypical rendering of Hebrew נפש. That is to say, the lexical choice is not based on
contextual appropriateness but on vertical demand.

I spoke of a perfectly principled solution to our commentator's problem. Given that the translated text has a vertical dimension, which, at
times, overrides its horizontal dimension, it makes no sense to insist at
all costs on the principle that, in lexicography (and grammaticography),
context determines meaning and rules supreme. Given that interference
from the source text is the rule rather than the exception and that the
interlinear assumption can accommodate all aspects of the translated text
(whereas the compositional assumption cannot), there is every reason to
avail oneself of interlinearity as a heuristic tool to explain the text, the
more when doing so accords with Occam's law of parsimony. That is to
say, when a word is used not because it suits the context of the target text
but because the source is seen as demanding it, no explanation is more
parsimonious than the assumption of interlinearity, an essential tool in
our commentator's toolbox (see Boyd-Taylor 2006, 2008, 2011 for more
on interlinearity).

Concretely, one will do well never to rely on a single lexicon, or on two
of the same kind, such as *GELS* and LEH. Moreover, every word definition
that does not fall within the semantic range of compositional usage should
be deemed *sub iudice*. As a rule of thumb, no lexical sense in the translated
LXX should be considered conventional usage unless it is attested in composition literature.

---

21. While *GELS* rightly ignores the semantic component of "slave" in Gen 12.5,
presumably because ψυχή is not a contextual misfit, it records ψυχή with the sense
of "corpse" in Leu 22.4 et al. While subentry 4 is duly marked with an asterisk (*),
indicating that this sense does not predate the LXX and thus has limited distribution,
it is included all the same as a bona fide semantic component, even though it occurs
exclusively in translation literature.

Flashar long ago suggested that a translator's semantic intent can typically be found where paired Hebrew and Greek lexemes intersect (Flashar 1912, 92). In an effort to formalize and restrict undisciplined recourse to the source text, NETS raised Flashar's suggestion to the level of principle, namely, the principle of the source text as arbiter of meaning. That is to say, the source text can be used to arbitrate between established meanings in the target language but *cannot* be used to create new meanings. Thus, far from superimposing the meaning of the Hebrew text onto the Greek, it in fact safeguards the Greek qua Greek.[22]

Conclusion

While the SBLCS Guidelines are about more than the text-as-produced in distinction from the text-as-received and conventional use of language versus nonconventional use, these two issues nonetheless play a central role. To the extent that that is correct, commentators will neglect them at their peril.

Bibliography

Barr, James. 1979. *The Typology of Literalism in Ancient Biblical Translations.* MSU 15. Göttingen: Vandenhoeck & Ruprecht.

Boyd-Taylor, Cameron. 2001. "The Evidentiary Value of Septuagintal Usage for Greek Lexicography: Alice's Reply to Humpty Dumpty." *BIOSCS* 34:47–80.

———. 2006. "In a Mirror, Dimly: Reading the Septuagint as a Document of Its Times." Pages 15–32 in *Septuagint Research: Issues and Challenges in the Study of the Greek Jewish Scriptures.* Edited by Wolfgang Kraus and R. Glenn Wooden. SCS 53. Atlanta: Society of Biblical Literature.

———. 2008a. "An Ear for an Eye—Lay Literacy and the Septuagint." Pages 127–46 in *Scripture in Transition: Essays on Septuagint, Hebrew Bible and Dead Sea Scrolls in Honour of Raija Sollamo.* Edited by Anssi Voitila and Jutta Jokiranta. JSJSup 126. Leiden: Brill.

———. 2008b. "Who Is Afraid of *Verlegenheitsübersetzungen*?" Pages 197–210 in *Translating a Translation: The LXX and Its Modern Translations*

---

22. For a specious misconstrual of this principle, see Muraoka 2008, 224. For a response to Muraoka's paper, see Pietersma 2013d.

in the Context of Early Judaism. Edited by Hans Ausloos, J. Cook, F. García Martínez, B. Lemmelijn, and M. Vervenne. BETL 213. Leuven: Peeters.

———. 2011. *Reading between the Lines: The Interlinear Paradigm for Septuagint Studies*. BTS 8. Leuven: Peeters.

———. 2015. "The Classification of Literalism in Ancient Hebrew-Greek Translation." Pages 121–42 in *Die Sprache der Septuaginta/The Language of the Septuagint*. Edited by Martin Karrer, Wolfgang Kraus, and Siegfried Kreuzer. Gütersloh: Gütersloher Verlagshaus.

Büchner, Dirk. 2009. "A Cultic Term (ἁμαρτία) in the Septuagint: Its Meaning and Use from the Third Century B.C.E until the New Testament." *BIOSCS* 42:1–17.

Flashar, Martin. 1912. "Exegetische Studien zum Septuagintapsalter," *ZAW* 32:81–116, 161–89, 241–68.

Frye, Northrop. 1976. *The Secular Scripture: A Study of the Structure of Romance*. Cambridge: Harvard University Press.

Honigman, Sylvie. 2003. *Septuagint and Homeric Scholarship in Alexandria: A Study in the Narrative of the Letter of Aristeas*. New York: Routledge.

Hossfeld, Frank Lothar, and Eric Zenger. 2011. *Psalms 3: A Commentary on Psalms 101–150*. Translated by Linda M. Maloney. Hermeneia. Minneapolis: Fortress.

Lee, John A. L. 1969. "A Note on Septuagint Material in the Supplement to Liddell and Scott." *Glotta* 47:234–42.

———. 2010. Review of *A Greek-English Lexicon of the Septuagint*, by T. Muraoka. *BIOSCS* 43:115–25.

Liddell, H. G., Robert Scott, and H. Stuart Jones. 1968. *A Greek-English Lexicon: A Supplement*. Edited by E. A. Barber. Oxford: Clarendon.

Muraoka, Takamitsu. 2008. "Recent Discussions on the Septuagint Lexicography with Special Reference to the So-called Interlinear Model." Pages 221–35 in *Die Septuaginta: Texte, Kontexte, Lebenswelten*. Edited by Martin Karrer and Wolfgang Kraus. WUNT 219. Tübingen: Mohr Siebeck.

Muses, Charles A., ed. 1954. *The Septuagint Bible: The Oldest Version of the Old Testament in the Translation of Charles Thomson*. Indian Hill, CO: Falcon's Wing Press.

Pietersma, Albert. 1998. "A Prospectus for a Commentary on the Septuagint." *BIOSCS* 31:43–48.

————. 2004. "A New English Translation of the Septuagint and a Commentary to Follow." *TLZ* 129:1008–16.

————. 2005. "The Seven Voices of the Lord: A Commentary on Septuagint Psalm 28." Pages 311–29 in *Interpreting Translation: Studies on the LXX and Ezekiel in Honour of Johan Lust.* Edited by F. García Martínez and M. Vervenne. BETL 192. Leuven: Peeters.

————. 2008. "Text-Production and Text-Reception: Psalm 8 in Greek." Pages 487–501 in *Die Septuaginta: Texte, Kontexte, Lebenswelten.* Edited by Martin Karrer and Wolfgang Kraus. WUNT 219. Tübingen: Mohr Siebeck.

————. 2010. "A Commentary on Psalm 15 in Greek: Text-Production and Text Reception." Pages 523–42 in *Die Septuaginta: Texte Theologien, Einflüsse.* Edited by Wolfgang Kraus and Martin Karrer. WUNT 252. Tübingen: Mohr Siebeck.

————. 2012. "Context Is King in Septuagint Lexicography—Or is It?" http://homes.chass.utoronto.ca/~pietersm/ContextisKing(2012).pdf.

————. 2013a. "Beyond Literalism: Interlinearity Revisited." Pages 359–78 in *A Question of Methodology: Albert Pietersma Collected Essays on the Septuagint.* Edited by Cameron Boyd-Taylor. BTS 14. Leuven: Peeters.

————. 2013b. "A New Paradigm for Addressing Old Questions: The Relevance of the Interlinear Model for the Study of the Septuagint." Pages 143–70 in *A Question of Methodology: Albert Pietersma Collected Essays on the Septuagint.* Edited by Cameron Boyd-Taylor. BTS 14. Leuven: Peeters.

————. 2013c. "A Panel Presentation on Ronald Troxel's *LXX-Isaiah.*" Pages 339–58 in *A Question of Methodology: Albert Pietersma Collected Essays on the Septuagint.* Edited by Cameron Boyd-Taylor. BTS 14. Leuven: Peeters.

————. 2013d. "A Response to Muraoka's Critique of Interlinearity." Pages 315–37 in *A Question of Methodology: Albert Pietersma Collected Essays on the Septuagint.* Edited by Cameron Boyd-Taylor. BTS 14. Leuven: Peeters.

————. 2013e. "Septuagintal Exegesis and the Superscriptions of the Greek Psalter." Pages 203–27 in *A Question of Methodology: Albert Pietersma Collected Essays on the Septuagint.* Edited by Cameron Boyd-Taylor. BTS 14. Leuven: Peeters.

Pietersma, Albert, and Benjamin G. Wright, eds. 2007. *A New English Translation of the Septuagint and the Other Greek Translations Tradi-*

tionally Included under That Title. Oxford: Oxford University Press. For updates, see the online version at http://ccat.sas.upenn.edu/nets/.

Rahlfs, Alfred. 1931. *Psalmi cum Odis*. SVTG 10. Göttingen: Vandenhoeck & Ruprecht.

———. 2006. *Septuaginta: Id est Vetus Testamentum graecum iuxta LXX interpretes*. Revised by Robert Hanhart. Stuttgart: Deutsche Bibelgesellschaft.

Schleusner, J. F. 1820–1821. *Novus Thesaurus philologico-criticus, sive lexicon in LXX. et reliquos interpretes Græcos ac Scriptores Apocryphos Veteris Testamenti*. Leipzig.

Swete, Henry Barclay. 1909–1922. *The Old Testament in Greek according to the Septuagint*. 3 vols. Cambridge: Cambridge University Press.

Toury, Gideon. 1995. *Descriptive Translation Studies and Beyond*. BTL 100. Amsterdam: Benjamins.

Troxel, Ronald L. 2008. *LXX-Isaiah as Translation and Interpretation: The Strategies of the Translator of the Septuagint of Isaiah*. JSJSup 124. Leiden: Brill.

In the Beginning: A Commentary on the Old Greek Text of Genesis 1.1–2.3

Robert J. V. Hiebert

Literature

Augustine. 1982. *The Literal Meaning of Genesis*. Vol. 1. ACW 41. Translated and annotated by John Hammond Taylor. New York: Paulist Press. ◆ **Brayford**, Susan. 2007. *Genesis*. Septuagint Commentary Series 5. Leiden: Brill. ◆ **Brown**, William P. 1993. *Structure, Role, and Ideology in the Hebrew and Greek Texts of Genesis 1:1–2:3*. SBLDS 132. Atlanta: Scholars Press. ◆ **Cassuto**, Umberto. 1961. *A Commentary on the Book of Genesis: From Adam to Noah*. Translated by I. Abrahams. Jerusalem: Magnes. ◆ **Davila**, James R. 1990. "New Qumran Readings for Genesis One." Pages 3–11 in *Of Scribes and Scrolls: Studies on the Hebrew Bible, Intertestamental Judaism, and Christian Origins Presented to John Strugnell on the Occasion of His Sixtieth Birthday*. Edited by Harold W. Attridge, John J. Collins, and T. H. Tobin. CTSRR 5. Lanham, MD: University Press of America. ◆ **Davila**. 1994. "4QGen^h," "4QGen^k." Pages 61–64, 74–78 in *Qumran Cave 4.VII: Genesis to Numbers*. DJD 12. Edited by Eugene Ulrich and Frank Moore Cross. Oxford: Clarendon. ◆ **Fenton**, Terry L. 1984. "'One Place,' *māqôm* ᵓ*eḥād*, in Genesis 1:9: Read *miqwîm*, 'Gatherings.'" VT 34:438–45. ◆ **Friedman**, Richard Elliott. 2003. *Commentary on the Torah: With a New English Translation and the Hebrew Text*. San Francisco: HarperSanFrancisco. ◆ **Grabe**, Johann E. 1707. *Septuaginta interpretum, Vol. 1: Octateuchum*. Oxford: Sheldonian Theatre, Smith. ◆ **Gunkel**, Hermann. 1910. *Genesis*. 3rd ed. HKAT 1. Göttingen: Vandenhoeck & Ruprecht. ◆ **Harl**, Marguerite. 1994. *La Bible d'Alexandrie 1: La Genèse*. 2nd ed. Paris: Cerf. ◆ **Hendel**, Ronald S. 1998. *The Text of Genesis 1–11: Textual Studies and Critical Edition*. Oxford: Oxford University Press. ◆ **Hiebert**, Robert J. V. 2000.

"Translation Technique in the Septuagint of Genesis and Its Implications for the NETS Version." *BIOSCS* 33:76–93. ♦ **Hiebert**. 2001. "Translating a Translation: The Septuagint of Genesis and the New English Translation of the Septuagint Project." Pages 263–84 in *X Congress of the International Organization for Septuagint and Cognate Studies: Oslo, 1998*. Edited by Bernard A. Taylor. SCS 51. Atlanta: Scholars Press. ♦ **Hiebert**. 2006. "The Hermeneutics of Translation in the Septuagint of Genesis." Pages 85–103 in *Septuagint Research: Issues and Challenges in the Study of the Greek Jewish Scriptures*. Edited by Wolfgang Kraus and Glenn Wooden. SCS 53; Atlanta: Society of Biblical Literature. ♦ **Hiebert**. 2007. "Genesis: To the Reader." Pages 1–6 in *A New English Translation of the Septuagint*. Edited by Albert Pietersma and Benjamin G. Wright. Oxford: Oxford University Press, 2007. ♦ **Hiebert**. 2013. "A 'Genetic' Commentary on the Septuagint of Genesis." *JSCS* 46:19–36; ♦ **Hiebert**, Robert J. V., and Nathaniel N. **Dykstra**. 2013. "Designing a New Septuagint Commentary: SBLCS and WATER." Pages 515–23 in *XIV Congress of the International Organization for Septuagint and Cognate Studies, Helsinki, 2010*. Edited by Melvin K. H. Peters. SCS 59. Atlanta: Society of Biblical Literature. ♦ **McEvenue**, Sean E. 1971. *The Narrative Style of the Priestly Writer*. AnBib 50. Rome: Biblical Institute Press. ♦ **Orlinsky**, Harry M. 1965. "The Textual Criticism of the Old Testament." Pages 140–69 in *The Bible and the Ancient Near East: Essays in Honor of William Foxwell Albright*. Edited by G. Ernest Wright. Garden City, NY: Anchor Books. ♦ **Plato**. 1871. *The Dialogues of Plato*. Translated by Benjamin Jowett. 4 vols. Cambridge: Cambridge University Press. ♦ **Polybius**. 1889. *The Histories of Polybius*. Translated by Evelyn S. Shuckburgh. London: Macmillan. ♦ **Rad**, Gerhard von. 1972. *Genesis: A Commentary*. Translated by John H. Marks. Rev. ed. OTL. Philadelphia: Westminster. ♦ **Runge**, Steven E. 2010. *Discourse Grammar of the Greek New Testament*. Lexham Bible Reference Series. Peabody, MA: Hendrickson. ♦ **Schmidt**, Werner H. 1973. *Die Schöpfungsgeschichte der Priesterschrift*. 3rd ed. WMANT 17. Neukirchen-Vluyn: Neukirchener Verlag. ♦ **Skinner**, John. 1930. *A Critical and Exegetical Commentary on Genesis*. 2nd ed. ICC. Edinburgh: T&T Clark. ♦ **Speiser**, E. A. 1964. *Genesis*. AB 1. Garden City, NY: Doubleday. ♦ **Tertullian**. 1885. *Adversus Hermogenem*. In vol. 3 of *The Ante-Nicene Fathers*. Edited by Alexander Roberts and James Donaldson. Translated by Peter Holmes. Repr., Peabody, MA: Hendrickson, 1994. ♦ **Toury**, Gideon. 1995. *Descriptive Translation Studies and Beyond*. BTL 4. Amsterdam: Benjamins. ♦ **Tov**, Emanuel. 1985. "The Nature and Background of Harmonizations in Biblical Manuscripts." *JSOT* 31:3–29. ♦

Wellhausen, Julius. 1899. *Die Composition des Hexateuchs und der historischen Bücher des Alten Testaments.* 3rd ed. Berlin: Reimer. ◆ **Wenham**, Gordon J. 1987. *Genesis 1–15.* WBC 1. Waco, TX: Word. ◆ **Wevers**, John William. 1993. *Notes on the Greek Text of Genesis.* SCS 35. Atlanta: Scholars Press.

Outline

As in the Hebrew source text, the initial creation account in Greek Genesis is framed by the structure of a week. Eight creative utterances by ὁ θεός with their corresponding enactments are distributed over the first six days, while the seventh day, which he blesses and hallows, is marked by the cessation of creative activity.

Commentary

It should be noted that this commentary takes as the English text for LXX Genesis the most recent version of *A New English Translation of the Septuagint* (NETS) that is posted online (http://ccat.sas.upenn.edu/nets/).

1.1

בְּרֵאשִׁית בָּרָא אֱלֹהִים אֵת הַשָּׁמַיִם וְאֵת הָאָרֶץ

Ἐν ἀρχῇ ἐποίησεν ὁ θεὸς τὸν οὐρανὸν καὶ τὴν γῆν.

In the beginning God made the sky and the earth.

G constructs this verse as an independent clause. This has commonly been the way that the Hebrew text has been understood, though as various interpreters from Rashi (eleventh century) and Abraham Ibn Ezra (twelfth century) onward have pointed out, it is possible to construe this verse as a dependent clause that is antecedent to either verse 3 or verse 2 (see *HALOT*, s.v. "רֵאשִׁית;" Wenham 1987, 11–12). In any case, the phrase Ἐν ἀρχῇ ἐποίησεν ὁ θεός and the concluding words of 2.3, ἤρξατο ὁ θεὸς ποιῆσαι, form an *inclusio* that delimits this first section of the book (Wevers 1993, 21; Brown 1993, 26). The *inclusio* has been fashioned by G through rendering the sequence בָּרָא ... לַעֲשׂוֹת in 2.3 as ἤρξατο ... ποιῆσαι, which provides a neat parallel to (Ἐν) ἀρχῇ ἐποίησεν in 1.1 with the matching word roots, whereas in the source text that does not hold true in the same way with its opening phrase (בְּ)רֵאשִׁית בָּרָא.

Ἐν ἀρχῇ. G's counterpart for ראשית is ἀρχή on all three occasions that it occurs in Genesis (1.1; 10.10; 49.3). As Wevers points out, "Gen did not understand בראשית as bound to the following clause, but simply as a prepositional phrase modifying ברא" (Wevers 1993, 1).

ἐποίησεν. ποιέω appears 165 times in Genesis, the counterpart to ברא in nine of eleven of its occurrences, including this one (1.1, 21, 27 [3x]; 5.1 [1°], 2 [2x]; 6.7 [1°]). The exception to this equivalence in the first creation account is in 2.3, where ἤρξατο (√ἄρχω) is the counterpart to ברא. As might be expected, ποιέω is most commonly employed by G to translate עשה, an equivalence that is attested 138 times, eight of which occur in the section under consideration (1.7, 16, 25, 26, 31; 2.2 [2°], 3). The use of ποιέω to render both of these Hebrew terms constitutes semantic leveling, a strategy from which later Greek versions at times depart (ברא: α' ἔκτισεν [1.1]; α' σ' θ' ἔκτισεν [1.27]; עשה: α' θ' ἐποίησεν [1.16]).

ὁ θεός. The term θεός occurs 280 times in Genesis. The counterpart in the MT involves some form of אלהים or אל in all but fifty cases, nine of which have no Hebrew equivalent at all. In 153 contexts in Genesis, including the present one, ὁ θεός appears as the counterpart to MT's anarthrous אלהים (not including equivalences such as κύριος ὁ θεός – אלהים). It is clear that G has not replicated in Greek the Hebrew author's decision to employ an anarthrous plural form to represent Israel's God. Instead the translator has opted for a singular arthrous form of the Greek generic term for deity. The effect of this strategy is to indicate that the reference is to THE god, that is, God.

τὸν οὐρανόν. οὐρανός occurs forty-four times in Genesis, always in the singular (which reflects classical usage) and always as the counterpart to the plural term שמים, except for three occasions when there is no corresponding Greek equivalent to the Hebrew. Of the thirty-six cases in which the Hebrew term is arthrous, in all but one (2.4 [1°]) that is also true in Greek Genesis.

1.2

והארץ היתה תהו ובהו וחשך על פני תהום ורוח אלהים מרחפת על
פני המים

ἡ δὲ γῆ ἦν ἀόρατος καὶ ἀκατασκεύαστος, καὶ σκότος ἐπάνω τῆς ἀβύσσου, καὶ πνεῦμα θεοῦ ἐπεφέρετο ἐπάνω τοῦ ὕδατος.

Yet the earth was invisible and unformed, and darkness was over
the abyss, and a divine wind was being carried along over the water.

ἡ δὲ γῆ. G's choice of the postpositive conjunction δέ as the counterpart
to the Hebrew conjunction ו constitutes a departure from his default rendering καί. The Greek lexicon includes a significantly greater selection of
conjunctions and particles than are attested in Biblical Hebrew, and Greek
authors in antiquity make creative use of that repertoire. More often than
not, however, G replicates the pattern of paratactic clause construction
that would have been found in his source text. Consequently, when that
does not occur, it must be regarded to be of expositional significance. In
this case, the use of δέ accords with Smyth's category of the copulative
δέ, which "marks transition, and is the ordinary particle used in connecting successive clauses or sentences which add something new or different,
but not opposed, to what precedes" (§2836; Runge 2010 §2.3). This raises
some interesting possibilities with respect to understanding the relationship between this verse and the preceding one, not unlike the ones that
arise for the interpreter of the source text. On the one hand, it could be
that G views verse 1 as an introductory summary statement for the entire
section (1.1–2.3), with the various stages in that process being detailed in
verses 2–31. On the other hand, it is possible that G regards verse 1 to be
a depiction of the first phase of God's creative work, which results in an
earth that exists in the state that is described in verse 2, and that the subsequent phases of God's work are spelled out in the verses that follow. Either
option is plausible, though in neither case does there appear to be sufficient evidence in the wording of the Greek text to support an argument
for the concept of *creatio ex nihilo*, which came to be articulated in subsequent centuries by authors like Theophilus of Antioch (*Autol.* 2.4) [second
century CE], Tatian (*Or. Graec.* 5) [second century CE], Irenaeus (*Haer.*
2.10.3–4) [second century CE], and Tertullian (*Herm.* 33–34) [second–
third centuries CE] (see the discussion in Brown 1993, 31–35).

Greek γῆ is the usual equivalent for Hebrew ארץ, and when the latter
is arthrous, γῆ is almost always accompanied by the article (163 out of a
total of 172 occurrences).

ἦν. Various forms of the verb εἰμί occur seven times in Gen 1, five times as
the equivalent of היה (1.2, 6, 14, 15, 29 [2°]) and twice in relative clauses
that correspond to the Hebrew relative pronoun אשר (ὃ ἦν [1.7]; ὅ ἐστιν
[1.29 (1°)]). γίνομαι is the counterpart to היה twenty-one times in Gen 1

(1.3 [2x], 5 [2x], 6, 8 [2x], 9, 11, 13 [2x], 14, 15, 19 [2x], 23 [2x], 24, 30, 31 [2x]). Throughout the book as a whole, εἰμί renders היה a total of 147 times and γίνομαι 151 times. G's choice of these two Greek equivalents for one Hebrew term is evidence of semantic differentiation, a phenomenon that is usually reflected in NETS by means of the verb *be* in the case of εἰμί and of expressions like *become* or *come to be* in the case of γίνομαι. In the present context, εἰμί is part of the description of the existential reality with respect to the state of ἡ γῆ.

ἀόρατος καὶ ἀκατασκεύαστος. G's rendering of the phrase תהו ובהו replicates the Hebrew sequence of two terms linked by a conjunction, but it also constitutes an exposition of this Hebrew "rhythmic pair" (Wevers 1993, 1) whose meaning is debated by scholars: "waste, void" (Wevers 1993, 1); "hodge-podge" (Brown 1993, 60, 74); "vide, désert, néant" (Harl 1994, 87); "formless" (Rad 1972, 49); "total chaos" (Wenham 1987, 2, 15–16).

The word ἀόρατος occurs in the translated corpus of the LXX only here as the counterpart to תהו and in Esa 45.3 as the counterpart to מסתר ("secret place" *HALOT*), as well as in 2 Makk 9.5. The characterization of the earth as ἀόρατος can be regarded as a logical inference from the fact that there is as yet no light (Josephus, *A.J.* 1.27; Wevers 1993, 1–2; Brown 1993, 48 n. 33). Another possible explanation for the use of this term here in Gen 1 is that it constitutes evidence of G having been influenced by the thinking of Plato, who employs ἀόρατος to describe the invisible, preexistent world of ideas (Hendel 1998, 19; Brown 1993, 48 n. 33). One work in which his conceptual framework in this regard is articulated is *Timaeus*:

> For the present we have only to conceive of three natures [γένη]: first, that which is in process of generation [τὸ μὲν γιγνόμενον]; secondly, that in which the generation takes place [τὸ δ' ἐν ᾧ γίγνεται]; and thirdly, that of which the thing generated is a resemblance [τὸ δ' ὅθεν ἀφομοιούμενον φύεται τὸ γιγνόμενον]. And we may liken the receiving principle to a mother, and the source or spring to a father, and the intermediate nature to a child; and may remark further, that if the model is to take every variety of form [ἐκτυπώματος ἔσεσθαι μέλλοντος ἰδεῖν ποικίλου πάσας ποικιλίας], then the matter in which the model is fashioned [τοῦτ' αὐτὸ ἐν ᾧ ἐκτυπούμενον ἐνίσταται] will not be duly prepared [παρεσκευασμένον εὖ], unless it is formless [ἄμορφον], and free from the impress of any of these shapes [τῶν ἰδεῶν] which it is hereafter to receive from without.... Wherefore, the mother and receptacle of all created and visible and in any way sensible things [τοῦ γεγονότος ὁρατοῦ καὶ πάντως αἰσθητοῦ], is

not to be termed earth, or air, or fire, or water, or any of their compounds
or any of the elements from which these are derived, but is an invisible and formless being [ἀνόρατον εἶδός τι καὶ ἄμορφον] which receives
all things and in some mysterious way partakes of the intelligible. (Plato,
Tim. 50c–d, 51a–b, trans. Jowett)

Philo was certainly influenced by Platonic ideas in his comments on the
creation narratives in Genesis, with his assertions that the creator first
fashioned an incorporeal (ἀσώματος) and invisible (ἀόρατος) cosmos that
served as the model (παράδειγμα) on the basis of which the corporeal
(σωματικός) and perceptible (αἰσθητός) cosmos was made (*Opif.* 29–36).
Hendel suggests that G's choice of the term ἀόρατος in Gen 1.2 "expresses
something of Platonic cosmology in biblical guise, perhaps joining the cos-
mologies of Plato and Moses, as was a commonplace in Hellenistic Jewish
thought, particularly in Alexandria" (Hendel 1998, 19). This is plausible,
though it is of course impossible to know for certain what may have motivated the translator to employ this term.

As for ἀκατασκεύαστος, the counterpart to בהו in this passage, it is
a *hapax legomenon* in the LXX and is, in fact, seldom attested in Greek
literature as a whole apart from texts that cite or refer to this passage in
Genesis. It may be noted that, in the passage cited above, Plato uses the
term παρεσκευασμένον ("prepared"), which is derived from the same basic
root as ἀκατασκεύαστος, when describing the ἐκτύπωμα ("model"). The
ἐκτύπωμα he portrays elsewhere as ἀνόρατον, and he asserts that it must be
ἄμορφον ("formless") in order for it to be ready to receive the perceptible
forms that constitute the visible creation. If κατασκευάζω (equip, furnish,
construct, prepare, establish), the verbal antonym of ἀκατασκεύαστος, can
be taken as an inverse indicator of what the adjective means, it can be
understood to connote lack of structure, form, or definition.

ἐπάνω. G employs ἐπάνω to render seven different Hebrew constructions
in Genesis. One of these, על פני, occurs here as well as in 1.29 and 7.18. It
is clear, however, that the translator does not replicate the Hebrew idiom
("upon the face of"), but with ἐπάνω opts for an interpretative Greek rendering that conveys the idea of being over something.

τῆς ἀβύσσου. G chooses ἡ ἄβυσσος as the equivalent for anarthrous תהום
all three times that the latter occurs in Genesis (1.2; 7.11; 8.2). The adjective ἄβυσσος denotes "bottomless, unfathomed" (LSJ), but it is substan-

tivized in the LXX. The Hebrew term signifies the "primaeval ocean" (*HALOT*), but this appears to be the first context in which ἄβυσσος comes to be associated with the primordial waters of ancient myth (Harl 1994, 87), though this does not mean that it takes on that specific component of meaning.

πνεῦμα θεοῦ. πνεῦμα is the equivalent for רוח in all seven places that the latter is found in Genesis (1.2; 6.3, 17; 7.15; 8.1; 41.38; 45.27). Both terms can mean "wind" or "spirit." In contrast to verse 1, however, in the present context anarthrous, singular θεός is the counterpart to anarthrous, plural אלהים. This equivalence occurs only eighteen times in Genesis (1.2, 27; 3.5; 5.1; 9.6; 17.7, 8; 23.6; 28.17, 21, 22; 30.2; 32.3, 29, 30[31]; 33.10; 35.5; 41.38) in comparison to the 153 cases mentioned above in which arthrous ὁ θεός is the counterpart to anarthrous אלהים. Since G here departs from his usual way of signifying the creator deity, it must be regarded as a deliberate move with semantic implications, namely that "the divine in an indefinite sense" is being signified by anarthrous θεός "rather than specifically *the* god = God" (Hiebert and Dykstra 2013, 523). If that is the case, and in view of the verb for which this noun pair serves as the subject, it would seem more likely that πνεῦμα is intended in the sense of "wind" rather than that of "spirit," a wind that is not itself divine in nature but that originates with the deity.

ἐπεφέρετο. The verb ἐπιφέρω appears three times in Genesis, on each occasion the counterpart to a different Hebrew verb: ἐπεφέρετο ("be carried along") – מרחפת ("sweep") (1.2); ἐπεφέρετο ("be carried along") – תלך ("float") (7.18); ἐπενέγκητε ("lay [a hand on]") – תשלחו ("lay [a hand on]") (37.22). In none of these cases is there semantic overlap between the Greek and Hebrew terms, so one is warranted in concluding that G has made expositional moves in his choice of equivalent.

τοῦ ὕδατος. Greek ὕδωρ is the equivalent for Hebrew מים in all fifty-four contexts in which the latter appears in Genesis. In all but four of those instances, ὕδωρ is singular in number in comparison to the plural form מים, as is the case here.

1.3

ויאמר אלהים יהי אור ויהי אור

καὶ εἶπεν ὁ θεός Γενηθήτω φῶς. καὶ ἐγένετο φῶς.

And God said, "Let light come into being." And light came into being.

In both the source text and in the LXX, this verse contains the first *Wortbericht*, or report of a divine creative word, and the first *Tatbericht*, or report of a divine creative act, in the initial creation account in Genesis (Schmidt 1973, 171).

Γενηθήτω … ἐγένετο. On G's use of γίνομαι to render היה, see the comment on verse 2 above. It would appear that in this context and others like it in the first section of the book where God speaks a creative word, implicit in the choice of γίνομαι is the idea of γένεσις, that is to say the origin and creation of the named entities, rather than the concept of simple existentiality that is associated with εἰμί (LSJ).

1.4

וירא אלהים את האור כי טוב ויבדל אלהים בין האור ובין החשך
καὶ εἶδεν ὁ θεὸς τὸ φῶς ὅτι καλόν. καὶ διεχώρισεν ὁ θεὸς ἀνὰ μέσον τοῦ φωτὸς καὶ ἀνὰ μέσον τοῦ σκότους.
And God saw the light, that it was good. And God separated between the light and between the darkness.

καὶ εἶδεν ὁ θεὸς τὸ φῶς ὅτι καλόν. G reproduces the Hebrew word order in the first sentence of this verse, which features two objects for the verb and involves "placing the subject of the ὅτι-clause [τὸ φῶς] outside the clause" in agreement with the Hebrew (Wevers 1993, 2; GKC §117h). There are a number of Greek counterparts to טוב in its forty-four occurrences in LXX Genesis, including ἀγαθός (4x) and its comparative form βελτίων (1x), and καλός (31x) and its adverbial cognate καλῶς (1x). In all seven cases in which טוב occurs in the *Hexaemeron* in the present section (1.4, 10, 12, 18, 21, 25, 31), καλός is the equivalent. Harl comments that the choice of καλός rather than ἀγαθός to render טוב connotes "non pas seulement ce qui fonctionne bien, mais ce qui a une valeur esthétique, morale, ordonnée" (1994, 88). Likewise, Wevers remarks that "[t]he divine recognition was more than functional; it was also an assessment of worth in and for itself" (Wevers 1993, 2). In view of the fact that καλός is G's usual rendering not only here but also throughout the book of Genesis, one must acknowledge, however, that it is not specifically marked here.

διεχώρισεν ... ἀνὰ μέσον ... καὶ ἀνὰ μέσον. While διαχωρίζω and בדל *hiphil* are more or less semantically equivalent, and ἀνὰ μέσον is an acceptable counterpart to בין (e.g., Οἱ δ᾽ Ἀπασιάκαι κατοικοῦσι μὲν ἀνὰ μέσον Ὄξου καὶ Τανάιδος ["The Apasiacae live between the rivers Oxus and Tanais" Polybius, *Hist.* 10.48; trans. Shuckburgh]), διαχωρίζω ... ἀνὰ μέσον does not represent standard usage in Greek literature unrelated to the Genesis creation texts. Furthermore, the repetition of ἀνὰ μέσον with the second noun of a pair in this kind of construction—first attested in the LXX—is, as Gideon Toury would put it, due the negative transfer of the idiom of the source text, בין ... בין (Toury 1995, 252–53, 274–76). In Genesis, ἀνὰ μέσον is repeated in nineteen contexts due to Hebrew influence (1.4, 7, 14, 18; 3.15; 9.12 [בין 3°], 15 [בין 3°], 16, 17; 10.12; 13.3, 7; 16.14; 17.2, 7, 10 [בין 3°]; 20.1; 26.28; 30.36), whereas in eleven contexts that is not the case (9.13; 13.8; 16.5; 17.11; 23.15; 31.44, 44[50b], 46c[48a], 48[51], 49; 32.16[17]). NETS replicates G's redundancy in those preceding nineteen instances. The Greek translator's decisions in rendering this construction do not, however, appear to be entirely arbitrary. In the majority of cases in which repetition does occur, the object of the second בין is a noun (1.4, 7, 14, 18; 3.15; 9.16, 17; 10.12; 13.3, 7; 16.14; 20.1; 30.36), whereas when repetition does not occur, that second object is usually a pronoun (9.12, 15; 13.8; 16.5; 17.10, 11; 23.15; 31.44, 44[50b], 46c[48a], 48[51], 49).

1.5

ויקרא אלהים לאור יום ולחשך קרא לילה ויהי ערב ויהי בקר יום
אחד

καὶ ἐκάλεσεν ὁ θεὸς τὸ φῶς ἡμέραν καὶ τὸ σκότος ἐκάλεσεν νύκτα. καὶ ἐγένετο ἑσπέρα καὶ ἐγένετο πρωί, ἡμέρα μία.

And God called the light Day and the darkness he called Night. And it came to be evening, and it came to be morning, day one.

καὶ ἐκάλεσεν ... τὸ φῶς ... καὶ τὸ σκότος ἐκάλεσεν. G does not attempt to reproduce the Hebrew idiom that involves the introduction of the object of קרא with ל, but quite appropriately uses the accusative case to mark the objects of ἐκάλεσεν.

καὶ ἐγένετο. See comments on ἦν in verse 2 and Γενηθήτω ... ἐγένετο in verse 3.

ἡμέρα μία. G follows the lead of the source text in employing a cardinal number.

1.6

ויאמר אלהים יהי רקיע בתוך המים ויהי מבדיל בין מים למים

Καὶ εἶπεν ὁ θεός Γενηθήτω στερέωμα ἐν μέσῳ τοῦ ὕδατος καὶ ἔστω διαχωρίζον ἀνὰ μέσον ὕδατος καὶ ὕδατος. καὶ ἐγένετο οὕτως.

And God said, "Let a firmament come into being in the midst of the water, and let it be a separator between water and water." And it became so.

στερέωμα. All nine occurrences of στερέωμα in Genesis are found in the first chapter of the book (1.6, 7 [3x], 8, 14, 15, 17, 20), and in each case it is the counterpart to רקיע. In Greek literature that antedates the LXX, στερέωμα denotes "solid body," "foundation," or "framework," and it is in LXX Genesis where it first comes to be associated with the idea of separation of the primeval waters. The Hebrew term רקיע is commonly understood to denote the vault or dome that the ancients imagined brought structure to the previously undefined watery mass depicted in verse 2, resulting in a habitable and functional space—beneath, around, and above which the waters were kept in check (Job 37.18; Pss 24.1–2; 136.5–6). This vault was apparently regarded to possess some form of solidity and substance that was also translucent or transparent (Ex 24.10; Ezek 1.22, 26; von Rad 1972, 53–54; Friedman 2003, 7–9). A στερέωμα is not, however, an entity with a predetermined shape or function, and if a domed structure had been what G envisaged, other terminology, such as that which appears in Esa 40.22, could have been employed (Harl 1994, 89): ὁ κατέχων τὸν γῦρον τῆς γῆς, καὶ οἱ ἐνοικοῦντες ἐν αὐτῇ ὡς ἀκρίδες, ὁ στήσας ὡς καμάραν τὸν οὐρανὸν καὶ διατείνας ὡς σκηνὴν κατοικεῖν ("It is he who holds the circle of the earth, and those who dwell in it are like grasshoppers, who has set up heaven like a vault and stretched it out like a tent to live in"). Thus G's choice of στερέωμα in Gen 1.6 represents a departure from what is envisaged in the source text.

καὶ ἔστω διαχωρίζον. G replicates the word order and structure of the source text, including employing a participial form of the finite verb that appears in verse 4.

ἀνὰ μέσον ὕδατος καὶ ὕδατος. G's strategy in representing בֵּין מַיִם לָמַיִם
results in an adequate, if less than elegant, explication of the thrust of the
source text (Toury 1995, 56–57). At least it is not as ponderous as what
"The Three" produced: α' μεταξὺ ὑδάτων εἰς ὕδατα, σ' ἐν μέσῳ ὕδατος καὶ εἰς
ὕδωρ, θ' ἀνὰ μέσον ὕδατος εἰς ὕδατα.

καὶ ἐγένετο οὕτως. G's placement of this "transition formula" (Tov 1985, 10)
at the end of the current verse, between the *Wortbericht* and the *Tatbericht*,
accords with the pattern that is exhibited in verses 9, 11, 15, and 24. The
OG and its source text agree on that sequence in those four contexts. In
the present case, however, the MT's transition formula וַיְהִי כֵן appears at
the end of verse 7. In the MT's version of the fifth day, it does not occur at
all, whereas in the OG, καὶ ἐγένετο οὕτως once again comes after the *Wortbericht* in verse 20. As for the sixth day, in both the LXX and its source text
the transition formula follows God's declaration that he has granted plant
life for food (v. 30). Summing up the situation, then, this formula occurs in
Gen 1 a total of seven times in the OG and six times in the MT, with disagreement between the two in regard to either its location (second day) or
presence (fifth day). The question arises as to whether the presence of καὶ
ἐγένετο οὕτως in verses 6 and 20 of the OG reflects a different source text
than the MT or is the result of harmonization with the pattern of verses
9, 11, 15, and 24. Emanuel Tov notes that harmonizations originating in a
source text are hard to distinguish from those introduced by a translator,
but then suggests a criterion for isolating the latter in parallel passages:

> If the translator took care to use the same Greek equivalents in both
> passages, and if at least a few equivalents are unique to the two parallel
> passages, harmonization in other details, too, is at least a possibility. If
> the translator varied the translation vocabulary of the two sections, har-
> monization is still possible, but unlikely (Tov 1985, 20).

The Greek wording of the transition formula is the same in all of its occurrences in Gen 1, though admittedly the translation equivalences are not
unique to the parallel passages in question. Hendel's position is that the
appearance of the formula in verses 6 and 20 is due to harmonization,
though he attributes that activity to the creator of what he calls proto-G,
namely G's source text, basing his argument on G's normally conservative
approach to rendering his *Vorlage* (Hendel 1998, 12, 16–18, 20–23; see
also Orlinsky 1965, 151 and Davila 1990, 11). The problem is, however,

that textual evidence for an alternative *Vorlage* in these two cases is lacking in the Qumran materials and SamPent. Occasional divergences from the pattern that recurs throughout the original Hebrew text of Gen 1.1–2.3 have been noted by various scholars over the years (Wellhausen 1899, 184; Cassuto 1961, 16; McEvenue 1971, 185). Yet it should not automatically be assumed that, where the extant Hebrew textual tradition is unanimous in departing from established patterns while the OG follows them, the Greek text provides evidence of an alternative source text. Although it is true that G's approach to the task of translation can often be described as quantitatively equivalent and isomorphic, it is equally true that the Greek translator does not always exhibit rigid conformity to his source text or consistently opt for stereotypical renderings (Hiebert 2007, 1; 2000, 76–93; 2001, 263–84; 2006, 85–103). In the light of the preceding considerations, it would seem preferable to attribute the transition formula's appearance after the OG's *Wortbericht* in verses 6 and 20 to G's harmonizing activity, carried out in order to "remedy" its anomalous placement in the source text after the *Tatbericht* in verse 7 and its absence following the *Wortbericht* in verse 20, than to conclude that καὶ ἐγένετο οὕτως in verses 6 and 20 of the OG and the MT's divergences in these two cases are due to scribal error or intentional alteration (Wevers 1993, 4; Hiebert 2013, 30–33).

1.7

ויעש אלהים את הרקיע ויבדל בין המים אשר מתחת לרקיע ובין
המים אשר מעל לרקיע ויהי כן

καὶ ἐποίησεν ὁ θεὸς τὸ στερέωμα, καὶ διεχώρισεν ὁ θεὸς ἀνὰ μέσον τοῦ ὕδατος, ὃ ἦν ὑποκάτω τοῦ στερεώματος, καὶ ἀνὰ μέσον τοῦ ὕδατος τοῦ ἐπάνω τοῦ στερεώματος.

And God made the firmament, and God separated between the water that was under the firmament and between the water that was above the firmament.

ἐποίησεν. G's usual equivalent for עשה in Genesis is ποιέω (see v. 1).

ὃ ἦν ... τοῦ 4°. G employs two different means of representing the Hebrew relative pronoun אשר in the present verse. The first features a relative pronoun plus the imperfect form of εἰμί, and the second involves simply an article that is functioning as a relative pronoun. There is no apparent reason for the different approach other than the translator's desire to vary the mode of expression.

ἀνὰ μέσον ... καὶ ἀνὰ μέσον. On the repetition of ἀνὰ μέσον in imitation of repeated בין, see verse 4.

ὑποκάτω τοῦ στερεώματος ... ἐπάνω τοῦ στερεώματος. The ὑποκάτω – מתחת equivalence occurs three times in Genesis (1.7, 9; 6.17), whereas ἐπάνω – מעל occurs twice (1.7; 40.17). The phrases that these prepositions initiate are not exact matches of the Hebrew in terms of replication of the specific constructions, but the translator has nonetheless chosen sensible equivalents. The Greek phrases are consistent with Greek idiom (ὑποκάτω + gen., ἐπάνω + gen.) and they represent the Hebrew expressions מתחת לרקיע and מעל לרקיע well.

As noted in the commentary on verse 6, the Greek equivalent of ויהי כן in the present verse follows the *Wortbericht* at the end of verse 6.

1.8

    ויקרא אלהים לרקיע שמים ויהי ערב ויהי בקר יום שני
    καὶ ἐκάλεσεν ὁ θεὸς τὸ στερέωμα οὐρανόν. καὶ εἶδεν ὁ θεὸς ὅτι καλόν.
    καὶ ἐγένετο ἑσπέρα καὶ ἐγένετο πρωί, ἡμέρα δευτέρα.
    And God called the firmament Sky. And God saw that it was good.
    And it came to be evening, and it came to be morning, a second
    day.

καὶ ἐκάλεσεν ὁ θεὸς τὸ στερέωμα οὐρανόν. Regarding the Greek rendering of the Hebrew construction ויקרא ... ל, see verse 5. This is the first context attested in Greek literature in which στερέωμα is associated with οὐρανός.

καὶ εἶδεν ὁ θεὸς ὅτι καλόν. This is the only place in Gen 1 where there is no counterpart in the MT to the "formula of divine approbation" (Wevers 1993, 4; cf. vv. 4, 10, 12, 18, 21, 25, 31). In view of the lack of evidence for an alternate Hebrew *Vorlage*, this would appear to be another example of the Greek translator's harmonizing activity (see v. 6; Hendel 1998, 23–24).

ἡμέρα δευτέρα. As in the case of "day one" (v. 5), G replicates his source text here and throughout the rest of the *Hexaemeron*. From this point onward, however, the numbers assigned to the days are ordinals.

1.9

ויאמר אלהים יקוו המים מתחת השמים אל מקום אחד ותראה
היבשה ויהי כן

Καὶ εἶπεν ὁ θεός Συναχθήτω τὸ ὕδωρ τὸ ὑποκάτω τοῦ οὐρανοῦ εἰς
συναγωγὴν μίαν, καὶ ὀφθήτω ἡ ξηρά. καὶ ἐγένετο οὕτως. καὶ συνήχθη
τὸ ὕδωρ τὸ ὑποκάτω τοῦ οὐρανοῦ εἰς τὰς συναγωγὰς αὐτῶν, καὶ ὤφθη
ἡ ξηρά.

And God said, "Let the water that is under the sky be gathered
into one gathering, and let the dry land appear." And it became
so. And the water that was under the sky was gathered into their
gatherings, and the dry land appeared.

Συναχθήτω τὸ ὕδωρ. The difference between the Greek and the source text
at this point is one of number, reflecting the states of the subject nouns that
govern the respective verbs. The verb συνάγω is employed by G to render
four different Hebrew roots in Genesis, all of which fall within the semantic range of "gather" or "collect": אסף, לקט, קבץ, קוה. This is the only place
in Genesis, however, in which συνάγω is the counterpart to קוה. The Greek
verb here simply relays the meaning of the Hebrew one, apart from the
difference in number.

τὸ ὑποκάτω. The article ensures that ὑποκάτω is read as an adjectival modifier of τὸ ὕδωρ, thus making explicit what is implicit in the source text.
Without the article, the adverb/preposition could be construed as specifying where the water is to be gathered, namely ὑποκάτω τοῦ οὐρανοῦ.

εἰς συναγωγὴν μίαν. Of the five times that συναγωγή occurs in Genesis, only
here is its MT counterpart מקום. It is therefore an anomalous rendering,
something that is reinforced by the fact that in all forty-six other appear-
ances of מקום in this book the Greek equivalent is τόπος. The question
then arises as to whether συναγωγή here is evidence of an interpretative
move by G or of his translation of an alternate source text. The readings
of Aquila, Symmachus, and Theodotion clearly reflect מקום inasmuch as
they substitute εἰς τόπον ἕνα for εἰς συναγωγὴν μίαν. Scholars have, however,
long pointed out that συναγωγή accords semantically with מקוה rather
than with מקום (e.g., Gunkel 1910, 107; Skinner 1930, 22; Speiser 1964,
6; Harl 1994, 90; Wenham 1987, 4; Hendel 1998, 24; *BHS*). The discovery
and publication of Dead Sea Scrolls manuscript 4Q8 (4QGen[h]) (Davila
1994, 61–62) has provided tangible support for the suggestion that מקוה

was the reading in G's *Vorlage*. The Greek συναγωγή is, of course, the substantival cognate of the preceding verb συναχθήτω, in the same way that the Hebrew מקוה and יקוו are etymologically related. This observation could be construed as evidence, either of harmonization that occurred in the Hebrew or the Greek textual history, or of an original symmetry that is now attested only in the LXX and 4Q8. On balance, the latter option seems more compelling. Graphic confusion involving the final letters of those two words, ה and ם, could account for the shift to מקום, a word that occurs in the MT canon far more frequently (401x) than מקוה root 2 does (4x: Gen 1.10; Exod 7.19; Leu 11.36; Esa 22.11). In the light of these statistics, a shift from an original מקום to מקוה seems less probable than the reverse option. Wevers's argument that מקוה is unlikely to have been the reading in G's parent text is based to a large extent on the fact that the Greek counterpart to מקוה in verse 10 is not συναγωγή but τὰ συστήματα, as it is in "The Three" (Wevers 1993, 5). This is a valid objection, but, in the broader context of verses 9–10, not ultimately fatal to the proposal that מקוה is the *Vorlage* for G in verse 9, as will be argued below. Terry Fenton's suggestion with respect to the interwoven textual histories of the LXX and the MT at this point—namely that, before the introduction of medial *matres lectionis*, מקום was the original consonantal form in verse 9a but that it was vocalized as *miqwîm*; that G's *Vorlage* did indeed read מקוים, but that the current MT reading came about as a result of the accidental loss of *yôd* resulting in the vocalization of מקום as *māqôm*; and that subsequently אחד was added to the clause יקוו המים מתחת השמים אל מקום in order to make for a more sensible reading (1984, 441–442)—while very ingenious, would appear to be a candidate for Occam's razor because of the complexity of the scenario that he sketches with its multiple stages and assumptions. No doubt the reading εις τας συναγωγας αυτων that is found in manuscripts 72 of the O group and 129 of the *f* group, and the anomalous reading εν ταις συναγωγαις μιαν that is attested by the corrector of manuscript 56 of the *f* group, are the result of harmonization with the latter half of the longer Greek text of the present verse (see below).

καὶ ἐγένετο οὕτως. Regarding the transition formula, see verse 6.

καὶ συνήχθη τὸ ὕδωρ τὸ ὑποκάτω τοῦ οὐρανοῦ εἰς τὰς συναγωγὰς αὐτῶν, καὶ ὤφθη ἡ ξηρά. This portion of the verse in the LXX constitutes the *Tatbericht* that is lacking in the MT. It is obelized in various Greek manuscripts (57–73–413 [ind mend] 343–344′). In the apparatus of *BHS*, it is retroverted into Hebrew: ויקוו המים מתחת השמים אל מקויהם ותרא היבשה. This is, in fact, the only instance in the present account in which a *Wortbericht* is not followed by a *Tatbericht* in the MT (see vv. 3–4, 6–7, 11–12, 14–18, 20–21, 24–25, 26–27). Wevers concludes that G "has intentionally restructured the creation account of ch. 1 in the interests of consistency" (Wevers 1993, 5). But there is evidence to suggest that the longer Greek reading may be based on a Hebrew text that differs from the MT. First, the Hebrew equivalent to the clause καὶ ὤφθη ἡ ξηρά appears to be partly preserved in 4Q10 (4QGen^k) (Davila 1994, 75–76): ותרא היב[שה]. Hendel argues that this phrase is not to be construed as belonging to verse 9a because the verb in this fragment is the short form preterite, which lacks the concluding ה of the jussive ותראה that does appear in verse 9a. He asserts that it "is very unlikely that a postexilic scribe would miswrite the long prefix form in verse 9a as a short prefix form, as the short form is virtually moribund in Late Biblical Hebrew" (1998, 25–26). Second, the possessive pronoun αὐτῶν that follows the phrase εἰς τὰς συναγωγάς does not agree in number with its antecedent τὸ ὕδωρ, but the plural pronoun can be accounted for as part of a Hebraistic rendering of אל מקויהם for which the plural noun המים is the antecedent of the Hebrew pronominal suffix. This would seem to be a more likely scenario than Wevers's proposal mentioned above that G has introduced the *Tatbericht* "in the interests of consistency" with the other parts of the *Hexaemeron* that feature the *Wortbericht-Tatbericht* pattern, since harmonizing pluses mirror the wording of the texts with which they are paralleled (see the discussion regarding καὶ ἐγένετο οὕτως in v. 6 and καὶ εἶδεν ὁ θεὸς ὅτι καλόν in v. 8). The wording of the *Tatbericht* in verse 9b (εἰς τὰς συναγωγὰς αὐτῶν) does not, however, mirror the wording of the *Wortbericht* in verse 9a (εἰς συναγωγὴν μίαν), and so it is more likely to be based on a non-MT source text. The absence of the *Tatbericht* in the MT could be the result of homoiarcton involving ויקוו verse 9b and ויקרא verse 10, or of homoioteleuton involving היבשה verse 9a and היבשה verse 9b (*BHS*; Wellhausen 1899, 184; Skinner 1930, 22; Fenton 1984, 443; Tov 1985, 21–22; Davila 1990, 11; Hendel 1998, 25–27).

1.10

ויקרא אלהים ליבשה ארץ ולמקוה המים קרא ימים וירא אלהים כי
טוב

καὶ ἐκάλεσεν ὁ θεὸς τὴν ξηρὰν γῆν καὶ τὰ συστήματα τῶν ὑδάτων
ἐκάλεσεν θαλάσσας. καὶ εἶδεν ὁ θεὸς ὅτι καλόν.

And God called the dry land Earth, and the systems of the waters
he called Seas. And God saw that it was good.

καὶ ἐκάλεσεν ὁ θεὸς τὴν ξηράν ... καὶ τὰ συστήματα. Regarding the Greek
rendering of the Hebrew construction ל ... ויקרא, see verse 5.

τὰ συστήματα τῶν ὑδάτων. There are a number of interesting matters to
consider with respect to how this phrase corresponds to the underlying
Hebrew and to verse 9. MT's counterpart in the present verse is מקוה
המים, and one notices at the outset the difference in number between τὰ
συστήματα and מקוה. On the basis of this LXX reading, Fenton maintains that the original Hebrew text must have been the plural construct
form מקוי, but that it "has obviously been accommodated to" מקום אחד
in verse 9a (1984, 442). His reconstruction of both the original LXX and
its source text in verses 9 and 10 therefore involves συναγωγάς and plural
forms of מקוה in all three relevant parts of these verses before they came
to be altered to their present form (1984, 442–45). Again the complexity
and speculative nature of this scenario is its Achilles's heel. Thus one must
begin with the acknowledgement that the Greek plural form in the present verse agrees in number with τὰς συναγωγάς in verse 9b but not with
συναγωγήν in verse 9a, whose presumed Hebrew counterparts are plural
and singular forms of מקוה, respectively. What is somewhat surprising,
then, is the choice of a different lexeme, σύστημα, as the equivalent for
מקוה here in verse 10. If G's *Vorlage* was, indeed, a form of מקוה in all
three places, then the employment of two different Greek lexemes for one
Hebrew term represents another case of semantic differentiation. It is clear
as well that when G talks about συναγωγὴ μία in verse 9a, on the one hand,
and about συναγωγαί in verse 9b and συστήματα in verse 10, on the other
hand, those are understood to be different entities. Presumably verse 9a
has to do with the general boundary that is drawn between a habitable
land mass and the primordial ocean, whereas verse 9b and verse 10 have
to do with the different bodies of water that are located on the earth, hence
the transition to plural terms. The switch in Greek lexemes may be due to
G's desire for variation. Noteworthy as well is the fact that the Greek term
for water is plural here, whereas in verses 6, 7, and 9 it is always singular.
This reinforces the idea that G is now referring to multiple bodies of water
rather than to the single undifferentiated watery expanse that is described
as existing prior to the emergence of the ξηρά.

καὶ εἶδεν ὁ θεὸς ὅτι καλόν. Regarding the divine approbation formula, see verse 8.

1.11

ויאמר אלהים תדשא הארץ דשא עשב מזריע זרע עץ פרי עשה פרי
למינו אשר זרעו בו על הארץ ויהי כן

καὶ εἶπεν ὁ θεός Βλαστησάτω ἡ γῆ βοτάνην χόρτου, σπεῖρον σπέρμα κατὰ γένος καὶ καθ᾽ ὁμοιότητα, καὶ ξύλον κάρπιμον ποιοῦν καρπόν, οὗ τὸ σπέρμα αὐτοῦ ἐν αὐτῷ κατὰ γένος ἐπὶ τῆς γῆς. καὶ ἐγένετο οὕτως.

And God said, "Let the earth put forth herbaceous vegetation, seeding seed according to kind and according to likeness, and a fruit-bearing tree producing fruit of which its seed is in it according to kind, on the earth." And it became so.

Βλαστησάτω ἡ γῆ βοτάνην χόρτου. The Greek text does not replicate the cognate wordplay in the source text between the verb and direct object in this clause (Βλαστησάτω ... βοτάνην – תדשא ... דשא). In the LXX, only here and in Ioel 2.22 do both these Greek and Hebrew verbs occur, whereas of the fourteen occurrences of the noun דשא, it is rendered by βοτάνη in five contexts including the present one (Gen 1.11, 12; 4 Rgns 19.26; Esa 66.14; Ier 14.5). The verbs are semantically equivalent, as are the nouns βοτάνη and דשא. While there is some degree of semantic overlap between χόρτος and עשב in that both can denote either animal or human food that comes from plants (see 1.29, 30), the former is also used of the place where animals feed, whether an enclosure or open pastureland (LSJ). The NRSV interprets עשב as a collective noun, but in rendering it as χόρτου in the singular, G reflects the number of his source text without signalling that it is to be understood as a collective (on Greek collective nouns, see Smyth §996; C-S §48). The fact that the Greek noun is an attributive genitive modifier of βοτάνην makes it clear that G construes the relationship between them to be different than what the Masoretes understand to be the case between דשא and עשב. In the present context, it appears that βοτάνην signifies the genus or general category of vegetation and χόρτου the species (Louw-Nida, s.v. "βοτάνη"; BDAG, s.v. "βοτάνη"), namely, of the herbaceous type (on the adjectival force of the adnominal gen., see Smyth §1291). In the MT, the disjunctive accent (zaqef qatan) over דשא signals an appositional relationship with what follows (Wevers 1993, 6; Harl 1994, 91; Brown 1993, 51 n. 48).

σπεῖρον σπέρμα. The verbal root σπείρω appears six times in Genesis; in five cases, including the current one, the Hebrew verb זרע is the counterpart (1.11, 12, 29; 26.12; 47.23), while in the remaining instance (47.19) there is no Hebrew equivalent. The cognate noun σπέρμα occurs sixty times in Genesis, in fifty-nine of which, including the present context, the Hebrew equivalent is זרע, whereas in the remaining case (21.23) the Hebrew counterpart is נין ("offspring" BDB). G's verb and noun choices here are thus default renderings. The Hebraism σπεῖρον σπέρμα, both here and in the following verse, represents a formally equivalent rendering of מזריע זרע in the source text. Wevers construes σπέρμα as the subject of the preceding predicative participle σπεῖρον, based on the assumption that this neuter verbal form could not be modifying either of the preceding nouns χόρτου (masc.) or βοτάνην (fem.) (Wevers 1993, 6). It seems likely, however, that σπεῖρον modifies or qualifies βοτάνην, despite the fact that they are not congruent in terms of gender, and that σπέρμα is its direct object. βοτάνην is to be understood as describing a class of object rather than an individual thing, and in such a circumstance, the use of the neuter gender for a generalizing modifier is not uncommon (Smyth §1048). G's rendering, then, communicates the idea that what the earth is to put forth is pastureland vegetation (βοτάνην χόρτου) that disseminates seed (σπεῖρον σπέρμα). Although in the initial portion of this *Wortbericht* there is formal equivalence between the OG and its source text—Βλαστησάτω ἡ γῆ βοτάνην χόρτου σπεῖρον σπέρμα – תדשא הארץ דשא עשב מזריע זרע—the syntax is different. Thus in contrast to the web of relationships in the OG described above, עשב מזריע זרע, to which χόρτου σπεῖρον σπέρμα corresponds formally, stands in apposition to דשא (βοτάνην).

κατὰ γένος καὶ καθ' ὁμοιότητα. These words are without counterpart in the MT, whereas in the *Tatbericht* of verse 12 they constitute a double translation of the first occurrence of למינהו. Given the fact that Hebrew evidence is lacking for them here and the fact that they mirror exactly the same Greek phrase in verse 12, this would appear to be a case of harmonization by G.

καὶ ξύλον κάρπιμον ποιοῦν καρπόν. The Greek conjunction does not have a counterpart in the MT in the present verse, though there is widespread versional support for it here (*BHS*), and in the *Tatbericht* in verse 12 where the Hebrew conjunction precedes עץ in agreement with the LXX. Once again G seems to have harmonized the present verse with verse 12.

The choice of ξύλον as the equivalent for עץ is consistent with the translator's usual practice, occurring twenty-five of the thirty times that עץ appears in Genesis. Harl points out that ξύλον is commonly employed in Classical Greek to signify "bois coupé," though she acknowledges that in the papyri it is attested with the same meaning as δένδρον ("arbre"; 1994, 91; cf. LSJ)—G's choice of equivalent on only three occasions in Genesis. ξύλον is therefore an unmarked rendering in Genesis. As in the case of χόρτου above, G does not indicate that ξύλον is to be read as a collective in the way that the NRSV interprets עץ. Thus OG should be understood to be referring to a tree that presumably serves as an exemplar of all such fruit-bearing trees.

The adjective κάρπιμος occurs in the LXX only here and in the following verse. The phrase ξύλον κάρπιμον constitutes a sensible rendering of the Hebrew noun pair עץ פרי in construct relationship.

κάρπόν. Apart from the two instances of κάρπιμος mentioned above, G's equivalent for פרי throughout Genesis is, as might be expected, καρπός (1.11, 12, 29; 3.2, 3, 6; 4.3; 30.2).

οὗ τὸ σπέρμα αὐτοῦ ἐν αὐτῷ κατὰ γένος. G reflects the various components of his source text, but not in the same sequence. κατὰ γένος corresponds to למינו, apart from the absence of a Greek pronominal modifier. That is how G usually translates this prepositional phrase in its various forms: of the seventeen cases of למין plus pronominal suffix in Genesis, all except three (1.21 [1°], 25 [3°]; 6:20 [3°]) involve κατὰ γένος without an accompanying pronoun. G consistently employs κατὰ γένος in conjunction with σπέρμα (Wevers 1993, 7), whereas in the present verse of the source text the linkage is between either פרי or עץ and למינו.

ἐπὶ τῆς γῆς. In a significant majority of cases in Genesis (24x), this phrase is G's equivalent for על הארץ, as opposed to six instances of ἐπὶ τὴν γῆν. The latter option does contrast with other equivalences that occur in proximity to it: בארץ – ἐπὶ τῆς γῆς (2.5; 6.17) or מעל הארץ – ἀπὸ τῆς γῆς (8.3) or בין הארץ – (ἀνὰ μέσον) τῆς γῆς (9.13). One also observes that in the contexts in which ἐπὶ τὴν γῆν appears as the equivalent to על הארץ, the passage has to do with natural phenomena that affect the earth from above: rain (2.5; 7.4), flood (6.17), wind (8.1), clouds (9.14), or sun (19.23). These are the kinds of factors that could have affected G's choice of case.

καὶ ἐγένετο οὕτως. Regarding the transition formula, see verse 6.

1.12

ותוצא הארץ דשא עשב מזריע זרע למינהו ועץ עשה פרי אשר זרעו
בו למינהו וירא אלהים כי טוב

καὶ ἐξήνεγκεν ἡ γῆ βοτάνην χόρτου, σπεῖρον σπέρμα κατὰ γένος καὶ
καθ᾽ ὁμοιότητα, καὶ ξύλον κάρπιμον ποιοῦν καρπόν, οὗ τὸ σπέρμα
αὐτοῦ ἐν αὐτῷ κατὰ γένος ἐπὶ τῆς γῆς. καὶ εἶδεν ὁ θεὸς ὅτι καλόν.
And the earth brought forth herbaceous vegetation, seeding seed
according to kind and according to likeness, and a fruit–bearing
tree producing fruit of which its seed is in it according to kind, on
the earth. And God saw that it was good.

καὶ ἐξήνεγκεν. In the *Tatbericht*, G follows his source text in choosing a different verb from the one employed in the *Wortbericht* in verse 11 to depict
the earth's role in generating plant life. The word ἐκφέρω occurs a total of
three times in Genesis (1.12; 14.18; 24.53), and all three times its semantically equivalent counterpart is יצא hiphil.

σπεῖρον σπέρμα. Regarding the translation of this phrase, see verse 11.

κατὰ γένος καὶ καθ᾽ ὁμοιότητα. G produces a double translation of למינהו
in his source text, the same wording that is employed in verse 11 for the
description of the σπέρμα produced by the βοτάνη χόρτου ("herbaceous
vegetation"), but there without a counterpart in the source text.

ξύλον κάρπιμον. In another move to harmonize the wording of the *Wortbericht* and the *Tatbericht*, G here supplies the adjective that modifies ξύλον
in verse 11, though his source text would have read simply עץ.

κατὰ γένος ἐπὶ τῆς γῆς. G's rendering of the second occurrence of למינהו
in this verse is now simply κατὰ γένος rather than the double translation
noted above. Thus the pattern observed in verse 11—with κατὰ γένος καὶ
καθ᾽ ὁμοιότητα used to characterize the σπέρμα generated by the βοτάνη
χόρτου, and only κατὰ γένος employed in connection with the σπέρμα con-
tained in the fruit of the ξύλον κάρπιμον—is replicated in the present verse.
    G here further harmonizes the *Tatbericht* with the *Wortbericht* by
adding the phrase ἐπὶ τῆς γῆς after κατὰ γένος in order to mirror the
wording of verse 11 where, however, the source text reads על הארץ.

Presumably the phrase ἐπὶ τῆς γῆς modifies the description of the pro-
pogation of both the βοτάνη χόρτου and the ξύλον κάρπιμον. G's addition
of the phrase here in verse 12 creates something of an *inclusio* for the
Tatbericht, like the one that exists in the *Wortbericht* of verse 11 in the
LXX and its source text.

καὶ εἶδεν ὁ θεὸς ὅτι καλόν. Regarding the divine approbation formula, see
verse 8.

1.13

ויהי ערב ויהי בקר יום שלישי

καὶ ἐγένετο ἑσπέρα καὶ ἐγένετο πρωί, ἡμέρα τρίτη.

And it came to be evening, and it came to be morning, a third day.

G replicates his source text as he does with the concluding formula for
each of the days of the *Hexaemeron*.

1.14

ויאמר אלהים יהי מארת ברקיע השמים להבדיל בין היום ובין הלילה
והיו לאתת ולמועדים ולימים ושנים

Καὶ εἶπεν ὁ θεὸς Γενηθήτωσαν φωστῆρες ἐν τῷ στερεώματι τοῦ
οὐρανοῦ εἰς φαῦσιν τῆς γῆς τοῦ διαχωρίζειν ἀνὰ μέσον τῆς ἡμέρας καὶ
ἀνὰ μέσον τῆς νυκτὸς καὶ ἔστωσαν εἰς σημεῖα καὶ εἰς καιροὺς καὶ εἰς
ἡμέρας καὶ εἰς ἐνιαυτούς,

And God said, "Let luminaries come into being in the firmament
of the sky for illumination of the earth, to separate between the
day and between the night, and let them be for signs and for seasons and for days and for years,

Γενηθήτωσαν φωστῆρες. The agreement in number between verb and subject in the Greek text is not matched in the source text, a situation that can
occur in Hebrew when the predicate precedes the subject (GKC §145o).
The word φωστήρ, which first appears here in extant Greek literature, is
the equivalent for מאור in four of its five occurrences in Genesis, once in
this verse and three times in verse 16. In verse 15, the LXX counterpart is
φαῦσις. Both φωστήρ and מאור are cognates of the nouns that are used in
verse 3 to designate light (φῶς, אור) and both denote a source of light or
luminary.

εἰς φαῦσιν τῆς γῆς. This phrase constitutes a plus in comparison to the MT. The Greek version here may reflect a source text similar to the SamPent in which להאיר על הארץ follows ברקיע השמים, as is the case in verses 15 and 17 in both the MT and the SamPent (Wevers 1993, 8; Tov 1985, 6, 23 n. 10; Hendel 1998, 28–29). It would appear, therefore, that the Sam-Pent reading in verse 14 consitutes evidence of harmonizing activity in the Hebrew textual history, which is subsequently reflected in the LXX (Hendel 1998, 29). It should be noted, however, that the Greek equivalent for להאיר על הארץ in verses 15 and 17 is ὥστε φαίνειν ἐπὶ τῆς γῆς, which is a more isomorphic rendering than εἰς φαῦσιν τῆς γῆς. The ὥστε + infinitive construction typically expresses result (Smyth §§2011, 2260–2263; LSJ s.v. "ὥστε" B.I), whereas εἰς with the accusative is often used in purpose clauses (Smyth §1686d; LSJ s.v. "εἰς" V.2). In verse 14, then, in comparison to the MT, G further emphasizes the purpose for the calling forth of the luminaries, whose "primary role in dividing day from night is the giving of light" on the earth (Wevers 1993, 8). Like φωστήρ, φαῦσις is noteworthy as a term whose first appearance in extant Greek literature is in the LXX (Gen 1.14, 15; Ps 74[73].16; Idt 13.13).

τοῦ διαχωρίζειν. G's equivalent for the Hebrew preposition + infinitive construct (להבדיל) is an articular infinitive, which is another standard Greek construction for signifying purpose (Smyth §1408).

ἀνὰ μέσον … καὶ ἀνὰ μέσον. On the repetition of ἀνὰ μέσον in imitation of repeated בין, see verse 4.

καὶ ἔστωσαν εἰς σημεῖα καὶ εἰς καιροὺς καὶ εἰς ἡμέρας καὶ εἰς ἐνιαυτούς. The specification of the luminaries' purpose continues. G has replicated his source text quantitatively, except for inserting the preposition εἰς prior to ἐνιαυτούς—without a corresponding ל—in order to continue the pattern established in the preceding list. This has the effect of specifying four distinct categories with respect to the functioning of the φωστῆρες rather than three (Wevers 1993, 8).

The significance of the choice of σημεῖον to designate one of these functions is as debatable as that of its counterpart אות in the source text. Presumably these terms refer in the present context to phenomena involving the celestial luminaries that may be interpreted as omens of one sort or another (e.g., 4 Rgns 20.8–11; Esa 38.7–8; Ier 10.2; Philo, Opif. 58–59). Elsewhere in Genesis, the σημεῖον – אות equivalence is associated with the mark placed on Kain (4.15), the covenant sign of the rainbow following the flood (9.12, 13, 17), and the covenant sign of circumcision (17.11).

G employs καιρός as the equivalent for מועד here, and for its other occurrences in Genesis, all three of which have to do with the appointed time of Isaak's birth (17.21; 18.14; 21.2). The Greek term typically pertains to times of special significance or import rather than to time in the generic, abstract, or durative sense that is more often associated with χρόνος (Gen 26.1, 15; see LSJ). In the present verse, καιρούς is an appropriate translation choice to convey the idea of מועדים, which likely refers to the cultic events on the Israelite liturgical calendar rather than to the seasons of nature (Wevers 1993, 8; Wenham 1987, 23).

G's choice of ἐνιαυτός to translate שנה is noteworthy inasmuch as it is not the usual equivalent. Of the total number of occurrences of שנה in Genesis, 110 are rendered by ἔτος whereas only five are rendered by ἐνιαυτός. In addition to the present context, which deals with the function of the celestial luminaries in demarcating annual cycles, in 17.21 the latter term is used in connection with the promised birth of Isaak in the coming year; in 26.12 the time reference pertains to the year in which Isaak experiences a hundredfold yield of barley; in 47.17 it has to do with the year of the famine in Egypt when Ioseph takes the Egyptians' livestock in exchange for bread; and in 47.28 it applies to the tally of "Iakob's days of the years of his life" (αἱ ἡμέραι Ἰακὼβ ἐνιαυτῶν τῆς ζωῆς αὐτοῦ). So whether the focus is on nature's calendar, a year that is associated with a singular event, or the reckoning of someone's age, there appears to be no evident rationale for the choice of ἐνιαυτός other than stylistic variation.

1.15

והיו למאורת ברקיע השמים להאיר על הארץ ויהי כן

καὶ ἔστωσαν εἰς φαῦσιν ἐν τῷ στερεώματι τοῦ οὐρανοῦ ὥστε φαίνειν ἐπὶ τῆς γῆς. καὶ ἐγένετο οὕτως.

and let them be for illumination in the firmament of the sky so as to give light upon the earth." And it became so.

Because of the presence of the phrase εἰς φαῦσιν τῆς γῆς in verse 14 (presumably a reflection of G's source text), the repetition of the creator's declaration here in the concluding section of the *Wortbericht* that the φωστῆρες are to illuminate the earth makes for even more redundancy in the LXX than in the MT.

εἰς φαῦσιν. This phrase, which reiterates the first purpose statement regarding the luminaries in the previous verse, is the counterpart to the MT's למאורת. Apart from the fact that φαῦσιν is singular and מאורת is plural, what further distinguishes these two terms is that φαῦσις describes function whereas מאור incorporates the element of identity, as is the case with φωστήρ, the equivalent for מאור in verses 14 and 16.

ὥστε φαίνειν ἐπὶ τῆς γῆς. This result clause corresponds isomorphically to the Hebrew source text להאיר על הארץ. See the discussion concerning the phrase εἰς φαῦσιν τῆς γῆς in verse 14, and the one that deals with ἐπὶ τῆς γῆς in verse 11.

καὶ ἐγένετο οὕτως. Regarding the transition formula, see verse 6.

1.16

ויעש אלהים את שני המארת הגדלים את המאור הגדל לממשלת
היום ואת המאור הקטן לממשלת הלילה ואת הכוכבים

καὶ ἐποίησεν ὁ θεὸς τοὺς δύο φωστῆρας τοὺς μεγάλους, τὸν φωστῆρα τὸν μέγαν εἰς ἀρχὰς τῆς ἡμέρας καὶ τὸν φωστῆρα τὸν ἐλάσσω εἰς ἀρχὰς τῆς νυκτός, καὶ τοὺς ἀστέρας.

And God made the two great luminaries, the great luminary for rulership of the day and the lesser luminary for rulership of the night, and the stars.

τὸν μέγαν ... τὸν ἐλάσσω. In the *Tatbericht* for the fourth day of creation, G distinguishes between "the two great luminaries" by employing an adjective in the positive degree for the first (τὸν μέγαν) and one in the comparative degree for the second (τὸν ἐλάσσω). In Hebrew there are, of course, no distinctive forms for comparatives or superlatives. In situations like this that involve correlative comparatives, the simple adjective with the article is used (GKC §133*a,f*): הגדל ... הקטן. Due to negative interference from the source text (Toury 1995, 274–6), G replicates this kind of construction in the case of the first adjective, but then conforms to Greek idiom in the case of the second (C-S §64; Thackeray §12, 13).

εἰς ἀρχάς ... εἰς ἀρχάς. G employs the plural form of the noun ἀρχή to render the singular Hebrew noun ממשלה, which in Genesis occurs only in this verse. This Greek construction may be understood in terms of an abstract plural that "refers to the single ... cases ... [or] manifestations of the idea expressed by the abstract substantive" (Smyth §1000.3; Brown 1993, 52 n. 58).

1.17

ויתן אתם אלהים ברקיע השמים להאיר על הארץ

καὶ ἔθετο αὐτοὺς ὁ θεὸς ἐν τῷ στερεώματι τοῦ οὐρανοῦ ὥστε φαίνειν ἐπὶ τῆς γῆς,

And God set them in the firmament of the sky so as to give light upon the earth

ἔθετο. Of the twenty-seven times that τίθημι occurs in Genesis, it serves as the equivalent to נתן on twelve occasions (1.17; 9.13; 15.10; 17.2, 5, 6; 30.40; 40.3; 41.10, 48 [2x]; 42.30). There is indeed semantic overlap between these two lexemes, though in both cases their semantic range is quite broad. In Genesis, τίθημι is G's choice of counterpart to four other Hebrew verbs (אסף, נוח hiphil, שים, שית), while נתן, which occurs 150 times in the book, is rendered by twelve other Greek verbs (ἀποδίδωμι, ἀφίημι, δίδωμι, ἐμβάλλω, ἐπιδίδωμι, ἵστημι, καθίστημι, παρατίθημι, περιτίθημι, ποιέω, προεκφέρω, προσδίδωμι).

ὥστε φαίνειν ἐπὶ τῆς γῆς. This result clause corresponds isomorphically to the Hebrew source text להאיר על הארץ (cf. v. 15). See the discussion concerning the phrase εἰς φαῦσιν τῆς γῆς in verse 14, and the one that deals with ἐπὶ τῆς γῆς in verse 11.

1.18

ולמשל ביום ובלילה ולהבדיל בין האור ובין החשך וירא אלהים כי
טוב

καὶ ἄρχειν τῆς ἡμέρας καὶ τῆς νυκτὸς καὶ διαχωρίζειν ἀνὰ μέσον τοῦ φωτὸς καὶ ἀνὰ μέσον τοῦ σκότους. καὶ εἶδεν ὁ θεὸς ὅτι καλόν.

and to rule the day and the night and to separate between the light and between the darkness. And God saw that it was good.

καὶ ἄρχειν τῆς ἡμέρας καὶ τῆς νυκτός. In his choice of ἄρχω + genitive direct object, G fashions an acceptable translation that conforms to the norms of the target language rather than attempting to replicate the Hebrew idiom משל ב (Toury 1995, 56–57). This equivalence occurs two other times in Genesis (4.7; 45.26). It seems unlikely in the present context that ἄρχειν is governed by ὥστε in the preceding verse, in the sense that ruling day and night is to be regarded as the result of the luminaries being set in the firmament. Instead, like למשל, this infinitive should be understood as purposive.

διαχωρίζειν. Unlike διαχωρίζειν in the *Wortbericht* in verse 14, the infinitive here is not preceded by the genitive article. As in that earlier verse, however, this is an infinitive of purpose like להבדיל.

ἀνὰ μέσον … καὶ ἀνὰ μέσον. On the repetition of ἀνὰ μέσον in imitation of repeated בין, see verse 4.

καὶ εἶδεν ὁ θεὸς ὅτι καλόν. Regarding the divine approbation formula, see verse 8.

1.19

ויהי ערב ויהי בקר יום רביעי

καὶ ἐγένετο ἑσπέρα καὶ ἐγένετο πρωί, ἡμέρα τετάρτη.

And it came to be evening, and it came to be morning, a fourth day.

G replicates his source text as he does with the concluding formula for each of the days of the *Hexaemeron*.

1.20

ויאמר אלהים ישרצו המים שרץ נפש חיה ועוף יעופף על הארץ על
פני רקיע השמים

Καὶ εἶπεν ὁ θεός Ἐξαγαγέτω τὰ ὕδατα ἑρπετὰ ψυχῶν ζωσῶν καὶ πετεινὰ πετόμενα ἐπὶ τῆς γῆς κατὰ τὸ στερέωμα τοῦ οὐρανοῦ. καὶ ἐγένετο οὕτως.

And God said, "Let the waters bring forth creeping things among living creatures and birds flying on the earth against the firmament of the sky." And it became so.

Ἐξαγαγέτω τὰ ὕδατα. As is often the case in Greek, here the neuter plural subject, which is historically regarded to be a collective, takes a singular verb (Smyth §§958–59; Thackeray §3). In the source text, however, both the verb, ישרצו, and its subject, המים, are plural. Of the total of seventeen occurrences of ἐξάγω in Genesis, it is the equivalent for the verb שרץ only in this verse and in the next one. This is not surprising, since their semantic ranges do not coincide. With the choice of ἐξάγω in the present context, G in fact assigns to the waters the same productive capacity that will be ascribed to the earth in verse 24 (Brown 1993, 53 n. 60). There the source text has יצא hiphil, with which ἐξάγω does correspond semantically. This latter equivalence occurs a total of twelve times in Genesis (1.24; 8.17; 15.5, 7; 19.5, 8, 12, 17; 38.24; 40.14; 43.23; 48:12), while ἐξάγω is the counterpart to יצא qal in one additional case (11.31), to רוץ hiphil once (41.14), and to תעה hiphil once (20.13).

ἑρπετὰ ψυχῶν ζωσῶν. G uses plural forms to render the constituent components of the collective construction of the source text שרץ נפש חיה. The Greek genitive noun with its attributive participial modifier (ψυχῶν ζωσῶν) denotes the whole, of which the noun it limits (ἑρπετά) constitutes a part (see Smyth §§1306–7, 1310). This corresponds functionally with the *nomen rectum* in the absolute state that is followed by its attributive adjective modifier, and the Hebrew *nomen regens* in the construct state (GKC §89a). There is no cognate connection between the verb Ἐξαγαγέτω and the object ἑρπετά, as there is in the Hebrew version ישרצו ... שרץ.

The counterpart to the segholate noun שרץ is ἑρπετόν both here and in the only other place that it occurs in Genesis (7.21). These terms are not really semantically equivalent, and ἑρπετόν is in fact also G's choice for translating the segholate noun רמש in all ten of the contexts in which it appears in Genesis (1.24, 25, 26; 6.7, 20; 7.14, 23; 8.17, 19; 9.3). G's equivalences here in 1.20 in the *Wortbericht* for the fifth day—Ἐξαγαγέτω [ישרצו] τὰ ὕδατα ἑρπετὰ [שרץ] ψυχῶν ζωσῶν—are understandable in the light of his rendering of the *Tatbericht* in verse 21: πᾶσαν ψυχὴν ζώων ἑρπετῶν [הרמשת], ἃ ἐξήγαγεν [שרצו] τὰ ὕδατα. The translation strategy is clearly to forge an explicit linkage between the *Wortbericht* and the *Tatbericht* by employing the same Greek verb (ἐξάγω) and noun (ἑρπετόν) in both, despite the fact that the corresponding noun (שרץ) and attributive participle (√רמש) in the source text are different. It should be noted that the participle is the verbal cognate of the noun רמש, which G consistently renders as ἑρπετόν.

With regard to ψυχή and נפש, they both have broad semantic ranges that overlap to a significant degree, as is the case here. The fact that ψυχή is G's translation choice in forty-one of the forty-three contexts in which נפש occurs in Genesis means that this equivalence is a nearly closed equation for him.

The attributive participial form of ζάω is an acceptable counterpart to the adjective חי. G employs this Greek root to render the Hebrew adjective twenty times in the book of Genesis (1.20, 24; 2.7, 19; 3.20; 8.21; 9.3, 10, 12, 15, 16; 25.6; 26.19; 43.7, 27, 28; 45.3, 26, 28; 46.30).

πετεινὰ πετόμενα. G again uses a plural noun (πετεινά) to translate a collective form (עוף) in his source text, which in and of itself is an appropriate strategy. The syntax of this part of the verse is, however, quite different in the two versions. In the LXX, the noun functions as the second part of the direct object of Ἐξαγαγέτω, and the participle that follows the noun of which it is a cognate form is an attributive modifier. This results in a rather odd scenario, given that the waters are called upon to bring forth birds in addition to sea creatures, a tradition that is perpetuated by "The Three": α' ἐξερψάτω τὰ ὕδατα ... πετηνὸν ἱπτάμενον, σ' ἐξερψάτω τὰ ὕδατα ... πετηνὸν πετόμενον, θ' ἐξερψάτωσαν τὰ ὕδατα ... πετηνὸν πετόμενον. Early commentators attempt to account for this peculiarity in different ways (Brown 1993, 53 n. 63). Philo explains that both types of creatures are "swimmers": ἑκάτερα γὰρ νηκτά (Opif. 63). Tertullian argues that material objects or beings have material origins of one sort or another:

> Whatever was made out of something, has its origin in something made [Etiamsi quid ex aliquo factum est, ex facto habet censum]: for instance, out of the ground was made the grass, and the fruit, and the cattle, and the form of man himself; so from the waters were produced the animals which swim and fly [ut ex aquis natatiles et volatiles animae] (Herm. 33; trans. Holmes).

Augustine propounds the idea that the environments that both sea creatures and winged creatures inhabit, and thus from which they would have emerged, are in fact aqueous:

> These two kinds of living creatures are described as produced from the waters [ex aquis productum esse]. Some water, therefore, is in a liquid and flowing state [undosum et fluidum est]; other water is in the rarified form of a vapor distributed in the air [vaporaliter tenuatum atque suspensum]. Both forms are classed under the moist element [utrumque tamen humidae naturae deputatur], the one being assigned to living creatures that creep [reptilibus] on the earth and the other to creatures that fly [volatilibus] (Gen. litt. 3.3.5; trans. Taylor).

As for G's source text, there is no indication in the textual history that the verb of which עוף is the subject would have been anything other than יעופף, namely the *polel* jussive form of the verbal cognate of the noun עוף. Thus in the Hebrew, the origin of birds is not ascribed to the waters, as is the case with the שרץ נפש חיה; instead the author's focus is on their flying about (BDB, s.v. "עוף I").

ἐπὶ τῆς γῆς. Regarding G's choice of this phrase to render על הארץ, see the discussion in verse 11.

κατὰ τὸ στερέωμα. As the description of the designated context for the flight of birds continues, G's choice for the counterpart to the prepositional construction על פני is κατά—the only place in Genesis where this particular equivalence is found. A quantitative rendering of the same Hebrew construction is κατὰ πρόσωπον, which occurs four times in the book (16.12; 25.18 [2x]; 32.21[22]). The focus of κατά + accusative in the present context, following the rather ambiguous phrase ἐπὶ τῆς γῆς, is on specifying further the location of birds in flight. Possible denotations for the Greek preposition in relation to τὸ στερέωμα include "throughout" and "in the region of" (LSJ). If, however, as seems likely, G is interested in describing things from the perspective of an observer looking upward, "against" would likely be the intended sense.

καὶ ἐγένετο οὕτως. G's transition formula has no counterpart in extant Hebrew texts, and so its presence here at the conclusion of the *Wortbericht*, as is usually the case in the *Hexaemeron*, is to be attributed to the harmonizing activity of the translator. See the relevant discussion in verse 6.

1.21
ויברא אלהים את התנינם הגדלים ואת כל נפש החיה הרמשת אשר
שרצו המים למינהם ואת כל עוף כנף למינהו וירא אלהים כי טוב
καὶ ἐποίησεν ὁ θεὸς τὰ κήτη τὰ μεγάλα καὶ πᾶσαν ψυχὴν ζῴων
ἑρπετῶν, ἃ ἐξήγαγεν τὰ ὕδατα κατὰ γένη αὐτῶν, καὶ πᾶν πετεινὸν
πτερωτὸν κατὰ γένος. καὶ εἶδεν ὁ θεὸς ὅτι καλά.
And God made the great sea monsters and every creature among creeping animals, which the waters brought forth according to their kinds, and every winged bird according to kind. And God saw that they were good.

καὶ ἐποίησεν. Regarding ποιέω as the translation of ברא, see verse 1.

τὰ κήτη τὰ μεγάλα καὶ πᾶσαν ψυχὴν ζῴων ἑρπετῶν. In the *Tatbericht* of the fifth day, G follows his source text in dividing ἑρπετὰ ψυχῶν ζωσῶν ("creeping things among living creatures") // שרץ נפש חיה ("swarms of living creatures") mentioned in the *Wortbericht* in verse 20 into two subgroups (Wevers 1993, 11).

τὰ κήτη τὰ μεγάλα. This is the only context in Genesis in which the term κῆτος appears, and it serves as the equivalent for the single occurrence of תנין in the book. Elsewhere in the LXX, κῆτος is associated with לויתן ("Leviathan," Iob 3.8), רהב ("Rahab," Iob 26.12; cf. 9.13), and דגה/דג ("fish," Ion 2.1 [2x], 2, 11). Wevers remarks that לויתן and רהב are "both mythological creatures," although in the present context the mention of τὰ κήτη "in itself has no mythological overtones and simply refers to large sea monsters or fish" (Wevers 1993, 11). The reference to התנינם in G's source text does not appear to have mythological connotations either, though elsewhere תנין is linked with לויתן (Isa 27.1) and רהב (Isa 51.9).

πᾶσαν ψυχὴν ζῴων ἑρπετῶν. As in the description of the sea creatures in verse 20, G here employs a genitive noun with its attributive modifier (ζῴων ἑρπετῶν) to signify the whole, of which the noun it delimits (ψυχήν) constitutes a part. There is something of a reversal with respect to the categories of whole and part, however, in that, whereas in verse 20 the former consists of ψυχῶν ζωσῶν ("living creatures") and the latter of ἑρπετά ("creeping things"), the former now consists of ζῴων ἑρπετῶν ("creeping animals") and the latter of πᾶσαν ψυχήν ("every creature"). G therefore makes use of the same lexical roots in both verses (ψυχ-, ζω-, ἑρπετ-), though in his source text there would be variation with respect to the counterparts for the third one of these (שרץ [v. 20], רמש [v. 21]; see the discussion of ἑρπετόν in v. 20). The grammar of the source text in verse 21 also differs from that of the Greek translation. G's combination of singular part (πᾶσαν ψυχήν) + plural whole (ζῴων ἑρπετῶν) is the counterpart to a Hebrew singular construction throughout, consisting of a construct phrase (כל נפש) + adjectival and participial attributive modifiers (החיה הרמשת).

ἃ ἐξήγαγεν τὰ ὕδατα. The specific antecedent for the neuter relative pronoun ἃ is τὰ κήτη, though undoubtedly the second component of the direct object of ἐποίησεν—namely, πᾶσαν ψυχὴν ζῴων ἑρπετῶν—is in view as well. Regarding the neuter plural subject τὰ ὕδατα with the singular verb ἐξήγαγεν, in contrast to the plurality of both subject and verb in the source text, see verse 20.

κατὰ γένη αὐτῶν ... κατὰ γένος. Because two genera of sea creatures are specified in the *Tatbericht*, G employs the plural γένη as the counterpart to the singular מין in his source text, the only time this occurs in Genesis. The genitive pronoun αὐτῶν corresponds to the plural pronominal suffix in the source text. All occurrences of מין in Genesis include pronominal suffixes. Elsewhere in OG Genesis, however, a suffix follows γένος only when ἑρπετά/ἑρπετόν precedes without an intervening reference to another kind of creature (1.25 [3°]; 6.20 [3°]; 8.19; but not 7.14 [3°]). True to form, in the present verse, γένος without an accompanying pronoun follows the mention of the genus of winged creature.

πᾶν πετεινὸν πτερωτόν. G produces an acceptable rendering of כל עוף כנף, the construct phrase of his source text. The attributive adjective πτερωτόν appropriately expresses the function of the *nomen rectum*, כנף.

καὶ εἶδεν ὁ θεὸς ὅτι καλά. This is the first place in the opening section of Genesis where the divine approbation formula concludes with a plural adjective (καλά) rather than a singular one (καλόν). G thereby highlights the plurality of the genera that God makes on the fifth day, a feature that טוב in his source text does not explicitly communicate. Regarding the divine approbation formula, see verse 8.

1.22

ויברך אתם אלהים לאמר פרו ורבו ומלאו את המים בימים והעוף
ירב בארץ

καὶ εὐλόγησεν αὐτὰ ὁ θεὸς λέγων Αὐξάνεσθε καὶ πληθύνεσθε καὶ πληρώσατε τὰ ὕδατα ἐν ταῖς θαλάσσαις, καὶ τὰ πετεινὰ πληθυνέσθω ἐπὶ τῆς γῆς.

And God blessed them, saying, "Increase, and multiply, and fill the waters in the seas, and let birds multiply on the earth."

καὶ εὐλόγησεν. G employs εὐλογέω as the equivalent for ברך *piel* all fifty-nine times that the latter occurs in Genesis. This translation choice appears to represent an innovation with respect to the incorporation of a new component of meaning into the semantic range of εὐλογέω. In pre-LXX and other nontranslation Greek literature, this verb typically denotes "speak well of, praise" (LSJ). In the present context and variously throughout the LXX, the intended sense seems to be that of the above-mentioned Hebrew verb, which, when God is the subject, has to do with bestowing power or benefits upon someone or something (*HALOT*, s.v. "ברך II"; BDAG, xxii; s.v. "εὐλογέω"; Hiebert 2001, 266–67).

λέγων. In the narrative to this point, God's direct speech has been introduced by the verb εἶπεν. This is the first of seventy-two instances in Genesis that a participial form of λέγω is used to render the Hebrew "uninflected direct speech marker" לאמר (Wevers 1993, 12), forty-four of which as in this context take the form of the masculine nominative singular present active participle.

Αὐξάνεσθε. The semantic ranges of αὐξάνω ("increase") and its counterpart in the source text, פרה *qal* ("be fruitful"), do not overlap. Nevertheless, for all fifteen occurrences of the verb פרה in Genesis—ten in the *qal* (1.22, 28; 8.17; 9.1, 7; 26.22; 35.11; 47.27; 49.22[2x]) and five in the *hiphil* (17.6, 20; 28.3; 41.52; 48.4)—G's equivalent is αὐξάνω. One might have expected a Greek equivalent such as καρπόω in the light of the fact that the καρπ- root is used throughout the book for the cognate noun פרי. G's strategy in this case, however, seems to have been to interpret the concept of fruitfulness in terms of its practical implications, namely growth in numbers.

πληθύνεσθε. G employs πληθύνω in twenty-five of the twenty-six contexts in which the רבה I verb occurs in his source text. These terms are semantically equivalent.

πληρώσατε. The verb πληρόω is G's equivalent for מלא *qal* in six of the eight contexts in which the latter appears in Genesis, including all three cases of the imperative volitional form which is employed here (1.22, 28; 9.1). These are likewise semantically equivalent terms.

καὶ τὰ πετεινὰ πληθυνέσθω. G replicates the word order of his source text in positioning the subject before the verb, which in both Greek and Hebrew involves the same root as the one used earlier in the present verse in the directive to sea creatures to multiply (πληθύνω, רבה). The Greek neuter plural subject τὰ πετεινά is the counterpart to the Hebrew collective העוף.

In both cases, the article marks generic usage (hence no article appears in either NETS or the NRSV), and both nouns take singular verbs. The neuter plural noun and singular verb combination in the Greek accords with what is found in verses 20 and 21, where the subject is τὰ ὕδατα and the verb is an aorist indicative singular form of ἐξάγω, though the Hebrew subject and verb in those cases are of course both plural. In the present context, a Greek third-person imperative (πληθυνέσθω) constitutes an acceptable equivalent to the Hebrew jussive (ירב).

ἐπὶ τῆς γῆς. G opts for this prepositional phrase nineteen times in Genesis to render the source text construction consisting of the ב preposition + articulated noun ארץ, typically when no attendant modifiers are involved. It is normally when modifiers are present (e.g., relative clauses, demonstrative pronouns) that the preposition employed is ἐν and its object is in the dative: ἐν τῇ γῇ, ᾗ ἄν σοι εἴπω (26.2); ἐν τῇ γῇ ταύτῃ (26.3); ἐν τῇ γῇ ἐκείνῃ (26.12; 35.21[22]). Perhaps the exception that proves the rule is found in the clause Παροικεῖν ἐν τῇ γῇ ἥκαμεν (47.4), where no such modifier is present. The ἐν + dative object phrase is almost always G's choice of equivalent when the corresponding prepositional phrase with ארץ is in a construct relationship with a following *nomen rectum* or it includes a pronominal suffix, either with the article (10x) or without one (43x). It is clear, therefore, that G has established certain patterns in rendering these constructions in his source text.

1.23

ויהי ערב ויהי בקר יום חמישי

καὶ ἐγένετο ἑσπέρα καὶ ἐγένετο πρωί, ἡμέρα πέμπτη.

And it came to be evening, and it came to be morning, a fifth day.

G replicates his source text as he does with the concluding formula for each of the days of the *Hexaemeron*.

1.24

ויאמר אלהים תוצא הארץ נפש חיה למינה בהמה ורמש וחיתו ארץ
למינה ויהי כן

Καὶ εἶπεν ὁ θεός Ἐξαγαγέτω ἡ γῆ ψυχὴν ζῶσαν κατὰ γένος, τετράποδα καὶ ἑρπετὰ καὶ θηρία τῆς γῆς κατὰ γένος. καὶ ἐγένετο οὕτως.

And God said, "Let the earth bring forth the living creature according to kind: quadrupeds and creeping things and wild animals of the earth according to kind." And it became so.

Ἐξαγαγέτω. Regarding G's use of ἐξάγω to render יצא hiphil, see verse 20.

ψυχὴν ζῶσαν. G employs the same equivalents for נפש חיה as in verse 20, except that in the present verse singular, rather than plural, forms are counterparts to the collective construction in the source text.

κατὰ γένος … κατὰ γένος. Regarding the translation pattern followed by G in rendering these מין constructions, see verse 21.

τετράποδα … ἑρπετά … θηρία. G employs plural forms for the collective nouns in his source text.

τετράποδα. G's choice of τετράπους as the counterpart to בהמה, only here and in 34.23, is a striking one, inasmuch as his usual equivalent in Genesis is κτῆνος (19x), including the case in the *Tatbericht* in the following verse. With no discernible pattern with respect to the choice of one equivalent or another, it appears as though G is motivated by the desire for stylistic variation when he departs from his default equivalence. Elsewhere in the Pentateuch, the respective ratios of τετράπους versus κτῆνος as equivalents for בהמה are: Exodus: 4–14; Leuitikon: 6–24; Numbers: 1–15; Deuteronomion: 0–14.

ἑρπετά. Regarding G's use of ἑρπετόν as the equivalent for both רמש and שרץ, see verse 20.

θηρία. G employs θηρίον as an acceptable equivalent for the noun חיה in seventeen of its eighteen occurrences in his source text. No attempt is made to reflect the different forms of the *nomen regens* in the present context and the following verse, חיתו and חית (GKC §90o).

καὶ ἐγένετο οὕτως. Regarding the transition formula, see verse 6.

1.25

ויעש אלהים את חית הארץ למינה ואת הבהמה למינה ואת כל רמש
האדמה למינהו וירא אלהים כי טוב

καὶ ἐποίησεν ὁ θεὸς τὰ θηρία τῆς γῆς κατὰ γένος καὶ τὰ κτήνη κατὰ
γένος καὶ πάντα τὰ ἑρπετὰ τῆς γῆς κατὰ γένος αὐτῶν. καὶ εἶδεν ὁ θεὸς
ὅτι καλά.

And God made the wild animals of the earth according to kind
and the cattle according to kind and all the creeping things of the
earth according to their kind. And God saw that they were good.

τὰ θηρία … τὰ κτήνη … πάντα τὰ ἑρπετά. Once again, G employs plural
forms to render the collectives in his source text. The sequence of genera
differs from that of the list in the preceding *Wortbericht*, though in both
verses there are three. As mentioned in the discussion regarding τετράποδα
in verse 24, in the present context the equivalent for בהמה is G's default,
κτῆνος.

κατὰ γένος … κατὰ γένος … κατὰ γένος αὐτῶν. Regarding the translation
pattern followed by G in rendering these מין constructions, see verse 21.

καὶ εἶδεν ὁ θεὸς ὅτι καλά. Regarding this version of the divine approbation
formula, see verse 21.

1.26

ויאמר אלהים נעשה אדם בצלמנו כדמותנו וירדו בדגת הים ובעוף
השמים ובבהמה ובכל הארץ ובכל הרמש הרמש על הארץ

καὶ εἶπεν ὁ θεὸς Ποιήσωμεν ἄνθρωπον κατ' εἰκόνα ἡμετέραν καὶ καθ'
ὁμοίωσιν, καὶ ἀρχέτωσαν τῶν ἰχθύων τῆς θαλάσσης καὶ τῶν πετεινῶν
τοῦ οὐρανοῦ καὶ τῶν κτηνῶν καὶ πάσης τῆς γῆς καὶ πάντων τῶν
ἑρπετῶν τῶν ἑρπόντων ἐπὶ τῆς γῆς.

Then God said, "Let us make humankind according to our image
and according to likeness, and let them rule the fish of the sea
and the birds of the sky and the cattle and all the earth and all the
creeping things that creep upon the earth."

ἄνθρωπον. G employs ἄνθρωπος as the counterpart to אדם twenty-seven
times in Genesis, including the present context, and in all but one of the
remaining twenty-six occurrences of the latter (where there is no Greek
counterpart), the equivalent is the proper noun Ἀδάμ. Here in 1.26, anarthrous ἄνθρωπον, like אדם, "denotes generic humanity" (Wevers 1993, 14;
LSJ).

κατ' εἰκόνα ἡμετέραν. G always employs εἰκών as an equivalent for צלם in Genesis (1.26, 27; 5.3; 9.6). Furthermore, both here and in the following verse, G's counterpart to בצלם is κατ' εἰκόνα. This translation differs from the more formally equivalent rendering ἐν εἰκόνι in 9.6, specifically in regard to the choice of prepositions. In 5.3, the phrase κατὰ τὴν εἰκόνα αὐτοῦ corresponds to כצלמו and features the prepositional equivalence κατά – כ that one would expect. This is the only place in the LXX Pentateuch where the possessive adjective ἡμέτερος is found. It thus provides a striking contrast to the fifty-seven occurrences in Genesis alone of the genitive plural personal pronoun ἡμῶν, which is the possessive form that typically modifies a substantive in the LXX.

καὶ καθ' ὁμοίωσιν. G departs from his source text by supplying the coordinating conjunction καί and not providing an equivalent for the first person plural pronominal suffix. The prepostion κατά, however, corresponds to כ. G's coordination of this phrase with the previous one gives rise to a syntactical, if not a semantic, distinction between them. In the source text, however, the second phrase without the conjunction may be interpreted as explicating the first one. The absence of a possessive form in the OG presumably reflects G's decision not to supply a counterpart to an element of the parent text that may be regarded as redundant (Wevers 1993, 14–15).

ἀρχέτωσαν. The verb ἄρχω is G's equivalent for רדה both here and in its only other occurrence in Genesis (1.28).

τῶν ἰχθύων ... τῶν πετεινῶν ... τῶν κτηνῶν ... πάσης τῆς γῆς ... πάντων τῶν ἑρπετῶν τῶν ἑρπόντων. The use of the genitive case for the items that comprise the direct object of ἄρχω conforms to standard Greek usage. G has therefore chosen a normal Greek construction to replace the Hebrew idiom that involves the preposition ב as a prefix for the constituent components of the object of the verb רדה. As has been noted in several previous contexts, G often renders Hebrew collective nouns as plurals: τῶν ἰχθύων – בדגת, τῶν πετεινῶν – בעוף, τῶν κτηνῶν – בבהמה, πάντων τῶν ἑρπετῶν τῶν ἑρπόντων – בכל הרמש הרמש הרמש. The other item in this sequence, בכל הארץ, is not, of course, a collective, and G shows his awareness of that fact by rendering the phrase πάσης τῆς γῆς.

ἐπὶ τῆς γῆς. See the discussion regarding this phrase as the rendering for
על הארץ in verse 11.

1.27

ויברא אלהים את האדם בצלמו בצלם אלהים ברא אתו זכר ונקבה
ברא אתם

καὶ ἐποίησεν ὁ θεὸς τὸν ἄνθρωπον, κατ᾽ εἰκόνα θεοῦ ἐποίησεν αὐτόν,
ἄρσεν καὶ θῆλυ ἐποίησεν αὐτούς.

And God made humankind;
according to divine image he made it;
male and female he made them.

ἐποίησεν. Regarding the ποιέω – ברא equivalence, see verse 1.

τὸν ἄνθρωπον. In contrast to what occurs in verse 26, G has represented
generic humanity by means of an arthrous form of ἄνθρωπος, undoubtedly
in order to distinguish the corresponding differences in his source text:
ἄνθρωπον – אדם in verse 26; τὸν ἄνθρωπον – את האדם in the present verse
(Wevers 1993, 14–15).

κατ᾽ εἰκόνα θεοῦ. G apparently decided to simplify things in comparison to
what could be regarded as a redundant sequence in his source text—בצלמו
בצלם אלהים—by representing only the last two words in his translation.
See verse 26 regarding the κατ᾽ εἰκόνα – בצלם equivalence.

ἄρσεν. In Genesis, ἄρσην is the counterpart to זכר, the noun denoting male,
nine times, while the cognate adjective ἀρσενικός (functioning as a substantive) is the equivalent in the other five contexts in which this Hebrew noun
occurs. G's translation choices in these contexts thus reflect his source text.

θῆλυ. G employs this Greek term for all six occurrences of נקבה in his
Genesis source text.

1.28

ויברך אתם אלהים ויאמר להם אלהים פרו ורבו ומלאו את הארץ
וכבשה ורדו בדגת הים ובעוף השמים ובכל חיה הרמשת על הארץ

καὶ εὐλόγησεν αὐτοὺς ὁ θεὸς λέγων Αὐξάνεσθε καὶ πληθύνεσθε καὶ
πληρώσατε τὴν γῆν καὶ κατακυριεύσατε αὐτῆς καὶ ἄρχετε τῶν
ἰχθύων τῆς θαλάσσης καὶ τῶν πετεινῶν τοῦ οὐρανοῦ καὶ πάντων τῶν

κτηνῶν καὶ πάσης τῆς γῆς καὶ πάντων τῶν ἑρπετῶν τῶν ἑρπόντων ἐπὶ τῆς γῆς.

And God blessed them, saying, "Increase, and multiply, and fill the earth, and subdue it, and rule the fish of the sea and the birds of the sky and all the cattle and all the earth and all the creeping things that creep upon the earth."

εὐλόγησεν. Regarding the εὐλογέω – ברך piel equivalence, see verse 22.

λέγων. Regarding the occurrence of λέγων in Genesis, see verse 22. In the present case, however, the counterpart in the MT to this participial form is not the uninflected direct speech marker לאמר that appears in verse 22 and is the usual equivalent, but the clause ויאמר להם אלהים. It will be noted that the present verse and verse 22 begin the same way in both the OG and the MT: καὶ εὐλόγησεν αὐτοὺς (αὐτὰ [v. 22]) ὁ θεός – ויברך אתם אלהים. But then, as indicated, whereas the speech introduction formula that follows is the same in both verses in the OG, namely, λέγων, in the MT it differs. Hendel argues that the appearance of λέγων in the present verse is likely due to harmonizing activity that has occurred in the *Vorlage* of LXX Genesis, which he calls proto-G (Hendel 1998, 30). Wevers maintains that this is a case of harmonization by G (Wevers 1993, 16). In the absence of Hebrew evidence to support Hendel's contention, I am inclined to agree with Wevers.

Αὐξάνεσθε … πληθύνεσθε … πληρώσατε. Regarding the αὐξάνω – פרה, πληθύνω – רבה I, and πληρόω – מלא equivalences, see verse 22.

κατακυριεύσατε αὐτῆς. Greek κατακυριεύω is semantically equivalent to Hebrew כבש. Like its simplex cognate, κυριεύω, it takes a genitive direct object. The only other appearance of κατακυριεύω in Genesis occurs in a context where the MT has no counterpart (9.1).

ἄρχετε. Regarding the ἄρχω – רדה equivalence, see verse 26.

τῶν ἰχθύων … τῶν πετεινῶν … πάντων τῶν κτηνῶν … πάσης τῆς γῆς … πάντων τῶν ἑρπετῶν τῶν ἑρπόντων. Regarding the use of the genitive case for the direct object of ἄρχω, the use of this construction as a replacement for the Hebrew idiom רדה ב, and the rendering of Hebrew collective nouns as plurals (τῶν ἰχθύων – בדגת, τῶν πετεινῶν – בעוף) see verse 26.

καὶ πάντων τῶν κτηνῶν καὶ πάσης τῆς γῆς. This section of the OG text has no counterpart in the MT. Except for πάντων, however, it mirrors the wording of verse 26—where the source text reads ובבהמה ובכל הארץ—following τῶν ἰχθύων τῆς θαλάσσης καὶ τῶν πετεινῶν τοῦ οὐρανοῦ. Once again in the present verse, Hendel posits harmonizing activity in proto-G (Hendel 1998, 30–31), while Wevers assumes it is the work of the LXX translator (Wevers 1993, 16). The absence of other textual evidence would appear to tip the scales in favor of G.

καὶ πάντων τῶν ἑρπετῶν τῶν ἑρπόντων. G has employed plural forms to render singulars in his source text. Furthermore, this is the only place in Genesis where ἑρπετόν is the counterpart to the noun חיה, in comparison to seventeen other contexts where the equivalent is θηρίον. This anomaly is once again undoubtedly due to harmonization with verse 26 by G.

1.29

ויאמר אלהים הנה נתתי לכם את כל עשב זרע זרע אשר על פני כל
הארץ ואת כל העץ אשר בו פרי עץ זרע זרע לכם יהיה לאכלה

καὶ εἶπεν ὁ θεός Ἰδοὺ δέδωκα ὑμῖν πᾶν χόρτον σπόριμον σπεῖρον σπέρμα, ὅ ἐστιν ἐπάνω πάσης τῆς γῆς· καὶ πᾶν ξύλον, ὃ ἔχει ἐν ἑαυτῷ καρπὸν σπέρματος σπορίμου—ὑμῖν ἔσται εἰς βρῶσιν—

And God said, "See, I have given to you any herbage, sowable, seeding seed, which is over all the earth, and any tree that has in itself fruit of sowable seed—to you it shall be for food—

δέδωκα. In OG Genesis, there are ninety-nine perfect indicative verbs, compared to some 891 Hebrew perfects (excluding *weqatal* forms) in the MT of the book. The default tense employed by G to render Hebrew perfects is the aorist, a verb form that occurs 2,585 times in Genesis. In the first ten chapters of the book, for example, the Greek equivalents for 110 of the 133 Hebrew perfects are aorist indicative verbs. The lone Greek perfect indicative in chapter 1 is δέδωκα in the present verse, the counterpart to the perfect verb נתתי in the source text. In the same chapter, there are nine Hebrew perfects, seven of which are translated by aorist indicatives, and the other one besides נתתי is היתה in verse 2, which is rendered by the imperfect indicative of εἰμί (ἦν), for which, of course, there is no aorist verb form. It is clear, therefore, that δέδωκα here constitutes a deliberate departure from the default for G, a move that has semantic implications in terms of signifying the perfective aspect of the verb.

ὑμῖν … ὑμῖν. G appropriately employs the pronoun in the dative case for the prepostional phrase לכם in the source text.

πᾶν χόρτον. Thackeray (§12, 4) points out that the neuter pronominal adjective πᾶν in combination with the masculine noun χόρτον in the present context is the first of a number of such constructions in the LXX (e.g., πᾶν οἰκέτην [Ex 12.44]; πᾶν λόγον [Routh 4.7; 1 Suppl 27.1(2x); 2 Suppl 19.11]; πᾶν ἄνδρα [1 Rgns 11.8; PsSal 3.8]; πᾶν πόνον [3 Rgns 8.37; 2 Suppl 6.28]; πᾶν βουνόν [3 Rgns 15.22; Ier 2.20; Iezek 20.28; 34.6]; πᾶν υἱόν [3 Rgns 21.15]; πᾶν τεκτόνα [4 Rgns 24.14]; πᾶν οἶκον [4 Rgns 25.9; Iezek 36.10; Idt 4.15; Ier 13.11]; πᾶν δὲ ὑβριστήν [Iob 40.11]; πᾶν λίθον [Iezek 28.13]; πᾶν φόβον [Iezek 38.21]). Outside the LXX corpus, other examples may be found: πᾶν ἄρτον (T. Reu. 1.10); πᾶν λόγον (P.Mil. 1.2 27, Milan, Università Cattolica P.Med. 1 Ro [b–c], 158 BCE [http://tinyurl.com/SBL0466e]; UPZ 1.99, Leiden, National Museum of Antiquities 410, 158 BCE [http://tinyurl.com/SBL0466f]; O.Petr. 334, London, UC Inv. Nr. 62038, third century CE [http://tinyurl.com/SBL0466g]); παν τὸν τόπον (UPZ 1.5, Paris, Louvre N 2359, 163 BCE [http://www.trismegistos.org/text/5967]). Thackeray suggests the possibility that πᾶν χόρτον in Gen 1.29 could be "a *syntactical* colloquialism rather than a vulgarism of *accidence*" (Thackeray §12, 4; italics original). Wevers understands this construction to be the result of G's construal of the masculine accusative noun χόρτον as a neuter (Wevers 1993, 17). It seems more likely, however, that this is a case of a neuter adjectival form πᾶν being used for a generalizing purpose (see the discussion regarding βοτάνην and σπεῖρον in v. 11). This has semantic and therefore interpretative implications with regard to G's choice of equivalent for כל. Given the generalizing sense of the neuter form, it seems best to translate πᾶν as *any* (LSJ, s.v. "πᾶς" D.III.2).

Greek χόρτος is the equivalent for Hebrew עשב all seven times that it occurs in Genesis. It has been noted in the discussion regarding this equivalence in verse 11 that both terms can denote food for animals or humans that is derived from plants (as is the case both here and in the next verse).

σπόριμον σπεῖρον σπέρμα. The words σπόριμον σπεῖρον are a doublet translation of the participle זרע. Although the adjective σπόριμον (which in Genesis occurs only in this verse) could be read here as a masculine singular attributive modifier of χόρτον, it seems more likely that it is parallel to σπεῖρον and therefore neuter. These apposite adjectival forms, in turn, modify the gender-incongruent pair πᾶν χόρτον, while σπέρμα, of course, is the direct object of the participle σπεῖρον. One may observe that G not only produces the Hebraism σπεῖρον σπέρμα to represent the cognate phrase זרע זרע (cf. σπεῖρον σπέρμα – מזריע זרע in vv. 11 and 12), but also, without warrant from his source text, heightens the tautology by introducing the additional Greek cognate form σπόριμον to create the doublet rendering. This addition does, however, have the effect of forging a connection with the phrase καρπὸν σπέρματος σπορίμου as the interpretative translation of פרי עץ זרע זרע later in this verse.

ὅ ἐστιν ἐπάνω πάσης τῆς γῆς. In the OG, a copulative verb follows the relative pronoun, though in the source text, of course, the pronoun אשר without any accompanying verbal form constitutes normal Hebrew idiom. The Greek clause is likely to be understood as a nonrestrictive relative, introduced in English by *which* and serving to provide incidental information about the antecedent—in this case πᾶν χόρτον rather than σπέρμα—rather than a restrictive one, introduced in English by *that* and serving to define or articulate the identity of the antecedent. Of the twelve occurrences of the phrase על פני כל הארץ in the MT, only here in the OG is it rendered as ἐπάνω πάσης τῆς γῆς. The other place in the OG where there is not an explicit equivalent for פני in the above-mentioned Hebrew phrase is Gen 7.3: ἐπὶ πᾶσαν τὴν γῆν. Elsewhere πρόσωπον is utilized as the equivalent for פני: ἐπὶ παντὶ προσώπῳ πάσης τῆς γῆς (Gen 8.9); ἐπὶ προσώπου πάσης τῆς γῆς (Gen 11.4); ἐπὶ πρόσωπον πάσης τῆς γῆς (Gen 11.8, 9; Deut 11.25; 1 Rgns 30.16; 2 Rgns 18.8; Zach 5.3; Dan 8.5 θ'); ἐπὶ προσώπου τῆς γῆς (Dan 8.5 OG). The same is true in contexts where the middle elements of the Hebrew phrase are reversed (at least in the MT if not in the relevant source texts): על כל פני ארץ – ἐπὶ πρόσωπον τῆς γῆς (Gen 19.28); על כל פני הארץ – ἐπὶ προσώπου πάσης τῆς γῆς (Gen 41.56; Iezek 34.6). Phrases in Genesis other than the one under consideration here in 1.29 where ἐπάνω is the counterpart to על פני include ἐπάνω τῆς ἀβύσσου for על פני תהום in 1.2 and ἐπάνω τοῦ ὕδατος for על פני המים in 1.2 and 7.18. In these cases, it seems that the focus in the OG is less on the topmost parts of the entities mentioned (abyss, water, ground), as על פני might suggest, than on their surfaces in general. Thus with respect to the herbage described here in verse 29, it would appear that ἐπάνω πάσης τῆς γῆς refers not specifically to the soil in which it grows but more generally to the earth's surface that it covers.

πᾶν ξύλον. This phrase parallels πᾶν χόρτον, which occurs earlier in the same verse, though in the present context but unlike the previous one, there is gender congruence inasmuch as both adjective and noun are neuter. The parallel nature of these phrases in the OG is evident as well by virture of the fact that the respective nouns in both cases are anarthrous whereas in the source text the earlier one is anarthrous (את כל עשב) while the later one is not (את כל העץ). It seems likely that the generalizing sense of πᾶν denoting *any* obtains in the present case as well.

ὃ ἔχει ἐν ἑαυτῷ. G employs a different copula verb than the one used in the relative clause earlier in this verse, and in combination with the prepositional phrase that includes the reflexive pronoun it constitutes a sensible rendering of אשר בו in the source text.

καρπὸν σπέρματος σπορίμου. G's translation offers an intelligible interpretation of the source text (פרי עץ זרע זרע, literally "fruit of a tree seeding seed"), which exhibits a redundancy in the form of the repetition of the noun עץ in the relative clause of which the present phrase is a part, despite that noun's earlier appearance in the antecedent phrase ואת כל העץ. In both the OG and the source text, however, the focus is on the fruit that contains the seed that is to be disseminated. Accordingly, σπέρματος σπορίμου is to be understood as a genitive of material or contents (Smyth §1323).

ἔσται. This verb, like the corresponding Hebrew verb in the source text, is singular. Presumably the antecedent to the "dummy subject" signified by "it" in NETS is the herbage and fruit tree combination construed as a single entity.

βρῶσιν. The word βρῶσις is G's choice to render אכלה here as well as in two additional contexts in Genesis (1.30; 9.3). In the only other occurrence of אכלה in the book (6.21), G opts for the aorist infinitive of ἐσθίω in an interpretative translation of the clause והיה לך ולהם לאכלה – καὶ ἔσται σοὶ καὶ ἐκείνοις φαγεῖν. The βρῶσις – אכלה equivalence may be contrasted with G's employment of the plural of βρῶμα as the counterpart to the noun אכל in fifteen of its sixteen occurrences, the one exception being βρῶσις in 47.24.

1.30

ולכל חית הארץ ולכל עוף השמים ולכל רומש על הארץ אשר בו נפש
חיה את כל ירק עשב לאכלה ויהי כן

καὶ πᾶσιν τοῖς θηρίοις τῆς γῆς καὶ πᾶσιν τοῖς πετεινοῖς τοῦ οὐρανοῦ
καὶ παντὶ ἑρπετῷ ἕρποντι ἐπὶ τῆς γῆς, ὃ ἔχει ἐν ἑαυτῷ ψυχὴν ζωῆς,
καὶ πάντα χόρτον χλωρὸν εἰς βρῶσιν. καὶ ἐγένετο οὕτως.

and to all the wild animals of the earth and to all the birds of the
sky and to every creeping thing that creeps on the earth that has
in itself the animating force of life, and all green herbage for food."
And it became so.

πᾶσιν τοῖς θηρίοις ... πᾶσιν τοῖς πετεινοῖς. Following his source text, G continues to detail the components of the indirect object of δέδωκα in verse
29—namely, all the living creatures for which the herbage and trees provide food—and he again employs the dative case to represent prepositional
phrases with ל. G's equivalents for the collective nouns חיה and עוף in the
construct state are arthrous plurals. Combined with the plural of πᾶς, this
communicates that all members of each named species are included. The
combination of כל with a collective suggests the distributive idea of *each,
every* (GKC §127b; cf. NRSV).

παντὶ ἑρπετῷ ἕρποντι. In this case, G renders the singular phrase לכל
רומש in the singular, which represents a departure from the translator's
approach in earlier contexts where this type of creature is mentioned: all
other references are to ἑρπετά in the plural (vv. 20, 21, 24, 25, 26, 28).
Preceded by the adjective πᾶς in the singular, this then constitutes a shift
from the type of expression that is inclusive of all members of a species to
one that communicates the distributive sense in terms of every member
of a species. The phrase ἑρπετῷ ἕρποντι is G's counterpart to the participle
רומש in the source text. The choice of noun plus attributive participle is
presumably due to harmonization by G with respect to that previously-
occurring combination: πάντων τῶν ἑρπετῶν τῶν ἑρπόντων – בכל הרמש
הרמש (v. 26); πάντων τῶν ἑρπετῶν τῶν ἑρπόντων – בכל חיה הרמשת (v. 28).

ὃ ἔχει ἐν ἑαυτῷ. Regarding this clause as the rendering for אשר בו, see verse 29.

ψυχὴν ζωῆς. Although in the present context, as in verse 24, the source text reads נפש חיה, G has correctly distinguished one meaning of that phrase from the other. Here G employs the genitive noun ζωῆς ("life") to specify what it is that constitutes the animating force (ψυχήν) of a living creature. In verse 24, the attributive participle ζῶσαν ("living") serves to characterize the essence of the creature (ψυχήν) itself.

καὶ πάντα χόρτον χλωρόν. This phrase, like that of its counterpart in the source text, constitutes the third and final component of the direct object of the main verb (δέδωκα – נתתי) in the divine declaration that begins in verse 29. In Wevers's edition (We^ed) cited here, it begins with καί, which is presented as uncontested in the textual history of the LXX, though not adopted in the editions of Johann Grabe and Alfred Rahlfs, who relegate this καί to the status of a variant to the OG. In the Brooke-McLean edition of the so-called Cambridge LXX, the Christian apologist Theophilus of Antioch is cited as the lone witness to a text without καί (*Autol.* 2.11.63). As for the translations of Aquila, Symmachus, and Theodotion, they too lack καί. This agrees with the textual tradition of the majority of Hebrew manuscripts in which the corresponding phrase does not begin with the ו conjunction. Fifteen Hebrew manuscripts do, however, attest the conjunction (*BHK*), something that Wevers surprisingly fails to mention, given the fact that this evidence could be marshalled in support of his conclusion regarding the originality of καί. Admittedly, the presence of this καί further complicates the already complex syntax of the sentence that spans verses 29–30, and its absence would mitigate the situation somewhat. Without καί, the text would exhibit a more symmetrical structure in which sowable herbage and fruit trees are allocated for food to humans and "green herbage" to the animals. If one were to accept the text cited by Theophilus and adopted by Grabe and Rahlfs as OG, the argument for the secondary introduction of καί would presumably run along the following lines: Very early in the textual history of the LXX, a copyist, confused by the anacoluthon that concludes verse 29 (ὑμῖν ἔσται εἰς βρῶσιν), inserted καί before the clause πάντα χόρτον χλωρὸν εἰς βρῶσιν, thus isolating it from what precedes. All subsequent Greek copyists replicated the longer reading, and any Greek manuscripts that would have attested the shorter one ultimately disappeared. As for the presence of וֹ in the fifteen above-mentioned Hebrew manuscripts, they would presumably attest to a parallel phenomenon that occurred in the Hebrew textual history, but independently of what happened in the Greek textual tradition.

The preceding scenario, however, is problematic. In the first place, the evidence of virtually the entire textual tradition of the LXX and of a substantial number of Hebrew manuscripts raises the very real possibility that G's source text was different than that of the majority of extant Hebrew manuscripts. Secondly, the presence of καί constitutes the *lectio difficilior*, which it seems easier to account for as the original reading (*pace* Grabe and Rahlfs) than as a complicating addition to an originally symmetrical and more easily understood text. Although καί does muddle the syntax somewhat, the result is not unintelligible. Translators of, and commentators on, this longer text have commonly understood καί to be adverbial, glossing it in various ways: "even" (Brenton 1844; Wevers 1993, 18; Brown 1993, 26), "also" (Thomson 1808), "aussi" (*BdA*), "auch" (LXX.D). Brayford (2007), however, translates this καί conjunctively as "and." Indeed, the fact that καί is G's default rendering for the וֹ conjunction makes it highly likely that this καί is conjunctive rather than adverbial. In Brayford's translation of the *Wortbericht* in verses 29–30, which includes the phrase being discussed here, one gets the impression that the same kinds of food are allotted to both humans and animals.

> Look, I have given you every sowable herbage reproducing seed, which is over all the earth; and every tree, which has in itself fruit of sowable seed; to you it will be for food, and for all the wild animals of the earth and all the birds of the heaven and every reptile that crawls on the earth, which has in itself animate being; and every green herbage for food. (Brayford 2007, 35).

Harl maintains that the phrase with καί, which she however renders adverbially ("aussi"), results in a declaration that humans and animals are accorded the same kinds of food (Harl 1994, 97). In Brayford's commentary on this passage, she asserts, contrary to what appears to be implied in her translation, that different types of food are designated for humans and animals.

> Best characterized as a vegetarian diet, what the human is to eat includes herbage and fruit from trees.... God provides a similar, but not identical,

diet for the other animate beings; they are to have χόρτον χλωρόν, literally "herbage of green" [*sic*] for food, presumably referring to grass (Brayford 2007, 224).

This interpretation of the text may best be assigned to its reception history, whereas her translation of the dangling clause introduced by a conjunctive καί comes nearer the mark of representing the meaning of the text as produced. That is to say, the dangling clause, understood the way it is translated in NETS, signifies that the animal genera mentioned in verse 30 are allocated, not an alternative, but an additional food source (green herbage) besides the types mentioned in verse 29 that they are to share with humans (sowable herbage, fruit trees). The fact that this appears to be an odd combination should not tempt the interpreter to allow the meaning of the text-as-produced to be overtaken by the meaning of the text-as-received.

In contrast to the gender-incongruent collocation πᾶν χόρτον in verse 29, here the pronominal adjective πάντα that precedes the masculine singular accusative noun χόρτον agrees with it in gender. This means that the idea of the whole ("all") is intended rather than the generalizing ("any") or distributive ("every") senses of the term. The noun plus attributive adjective sequence χόρτον χλωρόν represents a transposition of terms in the source text ירק עשב.

βρῶσιν. Regarding the βρῶσις – אכלה equivalence, see verse 29.

καὶ ἐγένετο οὕτως. Regarding the transition formula, see verse 6.

1.31

וירא אלהים את כל אשר עשה והנה טוב מאד ויהי ערב ויהי בקר
יום הששי

καὶ εἶδεν ὁ θεὸς τὰ πάντα, ὅσα ἐποίησεν, καὶ ἰδοὺ καλὰ λίαν. καὶ ἐγένετο ἑσπέρα καὶ ἐγένετο πρωί, ἡμέρα ἕκτη.

And God saw all the things that he had made, and see, they were exceedingly good. And it came to be evening, and it came to be morning, a sixth day.

τὰ πάντα, ὅσα. G employs plural forms to render the elements את כל אשר of the object clause in his source text. This highlights the fact that creation is comprised of many parts rather than the fact implied in the source text that all these parts taken together comprise an integrated whole.

καλὰ λίαν. The plural adjective καλά is congruent in number with the antecedent construction τὰ πάντα, ὅσα, but not with its singular counterpart טוב in the source text. As for the adverb λίαν, here, as in its only other occurrence in the Pentateuch (4.5), it is the equivalent for מאד in the source text. This represents a departure from G's default, however, since thirty-one other times in Genesis alone the Greek equivalent is σφόδρα, and once it is σφοδρῶς.

καὶ ἐγένετο ἑσπέρα καὶ ἐγένετο πρωί, ἡμέρα ἕκτη. G replicates his source text as he does with the concluding formula for each of the days of the *Hexaemeron*.

2.1

ויכלו השמים והארץ וכל צבאם
Καὶ συνετελέσθησαν ὁ οὐρανὸς καὶ ἡ γῆ καὶ πᾶς ὁ κόσμος αὐτῶν.
And the sky and the earth were finished, and all their arrangement.

συνετελέσθησαν. The aorist passive indicative of συντελέω is an appropriate equivalent for the *pual* perfect of כלה, a verb form whose counterpart in its only other occurrence in the LXX is, however, the aorist active indicative of ἐκλείπω (Ps 71[72].20).

ὁ κόσμος αὐτῶν. G fashions an interpretative translation of צבא in his source text, a term that often has to do with military forces and service, less frequently with service in the cult or compulsory labor of some sort, but also with heavenly bodies—especially the stars—and the divine entourage (*HALOT*). Understandably G does not opt here to employ the equivalent that he uses in the other three contexts where צבא appears in Genesis, where mention is made in each instance of Phichol who is the commander-in-chief of Abimelech's δύναμις ("army"; 21.22, 32; 26.26). In the present case, the choice of κόσμος—signifying "order" rather than "ornament," "adornment," or "universe" (LSJ, BDAG)—reflects the translator's focus on the creator's arrangement of the various components of his creation. "La belle ordonnance du monde" is a recurring theme in pagan Hellenistic literature as well as in Jewish and Christian texts (Harl 1994, 98; LSJ).

2.2

ויכל אלהים ביום השביעי מלאכתו אשר עשה וישבת ביום השביעי
מכל מלאכתו אשר עשה

καὶ συνετέλεσεν ὁ θεὸς ἐν τῇ ἡμέρᾳ τῇ ἕκτῃ τὰ ἔργα αὐτοῦ, ἃ ἐποίησεν,
καὶ κατέπαυσεν ἐν τῇ ἡμέρᾳ τῇ ἑβδόμῃ ἀπὸ πάντων τῶν ἔργων αὐτοῦ
ὧν ἐποίησεν.

And on the sixth day God finished his works that he had made,
and he left off on the seventh day from all his works that he had
made.

συνετέλεσεν. G employs συντελέω to render the *piel* of כלה—an acceptable
semantic equivalence both here and in the other five contexts in which this
Hebrew verb form occurs in Genesis (6.16; 17.22; 24.15, 45; 43.2).

τῇ ἕκτῃ ... τῇ ἑβδόμῃ. In the OG, as in SamPent and Pesh, the potential tension of the source text, which indicates that creator's work was finished on
both the sixth day (v. 1) and the seventh day (v. 2), is resolved. In verse 2,
G and these other versions intentionally diverge from the source text and
take pains to make it clear that the sixth day is the last one on which God
is active in creation, and that the seventh day is marked by the absence of
such activity.

τὰ ἔργα αὐτοῦ ... τῶν ἔργων αὐτοῦ. In this verse, as in the next one and
39.11, G renders מלאכתו—namely, the singular noun plus a third masculine singular pronominal suffix—with an arthrous plural form of ἔργον
plus the possessive pronoun.

κατέπαυσεν. Here, as well as in the other two contexts in Genesis where his
source text had שבת, G's equivalent is καταπαύω (2.3; 8.22). The essential
meaning of καταπαύω in its intransitive sense, as it is of שבת in the *qal*
stem, is to "cease" or "leave off" doing something.

2.3

ויברך אלהים את יום השביעי ויקדש אתו כי בו שבת מכל מלאכתו
אשר ברא אלהים לעשות

καὶ εὐλόγησεν ὁ θεὸς τὴν ἡμέραν τὴν ἑβδόμην καὶ ἡγίασεν αὐτήν, ὅτι
ἐν αὐτῇ κατέπαυσεν ἀπὸ πάντων τῶν ἔργων αὐτοῦ, ὧν ἤρξατο ὁ θεὸς
ποιῆσαι.

And God blessed the seventh day and hallowed it, because on it he left off from all his works that God had begun to make.

εὐλόγησεν. Regarding the εὐλογέω – ברך *piel* equivalence, see 1.22.

καὶ ἡγίασεν. This is the only place where the semantically equivalent verbs ἁγιάζω and קדש *piel* appear in Genesis.

ἀπὸ πάντων τῶν ἔργων αὐτοῦ. G employs plural forms to render the singular substantival components of the prepositional phrase מכל מלאכתו (see 2.2).

ὧν ἤρξατο ὁ θεὸς ποιῆσαι. G seems intentionally to have departed from his source text in fashioning the end component of an *inclusio* that is inaugurated with the words ἐν ἀρχῇ ἐποίησεν ὁ θεός in 1.1. While ποιέω is far and away his preferred equivalent for עשה (with 136 equivalences out of a total of 153 occurrences of עשה in Genesis), this is the only context among eleven occurrences of the verb ברא that the counterpart is ἄρχω.

Summary

An *inclusio* demarcates the limits of this segment of OG Genesis. Subsections are defined, as in the source text, by the days of the creation week, and structured according to a pattern of *Wortbericht*, transition formula, *Tatbericht*, and formula of divine approbation. Where the source text diverges from that pattern, G resorts to harmonization.

"Drawn from the Water": A Commentary on the Old Greek Text of Exodus 2.1–10

Larry Perkins

Literature

Aejmelaeus, Anneli. 1982a. *Parataxis in the Septuagint: A Study of the Renderings of the Hebrew Coordinate Clauses in the Greek Pentateuch.* AASF 31. Helsinki: Suomalainen Tiedeakatemia. ◆ **Aejmelaeus**. 1982b. *"Participium coniunctum* as a Criterion of Translation Technique." *VT* 32:385–93. ◆ **Aejmelaeus**. 1993. *On the Trail of Septuagint Translators: Collected Essays.* Kampen: Kok Pharos. ◆ **Boulluec**, Alain Le, and P. **Sandevoir**. 1989. *La Bible d'Alexandrie 2: L'Exode.* Paris: Cerf. ◆ **Chamberlain**, Gary A. 2011. *The Greek of the Septuagint: A Supplemental Lexicon.* Peabody, MA: Hendrickson. ◆ **Dozeman**, Thomas B. 2009. *Exodus.* ECC. Grand Rapids: Eerdmans. ◆ **Evans**, Trevor V. 2001. *Verbal Syntax in the Greek Pentateuch: Natural Greek Usage and Hebrew Interference.* Oxford: Oxford University Press. ◆ **Harl**, Marguerite. 1986. *La Bible d'Alexandrie 1: La Genèse.* Paris: Cerf. ◆ **Houtman**, C. 1993. *Exodus: Volume 1.* HCOT. Kampen: Kok . ◆ **Johannessohn**, M. 1928. *Der Gebrauch der Präpositionen in der Septuaginta.* MSU 4.1. Berlin: Weidmannsche Buchhandlung. ◆ **Lee**, John A. L. 1983. *A Lexical Study of the Septuagint Version of the Pentateuch.* SCS 14. Chico, CA: Scholars Press. ◆ **Louw**, Theo A. W. van der. 2007. *Transformations in the Septuagint: Towards an Interaction of Septuagint Studies and Translation Studies.* CBET 47. Leuven: Peeters. ◆ **Soisalon-Soininen**, Ilmari. 1965. *Die Infinitive in der Septuaginta.* AASF B 132. Helsinki: Suomalainen Tiedeakatemia ◆ **Soisalon-Soininen**. 1987. "Der Gebrauch des *Genetivus Absolutus* in der *Septuaginta.*" Pages 175–80 in *Ilmari Soisalon-Soininen: Studien zur Septuaginta-Syntax. Zu seinem 70. Geburtstag am 4. Juni 1987.* Edited by Anneli Aejmelaeus

and Raija Sollamo. AASF B 237. Helsinki: Suomalainen Tiedeakatemia.
♦ **Tenhunen**, K. 2008. "The Renderings of the Hebrew Preposition ל in
Predicate Expressions Denoting Transition and Becoming Something in
LXX Genesis and Exodus." Pages 1–16 in *Scripture in Transition: Essays on
Septuagint, Hebrew Bible and Dead Sea Scrolls in Honour of Raija Sollamo.*
Edited by Anssi Voitila and Jutta Jokiranta. JSJSup 126. Leiden: Brill. ♦
Thackeray, H. St. John. 1907. "The Greek Translators of the Four Books
of Kings." *JTS* 8:262–78. ♦ **Tov**, Emanuel. 1999. "Compound Words in the
Septuagint Representing Two or More Hebrew Words." Pages 129–52 in
The Greek and Hebrew Bible: Collected Essays on the Septuagint. VTSup 72.
Leiden: Brill. ♦ **Walser**, G. 2001. *The Greek of the Ancient Synagogue: An
Investigation on the Greek of the Septuagint, Pseudepigrapha and the New
Testament.* Studia Graeca et Latina Lundensia 8. Stockholm: Almqvist &
Wiksell. ♦ **Walters**, Peter. 1973. *The Text of the Septuagint: Its Corruptions
and Their Emendations.* Edited by D. W. Gooding. Cambridge: Cam-
bridge University Press. ♦ **Wevers**, John W. 1990. *Notes on the Greek Text
of Exodus.* SCS 30. Atlanta: Scholars Press. ♦ **Wevers**. 1992. *Text History of
the Greek Exodus.* MSU 21. Göttingen: Vandenhoeck & Ruprecht.

Outline

With various departures from and adaptations of his source text, G relates
Moyses's birth, his three-month concealment, his rescue from exposure in
the Nile marsh, and his adoption by Pharao's daughter, even as he is nursed
by his own mother.

Commentary

2.1

וילך איש מבית לוי ויקח את בת לוי

ἦν δέ τις ἐκ τῆς φυλῆς Λευί, ὃς ἔλαβεν τῶν θυγατέρων Λευὶ καὶ ἔσχεν
αὐτήν.

Now there was a certain man from the tribe of Leui who took one
of the daughters of Leui and married her.

ἦν δέ τις … ὅς. G emphasizes a break with the preceding discourse segment by using δέ, a nominal clause, and the indefinite pronoun τις for איש
to mark the beginning of the story of Moyses. The indefinite τις in turn
is defined by the following prepositional phrase and relative clause. The

71

phrase ἦν δέ τις marks a shift in discourse and sometimes the introduction of a new episode or a new character in Greek literature. Examples occur in Homer, *Il.* 5.9, ἦν δέ τις ἐν Τρώεσσι Δάρης ἀφνειὸς ἀμύμων ("Now there was amid the Trojans one Dares, a rich man and blameless" [LCL]); Xenophon, *Hell.* 4.1.29, ἦν δέ τις Ἀπολλοφανής Κυζικηνός, ὃς καὶ Φαρναβάζῳ ἐτύγχανεν ἐκ παλαιοῦ ξένος ("Now there was a certain Apollophanes of Cyzicus who chanced to be an old friend of Pharnabazus" [LCL]); and Plutarch, *Cor.* 22.1.1 ἦν δέ τις ἀνὴρ ἐξ Ἀντίου πόλεως διά τε πλοῦτον καὶ ἀνδρείαν καὶ γένους ἐπιφάνειαν ἀξίωμα βασιλικόν ("Now there was a certain man from the city of Antium both because of wealth and bravery and conspicuous lineage had the standing of a king" [LCL]).

This Greek idiom replaces ויֵּלֶךְ אִישׁ and creates a nominal sentence, with the subject modified by a relative clause, whereas the Hebrew has two standard *waw*-consecutive imperfect clauses. G used various strategies of subordination to represent Hebrew parataxis in this section: including the adverbial participle (ἰδοῦσα … ἀποστείλασα … ἀνείλατο [v. 5], ἀνοίξασα δὲ ὁρᾷ [v. 6], ἐλθοῦσα δὲ … ἐκάλεσεν [v. 8b], an adverbial temporal ἐπεί clause [v. 3]), and a genitive absolute (ἀδρυνθέντος δὲ τοῦ παιδίου εἰσήγαγεν [v. 10]). The translator's use of such diverse subordination indicates his tendency to pay attention to the target language requirements.

Other cases in Exodus where G renders Hebrew finite verbs other than היה with forms of εἶναι occur at 13.7, οὐκ ἔσται σοι ζύμη = וְלֹא יֵרָאֶה לְךָ שְׂאֹר; 22.15, ἔσται αὐτῷ ἀντὶ τοῦ μισθοῦ αὐτοῦ = בָּא בִשְׂכָרוֹ; 34.9, καὶ ἐσόμεθα σοί = וּנְחַלְתָּנוּ. However, none of these are similar to this case in 2.1.

δέ. G employs this particle frequently (vv. 1, 2, 3, 5, 6, 8 [2x], 9 [3x], 10) to render various uses of ו. Its ubiquity in Exodus reflects normal Greek usage and is one of the indicators that G seeks to accommodate the target language. It often signals change of subject, but not in every case (e.g., vv. 3, 6, 10a).

τις ἐκ τῆς φυλῆς Λευί. G provides an *ad sensum* rendering for בֵּית לֵוִי. The use of φυλὴ Λευί as the equivalent, while unique in Exodus, is certainly understandable, given that Λευί is one of the twelve tribes. The household of Levi, introduced in Exod 1.1–2 and defined more specifically in 6.19–27, over the intervening centuries has grown significantly, as had all the households connected with Jacob's offspring. Therefore φυλή is a more sensible reflection of this reality within the story, but anticipates later definitions of the Israelite organization.

Λευί. The personal name לוי is one of two in Exodus that possess a consonantal *waw*. The other is the gentilic חוי. In both cases the consonantal *waw* is transliterated with the diphthong –ευ: Λευί, Εὐαῖος (a declinable formation; see also 3.8).

ἔλαβεν. The verb λαμβάνω in Exodus and generally in the LXX is the default rendering of לקח ("take"; ca. 70x). The phrase λαμβάνω τῶν θυγατέρων occurs also at 6.25 and 34.16, but reflects a slightly different Hebrew construction (לקח מבנת). In Classical Greek the verb in some contexts can mean to "receive in marriage." LSJ references this usage in Herodotus, *Hist.* 1.199, 9.108, and Xenophon, *Hell.* 4.1.14. In 6.23 we find the expression ἔλαβεν … θυγατέρα … αὐτῷ γυναῖκα, reflecting the Hebrew *Vorlage*, meaning that a man married a daughter of someone (see v. 20 for a similar example).

τῶν θυγατέρων Λευί. The partitive plural genitive phrase τῶν θυγατέρων Λευί renders the singular את בת לוי, the object of the final verb. G had two options. He could translate it as "the daughter of Levi," but this chronologically is impossible, or he could construe it as a partitive genitive, that is, "one of the female clan members of Levi," which he did and thus avoided the chronological issue. Houtman (1993, 270) argues that "grammatically (unless one should think there is merit in appealing to Ges-K [GKC] §126q; Joüon §137n) it is unlikely that את בת לוי can mean something else than 'the daughter of Levi.'"

καὶ ἔσχεν αὐτήν. The last clause is in effect a literary addition filling out the sequence of events in four stages and enhancing the parallelism formed by these clauses. The common Greek verb ἔχειν only occurs seven times (2.1; 21.22; 28.28, 39; 33.12; 36.2, 31) in Exodus and usually is part of an idiomatic Greek translation. The sense of the clause in this verse is to cohabit with a wife and in this sense to be married. For example, we find in Aristotle, *Cat.* 15b.28, λεγόμεθα δὲ καὶ γυναῖκα ἔχειν καὶ ἡ γυνὴ ἄνδρα· … οὐδὲν γὰρ ἄλλο τῷ ἔχειν γυναῖκα σημαίνομεν ἢ ὅτι συνοικεῖ ("We say also that a man 'has' a wife and a wife has a husband … For we mean by this 'have' nothing more than that he cohabits" [LCL]). Later LXX translators use it in the sense to cohabit with a woman or man. Sometimes this occurs through normal marriage arrangements and sometimes through other events such as war (Deut 28.30; 1 Esd 9.18; Esa 13.16; 54.1 [τὸν ἄνδρα]). The verbal phrase may also imply sexual activity. It would seem that to a

Greek-speaking person the translation expresses that this person married one of the daughters of Levi and he cohabited with her. Aejmelaeus (1993, 101) notes, "the translator seems to be responsible for the divergence here, which, however, adds nothing to the content of the passage."

2.2

ותהר האשה ותלד בן ותרא אתו כי טוב הוא ותצפנהו שלשה ירחים

καὶ ἐν γαστρὶ ἔλαβεν καὶ ἔτεκεν ἄρσεν. ἰδόντες δὲ αὐτὸ ἀστεῖον ἐσκέπασαν αὐτὸ μῆνας τρεῖς.

And she conceived and bore a male child. Now when they saw that it was handsome, they sheltered it for three months.

While the translator resumes his more usual mode of serial fidelity, he incorporates numerous alterations. The use of ἄρσεν to render בן creates continuity with the preceding instruction by Pharaoh to kill all male infants.

καὶ ἐν γαστρὶ ἔλαβεν. The Greek text does not reflect האשה, its omission presumably an example of "implicitation" (van der Louw 2007, 81–82). The verb הרה, "conceive, become pregnant," only occurs at 2.2 in Exodus. The cognate adjective הרה, which means "pregnant," occurs at 21.22 and is rendered by the verbal phrase ἐν γαστρὶ ἔχουσαν. The LSJ in the entry "γαστήρ" remarks that ἐν γαστρὶ ἔχειν indicates pregnancy, whereas ἐν γαστρὶ λαμβάνειν refers to conception. Muraoka, *GELS*, follows this distinction in his entries related to ἔχειν and λαμβάνειν, as do LEH in their entry on γαστήρ. This distinction seems to be operative in 2.22 and 21.22, the only occurrences of this idiom in Greek Exodus, suggesting that the translator in choosing these different Greek idioms distinguishes between the Hebrew verb and the cognate adjective.

ἔτεκεν. τίκτω is the usual rendering for the verb ילד (7x) with one exception (γεννάω, 6.20).

ἄρσεν. Throughout this section (1.17, 18, 22; 2.2) the translator used ἄρσεν (a neuter form; the masculine form of the adjective is ἄρσην) to render בן and the plural הילדים. The word θῆλυ (also a neuter form) occurs in 1.16, 22, similarly rendering בת. The translator chose neuter gender terms to render בן and בת rather than the usual "υἱός ... θυγάτηρ."

ἰδόντες. Translating the third principle clause as an adverbial participle with the connecting particle δέ reflects normal Greek syntax. The adverbial participle occurs eight times in 2.1–10 to render coordinate Hebrew clauses. The participle ἰδών occurs frequently in this usage (Aejmelaeus 1993, 12–15). Temporal or causal connections often are expressed; the nuance of this participle is probably temporal. Whereas predicative participles in the nominative case almost always precede the principal verb in Exodus (and the rest of the Greek Pentateuch), in other contemporary non-LXX literature they tend to follow. This divergence reflects the translator's general commitment to serial fidelity in representing his source text (Walser 2001, 20–39). The translator used plural forms, even though the Hebrew text used the third person singular feminine form for each of the verbs. This creates ambiguity in the story because we do not know who the subject referent is specifically; logically it would be the parents, but this is left undefined. G continues with the plural formation in the next clause (v. 3a).

ἀστεῖον. G streamlines the כִּי clause in the source text as a predicate adjective. The translator's use of ἀστεῖον only occurs here in Exodus and is unique in the LXX as a representation of טוֹב. Given that it is applied to a newborn infant, its sense probably tends in the direction of handsome or well-proportioned, rather than charming or graceful. Perhaps the translator chose a term that had reference both to the child's beauty as well as charm.

The use of ἀστεῖοι by Aristotle (οἱ μικροὶ δ' ἀστεῖοι καὶ σύμμετροι, καλοὶ δ' οὔ in *Eth. nic.* 1123b7) suggests the idea of well-formed or well-proportioned, even though small. LXX.D renders it as "wohlgestaltet." However, material in Plato and Xenophon focus more on the sense of witty, charming, graceful. Xenophon *Cyr.* 8.4.23.6 writes ὥστε σοὶ ταῦτ' εἰρῆσθαι, καὶ ἀπαγγελθῆναι παρ' ᾗ εὐδοκιμεῖν βούλει ὅτι ἀστεῖος εἶ; ("would you not give a great deal to have made these jokes and to have them reported to the lady with whom you wish to have the reputation of being a witty fellow?" [LCL]). In Plato's *Phaed.*, 116.d, 5 Ὡς ἀστεῖος, ἔφη, ὁ ἄνθρωπος ("[Socrates] said, 'How charming the man is!'" [LCL]). In Judg 3.17 Eglon, king of Moab is said to be ἀνὴρ ἀστεῖος [בָּרִיא] σφόδρα. Holofernes acknowledges that Judith is ἀστεία … ἐν τῷ εἴδει (Idt 11.23). Susanna, the wife of Joachim is described as γυνεῖκα ἀστείαν τῷ εἴδει (Sus 7). The explicit reference to physical form in two of these contexts (as well as the usage in Aristotle) led me to use "handsome" as the appropriate rendering for ἀστεῖον in Exod 2.2, rather than "charming" or "graceful," which Muraoka, *GELS*, and Le Boulluec and Sandevoir ("gracieux") suggest. In its other two LXX occurrences the adjective defines ὁδός (Num 22.32, ירט) and λογισμός (2 Makk 6.23). I have not found a case apart from Exod 2.2 where this adjective is applied to an infant.

ἐσκέπασαν. The translation of צפן ("hide") by σκεπάζω ("shelter, protect") represents a slight shift in meaning. G has the plural (for the third-person plural, see above), as does the initial participle, in contrast to MT. Greek σκεπάζω occurs six times in Exodus for four different Hebrew verbs: including פסח (qal and hiphil are considered synonymous; "pass, spring over") (12.13, 27); שכה ("cover") (33.22); and סכך, hiphil ("screen, cover") (40.3, 19[21]). By using this verb in 12.13, 27 in relationship to the avenging angel the translator may be suggesting a parallel with the protection afforded to Moyses in 2.2. (I am indebted to Dirk Büchner for this last suggestion.)

μῆνας τρεῖς. The concealment lasted for μῆνας τρεῖς, the accusative case marking duration. The Greek word order diverges from the Hebrew order that in this case places the absolute form of the numeral first, followed by the object defined in apposition (GKC §134b). This is the only context in Exodus where μῆν renders ירח ("moon," "month," the latter occurring only here). In all other contexts (15x) μῆν represents חדש ("new moon"). G follows the Hebrew word order in these references to months except 2.2 where he reverses the word order, placing the numeral after the noun.

2.3

ולא יכלה עוד הצפינו ותקח לו תבת גמא ותחמרה בחמר ובזפת
ותשם בה את הילד ותשם בסוף על שפת היאר

ἐπεὶ δὲ οὐκ ἠδύναντο αὐτὸ ἔτι κρύπτειν, ἔλαβεν ἡ μήτηρ αὐτοῦ θῖβιν καὶ κατέχρισεν αὐτὴν ἀσφαλτοπίσσῃ καὶ ἐνέβαλεν τὸ παιδίον εἰς αὐτήν, καὶ ἔθηκεν αὐτὴν εἰς τὸ ἕλος παρὰ τὸν ποταμόν.

But when they could hide it no longer, its mother took a basket and plastered it with a mixture of pitch and tar, and she put the child in it and placed it in the marsh beside the river.

ἐπεί. G renders the first clause as a temporal subordinate clause, introduced by ἐπεί, but he still marks the advancing action by δέ. By simple juxtaposition of waw-consecutive clauses the Hebrew text may intend the initial clause to be read as a temporal clause. G may then have recognized this convention and translated accordingly (GKC §164a). This allows G to eliminate any equivalent for the ו that introduces the second clause.

οὐκ ἠδύναντο. ἠδύναντο represents יכלה (third-person feminine singular *qal*). Given G's use of plural formations in verse 2, he has to continue the plural rendering in verse 3. G normally renders יכל by forms of δύναμαι (with the exception of 4.13 and 7.18).

αὐτὸ ἔτι κρύπτειν. The word order αὐτὸ ἔτι κρύπτειν fronts the pronoun in the Greek text in contrast with the Hebrew placement. This reordering does occur elsewhere in Exodus (see 2.10) and suggests that G was marking it, perhaps giving some attention to Greek style. G used κρύπτω to render צפן in contrast to the rendering in verse 2, explainable as an example of μεταβολή ("variety") and indicative of G's literary interest. Lee (1983, 76–77) notes that σκεπάζω develops in usage the sense "to protect" or "to shelter" and documents this from third-century BCE papyri. However, he muses that "conceal" is the meaning for Exod 2.2–3, but acknowledges there is no attestation for this meaning. Le Boulluec and Sandevoir (1989, 80) render the Greek as "*ils* le mi*rent* à l'*abri*" [emphasis original]. The use of the present infinitive allows for a continuative sense, that is, "to keep on hiding." Greek ἔτι occurs as the equivalent of עוד nine times in Exodus (2.3; 4.18; 9.2, 17, 29; 11.1; 14.13; 17.4; 36.3; for other uses of ἔτι in Exodus see 8.29; 9.33; 10.17, 28; 15.18; 36.6.), but πάλιν occurs twice (3.15; 4.6) and οὐκέτι once (10.29).

ἔλαβεν. According to We^ed, G offered no equivalent for לו. This contrasts with Ra, which does read αὐτῷ. Wevers regards it as a hexaplaric addition because it is marked by an asterisk and metobelus in Syh (which precedes the equivalent of ἔλαβεν) and witnessed by B F O^{-426}-15′ *b d* 56′-129 370 *x* *y*^{-121} 68′-120′ 55 59 130 799 ^Lat cod 100 Ach Sa = Ra MT. As Wevers (1992, 169) notes, this textual variation is complicated by the question of the position of αὐτό relative to the preceding κρύπτειν. For example, F reads κρύπτειν αὐτό, ἔλαβεν αὐτῷ. This word order reflects MT.

ἡ μήτηρ αὐτοῦ. G clarifies by adding ἡ μήτηρ αὐτοῦ, as the subject shifts from plural in the first clause to feminine singular in the second. Personal endings of Greek verbs do not distinguish gender in contrast to Hebrew verb formations. SamPent reads אמו (even though the preceding verb was third-person feminine singular) and it is possible that this was in G's *Vorlage*. However, without additional Hebrew sources and noting the many amplifications in SamPent, it is more likely that both SamPent and G are independent in their activity.

θῖβιν. Thackeray (1907, 34) long ago noted θῖβις as one of the "Hellenized Semitic words in the LXX." Since θῖβις is attested in papyri from the third century BCE, it probably is a Greek loanword coined from Egyptian. Lee (1983, 115) notes: "The meaning of this loan-word is apparently 'basket.'" He gives examples from P. Cairo.Zen. 69.5 (257 BCE) ἐν θίβει νάρδου μαρσίππια ἐσφρα(γισμένα), as well as *UPZ* 149.21 (third century BCE) θῆβις τῶν ἄρτων, P. Petr. 3.51.4,13 (third century BCE), and P. Grenf.1.14.10 (second century BCE). The Hebrew term תבה ("ark, chest") would then be a Hebrew loanword from Egyptian. It only occurs in Exodus in 2.3, 5, but G used it a third time in 2.6 as well. Hebrew גמא describes reeds or papyrus materials and various hexaplaric witnesses add παπυρου in the text or a cognate formation in the margins. However, G did not provide an equivalent.

κατέχρισεν αὐτὴν ἀσφαλτοπίσσῃ. In order to waterproof the basket Moyses's mother plasters it with bituminous resin. The verb is modified by two prepositional phrases, the first of which contains a cognate noun (ותחמרה בחמר ובזפת), describing how she "plastered it with bitumen and pitch." G translates this idiomatically with a verb meaning to smear, plaster (κατέχρισεν) modified by the rare substantive ἀσφαλτόπισσα, which seems to be an alternative form of πισσάσφαλτος/πιττάσφαλτος which only occurs otherwise in a writing by Dioscordes Medicus, first century CE (*De materia medica* 1.73.1.9); ἀσφαλτόπισσα may be an alternative form of this compound noun formed by G to represent the order of two phrases בחמר ובזפת. This form's only other occurrence in extant Greek literature is in Philo, *Conf.* 106.4, referencing Exod 2.3; for the use of Greek compound words in LXX generally see Tov 1999. The noun זפת occurs twice in Isa 34.9 and in both cases the translator rendered it as πίσσα. G normally uses χρίω to render משח ("anoint") and the choice of the compound καταχρίω may suggest a sense of thoroughness. Diodorus Siculus, *Bibliotheca Historica* 2.9.2, 5, describes building processes using baked bricks plastered (κατέχρισεν) with bitumen.

The κατα- compound verb forms that occur in 2.1–10 include κατέχρισεν (v. 2), κατεσκόπευεν (v. 3), and κατέβη (v. 4). Note a similar sequence of such compounds in 1.10, 11, 13, 14.

ἐνέβαλεν ... ἔθηκεν. The final two clauses have the same verb form (ותשם). The first is marked by the object את הילד, but there is no expressed object in the second instance. G's varied rendering of these two instances semantically works well. In addition G alters the word order of the verbal modifiers in the first of these clauses (τὸ παιδίον εἰς αὐτήν) and may have added the accusative pronoun αὐτήν in the second clause to make clear what his mother placed εἰς τὸ ἕλος. However, it should be noted that 4Q13 (4QExod^b) apparently reads אותו and this may indicate that G had a textual warrant for αὐτήν. G used παιδίον to render ילד (nine times out of twelve), which becomes its default rendering, but at 4.20; 21.5; 22.24, it translates בן (υἱός is G's default rendering for בן [ca. 190x]). At 4.25, 26 the phrase τοῦ παιδίου μου is added by G. The cognate noun παῖς renders עבד eight times in Exodus.

ἕλος. G renders the collective noun סוף ("rushes, reeds") with ἕλος ("marsh"), which is defined by the following prepositional phrase παρὰ τὸν ποταμόν. In Exodus ἕλος twice renders סוף ("reeds, rushes") (2.3, 5), as well as the only two occurrences of אגמה ("pool, pond") (7.19; 8.5 [MT 8.1]). When סוף occurs in the descriptor ים סוף G rendered it with the stock phrase ἐρυθρὰ θάλασσα.

παρὰ τὸν ποταμόν. G used ποταμός ("river") as a default rendering for היאר (twenty-three of twenty-five occurrences). The word translated "the Nile" (היאר) in NRSV is a common noun in Hebrew (note the presence of the article) meaning stream, river, or watercourses of some nature. In the case of Egypt "the river" is the Nile. The translator had at his disposal the proper name Νεῖλος, which occurs as early as Hesiod, but opts consistently to render the Hebrew noun as ὁ ποταμός. The article consistently occurs with ποταμός when referencing the Nile, probably because the Hebrew noun always is marked by an article in Exodus. There are two exceptions in Exodus where the combination על נהרתם על יאריהם is rendered as ἐπὶ τοὺς ποταμοὺς αὐτῶν καὶ ἐπὶ τὰς διώρυγας αὐτῶν (7.19; see also 8.5[MT 1]). Having chosen ποταμός as the rendering for נהר the translator must select a different equivalent for היאר in these two contexts. At 23.31 the Hebrew expression עד הנהר is rendered in an expanded form as ἕως τοῦ ποταμοῦ τοῦ μεγάλου Εὐφράτου. In 1.22 יאר is marked uniquely in Exodus by the ה-locale, which the translator expresses using the preposition εἰς, a normal equivalent. G does not represent שפת ("lip") in this verse, but does so in 7.15.

The preposition παρά is distributed in Exodus with the following cases: accusative (2.3, 5; 11.5; 12.22 [2x]; 13.20; 14.9, 30; 15.27; 29.12; 33.12, 17; 35.22; 36.5; 40.6); genitive (3.22; 4.20; 11.2 [2x]; 12.35; 14.13; 18.11, 15;

22.12, 14; 25.2, 3; 27.21; 29.28 [2x]; 30.16; 33.16; 35.5; 36.3) and dative (22.25; 31.13; 33.12, 16, 21; 35.24; 36.3).

2.4

ותתצב אחתו מרחק לדעה מה יעשה לו

καὶ κατεσκόπευεν ἡ ἀδελφὴ αὐτοῦ μακρόθεν μαθεῖν τί τὸ ἀποβησόμενον αὐτῷ.

And his sister was watching from a distance to learn what would happen to him.

κατεσκόπευεν. Two matters are of interest here: (1) that G chooses κατασκοπεύω to render יצב ("set or station oneself, take one's stand"), and (2) that he uses the durative aspect representing Moyses's sister not merely standing (at a distance) but keeping a continuous watch. This is the only LXX context in which this verb functions as the equivalent for יצב. By these choices G clarifies that the child's sister will discover what happens to it because she is watching, not just standing. This is an example of "explicitation" (van der Louw, 2007, 81). This choice also emphasizes the source text's notion that Moyses's mother is not abandoning the child to the elements. In Greek Joshua this verb occurs seven times, usually with the sense of spying on territory that is about to be attacked. It renders the Hebrew verbs רגל (piel) (Ies 2.1; 6.21[22], 22[23], 24b[25b]; 14.7) and חפר (Ies 2.2, 3) and the noun מלאך (Ies 6.24a[25a]).

μακρόθεν. This adverb is the standard rendering for מרחק in Exodus (2.4; 20.18, 21; 24.1). In none of these cases does G represent the prefix (מן) with a separate lexeme. The −θεν affix is sufficient to reflect the ablative sense (Smyth §342). In contrast, the translator of Psalms twice rendered מרחק as ἀπὸ μακρόθεν (Ps 137[138].6 and 138[139].2; see also 2 Esd 3.13).

μαθεῖν. Although μανθάνω rarely renders ידע in LXX and only here in Exodus, it is very apt. The other occurrence of this equivalence in LXX is Est 4.5 in a similar context. G does not reflect specifically ל, the marker of the infinitive (e.g., לדעתה) in this chapter (Soisalon-Soininen 1965, 49–61).

τί τὸ ἀποβησόμενον αὐτῷ. G retains the indirect interrogative structure, but transforms the interrogative clause into a nominal clause with the future middle neuter substantival participle functioning as the subject. Again G's choice is idiomatic, but unique in Exodus to describe future events and as an equivalent for עשה; ἀποβαίνειν occurs with this sense in Iob 15.31, 35; 34.20; and 2 Makk 9.25. This particular usage occurs also in Polybius *Hist.* 5.33.4, 7: Πάντες δ' ἠναγκάσθημεν πρὸς αὐτὸν ἀποβλέπειν διὰ τὸ μέγεθος, δεδιότες τὴν συντέλειαν τῶν ἀποβησομένων ("All were compelled to watch it because of its magnitude, fearing the outcome of what would follow" [LCL]).

2.5

ותרד בת פרעה לרחץ על היאר ונערתיה הלכת על יד היאר ותרא
את התבה בתוך הסוף ותשלח את אמתה ותקחה

κατέβη δὲ ἡ θυγάτηρ Φαραὼ λούσασθαι ἐπὶ τὸν ποταμόν, καὶ αἱ ἅβραι αὐτῆς παρεπορεύοντο παρὰ τὸν ποταμόν· καὶ ἰδοῦσα τὴν θῖβιν ἐν τῷ ἕλει, ἀποστείλασα τὴν ἅβραν ἀνείλατο αὐτήν.

Now Pharao's daughter came down to the river to bathe, and her attendants were walking beside the river. And when she saw the basket in the marsh, she sent her attendant, and she picked it up.

κατέβη. Greek καταβαίνω is the usual equivalent for Hebrew ירד in Exodus (17x; exceptions are 9.19 [πέσῃ]; 15.5 [κατέδυσαν εἰς βυθόν]; 33.5 [ἀφέλεσθε]; at 24.16 καταβαίνω renders שכן ["settle down, dwell"]). The singular usage of the related verb ἀποβαίνω at the end of verse 4 with the following default rendering of καταβαίνω for ירד may reflect stylistic interest on the part of G.

λούσασθαι. The initial verb is completed by an infinitive of purpose (λούσασθαι = לרחץ). See comments regarding the infinitive μαθεῖν at 2.4. The medio-passive form of λούω defines "washing oneself, bathing." Active forms of λούω (29.4; 40.10) refer to the washing of Aaron and his sons at initial consecration for ministry. Other renderings in Exodus for רחץ include πλυνέω (washing sacrificial entrails, 29.17) and νίπτω (washing hands and feet in preparation for religious service 30.18, 19, 20, 21; 38.27 [2x = 40.30], 31, 32).

ἐπὶ τὸν ποταμόν. The Hebrew expression לרחץ על היאר means "to bathe at or in the river." It is unclear whether G intends this adverbial phrase to modify the primary verb of motion κατέβη or to accompany the infinitive λούσασθαι specifying something about the act of washing. If it modifies λούσασθαι, then ἐπί + accusative would have to have the sense of "near, by" which ἐπί + genitive normally would express (LSJ, s.v. "ἐπί" A. with genitive,

I.1. "at" or "near"). There is no textual evidence that G read ἐπὶ τοῦ ποταμοῦ. Neither is there evidence that ἐπί + accusative has the sense "at, by" (*GELS*, 265–67 offers no examples and neither does LEH). Given the case used with ἐπί in this context, I can only conclude that G meant this adverbial phrase to modify κατέβη (Johannessohn 1928, 317–24). Occasionally G used ἐπί + accusative after a verb of motion to describe movement in a certain direction (e.g., 7.15; 8.20; 22.13; 29.4, 10), representing a variety of Hebrew constructions. Alternatively it could be argued that G is merely following his default rendering of על as ἐπί + accusative, without regard for the difficulty this creates with the verbal form λούσασθαι. If this is the case, then the Hebrew text will act as the arbiter of meaning. According to We[ed] ἐπί + accusative occurs 172 times in Greek Exodus and for the most part it represents the preposition על. Eight times it renders ה-locale formations (ארצה 4.3 [2x]; 9.33; 34.8; המימה 7.15a; 8.20; המזבחה 29.13, 25); in twenty contexts the preposition ב (4.14; 7:4; 8.4 [MT 7:29] [3x], 21 [MT 17] [4x]; 9.22; 10.1, 13, 14, 22; 17.16 [case uncertain]; 27.18 [2x]; 33.5 (בקרבך); 37.7 [MT 38.9], 9 [MT 38.10]); and eleven times אל (14.5, 24; 18.22, 26; 19.20 [2x]; 21.6; 28.24, 26; 29.4; 36.27). It represents a variety of other source text formations, as well as plusses.

καὶ αἱ ἄβραι αὐτῆς. Twice in this verse the translator chose ἄβρα to represent two different Hebrew nouns: נערתיה and אמתה. This is the only context in LXX where אמה = ἄβρα. The more usual rendering in G is παιδίσκη (20.10, 17; 21.20, 32; 23.12). Both Hebrew nouns refer to female attendants, but אמה describes the personal attendant. In the second instance G used the singular articular form τὴν ἄβραν to identify one of the attendants as the chief personal attendant among all the others.

Wevers (1990, 14) indicates ἄβρα is borrowed from the Semitic (חברה). However, it occurs somewhat frequently in Menander (e.g., *Sik.*, 1.1: ἄβραν γὰρ ἀντωνούμενος ἐρωμένην), an Athenian playwright roughly contemporary with the translator of Exodus. Harl (1986, 204) notes its use in the Hellenistic era (e.g., Aristophanes Byzantinus, *Nomina aetatum (fragmenta)*, 279,22, ἐλέγοντο δὲ καὶ ἄβραι, ἀβροτέρως κοσμουμένων) and indicates an etymology related to the adjective ἁβρός, meaning "gracieux." It does not then seem to be a neologism created by the LXX translators. Nor is its choice here an attempt to reflect a specific nominal form in the Hebrew text. Ezekiel the Tragedian used this word in *Exagoge* as he writes κἄπειτα θυγάτηρ βασιλέως ἄβραις ὁμοῦ κατῆλθε λουτροῖς ("and then a daughter of the king came down together with servants to bathe" [my trans.]), reflecting G's rendering here. The pronoun αὐτῆς reflects the Hebrew pronominal suffix.

παρεπορεύοντο. G maintains the parataxis, but represents the sense of the Hebrew participle by using the durative aspect. The Hebrew structure (noun + participle) marks this clause as introducing background information and offline information. G used this verb three more times in reference to the census taken in 30.13, 14; 39.3. The tense form is present subjunctive, present participle, or imperfect. Lee (1983, 92) noted that this compound came into usage in the fourth century BCE as illustrated in Aristotle and the early third century Petrie papyri. He regards this compound verb as an example of "new formations" in Koine Greek emerging in the late fourth and early third centuries BCE. He also notes (1983, 85–86) that its usage in Exodus (and the rest of the Greek Pentateuch) reflects the use of πορεύομαι compounds "in the present and imperfect," whereas παρέρχομαι formations occur in contexts where future (12.23 [2x]; 23.5; 33.19) and aorist (3.3; 15.16 [2x]; 33.22 [2x]; 34.6) tense forms are chosen.

παρὰ τὸν ποταμόν. G uses the same phrase he employed in verse 3, but the preposition renders a different Hebrew construction עַל יִד, which means "beside."

καὶ ἰδοῦσα ... ἀποστείλασα ... ἀνείλατο. G renders three paratactic, independent clauses by means of two adverbial participles and one finite verb. Pharao's daughter probably is the intended subject of each action, but there is ambiguity, namely, did the attendant or Pharao's daughter pick up the basket? Greek ἀποστέλλω is the default rendering for שׁלח (qal forms [3.10, 12, 13, 14, 15; 4.13, 28; 5.22; 7.16; 9.15, 27; 23.20, 28] and piel forms [10.10; 15.7; 23.27]; ἀποστέλλω renders נפשׁ [only occurrence in Exodus] at 15.10.). The main verb in this clause ἀνείλατο (ἀναιρέω) in the middle voice means "take up, take away, carry off," which certainly expresses the sense of the Hebrew verb ותקחה. However, it is a marked equivalent in that G only used this equivalent for לקח in this context. This verb is used again in the etymology of Moyses's name in verse 10. Menander (Sam. 410: ἤκουσα καὐτὸς τῶν γυναικῶν ὅτι τρέφεις ἀνελομένη παιδάριον ["I myself heard from the women that you are nursing having taken up an infant"] [my trans.]) used this verb to describe the rescue of a child from exposure.

ἐν τῷ ἕλει. Greek ἐν usually renders the Hebrew preposition בְּ. The prepositional compound בְּתוֹךְ is rendered by ἐν five times in Exod (2.5; 9.24; 12.49; 25.7; 29.45). In three contexts it is translated in full by ἐν μέσῳ with τῆς θαλάσσης (14.29; 15.8, 19), that is, with a concrete noun, suggesting that G could have chosen ἐν μέσῳ here as well.

2.6

וַתִּפְתַּח וַתִּרְאֵהוּ אֶת הַיֶּלֶד וְהִנֵּה נַעַר בֹּכֶה וַתַּחְמֹל עָלָיו וַתֹּאמֶר מִילְדֵי הָעִבְרִים זֶה

ἀνοίξασα δὲ ὁρᾷ παιδίον κλαῖον ἐν τῇ θίβει, καὶ ἐφείσατο αὐτοῦ ἡ θυγάτηρ Φαραὼ καὶ ἔφη Ἀπὸ τῶν παιδίων τῶν Ἑβραίων τοῦτο.

Now when she opened it, she saw a child crying in the basket, and Pharao's daughter spared it and said, "This is one of the Hebrews' children."

ἀνοίξασα. G replaces the parataxis, using an adverbial participle; ἀνοίγω ("to open") renders both occurrences of פתח I ("open") in Exodus (2.6; 21.32), the standard equivalent in other sections of the LXX. It is also used in 4.12, 15 to describe Yahweh's promise to open Moyses's mouth (אהיה עם פיך). Here again G recognizes the temporal aspect inherent in the source text's juxtaposition and renders it as an adverbial participle that may have temporal force in this context.

ὁρᾷ. The pronominal suffix attached to the second verb (וַתִּפְתַּח וַתִּרְאֵהוּ) is omitted, probably because of its presumed redundancy (GKC §131.4b); ὁρᾷ is a present tense and functions as an historic present. "Of the 26 examples … of the historic present in Exodus, 24 correspond to Consecutive Imperfect," (Evans 2001, 120; see Thackeray 1907, 273–74) as in this case. Lee's discussion (1983, 131–40) of the use of ὁράω, "perceive by sight," in contrast with βλέπω indicates that Exodus reflects Greek usage in the third century BCE.

παιδίον. In this chapter MT uses two designations for the child, namely יֶלֶד and נַעַר, whereas G only has παιδίον. Because παιδίον is G's default rendering for יֶלֶד (see v. 3), and G uses νεανίσκος to translate נַעַר (10.9; 24.5; in 33.11 Joshua is described as יְהוֹשֻׁעַ בִּן נוּן נַעַר and this is translated as Ἰησοῦς υἱὸς Ναυὴ νέος), presumably G chose not to represent נַעַר in this context. For a different translation pattern consider Greek Genesis's use of παιδίον. As well, παιδίον here is anarthrous, whereas הילד is arthrous. G seems to reflect the perspective of Pharao's daughter, rather than that of the reader with prior knowledge. G also does not represent the interjection והנה. Possibly the entire phrase was omitted by parablepsis (from *daleth* to *resh*). Whatever the reason for this omission, G's text has less drama than that expressed in the Hebrew text.

κλαῖον. The verb κλαίω occurs only once in Exodus rendering the single usage of בכה ("weep, wail"). This is a regular equivalence throughout LXX. The participle can be read as either predicative or attributive.

ἐν τῇ θίβει. Whereas immediately prior G seems to streamline the text by omission, now he makes explicit what is implicit in the source text.

ἐφείσατο. External to the LXX a primary sense of φείδομαι is "to spare." LXX.D renders the Greek verb as "schonte" which suggests she "spared, saved, treated with consideration" the infant. Philoctetes, in Sophocles's play of the same name (l. 749), urges Neoptolemos to cut off his diseased foot. "Do not spare my life [μὴ φείσῃ βίου]," he pleads. Thucydides, *Hist.* 7.29.4.2 reports the outcome of battle in which τοὺς ἀνθρώπους ἐφόνευον φειδόμενοι οὔτε πρεσβυτέρα οὔτε νεωτέρας ἡλικίας ("they were killing the people, sparing neither old nor young in age" [my trans.]). The word φείδομαι only occurs this once in Exodus, reflecting the single occurrence of חמל ("spare, have compassion for"), which it often renders in other sections of LXX whenever the Hebrew verb also carries that meaning. We find similar usage in Greek Gen 19.16, ἐν τῷ φείσασθαι κύριον αὐτοῦ, describing Lot's escape from Sodom. Again in Gen 20.6 Kyrios promises to Abimelek in a dream καὶ ἐφεισάμην ἐγώ σου τοῦ μὴ ἁμαρτεῖν σε εἰς ἐμέ. Then in the testing of Abraham (Gen 22.12, 16) Kyrios acknowledges καὶ οὐκ ἐφείσω τοῦ υἱοῦ σου τοῦ ἀγαπητοῦ δι' ἐμέ. G seems to use φείδομαι here at Exod 2:6 with a similar sense "spare" because in his view Pharao's daughter is well aware of the king's decree to destroy every Hebrew male baby and yet she spares one from this destruction.

Le Boulluec and Sandevoir (1983, 82), however, emphasize the sense of "pity," translating this verb as "eut pitié de lui." They argue that this significance was known at the time of the translation. This may be. Perhaps the example that comes the closest to supporting their rendering might be Thucydides 7.29: "The Thracians, entering into Mycalessus, spoiled both houses and temples, slew the people without mercy on old or young" (Hobbes). "Not sparing old or young" works equally well as a translation. Philo, *Mos.* 1.15, interprets this text as καὶ δεδακρυμένον ὁρῶσαν ἐλεεῖν ("and seeing him weeping took pity on him"). But here Philo substitutes another term (ἐλεεῖν) for that used in the Old Greek translation, one that in his view better conveys the sense of the Hebrew text. This may be a subtle suggestion by Philo that the OG translation did not express the right nuance in its rendering. *GELS* and LEH also indicate that "pity" is the meaning for φείδομαι in this context.

ἡ θυγάτηρ Φαραώ. Although Pharao's daughter appears in verses 5, 7, 8, 9, 10 in both texts, here it is absent from MT. SamPent reads בת פרעה, as does 4Q13. Given the additional support of 4Q13 for this plus, it is possible that G read this in his source text. Conversely, G may be responsible for its addition. The same reason for this addition may have motivated scribes within the Hebrew tradition and G, namely the need to clarify who actually made the decision to spare the child, given the possible involvement of the attendants in the action of retrieving the basket.

καὶ ἔφη. G's default translation of אמר ("utter, say") in Exodus (as also throughout LXX) is λέγω/εἶπα. Surprisingly, here G uses φημί, its only occurrence in Exodus. Since it often has the sense "assert, affirm," perhaps G portrays Pharao's daughter as affirming the common reaction of the group.

ἀπὸ τῶν παιδίων τῶν Ἑβραίων. G indicates the child's origin and the group to which it belongs, with a partitive sense. Consider the instances of prepositional phrases such as ἐκ τῆς φυλῆς (v. 1) and ἐκ τῶν Ἑβραίων (v. 7) in contrast to τῶν θυγατέρων (v. 1).

2.7

ותאמר אחתו אל בת פרעה האלך וקראתי לך אשה מינקת מן
העברית ותינק לך את הילד

καὶ εἶπεν ἡ ἀδελφὴ αὐτοῦ τῇ θυγατρὶ Φαραώ Θέλεις καλέσω σοι γυναῖκα τροφεύουσαν ἐκ τῶν Ἑβραίων, καὶ θηλάσει σοι τὸ παιδίον;
And his sister said to Pharao's daughter, "Do you wish that I summon for you a nursing woman from the Hebrews, and she shall suckle the child for you?"

ἡ ἀδελφὴ αὐτοῦ. The proximity of Moyses's sister relates to prior instructions given in 2.4. In Exodus when referring to a person, ἀδελφή describes Miriam, Moyses's sister (2.7; 15.20), or Aaron's wife (6.23, ἀδελφὴν Ναασσών). The Hebrew noun is used to refer to parts of the tabernacle (26.3, 5, 6, 17), but is rendered by forms of ἕτερος or ἕκαστος.

Θέλεις καλέσω σοι. In most cases in Exodus the use of θέλω represents an idiomatic rendering of Hebrew finite verbs that do not mean specifically "wish/want" (2.7, 14; 8.32; 11.10), but as Evans (2001, 229) notes, the Greek verb still retains the sense of wish or desire. Exceptions might be 2.14, as well as 10.4, where לשלח ... מאן is rendered as μὴ θέλῃς ἐξαποστεῖλαι. Usually the Greek verb is complemented by an infinitive, with the exception of this context.

According to HRCS this is the only context in the LXX where a deliberative construction with θέλω occurs. Smyth (§1806) says that "βούλει, βούλεσθε (poet. θέλεις, θέλετε) *do you wish* often precedes the subjunctive," in this case a deliberative subjunctive (καλέσω). Examples would include Sophocles, *El.* 80: θέλεις μείνωμεν αὐτοῦ κἀπακούσωμεν γόων; ("Do you wish that we should remain here and listen to her cries?" [my trans.]) and *Oed. tyr.*, 651, τί σοι θέλεις δῆτ᾽ εἰκάθω; ("What then do you wish that I should grant you?" [my trans.]). If this idiom was still regarded as poetic in the early third century BCE, then this may suggest something about the linguistic register the translator chose for his work in the narrative sections.

The rendering of the ה interrogative by G is always contextually determined and usually no specific lexeme reflects it (2.7, 14; 4.11, 14, 18; 10.7; 14.11, 12; 16.4; 17.7; 33.16). This is the only context in Exodus where the deliberative subjunctive is used as an equivalent.

γυναῖκα τροφεύουσαν. G reflects the Hebrew by using an adjectival participle. The present aspect of the participle indicates a current activity. The verb τροφεύω is not attested in texts prior to Exodus. Chamberlain (2011, 192–94) lists it among those words "whose first known use is in the LXX, though they are also found in later secular Greek." Verbs ending in –ευω and formed from nouns "usually denote a *condition*, sometimes an *activity*. βασιλεύ-ω *am king, rule* (βασιλεύ-ς)" (Smyth §866.4). In the case of τροφεύω the activity is nursing, that is, feeding.

θηλάσει. G's use of this verb to render the Hebrew *hiphil* verb ינק, in the light of his use of τροφεύω immediately before to render the same verb, seems to express a semantic difference. Whereas τροφεύω suggests a general activity of nursing/feeding, θηλάζω specifically means "suckle." תניק is *hiphil* jussive and according to Evans (2001, 100) G renders a Hebrew jussive form by a future eleven times.

2.8

ותאמר לה בת פרעה לכי ותלך העלמה ותקרא את אם הילד

ἡ δὲ εἶπεν αὐτῇ ἡ θυγάτηρ Φαραώ Πορεύου. ἐλθοῦσα δὲ ἡ νεᾶνις ἐκάλεσεν τὴν μητέρα τοῦ παιδίου.

Then she, Pharao's daughter, said to her, "Go!" But the girl went and summoned the child's mother.

ἡ δὲ … ἡ θυγάτηρ Φαραώ. This formation is unusual. ἡ θυγάτηρ Φαραώ is in apposition to a pronominal ἡ. Probably the translator wanted to signal a change in subject, but then had to repeat that subject after the verb because of the Hebrew structure. It was not necessary to do this in order to communicate the sense of the Hebrew as we can see from the initial segment of verse 7. The Greek construction ἡ δὲ … αὐτῇ expresses normal idiom, but the translator, because of commitment to serial fidelity, feels obliged to represent בת פרעה.

Πορεύου. The main verbs in these paratactic clauses are all *waw*-consecutive forms. Within the direct speech we have the present imperative πορεύου rendering the Hebrew imperative. Note that G selects two different lexemes, πορεύου and ἐλθοῦσα, even though the source text reads לכי ותלך. Given the repetitive לכי ותלך, G may simply not want to repeat a form of the immediately preceding πορεύομαι. Lee (1983, 85–86), however, observed that in compounds formed from these two verbs, the present and future are supplied by πορεύομαι compounds and the future and aorist are supplied by "compounds of ἐλεύσομαι (Attic –ειμι), and -ἦλθον." Perhaps this lexical pattern is influencing G's selection of renderings in this instance also, even though they are not compound forms. If this is the case this variation is probably not stylistic, but may be idiomatic.

ἐλθοῦσα δέ. As we have seen, G often represents one clause in source text paratactical structures with an adverbial participle, perhaps marking emphasis with the finite verb form. Whether we should interpret the participle as attendant circumstance or temporal can be argued. ἔρχομαι normally renders בא ("come, go") in Exodus, but in three contexts G used it as the

equivalent for הלך (2.8 ἐλθοῦσα; 3.16 ἐλθών; 8.25 ἐλθόντες). In Greek Exodus
ἔρχομαι occurs primarily as an aorist form (19x), twice as a future form
(3.13; 22.9) and once as a present (5.20). The particle δὲ seems to convey a
mild adversative sense here as the young girl summons her mother, rather
than just any available nursing mother, as the reader might expect.

ἡ νεᾶνις. Both עלמה ("young woman") and νεᾶνις occur only here in
Exodus; νεᾶνις represents נערה more than twenty times in LXX and עלמה
four times. Both νεᾶνις and עלמה are girls of marriageable age. See verse
5 above.

2.9

ותאמר לה בת פרעה הֵילִיכִי את הילד הזה והינקהו לי ואני אתן את
שכרך ותקח האשה הילד ותניקהו
εἶπεν δὲ πρὸς αὐτὴν ἡ θυγάτηρ Φαραώ Διατήρησόν μοι τὸ παιδίον
τοῦτο, καὶ θηλασόν μοι αὐτό, ἐγὼ δὲ δώσω σοι τὸν μισθόν. ἔλαβεν δὲ
ἡ γυνὴ τὸ παιδίον καὶ ἐθήλαζεν αὐτό.
And Pharao's daughter said to her, "Take care of this child for
me, and suckle it for me, and I will give you your pay." Then the
woman took the child and kept suckling it.

εἶπεν δὲ πρὸς αὐτήν. After twice using εἶπεν + dative of indirect object (vv.
7–8) to render this Hebrew structure, G now switches to the prepositional
phrase marking the person addressed (for the first time in his translation).
Within Exodus אמר ל is rendered by λέγω/εἶπα + dative sixteen times
and λέγω/εἶπα + πρός + accusative three times. In comparison אמר אל is
rendered by λέγω/εἶπα + dative circa thirty-eight times (see 2.7) and λέγω/
εἶπα + πρός + accusative ca. eighty-two times. There is no apparent correla-
tion between the different Hebrew prepositions and the Greek rendering.

Διατήρησόν … τοῦτο. The translator creates parallelism through three connected clauses using the same structure: (conjunction) + verb + indirect
object + direct object. This parallelism is enhanced by the translator's
addition of μοι in the first clause and using the dative pronoun σοι in the
third clause, rather than the possessive σου (read by 376′ z Arm Co) as
MT reads. The verb διατήρησον renders הֵילִיכִי, which has the sense "carry
away." Wevers (1990, 15) indicates that this Hebrew form "is unique and
is usually emended to הוליכי" and regarded as *hiphil* imperative feminine

singular (e.g., GKC §69x regards this form as a second feminine imperative to be read as הוליכי). G used διατηρέω ("take care of, preserve") to
render four different Hebrew constructions (2.9; 9.16; 12.6; 34.7); the cognate noun διατήρησις twice translates משמרת (16.33, 34). The Greek verb
indicates care for and preservation, with a nuance of protection and does
not represent the sense of the Hebrew verb that means to "lead away" (Le
Boulluec and Sandevoir 1989, 82). Perhaps the translator references the
continued threat from Pharao's forces toward a Hebrew infant.

μοι τὸ παιδίον τοῦτο. G adds μοι. The placement of the dative pronoun
before the direct object occurs several times in Exodus in distinction
from his apparent source text (2.9; 6.8; 13.11; 16.32). It probably reflects
G's accommodation to Greek style. This word order occurs in each of
these parallel clauses, but in 2.7 σοι τὸ παιδίον reflects the Hebrew word
order.

θηλασόν. For this verb see verse 7 above. The aorist imperative, the second
in the series, renders a *hiphil* feminine singular imperative (היניקהו) introduced by a *waw*-conjunctive and completed by a third person masculine
singular pronominal suffix.

ἐγὼ δὲ δώσω σοι τὸν μισθόν. G reflects the pronominal suffix on the noun,
which usually would be rendered as σου (את שכרך), with the dative σοι.
The change probably enhances the parallelism with the first two clauses.
The initial ἐγὼ reflects the presence of אני. In representing את שכרך
("your wage") as τὸν μισθόν ("the wage"), G may express the idea of "the
appropriate wage." Nursing contracts dated to late first century BCE
(BGU 4, 1107) specify the wages to be paid for this service (μισθ[ὸν τοῦ
τε γάλακτος καὶ τῆς τροφείας κατὰ] μῆνα ἕκαστον ἀργυρίου δραχμὰς δέκα
καὶ ἐλαίου κοτύλας δ[ύ]ο, "the wage for milk and wet-nursing monthly
is ten silver drachmas and two half-pints of oil" [my trans.]). Presumably such contracts, informal or formal, were being created in the early
third century BCE, when the translation was occurring. For other Exodus
occurrences of μισθός rendering שכר, see 22.15. G also used the adjective
μισθωτός to render שכיר at 12.45 and 22.15.

ἔλαβεν δὲ ... καὶ ἐθήλαζεν αὐτό. The Hebrew narrative continues on with
two *waw*-consecutive verbs (ותקה ... ותניקהו) rendered by a Greek aorist
and past imperfect, marking the durative aspect. Given that the woman

is Moyses's mother and presumably had been nursing the infant before its exposure, the durative aspect probably conveys that she kept doing so (although it could also be inceptive, i.e., she began nursing the infant).

2.10

ויגדל הילד ותבאהו לבת פרעה ויהי לה לבן ותקרא שמו משה ותאמר
כי מן המים משיתהו

ἁδρυνθέντος δὲ τοῦ παιδίου εἰσήγαγεν αὐτὸ πρὸς τὴν θυγατέρα
Φαραώ, καὶ ἐγενήθη αὐτῇ εἰς υἱόν· ἐπωνόμασεν δὲ τὸ ὄνομα αὐτοῦ
Μωυσῆν λέγουσα Ἐκ τοῦ ὕδατος αὐτὸν ἀνειλόμην.

Now when the child grew up, she brought it to Pharao's daughter, and it became to her for a son. And she named his name Moyses, saying "I drew him out of the water."

ἁδρυνθέντος δὲ τοῦ παιδίου. G continues to vary the subordinate constructions used to represent coordinate structures in his source text. The genitive absolute is a standard Greek construction, used circa fourteen times by G. Aejmelaeus (1982a, 110–12; see also Soisalon-Soininen 1987, 175) indicates that "The cases of the *gen.abs.* in Ex and Deut are used to render verbal clauses." The genitive absolute in Greek Exodus frequently renders a bound infinitive with pronominal suffix (4.21; 5.20; 14.18; 16.1; 19.16; 34.29 [καταβαίνοντος δὲ αὐτοῦ ἐκ τοῦ ὄρους/בְּרִדְתּוֹ מִן הָהָר]; 38.27 [MT 40.32]). In other cases it represents expressions denoting time (12.18; 29; 34.22) or an interrogative (33.16) or a bound construction (16.13, probably construed as an infinitive). It also occurs in 40.15[17] in a plus. The genitive participle in 19.9 is most probably a supplementary participle. However, only in 2.10 does G use a genitive absolute construction to render an independent verbal clause. Here again G may recognize a circumstantial/temporal sense expressed in the Hebrew text by simple juxtaposition of the two clauses, so that with the genitive absolute he in fact communicates the sense of the Hebrew text in fine Greek form. In Classical Greek the "subject of the genitive absolute may be identical with the object of the leading verb" (Smyth §2073b), as is the case here (note the presence of αὐτό which is object of εἰσήγαγεν).

G rendered the two occurrences of גדל ("grow up, become great") differently reflecting its two meanings (2.10, 11). Here G correctly reflects the Hebrew verb's sense of maturation; ἁδρύνω in the passive within the LXX means to mature, grow (cf. Judg 11.2; 13.24; Routh 1.13; 2 Rgns 12.3 [lamb]; 4 Rgns 4.18; Ps 143[144].12 [growing plant]). External to LXX the verb describes maturation generally, applied, for example, to plants, embryos, and human beings (see Walters 1973, 86). Examples of these usages occur in Herodotus, *Hist.* 1.193.1: ἁδρύνεταί τε τὸ λήιον ("that ripens the crop"); Hippocrates, *Septim.* 1.9: ἁδρυνομένου τοῦ ἐμβρύου ("as the embryo matures"); T. Iss. 3.1: ὅτε οὖν ἡδρύνθην, τέκνα μου, ἐπορευόμην ἐν εὐθύτητι καρδίας ("when then I was grown up, my children, I began walking in uprightness of heart" [my trans.]). Chamberlain (2011, 3) proposed "weaned" as the meaning for Exod 2.10 and 4 Rgns 4.18, but this seems too specific for this context.

The particle δέ indicates additional information is being provided, which moves the story forward.

εἰσήγαγεν … πρός. The verb εἰσάγω occurs thirteen times in Exodus, usually rendering a *hiphil* form of בוא. Only here and 23.23 is it modified by πρός + accusative.

καὶ ἐγενήθη αὐτῇ εἰς υἱόν. Mayser (§ 2.2.269) provides examples from the early papyri (e.g., Teb. 40, 23 γενηθήτω τῶι ὑποτελεῖ τὸ δίκαιον [117ᵃ] ["let that which is due belong to the 'official'"]) for this use of the dative of possession or personal interest with forms of γίνομαι. However, the complete construction γίνομαι + dative of person + εἰς (relationship) does not, as far as I can determine, occur prior to usage in LXX. It reflects the Hebrew construction היה+ ל (pred.) + ל (pers.) "to be/become for someone for (a wife, son, refuge, etc.)" (BDB, 226). The same Hebrew structure occurs at 15.2 (ויהי לי לישועה) and the translator rendered it as ἐγένετό μοι εἰς σωτηρίαν (see also Gen 20.12; Harl 1986, 75; Tenhunen 2008, 4–5: "γίνεσθαι εἰς and εἶναι εἰς, as they come to mean 'to be/become/belong for someone *as something*' [such as … , Exod 2:10], are Hebraisms. The last two examples, Gen 20:12 and Exod 2:10 are the most clearly Hebraistic renderings in my material."). Here we see interference in the Greek syntax because of the influence of the Hebrew structure. G follows the Hebrew word order and sense exactly.

The aorist passive form of γίνομαι occurs eight times (2.10; 4.6; 10.13; 11.3; 12.29, 30; 14.24; 39.4) in Exodus. Wevers (1990, 16) notes that the aorist middle form was used twenty-five times and "the two forms seem to be almost indistinguishable lexically." In 2.11 the translator used ἐγένετο … μέγας γενόμενος.

ἐπωνόμασεν δὲ τὸ ὄνομα αὐτοῦ. G consistently renders the idiom קרא שם as ἐπονομάζω τὸ ὄνομα (2.10, 22; 15.23; 16.31; 17.7, 15). Occasionally, particularly in Plato's writings, we find ἐπονομάζω accompanied by τὸ ὄνομα with the sense "give a name to:" Plato, *Leg.* (816, b, 6): καὶ κατὰ λόγον (5) αὐταῖς θέμενος ὄνομα συμπάσαις ἐμμελείας ἐπωνόμασε ("and how rationally, giving a name to them all, he called them 'stately dances'" [LCL]); *Crat.* (406, a, 5) τὰς δὲ Μούσας ... ἀπὸ τοῦ μῶσθαι, ... καὶ ζητήσεώς τε καὶ φιλοσοφίας τὸ ὄνομα τοῦτο ἐπωνόμασεν ("and bestowed the name 'the Muses' ... from μῶσθαι, ... both searching and philosophy" [LCL]); *Tim.* (83, c, 1) καὶ τὸ μὲν κοινὸν ὄνομα πᾶσιν τούτοις ἤ τινες (c.) ἰατρῶν που χολὴν ἐπωνόμασαν ("and either certain of the physicians give the common name 'bile' to all these things" [LCL]). So G is using a known Greek idiom. Other uses of קרא usually are translated by forms of καλέω. The Greek expression occurs once (20.24) as the rendering for אזכיר את שמי. Herodotus also used this Greek verbal phrase but in the sense of "calling upon the name" (which is not the sense found in Exod 2.10); for example, *Hist.* 4.35.3, καὶ γὰρ ἀγείρειν σφι τὰς γυναῖκας ἐπονομαζούσας τὰ οὐνόματα ἐν τῷ ὕμνῳ τόν σφι Ὠλὴν ἀνὴρ Λύκιος ἐποίησε ("For the women collected gifts for them, calling upon their names in the hymn made for them by Olen of Lycia" [LCL]). Usually this expression occurs when he or one of his characters is speculating about why something or someone has a specific name.

Μωυσῆν. Dozeman (2009, 81) indicates that the Hebrew text incorporates two etymologies: "The first underscores the adoption of Moses by Pharaoh's daughter through the wordplay between 'son' in Hebrew (*ben*) and in Egyptian (*mose*)." The Egyptian word for "son" occurs in such names as Thutmose ("son of Thut"). The Greek translator shows no awareness of this etymology. The other etymology references the child's rescue from the river, but is based upon Hebrew language, not Egyptian. The verb משה seems to mean "draw." Greek cannot capture this etymology and so translates the verb as ἀνειλόμην.

The vowel cluster ωυ reflects Egyptian name formations contemporary with the translation according to Mayser (§1.138). He gives the following formations as examples: Ἀρθώυθου, Θαῶυτος, Πεκῶυτος, Πετῶυε, Πετῶυτος. However, the insertion of the υ in Μωυσῆς does not have warrant in the Hebrew form of the name. This proper noun also is inflected, one of the few in Exodus. These details suggest that G did not form this name, but rather it belonged to the lexical stock used by Egyptian Jews prior to the translation of the Pentateuch.

λέγουσα. See comments at verse 22 (λέγων Ὅτι κτλ.).

ἀνειλόμην. G used an aorist middle form of this verb previously in verse 5 with the sense "draw, take up" to represent לקה. In verse 10, G uses ἀναιροῦμαι to render the only use of משה ("draw") in Exodus. Le Boulluec and Sandevoir (1989, 83) observe that "elle renforce la cohérence narrative." Note the pre-posed αὐτόν at variance with the Hebrew word order (see also αὐτό at 2.3).

Summary

G's text demonstrates general serial fidelity to its source text but also shows considerable accommodation to the target language. Pluses (1–2, 3, 6) and minuses (3, 6) clarify or reduce redundancy, generating a more acceptable text. Shifts in person and number of verbs (e.g., 2–3a) reduce potential ambiguity. Alterations in source text word order also accommodate Greek word order preferences (e.g., 3, 9). G uses Greek subordinating structures in place of source text coordinating structures, assimilating in the direction of the target text (e.g., adverbial clauses [3], genitive absolute [10], frequent use of adverbial participles). Isomorphism does not seem to be a priority. Lexical variation occurs in the Greek text where the source text uses repeatedly the same lexical term (vv. 2–3, σκεπάζω … κρύπτω; v. 3, ἐμβάλλω … τίθημι; v. 7, τροφεύω … θηλάζω; vv. 6, 9, φῆμι … λέγω; v. 10, 11, ἀδρύνω … μέγας γενόμενος). Some of these may be examples of μεταβολή. Conversely, the Greek text reduces lexical variation (e.g., ἀναίρω, vv. 5, 10), perhaps again in the service of literary coherence.

Leuitikon 3.1–17: The Sacrifice of Deliverance

Dirk Büchner

Literature

Athenaeus. 1927. *The Deipnosophists in 9 Volumes*. Translated by Charles Burton Gulick. LCL. Cambridge: Harvard University Press. ♦ **Bergquist**, Brigitte. 1993. "Bronze Age Sacrificial Koine in the Eastern Mediterranean? A Study of Animal Sacrifice in the Ancient Near East." Pages 11–43 in *Ritual and Sacrifice in the Ancient Near East*. Edited by Jan Quaegebeur. OLA 55. Leuven: Peeters. ♦ **Boulluec**, Alain Le, and P. **Sandevoir**. 1989. *La Bible d'Alexandrie 2: L'Exode*. Paris: Cerf. ♦ **Bowie**, Angus M. 1995. "Greek Sacrifice: Forms and Functions." Pages 463–82 in *The Greek World*. Edited by Anton Powell. New York: Routledge. ♦ **Boyd-Taylor**, Cameron. 2004. "Linguistic Register and Septuagintal Lexicography." Pages 149–66 in *Biblical Greek Language and Lexicography: Essays in Honor of Frederick W. Danker*. Edited by Bernard A. Taylor, John A. L. Lee, Peter R. Burton, and Richard E. Whitaker. Grand Rapids: Eerdmans. ♦ **Büchner**, Dirk. 1997. "Jewish Commentaries and the Septuagint." *JJS* 48:250–61. ♦ **Büchner**. 2014. "Brief Remarks on the Occurrence and Value of Blood in Greek Sources from Epic Literature to Early Christianity." Pages 255–71 in *Die Septuaginta—Text, Wirkung, Rezeption: 4. Internationale Fachtagung veranstaltet von Septuaginta Deutsch (LXX.D), Wuppertal 19.–22. Juli 2012*. Edited by Wolfgang Kraus and Siegfried Kreuzer. WUNT 325. Tübingen: Mohr Siebeck. ♦ **Burkert**, Walter. 1966. "Greek Tragedy

I am grateful to Al Pietersma for spending a great deal of time and effort critiquing this piece of commentary. Though we did not agree on all points, many of his suggestions and corrections have been incorporated into the final draft. Cameron Boyd-Taylor, Spencer Jones, and the other contributors to this volume also offered helpful advice.

and Sacrificial Ritual." *GRBS* 7:87–121. ✦ **Burkert**. 1997. *Homo Necans: Interpretationen altgriechischer Opferriten und Mythen.* 2nd ed. RVV 32. Berlin: de Gruyter. ✦ **Crawley**, Richard. 1934. *The Complete Writings of Thucydides: The Peloponnesian War.* New York: Modern Library. ✦ **Daniel**, Suzanne. 1966. *Recherches sur le Vocabulaire du Culte dans la Septante.* EeC 61. Paris: Klincksieck. ✦ **Détienne**, Marcel. 1989. "Culinary Practices and the Spirit of Sacrifice." Pages 1–20 in *The Cuisine of Sacrifice among the Greeks.* Edited by Marcel Détienne and Jean-Pierre Vernant. Translated by Paula Wissing. Chicago: University of Chicago Press. ✦ **Durand**, Jean-Louis. 1989. "Greek Animals: Toward a Topology of Edible Bodies." Pages 87–118 in *The Cuisine of Sacrifice among the Greeks.* Edited by Marcel Détienne and Jean-Pierre Vernant. Translated by Paula Wissing. Chicago: University of Chicago Press. ✦ **Fraser**, Peter M. 1972. *Ptolemaic Alexandria, Volume 1: Text.* Oxford: Clarendon. ✦ **Gill**, David. 1966. "Thysia and Selāmīm: Questions to R. Schmid's Das Bundesopfer in Israel." *Bib* 47:255–62. ✦ **Goodwin**, William W. 1930. *Greek Grammar.* Revised by Charles Burton Gulick. Boston: Ginn. ✦ **Gould**, John. 1985. "On Making Sense of Greek Religion." Pages 1–33 in *Greek Religion and Society.* Edited by Pat E. Easterling and John V. Muir. Cambridge: Cambridge University Press. ✦ **Graf**, Fritz. 2002. "What Is New about Greek Sacrifice?" Pages 113–25 in *Kykeon: Studies in honor of H. S. Versnel.* Edited by Herman F. J. Horstmanshoff, H. W. Singor, F. T. van Straten, and Johan H. M. Strubbe. RGRW 142. Leiden: Brill. ✦ **Harlé**, Paul, and Didier **Pralon**. 1988. *La Bible d'Alexandrie 3: Le Lévitique.* Paris: Cerf. ✦ **Honea**, Sion M. 1993. "Homer's Daitos Eises: The Greek Sacrificial Meal." *JRitSt* 7:53–68. ✦ **Herodotus**. 1920. *The Persian Wars, Volume I: Books 1–2.* Translated by A. D. Godley. LCL 117. Cambridge: Harvard University Press. ✦ **Huber**, Karl. 1916. *Untersuchungen über den Sprachcharakter des griechischen Leviticus.* Giessen: Töpelmann. ✦ **Huffman**, Carl A. 1993. *Philolaus of Croton: Pythagorean and Presocratic; A Commentary on the Fragments and Testimonia with Interpretive Essays.* Cambridge: Cambridge University Press. ✦ **Jameson**, Michael H. 1988. "Sacrifice and Ritual." Pages 2:959–79 in *Civilization of the Ancient Mediterranean.* Edited by Michael Grant and Rachel Kitzinger. New York: Scribner. ✦ **Jones**, Spencer. 2015. "Syntax in the Septuagint: With Special Reference to Relative Clauses in Greek Numbers." MA thesis, Trinity Western University. ✦ **Kirk**, Geoffrey S. 1981. "Some Methodological Pitfalls in the Study of Ancient Greek Sacrifice (in Particular)." Pages 41–90 in *Le Sacrifice Dans l'Antiquité: Entretiens sur l'Antiquité Classique, Vandœuvres-Genève, 25–30 août 1980.* Edited by Jean Rudhart and Olivier Reverdin. EnAC 27. Geneva: Vandoeuvres. ♦ **Levinsohn**, Stephen H. 1992. *Discourse Features of New Testament Greek.* Dallas: Summer Institute of Linguistics. ♦ **Meuli**, Karl. 1946. "Griechische Opferbräuche." Pages 185–288 in *Phyllobolia für Paul von der Mühll zum 60. Geburtstag am 1. August 1945.* Edited by Olof Gigon and Karl Meuli. Basel: Schwabe. ♦ **Milgrom**, Jacob. 1991. *Leviticus 1–16: A New Translation with Introduction and Commentary.* AB 3. New York: Doubleday. ♦ **Soisalon-Soininen**, Ilmari. 1987. *Studien zur Septuaginta-Syntax: Zu seinem 70. Geburtstag am 4. Juni 1987.* Edited by Anneli Aejmelaeus and Raija Sollamo. AASF B 237. Helsinki: Suomalainen Tiedeakatemia. ♦ **Spicq**, Ceslas. 1994. *Theological Lexicon of the New Testament.* Translated by James D. Ernest. 3 vols. Peabody, MA: Hendrickson. ♦ **Stengel**, Paul. 1972. *Opferbräuche der Griechen.* Stuttgart: Teubner. ♦ **Straten**, Folkert van. 1987. "Greek Sacrificial Representations: Livestock Prices and Religious Mentality." Pages 159–70 in *Gifts to the Gods: Proceedings of the Uppsala Symposium, 1985.* Edited by Tullia Linders and Gullög Nordquist. AAU 15. Uppsala: ACTA Universitatis Uppsaliensis. ♦ **Straten**. 1988. "The God's Portion in Greek Sacrificial Representation: Is the Tail Doing Nicely?" Pages 51–68 in *Early Greek Cult Practice: Proceedings of the Fifth International Symposium at the Swedish Institute at Athens, 26–29, June, 1986.* Edited by Robin Hägg, Nannó Marinatos, and Gullög C. Nordquist. Skrifter Utgivna Av Svenska Institutet i Athen 38. Stockholm: Svenska Institutet i Athen. ♦ **Tarn**, William W. 1933. "Two Notes on Ptolemaic History." *JHS* 53:57–68. ♦ **Ulrich**, Eugene. 1994. "4QLev[b]." Pages 177–87 in *Qumran Cave 4.VII: Genesis to Numbers.* Edited by Eugene Ulrich, Frank Moore Cross, James R. Davila, Jastram Nathan, Judith E. Sanderson, Emanuel Tov, and John Strugnell. DJD 12. Oxford: Clarendon. ♦ **Vahrenhorst**, Martin. 2009. "Leuitikon." in LXX.D. ♦ **Vernant**, Jean-Pierre. 1989. "At Man's Table: Hesiod's Foundation Myth of Sacrifice." Pages 21–86 in *The Cuisine of Sacrifice among the Greeks.* Edited by Marcel Détienne and Jean-Pierre Vernant. Translated by Paula Wissing. Chicago: University of Chicago Press. ♦ **Wevers**, John W. 1986. *Text History of the Greek Leviticus.* MSU 19. Göttingen: Vandenhoeck & Ruprecht. ♦ **Wevers**. 1997. *Notes on the Greek Text of Leviticus.* SCS 44. Atlanta: Scholars Press.

Outline

This chapter concerns gifts from the animal groups cattle, sheep, and goats that may be brought as victims for the sacrifice of deliverance (θυσία σωτηρίου) and in each case, an additional offering (κάρπωμα) is made of some of the animals' internal parts, as a kind of ritual within the ritual. The role of the respective agents, whether suppliant or priests, is not always clear. The anatomical terminology is also rather imprecise and together these two matters will provide some indication of the translator's purpose in creating a Greek version of a Hebrew ritual.

Commentary

3.1

ואם זבח שלמים קרבנו אם מן הבקר הוא מקריב אם זכר אם נקבה
תמים יקריבנו לפני יהוה

Ἐὰν δὲ θυσία σωτηρίου τὸ δῶρον αὐτοῦ τῷ κυρίῳ, ἐὰν μὲν ἐκ τῶν
βοῶν αὐτὸ προσαγάγῃ, ἐάν τε ἄρσεν ἐάν τε θῆλυ, ἄμωμον προσάξει
αὐτὸ ἔναντι κυρίου.

Now if his gift to the Lord is a sacrifice of deliverance, if he brings it from the cattle, whether male or female, he shall bring it without blemish before the Lord.

ἐάν. When viewed as a whole, the verse consists of a conditional sentence with multiple protases and a single apodosis. The structure of the Hebrew is carefully modeled in Greek; one notices for instance four occurrences of ἐάν for the four of אם. The first protasis is verbless. Normally, the verb in the protasis is suppressed when it is understood to be the same as the one in the apodosis; for example, in 2.5, ἐὰν δὲ θυσία ἀπὸ τηγάνου τὸ δῶρόν σου σεμίδαλις πεφυραμένη ἐν ἐλαίῳ ἄζυμα ἔσται but that is not the case here (cf. Smyth §2345).

δέ. NETS renders "now" to indicate that this particle is standing in for Hebrew *waw* in a statement that is not adversative but rather introducing information that builds on what precedes it, in this case the statement of 1.3 (cf. Levinsohn 1992, 112). An example is found in P.Rev. Laws, col. 43.3–4 (259 BCE): Ὅσαι δ᾽ ἐν δωρεῖα κῶμαι εἰσιν, ἐν ταύταις δὲ ἐλαιουργῖον μηθὲν καθιστάτωσαν ("Now whichever villages are held in gift, in these they shall set up no oil factory"; see Jones 2015, 157).

θυσία. The pairing of θυσία with זבח occurs twice in Genesis and three times in Exodus. The Exodus translator employed along with it three other nominal cognates of θύω, but it was the Leviticus translator who cemented this particular match and subsequently it appears to have become the standard. There may be little else to say about the word's employment in this chapter besides the fact that it is the most self-evident translational equivalent due to its semantic closeness to the Hebrew noun.

However, there is a sense in which cultic words belong to a special category, and having some understanding of this word's cultural value as well as its performance aspects will be essential if we are to form a judgment of the translator's depiction of the procedure in the verses that follow. One could imagine that as he worked, searching for vocabulary of sacrifice from sources familiar to him, he would no doubt have become aware that the ritual described here in his Hebrew text and the Greek θυσία are virtually identical in practice. Both belong to what is known as the alimentary communion sacrifice, in which meat for human consumption is slaughtered in a sacral setting. Hebrews as well as Greeks ate meat only under such conditions. In both cultures, depictions of the sacrifice paid more attention to the post-kill ceremony than to the act of slaughter. Of special interest for this chapter is that both required their deities to be given a special due consisting of some of the internal parts. Lastly, in both cultures the victim's flesh was afterward eaten by the wider community in a festal setting. There are of course divergences too. The god's special portion offered by Greeks was not quite identical to that given by Jews, and its giving was motivated by a different understanding of the deity's participation (Gill 1966, 255 and n. 1 for bibliography). Hebrew participants did not partake of the internal organs as their Greek counterparts were accustomed to, and neither was the Hebrew ritual accompanied by a procession, music, or gifts of barley and wine. A Greek θυσία had women and sometimes a μάγειρος officiating whereas Jewish sacrifice permitted only priests. Nevertheless the fact of the rituals' broadly identical procedures is significant and will constantly be in the background as we ask whether the translator (G) fully understood the terminology found in his *Vorlage* and whether he was concerned about the suitability of the Greek cultic terminology he chose for his translation. Behind these questions lies a statement made by the notable historian Peter Fraser, that in Alexandria, Greek-speaking foreigners writing about their religious practices gave them an *interpretatio graeca* to which Jews would have been no exception (1972, 190). Whether or not this may be true for Leu 3 will be demonstrated below. In preparing the commentary for this chapter it became clear that some background knowledge of the Greek sacrificial vocabulary was necessary in order to come to an understanding of what G tried to pass on to his reader.

Of the alimentary ritual's performance aspects we know a great deal, since it is the cultic procedure most often recounted in Greek literature. Textual as well as epigraphic evidence show that from as far back as Hesiod and Homer through to Appollonius in the third century, the θυσία remained essentially the same. Of all retellings, the epic material is most well known and receives the bulk of attention in scholarship. Among later texts that describe it are Sophocles, *Ant.* 1020 and Apollonius Rhodius, *Argon.* 698. On Hesiod, see Burkert 1966, 104 and especially n. 37 for bibliography; on the Homeric material, Kirk 1981, 63–80. On the epigraphic evidence, Jameson 1988, 971; Durand 1989, 87–118; and van Straten 1987, 160; see also Bowie 1995, 464–65; and Honea 1993, 56–57.

As a starting point it must be asserted that the Leviticus translator was familiar with the terminology associated with θυσία, and drew from it the vocabulary items he needed in order to create a Greek version of the Hebrew meal sacrifice. But this selection appears to have been made arbitrarily and without care. We notice for example, that technical terms that would have stood him in good stead, such as γέρας, or σπλάγχνα are absent. Other Greek words like μηρία and ὀσφῦς were simply slotted into his telling like pieces of a puzzle where they neither fitted well nor brought across the semantic value of their Hebrew counterparts. This can only be explained by the fact that G was primarily concerned with representing the linguistic features present in the source text piece by piece; in other words, he was faithfully translating a sacred text as it was demanded of him by convention. He therefore tended to rely on established equivalents, rather than employ words that more adequately communicated the meaning of the Hebrew. This is why the bound formation זבח שלמים is represented by a Greek genitival compound: θυσία σωτηρίου. If such care to faithfully render item by item had not been his guiding principle, he might have recognized that זבח שלמים and θυσία are so similar that the latter term by itself could serve as the most fitting descriptor, fully adequate for Greek speakers to grasp the content and cultural value of the Hebrew ritual. But instead, he gave his version of the alimentary sacrifice a compound title, a hybrid no Greek speaker would have recognized, and this out of concern that the vocabulary of the source text be represented in a quantitatively equivalent fashion.

σωτηρίου. NETS's chosen rendering "sacrifice of *deliverance*" is supported by LXX.D's "*Rettungs*opfer" and *BdA* "offrande de *salut*." The precise meaning of שלמים has always been unclear. The targumim, for instance, offer no help with their rendering נבסת קודשיא. Hebrew שלמים carries the sense of well-being, health, completeness or finality, but there is little consensus on how exactly such meanings are to be understood in relation to a ritual associated with the rare activity of eating meat. The explanation found in rabbinic tradition is that the שלמים are so called because they give peace, or provide release from vows (Daniel 1966, 274; cf. Milgrom 1991, 220). It is doubtful whether G was himself certain of the Hebrew or aware of any contemporary attempts at making sense of it. It is safer to say that here, as in similar cases, he follows the lead of the Exodus translator (25.5 and 32.6) who selected for it a neuter adjective in the genitive, denoting "safety" or "deliverance" (LSJ, s.v. "σωτήριον" I.b). Why this should have been G Exodus's rendition is uncertain since there is no discernible semantic overlap between the Hebrew and Greek terms (Le Boulluec and Sandevoir 1989, 244). Anyone living in third century Ptolemaic Alexandria hearing the word σωτήριον used in a ritual context would have associated it not with an alimentary sacrifice but rather with a civic offering for deliverance called τὸ σωτήριον ἱερόν or frequently τά σωτήρια ἱερά, (LSJ, s.v. "σωτήριον" II.2). The *Soteria* in third-century Alexandria included music, sacrifices, and libations by Dionysiac artists to the θεοί σωτῆρες Philadelphus and Arsinoë I (Tarn, 1933, 60). Athenaeus *Deipn.* 11.97 cites the third century lyric poet Theocles as follows: ἐθύσαμεν γὰρ σήμερον Σωτήρια πάντες οἱ τεχνῖται· μεθ' ὧν πιὼν τὸ δίκερας ὡς τὸν φίλτατον βασιλέα πάρειμι ("All we artists have to-day celebrated with sacrifice the festival of Salvation; in their company I have drunk the double horn and am come into the presence of our dearest king," trans. Gulick). The presence of τεχνῖται and δίκερας helps to situate this ritual in the Ptolemaic cult. Beyond Egypt, the σωτήριον was a regular sacrifice according to a set calendar that required neighboring dignitaries to attend (Polybius, *Hist.* 4.49), and a sacrifice offered out of gratitude for, or even to achieve deliverance, perhaps in the realm of personal safety or health (Xenophon, *Anab.* 3.2.9). Daniel (1966, 278 and esp. 279) mentions a number of similar occurrences of this term that postdate the Greek Pentateuch.

It is therefore difficult for the modern commentator to account for G's use of this word. Obviously, he did not intend his readership to take it to connote what it did for pagan Alexandrians. Philo, perhaps anxious to rule out such a possibility, points out that the σωτήρ in this sacrifice is the God of the Jews (*Spec. Laws* 1.252). If all we can say is that G simply went along with the Exodus translator, it is likely that he was uncertain about the meaning of the Hebrew. Neither was he concerned about any discord caused by including in his nomenclature an adjectival element known to refer to a pagan rite. Later translators in an effort to resolve this tried other alternatives. Reigns and Proverbs, for example, made use of the etymological rendering εἰρηνικός, while Josephus (*A.J.* 3.228) reformulated it as a χαριστήρια θυσία.

τῷ κυρίῳ. This may be a *Vorlage*-based harmonization as it is found also in 4Q24 (4QLevᵇ) (Ulrich 1994, 180).

ἐάν μέν … ἐάν τε … ἐάν τε. G is careful to represent each element of the אם clauses with corresponding morphemes. The μέν can either be viewed as solitary, "if in fact" (Wevers 1997, 23) or as resolved by δέ in verses 6 and 12. The double ἐάν τε … ἐάν τε accompanying the subjunctive προσαγάγῃ renders the two Hebrew disjunctive clauses (Joüon §175e) and the result finds analogy in, for example, Thucydides 4.98.2: τὸν δὲ νόμον τοῖς Ἕλλησιν εἶναι, ὧν ἂν ᾖ τὸ κράτος τῆς γῆς ἑκάστης ἥν τε πλέονος ἥν τε βραχυτέρας, τούτων καὶ τὰ ἱερὰ αἰεὶ γίγνεσθαι ("The law of the Hellenes was that conquest of a country, whether more or less extensive, carried with it possession of the temples in that country," trans. Crawley; cf. Smyth §2852a).

αὐτὸ προσαγάγῃ. Here and in verse 7 (cf. 21.8) הוא מקריב must be understood as a fientive verb expressing "a single and comparatively transitory act" (GKC §116f; cf. IBHS §37.3b) and G renders appropriately with an aorist subjunctive. Although the meaning is not identical with the Hebrew, G by adding the objective pronoun manages to maintain the Hebrew word order, but also provide his reader with additional information. A chiasm results with προσάξει αὐτό later in the verse.

ἄμωμον. The adjective can be applied to concretes (the male victim) as well as to abstracts (the gift). Herodotus speaks of ἀμώμῳ νόμῳ ([by] "a perfect law" *Hist.* 2.177, trans. Godley).

ἄμωμον προσάξει αὐτό. The Hebrew formula תמים יקריבנו is one in which an indefinite adjective expressing a state is placed before or after a verb (GKC §118n.a) here referring to the verb's object and the feature it possesses at the time of the verbal action (*IBHS* §10.2.2.d, esp. n. 19). There is therefore more than simple juxtaposition at play, or else an attributive might have been employed with the noun itself. The question for the analyst of the Greek to settle is this: If the translator was aware of such a sense, and tried to express it by means of Greek that nevertheless strictly maintains the word order of the Hebrew, did he succeed in producing a comparable effect? This is not impossible to imagine, if one regards the adjective as a nominal accusative of specification in apposition to the pronoun, in other words, "he shall bring it (as something) without blemish." What is the referent of the adjective ἄμωμον and the pronoun αὐτό? In Hebrew, most of the nouns are masculine, so that the masculine verbal suffix could refer to any one of the offering, the sacrifice, or the male and female animal (1.3, 10; 3.1, 6) but most likely it is the animal itself that is intended. The Greek neuter pronoun can refer only to δῶρον or ἄρσεν to be brought as something without defect. The same considerations will obtain in verse 6, but similar wording in verse 9 causes some complications.

3.2

וסמך ידו על ראש קרבנו ושחטו פתח אהל מועד וזרקו בני אהרן
הכהנים את הדם על המזבח סביב

καὶ ἐπιθήσει τὰς χεῖρας ἐπὶ τὴν κεφαλὴν τοῦ δώρου καὶ σφάξει αὐτὸ παρὰ τὰς θύρας τῆς σκηνῆς τοῦ μαρτυρίου· καὶ προσχεοῦσιν οἱ υἱοὶ Ἀαρὼν οἱ ἱερεῖς τὸ αἷμα ἐπὶ τὸ θυσιαστήριον τῶν ὁλοκαυτωμάτων κύκλῳ.

And he shall lay his hands on the head of the gift, and he shall slaughter it at the entrance to the tent of witness, and the sons of Aaron the priests shall pour out the blood against all sides of the altar of whole burnt offerings.

τάς χεῖρας. Three times in this chapter, in contrast to chapter 1, hands are plural. Paul Harlé and Didier Pralon (1988, 91) contend that this is following an oral tradition, which one sees reflected in m. Menaḥ. 9:8. There is no doubt that some known traditions of correct cultic procedure will color our interpretation of what is found in the LXX's version of biblical prescriptions (see Büchner 1997). But the question of whether or not G took care to be legally precise for the benefit of a living community will raise itself a number of times in this chapter, and the answer appears most often to be in the negative. Instances in which there are analogies between the OG's wording and later Jewish writings seem to be balanced out by the times when the Greek is so vague that any concern for legal clarity must be out of the question.

δώρου. If G were composing a text in which he wanted to convey the details of a ritual, he might have preferred to employ a more suitable Greek word that specifies the victim (gifts tend not to have heads), such as σφάγιον or ἱερεῖον. But as a translator he was determined not to vary the pairing of קרבן and δῶρον he established in 1.2.

σφάξει αὐτό. In chapter 1 G changed the singular of the Hebrew (which is consistently so) to a plural but here, as Harlé and Pralon (1988, 91) suggest, the primitive tradition appears unchanged: the suppliant slaughters and the priests participate only by manipulating the parts. Not so in verse 13! One notices that here G represents the Hebrew verbal suffix, a practice he does not follow throughout. That he does not render the suffix on "hands" is simply because it is good Greek to omit a suffix when the possessor is obvious.

προσχεοῦσιν ... αἷμα. Again, G appears not to take great pains to reproduce the Hebrew ritual in a pedantic way (pouring on is not sprinkling), but rather to represent a Hebrew action with a loosely corresponding Greek one, already familiar from Exodus. In extrabiblical Greek literature blood as the object of χέω and cognates is found mostly in reference to human bloodshed, not animal sacrifice. Artistic and literary depictions of animal sacrifice do show animal blood being splashed onto altars, and the regular terms for this action are αἱμάσσω and αἱματόω. But unlike the Hebrews, Greeks did not assign any special operative value to blood in animal sacrifice and so it is hardly ever mentioned in recollections of the θυσία. It was merely abandoned as something that belongs to the gods (Durand 1989, 95 and for a fuller discussion of blood in the Greek and Hebrew worlds see Büchner 2014, 256–71). Our translator may have preferred to employ a word like αἱμάσσω, but once again he prefers to retain an established Hebrew-Greek relation, for the sake of his audience.

τάς θύρας. Though θύρα can mean "entrance" as well as "door," in NETS "door" is used for the singular, and "entrance" for the plural. The translator alternates randomly between the two for the Hebrew singular (Wevers 1986, 73).

τῶν ὁλοκαυτωμάτων. The Hebrew מזבח העלה likely underlying this addition occurs several times in Exodus, but there עלה is only rendered by ὁλοκαύτωμα once. In the case of Leviticus the match of עלה with ὁλοκαύτωμα occurs repeatedly in chapter 4, and if Wevers is correct (1997, 25), the translator is harmonizing from a knowledge of the Hebrew text of that chapter. Milgrom (1991, 205) feels that if the addition is for clarification it is unnecessary since there is no doubt that the outer altar is meant.

3.3

והקריב מזבח השלמים אשה ליהוה את החלב המכסה את הקרב
ואת כל החלב אשר על הקרב

καὶ προσάξουσιν ἀπὸ τῆς θυσίας τοῦ σωτηρίου κάρπωμα κυρίῳ, τὸ στέαρ τὸ κατακαλύπτον τὴν κοιλίαν καὶ πᾶν τὸ στέαρ τὸ ἐπὶ τῆς κοιλίας,

And they shall bring from the sacrifice of deliverance an offering to the Lord: the fat that covers the entrails and all the fat that is on the entrails

προσάξουσιν. The verb can take a double accusative like other verbs of bringing and offering. In Hebrew constructions that contain two objects, the predicate accusative is usually marked by indefiniteness (GKC §118; Joüon §129a). In this case indefinite "offering" is followed by definite "fat." For the most part, G is careful to follow the Hebrew word order and to supply the article in Greek when present in the Hebrew, and vice versa. As in Hebrew, the Greek predicate accusative is usually distinguishable from the direct object by the former's lacking the article (BDR §273, Smyth §1150, 1614). The same formula is found in verses 7, 9, and 14. The sense conveyed in all three instances is that the fat and the other ingredients are separated off to make up a suboffering, a κάρπωμα.

G pluralizes, since in his understanding the priests are manipulating the separated parts (recall chs. 1–2). It brings this verse into conflict with 7.20 [MT 30]. That he fails to pluralize the future verb at the end of 3.4 presents numerous difficulties discussed by Wevers (1997, 24). In NETS we have made no effort at a resolution. From the perspective of modern sensibilities, the translation ends up trapped between an alteration in verse 3 that is not carried over into verse 4. But this kind of logical inconsistency is to be attributed to what Soisalon-Soininen identified as the translators' mode of work (1987, 88): they proceeded phrase by phrase in a forward direction and often ignored the wider context, in this case the sentences preceding and following.

θυσίας ... κάρπωμα. In chapter 1 and in 23.37, these two terms are used appositionally, referring to the gift itself. But in this verse and elsewhere κάρπωμα comprises of internal organs removed from the victim. G chose to render the Hebrew sacrificial terms only very generally, a matter that has caused generations of interpreters varying degrees of surprise. Greek to Hebrew equivalence is not always helpful as an indicator of G's intentionality since he uses Greek words interchangeably for more than one Hebrew word: אשה – θυσία nine times; זבח – θυσία thirty-two times; אשה – κάρπωμα nineteen times; and אשה – ὁλοκαύτωμα seven times. While consistent matching was not carried out in all cases, quantitative representation appears to have been a commensurate goal.

κάρπωμα. This term succeeds as a stand-in for אשה because, as Paul Stengel (1972, 166) pointed out, it is a burnt offering—the cognate verb καρπόω does not mean "bring a fruit offering" but "make a burnt offering" (cf. LXX.D "Feueropfer"; this pairing has already been employed in Exodus). Stengel cites there an inscription that describes the sacrifice of a cock to Osiris and Nephthys who receive their share before the suppliants consume the rest. Viewed from a religio-cultural perspective, κάρπωμα is not at home in the semantic domain of θυσία. It is never used to refer to the firstfruits offering within the alimentary sacrifice, that is, the deity's special portion—the usual terms are γέρας, ἄργματα or θυελαί. G again chooses not to select a field-specific term, but prefers to make use of an established pairing.

To aid us in evaluating G's choice of vocabulary for the ingredients of his κάρπωμα, a knowledge of the Greek firstfruits offering will be of some value. Apart from the σπλάγχνα the most significant of its ingredients were the ὀσφῦς (haunches with tail), νῶτος or ῥάχις (tender meat from the back and the loin), and the μηροί or μηρία (thighs or thighbones) onto which a double layer of fat was laid (any of πιμελή, πῖαρ, πίων, δημός, κνίση).

στέαρ. Though στέαρ is not found among the other words for fat in standard recollections of the Greek ritual, it is found here as we have come to expect, by reason of being the standard equivalent for חלב found already in Genesis and Exodus (and will remain so in the rest of the LXX). G is unique in rendering also פדר by στέαρ. The word στέαρ is more commonly encountered in anatomical descriptions, and if this was a concern of G's it is used correctly here. The fact that he is not employing any of the other five terms mentioned above, shows again that he is not overly concerned to contextualize, but rather to abide by established pairings, so that when Greek equivalents appear, they will be recognized by the audience as the representative of Hebrew words perhaps known to them.

κοιλίαν. In Genesis and Exodus the word levels בטן, גחן, and קרב ("intestines"), and it is likely that Exod 29.13 and 22 served as basis for G's selection in this case. Though κοιλία can also mean the intestines in addition to the cavity (LSJ), the more usual word in Greek parlance is ἔντερα, contrasting with σπλάγχνα (the noble viscera), neither of which occurs in the LXX's cultic contexts. G's equivalent makes no effort to clarify the Hebrew although the word by its dual sense may communicate that there are two kinds of fat—the first kind enclosing the innards and the second kind found on the organs or on the body cavity.

3.4

ואת שתי הכלית ואת החלב אשר עלהן אשר על הכסלים ואת היתרת
על הכבד על הכליות יסירנה

καὶ τοὺς δύο νεφροὺς καὶ τὸ στέαρ τὸ ἐπ᾽ αὐτῶν, τὸ ἐπὶ τῶν μηρίων,
καὶ τὸν λοβὸν τὸν ἐπὶ τοῦ ἥπατος, σὺν τοῖς νεφροῖς περιελεῖ,

and the two kidneys and the fat that is on them at the thighs, and he shall remove the appendage that is on the liver with the kidneys.

νεφρούς. To the Greeks, kidneys and liver were regarded as congealed blood and belonged to the category of σπλάγχνα, whose spitting and roasting comprised one of the most sacred moments of the sacrifice, the moment of communing with the gods (see below). Semites, on the other hand, regarded the kidneys as suet (Milgrom 1991, 207) and did not eat them. In any case, the kidneys are found in the deity's portion here just as they are in the Greek ritual.

μηρίων. The word μηρία (used five times in Leuitikon and in the LXX only ever again in Iob 15.27), meaning "thighs" or "thighbones" (LSJ; cf. BdA "cuisse," pace LXX.D "Lendenstücke") is by far the most weighty technical term of the Greek θυσία. The thighbones were part of the γέρας or firstfruits, overlaid with fat and burned as the deity's portion. G chose this part of the anatomy as a match for כסל, which Milgrom (1991, 207) translates as "sinews," noting its Akkadian cognate "the transverse process of the vertebra," and not "loins" as HALOT and NRSV. There is therefore neither lexical nor anatomical connection between כסל (the inner spine) and μηρία (the upper legs), whose pairing is without prior precedent. It is likely that G was uncertain of a Hebrew term and provided for it a word suitable only by virtue of its prominence in the linguistic environment of θυσία (see next entry). It is almost as if his depiction would have been incomplete without inclusion of the μηρία, and the best opportunity for him to do so was here.

τὸ στέαρ τὸ ἐπ' αὐτῶν, τὸ ἐπὶ τῶν μηρίων. The structure of G's clauses here, in verse 10 and in verse 15 follows the Hebrew exactly, so that the presence of the Hebrew relative is carefully indicated each time. Whenever אשר occurs with a prepositional phrase as it does here, G renders almost without exception by the adjectival use of the article, producing a restrictive sense that provides essential information about otherwise referentially nonspecific substantives (Jones 2015, §3.6.2.). This makes the current clause all the more jarring, since kidneys are nowhere near thighs, and what little fat is on the flesh of the thighs is not easily separable. NETS tries to convey this somewhat nonsensical aspect of the OG, in contrast to Brenton's "he shall take away that which is on the thighs" which is not entirely faithful to the Greek since the article in the adjectival phrase refers back to στέαρ (cf. BdA, 92). G's choice of μηρία and especially as something supposedly covered in the fat found in the region of the kidneys, shows that he is quite unconcerned with giving precise instructions by which members of a living community are to observe a rite.

τὸν (ἐπὶ τοῦ ἥπατος). An אשר is presumed to occur here in the same fashion as it does before על twice in the rest of this verse.

καί τόν λοβόν ... περιελεῖ. NRSV's "the appendage of the liver, which he shall remove with the kidneys" reads the final clause of verse 3 as an asyndetic relative clause subordinate to הקריב at the beginning of the previous verse. The NJB regards the objective suffix of יסירנה to resume an object other than the lobe of the liver, thus "the mass of fat which he will remove from the liver and kidneys." There is some value in that, since Milgrom intimates that the Hebrew is concerned with three kinds of fat (1991, 205). But G regards the predicate of καί προσάξουσιν beginning the previous verse to end at μηρίων after which a new sentence begins, emphasizing that the lobe on the liver is to be removed together with the kidneys. G reads the relative clause as beginning with a casus pendens of the object (Joüon §156c) with that object resumed in the suffix.

σύν. Though occurring also in Pesh and followed by Ibn Ezra and 11Q19 (11QTemple) 23.15 (Milgrom, 1991, 208) σύν may be regarded here as an explanatory rendering that represents the correct value of the Hebrew preposition as "in addition to."

περιελεῖ. In contrast with σφάξει αὐτό above, the objective suffix is not rendered here nor in verse 10. In Hebrew the appendage of the liver is intended by the suffix but the Greek may be viewed as referring to everything that must be removed with the kidneys (cf. Wevers 1997, 25), although NETS reflects the equally possible view that only the lobe is the verb's intended object.

3.5

והקטירו אתו בני אהרן המזבחה על העלה אשר על העצים אשר על האש אשה ריח ניחח ליהוה

καὶ ἀνοίσουσιν αὐτὰ οἱ υἱοὶ Ἀαρὼν οἱ ἱερεῖς ἐπὶ τὸ θυσιαστήριον, ἐπὶ τὰ ὁλοκαυτώματα ἐπὶ τὰ ξύλα τὰ ἐπὶ τοῦ πυρός· κάρπωμα, ὀσμὴ εὐωδίας κυρίῳ·

And the sons of Aaron the priests shall offer them up on the altar, on the whole burnt offerings on the wood that is on the fire; it is an offering, an odor of fragrance to the Lord.

ἀνοίσουσιν. This verb is not normally employed in cultic descriptions. It is found here most probably as a result of its initial etymological pairing with עלה in Genesis. By the time of Exodus this is extended also to קטר (3x) although Exodus was also fond of using θυμιάω (4x). The primary sense of ἀναφέρω here is the act of lifting up onto the altar, and perhaps "offer up" of NETS goes a little too far in the direction of the Hebrew meaning.

αὐτά. G pluralizes the objective suffix in this instance, probably to specify the ingredients themselves. The reason may be that in similar contexts (4.10, 35; 7.5) the object of the Hebrew verb is plural, and he levels for the sake of consistency. That he does not pluralize in all occurrences of multiple ingredients is due to his disinterest in standardizing, and neither will he rework any rendering on the basis of another, as we shall see shortly.

ἐπί. In reflecting every על in this way G lumps everything together on the altar as in 1.7–9. Wevers suggests a meaning like "alongside" for ἐπί (1997, 26) but NETS by repeating "on" conveys that the Hebrew preposition is rendered consistently, at least here, and that he chose not to make use of σύν as in the previous verse.

ὁλοκαυτώματα. Harlé and Pralon (1988, 91) regard this pluralizing as perhaps referring to the daily sacrifices. In other words, the κάρπωμα will be burned alongside the regular whole burnt offerings performed by the Aaronides.

3.6

ואם מן הצאן קרבנו לזבח שלמים ליהוה זכר או נקבה תמים יקריבנו

Ἐὰν δὲ ἀπὸ τῶν προβάτων τὸ δῶρον αὐτοῦ, θυσίαν σωτηρίου τῷ κυρίῳ, ἄρσεν ἢ θῆλυ, ἄμωμον προσοίσει αὐτό.

But if his gift, a sacrifice of deliverance to the Lord, is from the sheep, male or female, he shall present it without blemish.

Ἐὰν δὲ ἀπὸ τῶν προβάτων. The case begun by ἐὰν μὲν ἐκ τῶν βοῶν in verse 1 is now expanded.

θυσίαν. It is hard to account for this accusative found in a nominal sentence. If we ask what lies behind it in the source text, the answer must be the *lamed* of the datival goal referring to a change in status, almost without exception rendered in Leuitikon by a preposition (εἰς and more seldom περί) with the accusative (compare εἰς ὁλοκαύτωμα for לעלה in 1.10, also in a nominal sentence). Here, however, the *lamed* is not rendered at all, but the accusative remains. It may have been intended to function as a kind of accusative of respect, although such a construction does better with a verb or an adjective (see Smyth §1601c.). Wevers suggests that the accusative θυσίαν may be viewed as direct object of a proleptic προσφέρω: "(when presenting) a sacrifice of deliverance to the Lord, ... he shall present it" (1997, 27 and cf. *BdA* "si son présent est fait de petit bétail en offrande," 92). Perhaps a rendering such as "if his gift, *for* a sacrifice of deliverance to the Lord," would suggest that grammatically speaking the gift is related in some *respect* to the sacrifice.

προσοίσει. This verb can mean both "present" or "offer" and is a preferable choice to ἀναφέρω to indicate the act of bringing a sacrifice (Spicq 1994, 3:118).

ἄμωμον προσοίσει αὐτό. See comment at verse 1.

3.7

אם כשב הוא מקריב את קרבנו והקריב אתו לפני יהוה

ἐὰν ἄρνα προσαγάγῃ τὸ δῶρον αὐτοῦ, προσάξει αὐτὸ ἔναντι κυρίου

If he brings a lamb as his gift, he shall bring it before the Lord

ἐὰν ἄρνα ... τὸ δῶρον αὐτοῦ. As in verse 3, it would be natural to regard the indefinite noun (in this case the animal kind) as predicate accusative. Although NETS takes indefinite ἄρνα as the direct object, it would be preferable to say "his gift by way of a lamb," as does LXX.D with "seine Gabe in Gestalt eines Lammes" (101).

προσαγάγῃ. See above at verse 1.

3.8

וסמך את ידו על ראש קרבנו ושחט אתו לפני אהל מועד וזרקו בני
אהרן את דמו על המזבח סביב

καὶ ἐπιθήσει τὰς χεῖρας ἐπὶ τὴν κεφαλὴν τοῦ δῶρου αὐτοῦ καὶ σφάξει αὐτὸ παρὰ τὰς θύρας τῆς σκηνῆς τοῦ μαρτυρίου· καὶ προσχεοῦσιν οἱ υἱοὶ Ἀαρὼν οἱ ἱερεῖς τὸ αἷμα ἐπὶ τὸ θυσιαστήριον κύκλῳ.

and he shall lay his hands on the head of his gift and he shall slaughter it at the entrance of the tent of witness. And the sons of Aaron the priests shall pour out the blood against all sides of the altar.

Comparing 3.8 with 3.2, one notices that the Greek is quite similar, but for the addition of αὐτοῦ here and the omission of τῶν ὁλοκαυμάτων which was added there. Besides that, G appears to be rendering a text very similar to the MT of verse 2, having פתח instead of לפני and the addition of הכהנים after the sons of Aaron (cf. Milgrom 1991, 210). It is hard to know whether a translator has a previous Greek sentence in memory and harmonizes the present one toward it, or harmonizes the present sentence to a Hebrew verse in memory from elsewhere in the book, although both are possible. This phenomenon is further discussed in Spencer Jones's commentary on Num 22 (p. 147).

3.9

והקריב מזבח השלמים אשה ליהוה חלבו האליה תמימה לעמת
העצה יסירנה ואת החלב המכסה את הקרב ואת כל החלב אשר
על הקרב

Büchner

καὶ προσοίσει ἀπὸ τῆς θυσίας τοῦ σωτηρίου κάρπωμα τῷ θεῷ, τὸ
στέαρ καὶ τὴν ὀσφὺν ἄμωμον· σὺν ταῖς ψόαις περιελεῖ αὐτό· καὶ τὸ
στέαρ τὸ κατακαλύπτον τὴν κοιλίαν, καὶ τὸ στέαρ τὸ ἐπὶ τῆς κοιλίας,
And he shall present some of the sacrifice of deliverance as an
offering to God: the fat and the lower back without blemish (he
shall remove it with the loin muscles), and the fat that covers the
entrails and the fat that is on the entrails,

ἀπό. NETS, with its "some of" rather than repeating "from" at verse 3
(whose Greek text is identical, apart from the initial verb) indicates to the
English reader that the מִן of the parent text is represented carefully, and
that the Greek word, like its Hebrew counterpart, may be understood in
these two ways.

τῷ θεῷ. The variation of ὁ θεός and κύριος for the Tetragrammaton is hap-
hazard and cannot be regarded as having any significance.

ὀσφύν. The anatomical term ὀσφῦς refers to the "lower back" (LSJ, cf. LEH,
449), "waist, loins" (LSJ, cf. GELS, 510) of a sacrificial animal. The pairing
of אַלְיָה ("fat tail") and ὀσφῦς is an innovation of G, and it is uncertain
why he made this choice, since there is no semantic affinity between the
two words. This fact motivated the Three to render אליה by κέρκιον and
Josephus in A.J. 3.228 to speak of οὐρά (Wevers 1997, 28; Harlé and Pralon
1988, 92), which is what Herodotus calls the fat tail of the Arabian sheep
(Hist. 3.113). In contrast, ὀσφῦς refers to the lumbar region and the flesh-
covered bones of the haunches as in Xenophon's description of the horse
(Eq. 1:12:3) and the hunting hound (Cyn. 4.1.9, whose long tail, incidentally, is also οὐρά). In Aristophanes, Pax 1053–1055 and in the scholiast on
that passage, ὀσφῦς and κέρκος appear together in a way that shows there is
this distinction between them.
    As a cultic term ὀσφῦς is noteworthy because like μηρία it is a promi-
nent ingredient in post-Homeric descriptions of the firstfruits ritual, in
which it is burned on the altar (for instance Aeschylus, Prom. 495). Furthermore, an ὀσφῦς on the altar is one of two most frequent motifs found
on Attic vase paintings depicting the θυσία, the other being the roasting
of the σπλάγχνα on skewers. Spitting the noble viscera is the moment of
communion with the gods and the action of the ὀσφῦς in the fire is the
means by which the gods communicate their favor (or otherwise) toward
the sacrifice (Jameson 1988, 971; Durand 1989, 102). Brigitte Bergquist

(1993, 16, 18) and Folkert van Straten (1988, 57–60) provide detailed sets of illustrations depicting the sacrum with tail. In Herodotus's account of the Egyptian alimentary sacrifice (*Hist.* 2:40) the ὀσφῦς is removed with the edible portion, while what remains is burned with honey and frankincense.

In our passage, the Hebrew understanding is that the fat tail is classed as suet to be removed with the rest of the inedible parts and burned up, since YHWH, in contrast to Greek and Canaanite deities, does not partake of the meal (Milgrom 1991, 221). As with his rather reckless inclusion of the word μηρία above, G most likely chose ὀσφῦς above the purely anatomical terms for tail (κέρκος or οὐρά) purely by reason of the special place it holds within the lexical domain of θυσία. The result is that another important ingredient of the Greek γέρας or firstfruits now becomes also an ingredient of the LXX's κάρπωμα, as will the flesh of the ψόα (see next entry), all of which may have come as some surprise to Jews. This unease is noticeable in the alternative suggestions made by revisers of the text. Again it is not likely that by choosing this word G wanted to express anything of a cultural nature. He merely adopted a vocabulary item from the field of θυσία as a match for a Hebrew anatomical term of which he was perhaps unsure.

σὺν ταῖς ψόαις. The clause לעמת העצה means "close to the lower back." G by his choice of σύν now marks for inclusion in the κάρπωμα also the ψόαι, the muscles on the inside of the spine. Clearchus (Pollux II 185 [*FGH* 2:324]) clarifies: οἱ δὲ ἔνδοθεν κατὰ τὴν ὀσφῦν μύες καλοῦνται ψόαι ("the inner muscles against the lower back are called ψόαι"). In the older recollections of θυσία, part of the firstfruits ritual would include the placing of fine meat on top of the deity's portion, an action known as ὠμοθετεῖν (Bowie 1995, 469; Burkert 1966, 108). Together with the lower back and the thighbones, the addition now also of choice, edible bits of flesh without pretext in the Hebrew, means that G obviously relied on the Greek conceptual world to mold his portrayal of the subritual. It is hard to draw any conclusions about his intention for doing so, beyond observing that he felt no need to suppress anything that alluded to pagan notions, a fact that must be borne in mind when we evaluate his rendering of לחם in verse 11.

προσοίσει … κάρπωμα … τὸ στέαρ καὶ τὴν ὀσφῦν ἄμωμον· σὺν ταῖς ψόαις περιελεῖ αὐτό. An explanation of the difficult Greek syntax may now be attempted. Distinguishing direct object from object complement is the first task and for this we must invoke the usual rule of the article. Accordingly, the definite direct objects of the verb appear to be στέαρ and ὀσφύν, with indefinite κάρπωμα as the predicate accusative, as NETS has it. The next question to settle is to which words ἄμωμον and αὐτό hearken back, since they are singular appearing among a list of multiple items, and perhaps at least the pronoun might have been pluralized as it was in verse 5. What is certain is that the Hebrew word order and syntax is being scrupulously represented, apart from the *waw* of the suffix on στέαρ being read as a copulative with ὀσφῦς. What is unclear is whether G chose to maintain grammatical concord at the expense of sense, or sense at the expense of concord. If we take the first option, ἄμωμον modifies κάρπωμα attributively and αὐτό is the latter's anaphor. In other words, an unblemished offering is removed with the loin-muscles and nothing further needs to be said. The *grammatical* make-up of the text is all we have to work with and the only measurable result is that Hebrew items are represented at the expense of logical sense. But if we take the second option and suppose that the translator wanted to produce some kind of coherent sense, it would have to mean that he allowed some laxity of syntax. In fact, there is enough evidence for G's loose syntax to suggest that this was indeed the case. We begin with αὐτό. What single item in the neuter is being removed together with the ψόα? Though there is grammatical agreement between αὐτό and κάρπωμα, it makes no sense that the κάρπωμα is to be removed, when as predicate accusative it represents the sum of the ingredients listed for separating off and presenting to God. Once the list is complete, the final action of ἀναφέρειν in verse 11 applies to the κάρπωμα. Alternatively, the pronoun αὐτό refers to στέαρ—the other neuter singular noun—but again it hardly makes sense that "the fat" in general is singled out for removal with the ὀσφῦς after which two more specific kinds of fat are mentioned. Wevers observes a number of times that G is prone to employ neuter pronouns to refer to the foregoing in a general way with no particular identifiable antecedent (e.g., 1997, 357). Karl Huber also (1916, 34–35) drew attention to this verse as another of many cases in which G employs the neuter singular pronoun in lockstep with a corresponding Hebrew item in the singular, without concern for agreement with antecedents. The neuter pronoun refers to a masculine antecedent in 1.16, καὶ ἀφελεῖ τὸν πρόλοβον σὺν τοῖς πτεροῖς καὶ ἐκβαλεῖ αὐτὸ (והשליך אתה) and to a feminine in 2.11, πᾶσαν γὰρ ζύμην καὶ πᾶν μέλι οὐ προσοίσετε ἀπ᾽ αὐτοῦ (ממנו). What is then being removed here with the loin-muscles appears to be an unspecified, general item.

For ἄμωμον there are two possible grammatical explanations. It can be a neuter attributive adjective agreeing with κάρπωμα some words distant, but this may be no more than fortuitous. It is more probable that ἄμωμον is simply employed as the expected stand-in for תמימה, again without too much concern shown for agreement with an antecedent, as we saw in the case of αὐτό. Again a precedent exists for disagreement in gender when neuter adjectives are employed. In Exod 12.9 we notice οὐκ ἔδεσθε ἀπ᾽ αὐτῶν ὠμὸν οὐδὲ ἡψημένον ἐν ὕδατι ἀλλ᾽ ἢ ὀπτὰ πυρί ("You shall not eat from it raw or boiled with water but rather roasted in fire" NETS). Comparable cases in Leuitikon are ζυμωτόν in 2.11 (for ζυμωτήν), ἄθυτόν in 19.5-7 (for ἄθυτός), ἄμωμον and δεκτόν in 22.21 (for ἄμωμός and δεκτήν). There is, however, another way of viewing ἄμωμον. If it is a predicate adjective then some of the difficulty is removed. It may function as a predicate to the verbal action, that is, as a quality of the *subject*, where in English we would use an adverb (Goodwin 1930, §926, Smyth §1042). The phrase πᾶσαν θυσίαν ἣν ἂν προσφέρητε κυρίῳ οὐ ποιήσετε ζυμωτόν of 2.11 also fits this category. A meaning like "present … the fat and the lower back, in a perfect way" would not sit uncomfortably here. Then *pace* Wevers (1997, 29), G was not unaware of the adverbial sense of the Hebrew "the broad tail completely removed close to the sacrum" (so Milgrom 1991, 210).

3.10

ואת שתי הכלית ואת החלב אשר עלהן אשר על הכסלים ואת היתרת
על הכבד על הכלית יסירנה

καὶ ἀμφοτέρους τοὺς νεφροὺς καὶ τὸ στέαρ τὸ ἐπ᾽ αὐτῶν, τὸ ἐπὶ τῶν μηρίων, καὶ τὸν λοβὸν τὸν ἐπὶ τοῦ ἥπατος, σὺν τοῖς νεφροῖς περιελών
and both the kidneys and the fat that is on them at the thighs, having also removed the appendage which is on the liver with the kidneys,

ἀμφοτέρους. Here is an example of the translator's tendency to use variation within a goal of quantitative equivalence. Such variation happens in Genesis and Exodus too but the ratio of δύο to ἀμφότερος is 130:22 in the entire LXX and 31:7 in Leuitikon.

περιελών. The same applies to this circumstantial participle that appears as alternative to περιελεῖ of verse 4. It is a regular practice of G to indicate to his readership that a Hebrew clause can be rendered by alternative ways in Greek.

3.11

והקטירו הכהן המזבחה לחם אשה ליהוה

ἀνοίσει ὁ ἱερεὺς ἐπὶ τὸ θυσιαστήριον ὀσμὴν εὐωδίας· κάρπωμα κυρίῳ.
the priest shall make an offering on the altar, an odor of fragrance,
an offering to the Lord.

ἀνοίσει. This verb signals the culmination of the activity begun in verse 9
with the removal of the ancillary offering's various ingredients. Together,
they are now manipulated on the altar as the κάρπωμα.

ὀσμήν εὐωδίας. MT has לחם, which means that the offering by fire is
YHWH's food. Milgrom (1991, 213) puts the notion of YHWH feeding
on sacrifices down to an archaism—a linguistic fossil—since it is rejected
by later parts of the Hebrew Bible. G replaces the mention of food with
the formula found in verse 5. The result is that the κάρπωμα appears to
be no more than an odor of fragrance. This reading, against all the versions, is surprising and calls for some attention. It may be a simple case
of antianthropomorphism (Vahrenhorst 2009, 352) and we will return to
this suggestion below. But it also hints at something noticed by historians
of religion: ancient writers are uncomfortable about the idea that a deity
should be given, and even request, an offering that from a human perspective consists of inedible parts. In the Prometheus myth, for example,
the gods feel tricked by being given the thighbones disguised by fat and
retaliate by creating womankind. The reason why there should be this
unease has been a topic of debate for some time. If the gods are given
the worst portion of the alimentary sacrifice, what do they do with it?
And so we are back to the matter of eating. Gould (1985, 17–19) spells
out the range of possibilities offered by the texts on their own, but sus-
pends judgment on whether or not the gods are actually understood to
eat their portion, noting the seminal work of Meuli (1946, 215–23) and
Burkert (1966, 105–6). Burkert, in following Meuli's view that the word
μηρία refers to bones and only bones, argues that humans as primeval
hunters feel guilty about taking animal life. Thus, θυσία is in fact nothing
more than ritualized slaughter in which the Olympian deities are given
the bones to symbolize a returning of the animal's marrow to the divine
to ensure its continued existence (1997, 1–25). In contrast to this view,
the so-called Lausanne School, represented by scholars such as Détienne
and Vernant, prefer to think of sacrifice as being more about eating than
killing. And so the gods are seen to eat at a distance through the savor of

smoke (Détienne 1989, 7; Vernant, 1989, 24). The difference in diet effects the distance as well as signifies bridge-building between the different realms that they who once shared the same table currently occupy—gods feed on the incorruptible bones but humans on the dead flesh. Humans eat meat and suffer hunger and death, while the immortal gods feed on the superior food of perfumed smoke. Further support may be found in Gill 1966, 261, Jameson 1988, 966, and Kirk 1981, 78–79. This may be of help in deciding why in this verse the אשה that is called לחם for YHWH is rendered by ὀσμή εὐωδίας rather than ἄρτος, the default rendering of לחם throughout the Greek Pentateuch. We know already that G is not trying to avoid anything reminiscent of the pagan firstfruits offering and rather deliberately includes the kinds of ingredients in the Lord's portion favored by Greek deities. So it is not convincing to suggest that the Lord cannot be regarded as partaking in the meal (Harlé and Pralon 1988, 93), or that G made the change out of reaction to Egyptian-Greek deities who partake in sacred meals (Wevers 1997, 29). It has been suggested that G is simply harmonizing since the Hebrew formula occurring in verses 5 and 16 is missing here (Daniel 1966, 139). However, adding a missing formula for the sake of consistency is not the same as failing to render an important word like לחם. It is significant that also in chapter 21 לחם is replaced by δῶρον six times, although there it is perhaps for a differ-ent reason. The answer may lie in the fact that here the Hebrew word for food edible by humans is replaced with one that connotes the food of the gods. The way deities partake in the sacrificial meal is by way of the savory smoke (see Graf 2002, 120 and below at v. 16). So perhaps it is a true antianthropomorphism.

3.12

ואם עז קרבנו והקריבו לפני יהוה

Ἐὰν δὲ ἀπὸ τῶν αἰγῶν τὸ δῶρον αὐτοῦ, καὶ προσάξει ἔναντι κυρίου,
But if his gift is from the goats, he shall both do the presenting before the Lord,

Ἐὰν — δῶρον αὐτοῦ. The verbless protasis of the G follows the syntax of the Hebrew.

ἀπὸ τῶν αἰγῶν. G appears to maintain his regular introduction of the animal kind even though MT varies it at this point.

καί. In NETS we have attempted to show that the apodotic καί is faithfully rendered, and though it is not the best Greek usage, it can make sense if it is understood to lead to the next sentence in adverbial fashion. A new sentence is produced where G pluralizes again for the priests. Compare verses 1 and 6 where the Hebrew has no apodotic copulative word and G is able to provide standard apodoses.

προσάξει. The verbal suffix is not rendered here, in contrast to the object of σφάξουσιν of the next verse, and hence NETS reflects this, even though to a Greek reader the referent of the missing pronoun would have been obvious.

3.13

וסמך את ידו על ראשו ושחט אתו לפני אהל מועד וזרקו בני אהרן
את דמו על המזבח סביב

καὶ ἐπιθήσει τὰς χεῖρας ἐπὶ τὴν κεφαλὴν αὐτοῦ· καὶ σφάξουσιν αὐτὸ ἔναντι κυρίου παρὰ τὰς θύρας τῆς σκηνῆς τοῦ μαρτυρίου καὶ προσχεοῦσιν οἱ υἱοὶ Ἀαρὼν οἱ ἱερεῖς τὸ αἷμα ἐπὶ τὸ θυσιαστήριον κύκλῳ.

and he shall lay his hands on its head, and they shall slaughter it before the Lord at the entrance of the tent of witness, and the sons of Aaron the priests shall pour out the blood against all sides of the altar.

σφάξουσιν. Here, in contrast to verses 2 and 8, in which the suppliant slaughters but the priests manipulate the blood, G pluralizes the act of slaughter, which is singular in Hebrew.

ἔναντι κυρίου. It is noteworthy that in MT as well as the OG this formula is absent from the prescriptions for cattle or sheep. But here, only the goat's slaughter is given this designation by G against the Hebrew, which until now has occurred in Exod 29.11 (Greek = Hebrew) and Leu 1 (2x; Greek = Hebrew) and will occur again in chapter 4 (3x; Greek = Hebrew). Notably in 16.15 this formula is again added by G against the Hebrew for the goat of the sin offering. Wevers comments that of the ancient witnesses it is only G who singles out the goat for priestly slaughter since the layman cannot sacrifice at the altar, only at the doors (1997, 30). It is known that the goat is slaughtered in the onomastic cult of the Ptolemies, but whether this has anything to do with the addition is uncertain.

3.14

והקריב ממנו קרבנו אשה ליהוה את החלב המכסה את הקרב ואת
כל החלב אשר על הקרב

καὶ ἀνοίσει ἀπ' αὐτοῦ κάρπωμα κυρίῳ, τὸ στέαρ τὸ κατακαλύπτον
τὴν κοιλίαν καὶ πᾶν τὸ στέαρ τὸ ἐπὶ τῆς κοιλίας,

And he shall offer up of it as an offering to the Lord: the fat that
covers the entrails and all the fat that is on the entrails,

ἀνοίσει. As Wevers notes, G probably mistakenly read והקטיר here unless
for variation he chose this as a singular pairing, which is not unusual, but
unlikely. One has to agree with his view that a better translation of this
verb is "take up" (1997, 31).

κάρπωμα. G omitted rendering קרבנו and the result is a much smoother
reading. He also omits to translate the suffix, presumably because he wants
his sentence to be equivalent to the other times the formula appears in the
chapter, for example, verse 9.

τὸ ἐπὶ τῆς κοιλίας. Once again the Hebrew relative with prepositional
phrase is rendered by the adjectival use of the article.

3.15

ואת שתי הכלית ואת החלב אשר עלהן אשר על הכסלים ואת היתרת
על הכבד על הכלית יסירנה

καὶ ἀμφοτέρους τοὺς νεφροὺς καὶ πᾶν τὸ στέαρ τὸ ἐπ' αὐτῶν, τὸ ἐπὶ
τῶν μηρίων καὶ τὸν λοβὸν τοῦ ἥπατος, σὺν τοῖς νεφροῖς περιελεῖ·

and both the kidneys and all the fat that is on them at the thighs,
and he shall remove the appendage of the liver with the kidneys.

πᾶν. An addition not reflected in the versions.

τοῦ ἥπατος. Here G varies from his renderings in verses 4 and 10 in representing the Hebrew quite idiomatically. Again it appears as if he first
provides a more literal rendition of a Hebrew syntagm, and then an alternative. The benefit to the Greek reader lies on the level of understanding
something about the way Hebrew works.

3.16

והקטירם הכהן המזבחה לחם אשה לריח ניחח כל חלב ליהוה

καὶ ἀνοίσει ὁ ἱερεὺς ἐπὶ τὸ θυσιαστήριον κάρπωμα, ὀσμὴν εὐωδίας τῷ κυρίῳ. πᾶν τὸ στέαρ τῷ κυρίῳ.

And the priest shall offer on the altar an offering, an odor of fragrance to the Lord. All the fat is the Lord's.

ἀνοίσει. The verbal suffix is not rendered, and neither is לחם so that the emphasis is no longer on the constituent parts of the אשה as the Deity's food, but rather on the fact that the κάρπωμα as a whole is pleasing to the Deity.

This chapter shows the interface between variability in the source as well as target texts and one notices the following:

3:5: κάρπωμα ὀσμὴ εὐωδίας

3:11: ὀσμὴν εὐωδίας κάρπωμα

3:16: κάρπωμα ὀσμὴν εὐωδίας

In so doing, G represents three times in full the Hebrew terms first occurring in verse 5, that is אשה ריח ניחח, with a variation in word order. Twice he avoids rendering לחם. Here too the *lamed* of the datival goal is not rendered by εἰς but by a simple accusative.

3.17

חקת עולם לדרתיכם בכל מושבתיכם כל חלב וכל דם לא תאכלו

νόμιμον εἰς τὸν αἰῶνα εἰς τὰς γενεὰς ὑμῶν ἐν πάσῃ κατοικίᾳ ὑμῶν· πᾶν στέαρ καὶ πᾶν αἷμα οὐκ ἔδεσθε.

It shall be a precept forever throughout your generations, in all your settlement; you shall not eat any fat and any blood.'"

εἰς τὸν αἰῶνα. G renders the Hebrew attributive genitive correctly and provides an idiomatic adverbial rendering. Something needs to be said for the meaning of αἰών in relation to Hebrew עולם, both of which carry the sense of enduring time and both of which carry the gloss "eternity" in the lexica. The idea of eternity is philosophically complex and must have meant different things to different cultures. The idea of the eternity of the world was a theme first developed by Aristotle (Huffman 1993, 343), but it is hard to tell in what way the Greek philosophical notion of eternity overlaps with the Hebrew notion of duration. When referring to enduring time the prepositional phrase δι᾽ αἰῶνος is found in apposition to a word like ἄπαυστος; for example, in Aeschylus, *Suppl.* 574 referring both to the unending rule of Zeus and the lasting blessedness of his offspring. When used for the future, the phrase occurs with something like μόρσιμος to refer to an appointed time (*Suppl.*, 46). The expression εἰς αἰῶνα is well attested before the LXX. The Pythagorean Philolaus of the fifth century BCE uses the expression ἐξ αἰῶνος ἐς αἰῶνα of the universe remaining constant and unchanging in the past and the future (DK B. 21). Similarly, Isocrates (10.62) can use the expression εἰς ἅπαντα τὸν αἰῶνα to speak of the permanence of immortal Menelaus's sharing of Helen's throne. More concretely, Lycurgus speaks in real time of Troy being forever deserted (1.62) or about Tyrtaeus the Athenian whose influence benefited Sparta forever (1.106). The latter two instances suggest an understanding that does justice to the Hebrew phrase in this verse, of a perpetual ordinance, remaining in place as long as the living are able to conceive of it or recognize its validity. It is worth noting that some receptors of this Septuagintal expression found it in need of rephrasing. The Epistle to the Hebrews, in addition to frequently employing εἰς αἰῶνα, also makes use of εἰς τὸ παντελές (7.25) and εἰς τὸ διηνεκές (10.1) "forever" and "in perpetuity," and one wonders if these would have been more clearly understood by a Jewish Greek audience, than the former.

καί πᾶν αἷμα. The conjunction καί is used in affirmative, not adversative sentences, so that we have reflected this in NETS. We could also have translated, "you must not eat any fat, even any blood."

κατοικία. Why a singular? Exodus 35.3, in which the Greek is also singular for the Hebrew plural, is perhaps the example he follows. The Hebrew word is always plural in Leviticus and G will singularize another five times, except for the very last time he encounters the word (23.31), where a plural appears for no discernible reason.

Summary

The translator's intention can now be stated as one that was not to create a culturally or technically accurate portrayal of a ritual, or a set of instructions that could function in a liturgical setting. Moments of specifying appropriate procedure, such as attributing the slaughter to the priests rather than to the suppliant, must be balanced by the lack of consistency in such matters and the relative freedom with which the closer prescriptions are handled. What is clear, however, is that he intended to provide a conduit to the language units of the original through etymologizing or through existing translational precedent. Here we may call upon Cameron

Boyd-Taylor's distinction between field-specific vocabulary and transla-
tion-specific vocabulary (2004, 154).

Balaam, Pagan Prophet of God:
A Commentary on Greek Numbers 22.1–21

Spencer A. Jones

Literature

Aejmelaeus, Anneli. 1982. *"Participium coniunctum* as a Criterion of Translation Technique." *VT* 32:385–93. ♦ **Aejmelaeus**. 1993. *On the Trail of Septuagint Translators: Collected Essays.* Kampen: Kok Pharos. ♦ **Boyd-Taylor**, Cameron. 2006. "Toward the Analysis of Translational Norms: A Sighting Shot." *BIOSCS* 39:27–47. ♦ **Dorival**, Gilles. 1994. *La Bible d'Alexandrie 4: Les Nombres.* Paris: Cerf. ♦ **Evans**, Trevor V. 2001. *Verbal Syntax in the Greek Pentateuch: Natural Greek Usage and Hebrew Interference.* Oxford: Oxford University Press. ♦ **Holmstedt**, Robert, and Andrew **Jones**. 2014. "The Pronoun in Tripartite Verbless Clauses in Biblical Hebrew: Resumption for Left-Dislocation or Pronominal Copula?" *JSS* 59:53–89. ♦ **Hunt**, A. S., and C. C. **Edgar**, trans. 1932. *Select Papyri: Volume 1; Non-literary Papyri, Private Affairs, Private Documents.* LCL. Cambridge: Harvard University Press. ♦ **Jastram**, Nathan R. 1994. "4QNum[b]." Pages 205–68 in *Qumran Cave 4.VII: Genesis to Numbers.* Edited by Eugene Ulrich, Frank Moore Cross, James R. Davila, Jastram Nathan, Judith E. Sanderson, Emanuel Tov, and John Strugnell. DJD 12. Oxford: Clarendon. ♦ **Louw**, Theo A. W. van der. 2007. *Transformations in the Septuagint: Towards an Interaction of Septuagint Studies and Translation Studies.* CBET 47. Leuven: Peeters. ♦ **Meer**, Michaël van der. 2012. "The Natural and Geographical Context of the Septuagint." Pages 387–421 in *Die Septuaginta—Entstehung,*

Thanks are due to Dirk Büchner who offered many helpful suggestions and saved me from many errors.

Sprache, Geschichte: 3. Internationale Fachtagung veranstaltet von Septuaginta Deutsch (LXX.D), Wuppertal 22.–25. Juli 2010. Edited by Siegfried Kreuzer, Martin Meiser, and Marcus Sigismund. WUNT 286. Tübingen: Mohr Siebeck. ◆ **Rösel**, Martin, and Christine **Schlund**. 2011. "Arithmoi/ Numeri/Das vierte Buch Mose." Pages 431–522 in *Septuaginta Deutsch: Erläuterungen und Kommentare zur griechischen Alten Testament; Band I. Genesis bis Makkabäer.* Edited by Martin Karrer and Wolfgang Kraus. Stuttgart: Deutsche Bibelgesellschaft. ◆ **Tjen**, Anwar. 2010. *On Conditionals in the Greek Pentateuch: A Study of Translation Syntax.* LHBOTS 515. New York: T&T Clark. ◆ **Tov**, Emanuel. 1985. "The Nature and Background of Harmonizations in Biblical Manuscripts." *JSOT* 31:3–29. ◆ **Tov**. 1999. "Renderings of Combinations of the Infinitive Absolute and Finite Verbs in the Septuagint—Their Nature and Distribution." Pages 247–56 in *The Greek and Hebrew Bible: Collected Essays on the Septuagint.* VTSup 72. Leiden: Brill. ◆ **Wevers**, John W. 1982. *Text History of the Greek Numbers.* MSU 16. Göttingen: Vandenhoeck & Ruprecht. ◆ **Wevers**. 1998. *Notes on the Greek Text of Numbers.* SCS 46. Atlanta: Scholars Press.

Outline

When the Israelites encamp on the western edge of Moab (ἐπὶ δυσμῶν Μωάβ), the Moabites become afraid. Balak, the king of Moab, had observed Israel's destruction of the Amalekites (Num 21) and so he calls together various regional elders of Madiam (ἡ γερουσία Μαδιάμ) to summon the renowned prophet Balaam (22.1–7). Although Balaam turns Balak's envoy away for the first time when θεός denies him permission (vv. 8–14), Balak repeats his request—this time sending more honorable emissaries and promising rich rewards (vv. 15–19). Balaam is granted permission by θεός on the one condition that Balaam will only do whatever the deity speaks (22.20). Thus, Balaam departs on his she-donkey with Balak's elders (22.21).

Commentary

22.1

ויסעו בני ישראל ויחנו בערבות מואב מעבר לירדן ירחו

Καὶ ἀπάραντες οἱ υἱοὶ Ἰσραὴλ παρενέβαλον ἐπὶ δυσμῶν Μωὰβ παρὰ τὸν Ἰορδάνην κατὰ Ἰεριχώ.

And after[a] the sons of Israel set out, they[a] encamped on the west of Moab by the Jordan opposite Iericho.

a-a The MT as well as Greek MS 314 have a conjunction (ו – καί) before παρενέβαλον (NETS, "the sons of Israel set out and encamped"; BdA, "les fils d'Israël décampèrent et campèrent"). The translation represented here agrees with We^ed and the majority of OG manuscripts; see also LXX.D: "Und nachdem die Israeliten aufgebrochen waren, lagerten sie." The major difference is the omission of καί before παρενέβαλον, which indicates that ἀπάραντες is an adverbial participle and should thus be rendered as a dependent temporal clause.

Καὶ ἀπάραντες. G at times renders the first wayyiqtol form in a coordinate sequence with an adverbial participle—as he does here. This change in grammatical category makes for more idiomatic Greek and betrays G's concern to produce an *acceptable* translation and avoidance of awkward polysyndeton (see 21.13, 33; 22.14; but not with high consistency). However, he leaves the introductory καί – ו which is not idiomatic with *participia coniuncta*. Acceptability is understood to denote an attempt to employ language that suits the linguistic and textual norms of the target language (Boyd-Taylor 2006, 29–30). Having used the *participium coniunctum*, a conjunction between Ἰσραὴλ and παρενέβαλον is unnecessary and so omitted (see also vv. 13, 14, 21 in this chapter). Nevertheless, the introductory καί is unusual and not idiomatic in the *participium coniunctum* construction. Likely, the nuance of the participle is temporal, "*after* setting out." For a taxonomy of *participia coniuncta* in the LXX, see Aejmelaeus 1982, especially 389–93.

οἱ υἱοὶ Ἰσραήλ. G always renders בני ישראל—when in the nominative— with the definite article (e.g., Num 9.19, passim; see Wevers 1982, 105). There is no clear pattern in other cases.

παρενέβαλον ἐπὶ δυσμῶν Μωάβ. Whereas παρεμβάλλω is common for חנה, this is the first occurrence of the match between ערבה ("desert") and δυσμή ("setting of the sun," and by extension, "west"; see 33.48, 49, 50; 35.1; 36.13; also Deut 34.8). G later equivocates and transliterates it as a proper noun, Ἀραβώθ (26.3, 63; 31.12). NETS here takes the phrase as a direction, "in the western parts" (also, LXX.D, "westlich von Moab").

How G derived δυσμή from ערבות is subject to some speculation. Wevers states that it was a different vocalization of the consonantal text, but he does not indicate to which Hebrew word it could plausibly be vocalized (1998, 360). Possibly, the Hebrew word is עֶרֶב, as Gilles Dorival explains:

"Au lieu du [MT] ʿarebōt, qui est le pluriel de ʿarābā, 'désert, steppe, plaine aride,' la LXX lisait probablement ʿarābōt, qui est un des pluriels de ʿèrèb, 'soir, couchant'" (1994, 413). There is, however, no indication that עֶרֶב can denote the cardinal direction in Hebrew (see *HALOT*, s.v. "עֶרֶב"). Hebrew עֲרָבָה ("desert") is also confused with עֶרֶב ("evening") in 1 Rgns 23.24, although δυσμή is not selected nor is the cardinal direction indicated: וַיֵּלְכוּ בָעֲרָבָה מָעוֹן בְּמִדְבַּר וַאֲנָשָׁיו וְדָוִד שָׁאוּל לִפְנֵי זִיפָה – ἐπορεύθησαν [οἱ Ζιφαῖοι] ἔμπροσθεν Σαουλ, καὶ Δαυιδ καὶ οἱ ἄνδρες αὐτοῦ ἐν τῇ ἐρήμῳ τῇ Μααν κατʼ ἑσπέραν ("the Ziphites set out and went ahead of Saoul, and Dauid and his men were in the Maan wilderness *in the evening*," NETS). Elsewhere in Numbers, G renders עֶרֶב with ἑσπέρα ("evening") consistently, thirteen times in total (e.g., 9.11, 15, 21; 19.7, 8, 10). Whereas both δυσμή and ἑσπέρα can indicate "west" (see LSJ, s.v. "ἑσπέρα," II and "δυσμή," II), δυσμή usually indicates the setting of the sun and ἑσπέρα is a temporal term for evening. In light of this, it is curious that G selects δυσμή over against ἑσπέρα to indicate "west" here.

παρὰ τὸν Ἰορδάνην. G's rendering of the idiomatic מֵעֵבֶר לַיַּרְדֵּן with the preposition παρά quite succinctly captures the gist of the Hebrew. In other instances, the phrase is rendered literally with ἐν τῷ πέραν or something similar (21.13; 32.19, 32; 34.15; 35.14; cf. διάβασις of Gen 32.23).

κατὰ Ἰεριχώ. Whereas the relationship between יְרֵחוֹ and לַיַּרְדֵּן in the MT is that of a simple genitive, G adds κατά to add further specificity to the relationship. NETS renders this as "opposite Jericho" (LXX.D, "gegenüber"; BdA, "face à Jéricho"). Although in every following instance the Hebrew text has no more than the simple genitive as it does here, G uses this rendering consistently henceforth (26.3, 63; 31.12; 33.48, 50; 34.15; 35.1; 36.13).

22.2

וַיַּרְא בָּלָק בֶּן־צִפּוֹר אֵת כָּל־אֲשֶׁר־עָשָׂה יִשְׂרָאֵל לָאֱמֹרִי

Καὶ ἰδὼν Βαλὰκ υἱὸς Σεπφὼρ πάντα, ὅσα ἐποίησεν Ἰσραὴλ τῷ Ἀμορραίῳ,

And when Balak son of Sepphor saw all that Israel had done to the Amorrite,

Καὶ ἰδὼν Βαλὰκ. The adverbial participle is again used for the *wayyiqtol* (see also v. 1). However, the syntax breaks down in verse 3 where a conjunction, καὶ, is used, thus making this clause pendent. Balak is introduced, described, and the conflict that gives rise to the following sequence of events given in this pendent clause (with an embedded relative clause). Likely, in G's unit-by-unit translation style, he began with a *participium coniunctum* and then noticed the change in subject to Moab in the next clause and so abandoned the construction. If, as Dorival suggests, this is a nominative absolute in which the nominative (Βαλάκ) is resumed in the main clause (v. 3) (see Dorival 1994, 419), then Μωάβ of verse 3 is taken to refer to Βαλάκ. However, in standard Greek nominative absolute constructions, a *pronoun* resumes the pendent element *in a different case* (see BDF §466 and the examples cited there). Since this construction looks very little like a nominative absolute, it is better to see it as Hebrew interference.

υἱὸς Σεπφώρ. The epithet צפור בן is applied to Balak in three places in this narrative (22.2, 4, 16). In this occurrence and in verse 4, υἱὸς Σεπφώρ translates the phrase; however, ὁ τοῦ Σεπφώρ appears inexplicably at 22.16 (also Ies 24.9). The transliteration of צפור with Σεπφώρ is relatively stable (outside of Numbers, see Ies 24.9; Judg 11.25). Balak is only later introduced as king (v. 4).

τῷ Ἀμορραίῳ. The collective gentilic אמרי is rendered with the singular τῷ Ἀμορραίῳ, which is unusual for G. The account of the destruction of the Amorites has just been told in 21.21–32, where G translates the singular form with a plural (21.13, 21, 25, 26, 29, 31, 34; compare the singular in 21.32). Here the singular would most likely refer to the king of the Amorites, Seon. Although Seon had formerly fought against Moab (21.26), the defeat of Moab's former enemy is clearly taken as a bad omen rather than as a stroke of luck: Balak understands the defeat of Seon to forebode the destruction of Moab.

22.3

ויגר מואב מפני העם מאד כי רב הוא ויקץ מואב מפני בני ישראל
καὶ ἐφοβήθη Μωὰβ τὸν λαὸν σφόδρα, ὅτι πολλοὶ ἦσαν, καὶ προσώχθισεν Μωὰβ ἀπὸ προσώπου υἱῶν Ἰσραήλ.
also Moab feared the people very much, because they were many, and Moab was vexed because of the presence of Israel's sons.

καὶ ἐφοβήθη Μωὰβ τὸν λαὸν σφόδρα. The Hebrew form ויגר is rendered with ἐφοβήθη. Hebrew גור normally takes מן + pronominal suffix (see Deut 18.28; Ps 38[37].18) as a complement in order to indicate the cause of fear (here מפני). However, given G's choice of φοβέομαι for גור, a literal rendering of מפני—ἀπὸ προσώπου—would create nonsensical Greek and thus the grammatically requisite accusative, τὸν λαόν, is used and מפני not rendered (see also Num 14.9, 21.34; on the accusative with φοβέω, see LSJ, s.v. "φοβέω," B.II.6). Later in this verse, G reverts to isomorphism and gives προσώχθισεν Μωὰβ ἀπὸ προσώπου for ויקץ מואב מפני. Greek σφόδρα consistently renders Hebrew מאד, except in 22.17, where it is omitted.

Whereas Balak was introduced in the preceding sentence, the Moabite people are the subject here. The incongruity leads Tg. Onq. to render both occurrences of מואב with מואבאה. G, faithful as he is to his parent text, retains Moab as the subject despite the incongruity (cf. Tg. Onq., which reads מואבאה ["Moabite"] here). Greek does also allow for the name of a nation to represent an individual member, such as the king, but this use usually takes the definite article (see Smyth §996b) and so it is unlikely to be the case here.

πολλοὶ ἦσαν. The Hebrew bipartite nominal (or verbless) clause, רב הוא, is singular in both elements. However, G transforms these into plural and produces a *constructio ad sensum*, having its antecedent in τὸν λαόν/העם.

ἦσαν. The Hebrew pronoun in the bipartite nominal clause is certainly pronominal in force, unlike in certain tripartite nominal clauses where it can take on a copular function (see Holmstedt and Jones 2014). G, however, consistently renders the pronoun in bipartite nominal clauses with a form of εἰμί, and selects the best tense for the context, in this case, the imperfect (also in Num 5.28; present tense is used in 12.7; 13.8; 15.25).

καὶ προσώχθισεν. Greek προσοχθίζω renders Hebrew קוץ both times it appears in Numbers; קוץ is variable in its meaning depending on the preposition that appears with it. With מפני, it carries the sense of "dread" as it does here (cf. Exod 1.12, also using βδελύσσομαι). But with the ב preposition, it carries the sense of "abhor," as in Num 21.5. G does not distinguish and translates with the same lexeme in both locations. Here, unlike in 21.5, the selected lexeme, προσοχθίζω, fits well. Outside of the LXX, προσοχθίζω is rare. The earliest attestation is in P.Oxy. 9.1176 (third century BCE), a fragment of Satyrus's *Vita Euripidis*; it reads, προσώ[χθ]ισεν δὲ τῶι [γ]ένει τούτων χάριν ("he was angry with the generation on account of these things"). Also, see in Sib. Or. 3.272: πᾶς δὲ προσοχθίζων ἔσται τοῖς σοῖς ἐθίμοισιν ("each one will be angered with your customs"). Dorival, who does not mention the use in P.Oxy 9.1176, seems to think that this appeared first in the LXX (1994, 400); this is unlikely in my opinion. From its cognate simplex, ὀχθέω and the later developed ὀχθίζω, its meaning is clear: "to be angry, vexed in spirit" (see LSJ, s.v. "ὀχθέω").

ἀπὸ προσώπου υἱῶν Ἰσραήλ. This is a clear instance of a literal rendering resulting in a grammatically possible but thoroughly unidiomatic construction. The phrase ἀπὸ προσώπου appears six times in Numbers, rendering מלפני (17.11, 24) and מפני (20.6; 22.3; 32.21; 33.55). The former Hebrew expression appears only three times and is rendered with ἀπέναντι (20.9). The latter occurs ten times and is rendered in variable fashion: with πρὸ προσώπου (33.52), freely with διά (32.17), and omitted (10.35; 22.3 [1°]) or misrendered (22.33). In his literal rendering here, G allows interference from the Hebrew form, since in Greek idiom προσοχθίζω would prefer a bare dative (see P.Oxy. 9.1176; Sib. Or. 3.272; Leu 18.25, 28; 26.44; Ps 21.25). Compare Gen 27.46, where the idiomatic διά + accusative replaces מפני in order to denote the cause of provocation. Curiously, this instance of interference appears directly after G used an idiomatic rendering of מפני, disallowing such interference in the phrase ἐφοβήθη Μωὰβ τὸν λαόν.

Whereas the nominative υἱοὶ Ἰσραήλ always appears with the definite article (42x in Numbers), the oblique cases are less consistent. Anarthrous forms are less common than the articular form with oblique cases, with ca. thirty-eight occurrences in Numbers.

22.4

ויאמר מואב אל זקני מדין עתה ילחכו הקהל את כל סביבתינו כלחך
השור את ירק השדה ובלק בן צפור מלך למואב בעת ההוא

καὶ εἶπεν Μωὰβ τῇ γερουσίᾳ Μαδιάμ νῦν ἐκλείξει ἡ συναγωγὴ αὕτη πάντας τοὺς κύκλῳ ἡμῶν, ὡς ἐκλείξαι ὁ μόσχος τὰ χλωρὰ ἐκ τοῦ πεδίου. καὶ Βαλακ υἱὸς Σεπφωρ βασιλεὺς Μωαβ ἦν κατὰ τὸν καιρὸν ἐκεῖνον.

And Moab said to the council of elders of Madiam, "Now this gathering will lick up all those who are around us, as the bull calf might lick up the greenery of the plain." And Balak son of Sepphor was king of Moab at that time.

This verse is marked by subtle changes—changes in number, minor plusses—that interpret but do not depart far from the MT. The style employs good Greek idiom.

καὶ εἶπεν Μωὰβ τῇ γερουσίᾳ Μαδιάμ. G preserves the somewhat awkward מואב, although the identity of the speaker is unclear (cf. again Tg. Onq. which reads מואבאה ["the Moabite"]). For the plural זקני מדין, a collective singular γερουσία is used, which in Numbers appears only here and 22.7. Elsewhere, it translates the plural זקן in a genitive construction (see Exod 3.16, 18; 4.29; 12.21; 24.9; Leu 9.1 [cf. 9.3: בני ישראל]; Deut 5.23; 21.2; 25.7) or absolute (Deut 25.9). Outside of the Pentateuch, it appears only rarely (e.g., Ies 23.2; 2 Makk 11.27). According to LSJ, γερουσία refers to a council of elders or a senate. Thus, G's rendering makes explicit what is implicit here: the elders form a governing body. Theo van der Louw calls this type of translation strategy "explicitation" (2007, 81). However, the match πρεσβύτεροι – זקן appears slightly more often (Num 11.16, 24, 25, 30; 16.25; cf. Exod 10.9; 17.5; 18.2). It seems that consistency is not of particular concern for G.

ἐκλείξει ἡ συναγωγὴ αὕτη. The Hebrew verb לחך piel ("lick up") is rare, appearing only here in the Pentateuch. In the rest of the LXX, G's translation of לחך (or a cognate thereof) becomes standard (see 3 Rgns 18.38; Ps 71[72].9; Esa 49.23; Mich 7.17). The Hebrew verb is plural with the collective קהל serving as the subject (see Joüon §150.e). G retains the singular subject but brings the number of the verb into alignment. There is some question whether this simply reflects his *Vorlage* since SamPent reads a singular here as well (ילחך). However, throughout Numbers, G's renders plural Hebrew verbs with singulars when the subject is a collective, but grammatically singular subject (see 10.3; 11.8; 14.1 [2x], 10, 39; 15.14, 24, 36 [1°]; 20.29; 22.4; 34.14; 35.24, 25). Only twice does he reflect the plural Hebrew verb with a collective, singular subject (15.36 [2°]; 34.25 [2°]). Therefore, if G did render the MT's plural ילחכו with the singular ἐκλείξει, it would at least square with his translation technique elsewhere.

Greek συναγωγή translates Hebrew קהל, but also often translates עדה (e.g., 16.21; 17.10). The near demonstrative αὕτη is lacking in the MT but present in OG, SamPent, Tg. Neof., and Pesh. G has a near demonstrative pronoun in only a few places where they are not present in the MT; it is noted that they are always definite nouns (5.18 [probably harmonizing with 5.19]; 14.22; 22.19, 20; 27.16 [with συναγωγή]; 29.12; 32.11). It is possible that one could ascribe this addition to translation technique; however, given that other ancient versions and SamPent attest it as well, it is likely that it was present in the *Vorlage*.

πάντας τοὺς κύκλῳ ἡμῶν. G's rendering of סביבתינו כל את is quite near the Hebrew but departs in one significant way. The Hebrew speaks about surrounding *areas*, while G speaks about surrounding *people* (so Wevers 1998, 361). This indicates a nuanced understanding of the dialogue. Implicit in the statement of Israel's military threat is Moab's request for an alliance to fight back the Israelites. G interprets this to mean that Midian will be destroyed as well as Moab.

ὡς ἐκλείξαι ὁ μόσχος. The optative verb captures the sense of Hebrew simile, that is, "as a bull *might* lick up" (so Wevers 1998, 361). The MT merely has an infinitive construct with a prefixed כ preposition. Again, G displays a nuanced understanding of the force of the Hebrew and chooses an idiomatic expression for rendering a simile into Greek. Trevor Evans argues that this is a reflection of Homeric similes—which could have influenced G's selection of the otherwise rare optative (2001, 190–7).

τὰ χλωρὰ ἐκ τοῦ πεδίου. Although ירק is found rarely, a precedent has been set in Gen 1.30 and Exod 10.15 to translate it with χλωρόν (cf. λάχανον in Gen 9.3). The substantival adjective captures the sense of "greenery," without tying itself slavishly to the singular form. The Hebrew direct object phrase, השדה ירק את, employs a simple genitive to denote the relationship between the two substantives. However, G adds the preposition ἐκ, deriving this particular preposition from the verb ἐκλείχω. The clear reference to the Israelites annihilating the surrounding nations *from* an area is thereby strengthened. In other words, instead of describing the greenery with the phrase "of the field," the greenery is annihilated *"from the field"*; πεδίον is not an altogether unusual choice for שדה, appearing previously in 19.16 and 21.20 (but ἀγρός in 16.4; 20.17; 21.22; 23.14). It may look back to 21.20 where the region around Moab is called a πεδίον.

καὶ Βαλὰκ υἱὸς Σεπφὼρ βασιλεὺς Μωὰβ ἦν. This is most likely to be taken as "Balak, son of Sepphor *was* king of Moab." The string of Hebrew nouns is not entirely clear without an explicit copula, to which G accordingly adds one in order to mitigate ambiguity (cf. Pesh's placement of a copula between Balak and son of Beor).

κατὰ τὸν καιρὸν ἐκεῖνον. Greek καιρός stands in the place of Hebrew עת, both of which denote a delimited period of time. The phrase κατὰ τὸν καιρόν has

been used only once before by G at 9.13, where it translates במועדו (see
also Exod 23.15). The translator of Genesis, when rendering the prepositional phrase בעת, alternates between the adverb ἡνίκα (31.10; 38.27) and
ἐν τῷ καιρῷ (21.22; 38.1; also 15x in Deut). Although G's rendering of בעת
with κατά is unique, it is an adequate translation. κατά probably indicates
duration; in other words, through the course of the following events, Balak
was king (LSJ, s.v. "κατά," B.VII).

22.5

וישלח מלאכים אל בלעם בן בעור פתורה אשר על הנהר ארץ בני
עמו לקרא לו לאמר הנה עם יצא ממצרים הנה כסה את עין הארץ
והוא ישב ממלי

καὶ ἀπέστειλεν πρέσβεις πρὸς Βαλαὰμ υἱὸν Βεὼρ Φαθούρα, ὅ ἐστιν
ἐπὶ τοῦ ποταμοῦ γῆς υἱῶν λαοῦ αὐτοῦ, καλέσαι αὐτὸν λέγων Ἰδοὺ
λαὸς ἐξελήλυθεν ἐξ Αἰγύπτου, καὶ ἰδοὺ κατεκάλυψεν τὴν ὄψιν τῆς
γῆς, καὶ οὗτος ἐγκάθηται ἐχόμενός μου.

And he sent ambassadors to Balaam son of Beor of Pathoura,
which is on the river of the land of his people's sons, to call him,
saying, "Behold, a people has come out of Egypt, and behold, it
has covered the sight of the earth, and it is lying in wait next to me."

In 22.5b–6, Balak gives a message to his messengers for Balaam. Balaam
repeats these words to God in 22.11. In these parallel passages, there are
only a few differences in the MT, but still less in G's translation. G prefers
to be consistent and to follow patterns for larger units such as this.

καὶ ἀπέστειλεν πρέσβεις. Balak is clearly the subject, having been identified
in the last clause of 22.4. This is the second occurrence of πρέσβυς in Numbers and carries the sense of "ambassador" (see LSJ, s.v. "πρέσβυς," A.II).
It was also just used to render מלאכים in Num 21.21, where Moses sent
ambassadors to Seon, king of the Amorites. Elsewhere in the Pentateuch,
Greek Genesis and Exodus use ἄγγελος for מלאך (15x in Gen, first at 16.7;
5x in Ex, first at 3.2). At times, G also employs ἄγγελος, as in 20.14. Wevers
postulates that G uses πρέσβεις "probably to harmonize with v[erse] 7,
where they are called זקני מואב וזקני מדין" (1998, 360). This is of course
possible; however, G renders the זקני phrases with the collective γερουσία
in both instances and so the harmonization would not be felt on the level
of target language.

Alternatively, it may be that G wants to distinguish between heavenly messengers and earthly messengers in this account. Although in two previous instances (20.14, 16) he follows the conventional match of מלאך – ἄγγελος, he uses πρέσβεις or γερουσία here to refer to the human messengers. A divine messenger (מלאך), rendered with ἄγγελος, will appear shortly (22.22). However, G reverts to ἄγγελος to refer to human messengers in 24.12 once the divine messenger is off the scene.

πρὸς Βαλαὰμ υἱὸν Βεὼρ Φαθούρα. G transliterates the place name פתור as well as the directive ה. If the large number of variants for Φαθούρα is any indicator, it is likely that the location was not known to the translator and subsequent coypists. That the directive ה is transliterated as well further confirms this.

λαὸς ἐξελήλυθεν ἐξ Αἰγύπτου. The Hebrew qatal, יצא, is rendered with a perfect by G rather than an aorist. The Greek perfect tense coheres better with the context by focusing on the people's present location, staging on the borders of Moab (see Smyth §434). The perfect is again used in the parallel text in 22.11, although there is some variance in the MT. On this, see at 22.11.

ὅ ἐστιν ἐπὶ τοῦ ποταμοῦ γῆς υἱῶν λαοῦ αὐτοῦ. G does not depart from an isomorphic rendering to clarify the location. In fact, the string of genitives leaves the location—assuming that Φαθούρα was unknown—quite ambiguous. Whereas the MT and G have λαοῦ αὐτοῦ/עמו ("his people"), SamPent, Pesh, and the Vulgate all have the proper name עמון (Ammon) or its equivalent (see also ESV, RSV). For G, this phrase adds little more than to say Balaam's homeland was near a river. The Hebrew phrase "the river" is an idiom denoting the Euphrates (as Tg. Onq. makes explicit here; see also NRSV; Exod 23.31 OG) and the idiom is not meaningfully conveyed in this literal rendering (see also Gen 31.21; 36.37). Moreover, the Nile (יאר) is consistently translated with ὁ ποταμός throughout the LXX (e.g., Gen 41.1, Exod 1.22; see van der Meer 2012, 388). On the level of text-as-received, a later reader could easily take this as a reference to the Nile. On the level of text-as-produced, G was simply giving the convenient match for הנהר and was not concerned with referential clarity.

γῆς υἱῶν λαοῦ αὐτοῦ. In what appears to be an effort to imitate the formal shape of the Hebrew, G does not add a definite article on these three nouns, all of which are perforce definite in the original.

καλέσαι αὐτόν. The Greek καλέω here renders Hebrew קרא. The polyvalence of קרא is handled well by G, who employs a different construction or lexeme depending on whether קרא indicates summoning (קרא – [ἐπι] καλέω: 11.3, 35; 12.5; 16.12; 22.20; 21.3; 22:37; 24.10; 25.2), meeting in person (קרא – εἰς συνάντησιν: 20.18, 20; 21.33; 22.34, 36; 23.3; 24.1; 31.13), meeting in battle (קרא – παρατάσσω: 21.23), or naming something (קרא – ἐπονομάζομαι: 13.16, 24; 32.38; 32.41, 42). Here, of course, Balak is summoning Balaam and so καλέω is appropriately used. This suggests that G is sensitive to his context and does not simply render קרא with a stereotyped equivalent every time it appears.

καὶ ἰδοὺ κατεκάλυψεν τὴν ὄψιν τῆς γῆς. The obscure Hebrew phrase כסה את עין הארץ is found in Exodus twice (10.5, 15) and Numbers twice (22.5, 11). In the LXX, ὀφθαλμός renders עין 510 times whereas ὄψις appears for עין only 7 times (Exod 10.5, 15; Leu 13.55; Num 22.5, 11; Iezek 1.27; 10.9). G, who does not take the easy road of using ὀφθαλμός as the standard equivalent of עין, went the way of his colleague in Exod 10.5 and 15, perhaps allowing the reader to recall the passage and also making a sly comparison between Israel and the plague of locusts in Egypt. Irrespective of whether G is relying on the translator of Exodus, ὄψις represents a deliberate choice to avoid the "easy" equivalent for a more contextually sensitive reading. In the plural, ὄψις can refer to the organs of sight (LSJ, s.v. "ὄψις," II.c.) but is more commonly used of things that are seen, that is, "aspect, appearance." Thus, as the NETS rendering "sight" suggests, Balak's own ability to see the land is clouded by the host of the Israelites.

οὗτος ἐγκάθηται. The near demonstrative οὗτος for הוא in verbal clauses is a usual equivalent throughout the Pentateuch. Whereas the Hebrew has the neutral "to dwell" (ישב), G employs a more contextually sensitive lemma, ἐγκάθημαι, implying not only Israel's presence near Moab but also their intent to invade. LSJ defines ἐγκάθημαι as it relates to garrisons as "lie in place"; such a use appears in Polybius *Hist.* 18.11: οὔτε γὰρ Πελοποννησίους ἀναπνεῦσαι δυνατὸν ἐν Κορίνθῳ βασιλικῆς φρουρᾶς ἐγκαθημένης ("For neither were the Peloponnese able to breathe while the royal garrison was stationed in Corinth"). When used with τρίβος ("ambush"), it means "to lie in ambush," as in Gen 49.17: καὶ γενηθήτω Δὰν ὄφις ἐφ' ὁδοῦ ἐγκαθήμενος ἐπὶ τρίβου ("And let Dan become a snake on the road lying in ambush on the path," NETS).

However, this also betrays a knowledge of the coming events—from MT's perspective, Israel in Balak's mouth is simply present and their motive insinuated from their actions towards the Amorites (22.2). From the translator's perspective, Israel is present in order to invade and conquer.

ἐχόμενός μου. The phrase ἐχόμενός μου stands in place of the prepositional phrase ממלי, employing a rare use of ἔχω, meaning "being close to, bordering" (LSJ, s.v. "ἔχω," C.IV.3; see also Gen 41.23; Exod 26.3; Leu 6.3; Deut 11.30). Although the construction is not attested often, it is an established meaning and denotes close proximity. In other words, G portrays Balak's description of Israel as pressed up against their border and staging for war. The Hebrew simply denotes that they are opposite (see *HALOT*, s.v. "מול").

22.6

ועתה לכה נא ארה לי את העם הזה כי עצום הוא ממני אולי אוכל
נכה בו ואגרשנו מן הארץ כי ידעתי את אשר תברך מברך ואשר
תאר יואר

καὶ νῦν δεῦρο ἄρασαί μοι τὸν λαὸν τοῦτον, ὅτι ἰσχύει οὗτος ἢ ἡμεῖς·
ἐὰν δυνώμεθα πατάξαι ἐξ αὐτῶν, καὶ ἐκβαλῶ αὐτοὺς ἐκ τῆς γῆς·
ὅτι οἶδα οὓς ἂν εὐλογήσῃς σύ, εὐλόγηνται καὶ οὓς ἂν καταράσῃ σύ,
κεκατήρανται

And now come, curse for me this people, since it is stronger than we are, if we may be able to strike some of them, and I will cast them out from the land. For I know that whomever you bless are blessed, and whomever you curse are cursed."

καὶ νῦν δεῦρο. The Hebrew has a double imperative construction without a conjunction, ועתה לכה נא ארה לי. As this would make for quite awkward Greek if represented in the same manner; G represents the first imperative as the adverbial interjection δεῦρο (disregarding נא; cf. 22.16). This accurately captures the semantic force of לכה if not its grammatical category, following the precedent set in Genesis and Exodus, in each of which לכה is matched by δεῦρο (Gen 19.32; 31.44; 37.13; Exod 3.10; also Num 10.29; 22.11; 23.7, 13, 27; 24.14).

ἄρασαί μοι. In the Pentateuch, ἀράομαι appears only in the Balaam account (22.6, 11; 23.7, 8). Incidentally, this match is one of the few instances in which the Greek root ἀράομαι appears to match phonetically the Hebrew ארר, which may have influenced the selection of ἀράομαι. However, as καταράομαι also renders ארר later in this verse, this line of argument should not be pushed too far. The Balaam account employs καταράομαι as well (22.6, 12; 23.8; 13, 25, 27, 24.10) and ἐπικαταράομαι (22.17; 23.7), translating alternatively ארר, קבב, and זעם (once, in 23.7). There does not appear to be a discernible pattern here except that G employs καταράομαι and ἀράομαι as synonyms (see, e.g., 22.6; 23.8).

ὅτι. The conjunction ὅτι is usually used to represent direct causality in Greek; here, however, G has used ὅτι to represent indirect causality due to the stereotyped match between כי and ὅτι (see Aejmelaeus 1993, 11–30). Here, of course, the ὅτι clause is providing a motivation for the imperative clause and under normal Greek constraints, γάρ would have been preferred.

ἰσχύει οὗτος ἢ ἡμεῖς. The Hebrew employs a nominal comparative clause, indicated by מן + pronoun. G transforms this into a comparative verbal clause; οὗτος, standing for הוא, is clearly referring to ὁ λαός. Rather than an adjectival form—positive (πολύ in Num 14.12) or comparative (ἰσχυρότερος in Deut 9.1; 11.23)—G employs the verbal form ἰσχύω + ἤ; ἰσχύω implies not simply immensity of size, but strength or ability of Israel's military capacity. Consistent with G's rendering of the previous verse with οὗτος ἐγκάθηται ἐχόμενός μου ("this [people] is lying in wait next to me"), G continues to insinuate the militaristic intentions of Israel. For an example of a similar use of ἰσχύω with militaristic connotations, see Thucydides, *Hist.* 3.46.3: ἰσχύομεν δὲ πρὸς τοὺς πολεμίους τῷδε ("But we are strong against our enemies in this").

G's use of ἤ is not uncommon throughout the rest of the Pentateuch for the מן comparative forms (Gen 29.19, 30; 38.26; 49.12; Exod 14.12 [cf. Exod 18.18]; Deut 7.17; Deut 11.23). The plural ἡμεῖς renders the suffixed first person common singular pronoun (ממני) of the MT. Logically, it must be plural as Balak is speaking through messengers concerning the ability of his people vis-à-vis that of Israel.

From these data a few remarks can be made. First, G as one of the Pentateuch translators resists characterization as either *literal* or *free*. G's rendering of ὅτι is literalistic, but ἐγκάθημαι, ἐχόμενος + genitive, and the comparative ἤ are all somewhat "free" and idiomatic. Second, he was quite capable, and fond of translating idiomatically but appears to value equally highly the practice of letting the Hebrew word order determine the shape of the Greek product.

ἐὰν δυνώμεθα πατάξαι ἐξ αὐτῶν. The status of the Hebrew particle אולי is debated among Hebrew grammarians (see Tjen 2010, 15, for a synopsis). According to Waltke and O'Connor, it is not a conditional but a *sentence adverb* or *disjunct*, a subclass of adverbs that relate the speaker's attitude toward the proposition (*IBHS* §39.3.4b); אולי ("perhaps") then connotes that Balak is uncertain regarding his ability to strike the Israelites. Accordingly, the striking and the driving out are then two potential or hoped for outcomes of Balaam's acquiescence to come and curse the Israelites. In other words, these serve as *effects* of Balaam's actions related in the first clause.

G transforms this, effectively introducing his own syntactic division. Tjen notes that of the eighteen occurrences of אולי in the Pentateuch, eleven are translated with conditionals (2010, 94). In Numbers, אולי appears only in the Balaam episode (5x) and is translated variously: ἐὰν (22.6), εἰ ἄρα (22.11), εἰ μή (22.33), εἰ (23.3, 27). By rendering אולי with ἐάν, G introduces the protasis to a conditional statement rather than a clause grammatically connected to the preceding clause, as in MT.

πατάξαι. This infinitive renders נכה; נכה is difficult to identify: although it appears to be a *hiphil yiqtol* first-person plural, an infinitive is expected here; *HALOT* states that this could be a *piel* infinitive (s.v. "נכה," hiphil, 1.b.). That נכה does not occur in the *piel* makes this unlikely. Thus, I will tentatively take it as a finite *hiphil* form. G renders this consecution well by transforming אוכל into a first-person common plural and rendering נכה with an infinitive.

ἐξ αὐτῶν. The prepositional phrase ἐξ αὐτῶν is likely intended to represent בו and is best understood as a substantival prepositional phrase that serves as the direct object, that is, "some of them" (NETS). A ב preposition that indicates *not instrument* but *object* is not attested frequently with נכה (see Exod 12.13; 17.6). In Exod 12.13, the ב preposition is rendered with ἐν; in Exod 17.6 the preposition is ignored and a simple accusative is used. Here, G avoids giving a stereotyped rendering of ב but still retains quantitative equivalence. The resultant text indicates that Balak is not hoping to destroy them but simply kill enough that they will retreat from his borders. In this way, G in fact hints at the immensity of Israel vis-à-vis Moab—Balak cannot hope for more than a partial defeat.

καὶ ἐκβαλῶ αὐτοὺς ἐκ τῆς γῆς. G opts for quantitative equivalence and renders the apodotic *waw* with καί, despite the fact that it is not idiomatic. If Greek marks the apodosis with a conjunction, it prefers δέ or ἀλλά (see Smyth §2837; Tjen 2010, 36–37). According to Tjen, G renders the apodotic *waw* with a καί 65.8 percent of the time (2010, 215). NETS passes this unidiomatic construction on to the reader by rendering the καί with an equally awkward "and" before the apodosis.

οὓς ἂν εὐλογήσῃς σύ ... οὓς ἂν καταράσῃ σύ. The objects of blessing or cursing are the contingent elements, thus "whomever" in NETS. G adds the independent pronoun σύ, which is not necessary from a grammatical standpoint in either Hebrew or Greek. Rhetorically, however, this enhances Balak's plea to Balaam by emphasizing the subject: "whomever *you* should bless."

Although אשר, as a relative complementizer, is unmarked with respect to number, the singular participle מברך that follows would dictate that the headless relative envisions a singular entity. However, G renders these participles with a plural (εὐλόγηνται, κεκατήρανται) and so also the relative pronouns (οὕς). This further strengthens Balak's plea: instead of "the one whom you bless," G has "whomever [pl.] you should bless." However, this increase of emphasis comes at the cost of a few departures from his *Vorlage*. These subtle changes from the Hebrew merely make explicit the implicit sense of the Hebrew: Balak is flattering Balaam in order to coax him to come and curse Israel.

εὐλόγηνται ... κεκατήρανται. With the participle מברך, G has a choice: render the participle with a participle and thus be required to add ἔστιν and so be inconsistent vis-à-vis the following finite form of κεκατήρανται, or render with a finite form. G chose the latter which allows him to retain isomorphism and consistency. Beyond a transformation of grammatical category, G renders both with plural forms, as his choice of the plural relative pronoun demands (see above on "οὓς ἂν εὐλογήσῃς σύ ... οὓς ἂν καταράσῃ σύ").

22.7

וילכו זקני מואב וזקני מדין וקסמים בידם ויבאו אל בלעם וידברו אליו
דברי בלק

καὶ ἐπορεύθη ἡ γερουσία Μωὰβ καὶ ἡ γερουσία Μαδιάμ, καὶ τὰ
μαντεῖα ἐν ταῖς χερσὶν αὐτῶν, καὶ ἦλθον πρὸς Βαλαὰμ καὶ εἶπαν αὐτῷ
τὰ ῥήματα Βαλάκ.

And the council of elders of Moab went, and the council of elders
of Madiam, and the instruments of divination were in their hands,
and they came to Balaam and said to him the words of Balak.

ἐπορεύθη ἡ γερουσία Μωὰβ καὶ ἡ γερουσία Μαδιάμ. On γερουσία, see 22.4.
Curiously, MT has a plural verb, וילכו, whereas G employs a singular form
of πορεύομαι, despite also having two subjects. Wevers notes that this is G's
pattern: "When a compound subject immediately follows a verb the verb
is singular if the first element is singular, but in the following narration the
verb is in the plural" (1982, 122; cf. 1.17, 12.1, 14.45; 20.6; 22.7 [he also
cites 20.10 as an exception]). Although that is G's pattern, this is the only
place where he translates a *plural Hebrew verb* as a singular. In the other
instances just mentioned, the Hebrew *Vorlage* employs a singular verb
with a compound subject following and G merely represents this. Compare this to 20.10: the plural Hebrew verb *is* translated by a plural, despite
the fact that a compound subject follows it. Here, then, G is emphasizing
the first subject, ἡ γερουσία Μωάβ, as the primary actors, which can safely
be assumed from the preceding narrative of Balak's initiation (see Smyth
§966: "The verb may agree with the nearest or most important of two or
more subjects").

καὶ ἐπορεύθη ... καὶ ἦλθον ... καὶ εἶπαν. The MT has the normal *wayyiqtol*
structure for a sequence of actions in a narrative. G, instead of departing
from this as he does in 22.1, retains the clumsier polysyndeton. Here, the
tendency towards faithful representation of G's *Vorlage* comes through.

τὰ μαντεῖα. The word μαντεῖον appears for the first time in the LXX here. It
renders קסם, usually "divination" or "oracular response" (see Num 23.23;
1 Rgns 15.23; Prov 16.10; Ier 14.14). Since Balaam is the one who is to offer
the divination, it is unlikely that they are bringing him divinations and so
the Hebrew word is usually understood as *payment* for divination. Outside
the LXX, μαντεῖον is used in the meanings of "oracular response, method
or process of divination, seat of divination" (LSJ). It therefore carries a
similar semantic range to קסם and although LSJ notes "payment for divination" as a possible gloss, it only finds support here in the LXX (see Dorival 1994, 421 for the tradition related to this interpretation). The two LXX

lexica gloss μαντεῖα in this context variously: LEH have "things attached to divination"; *GELS*, glosses "fees for divination" (so *BdA*, "l'argent de la divination"). LEH's conservative gloss is probably best. In Num 23.23, קסם denotes a divination and is rendered with the cognate noun μαντεία. It seems most likely, then, that G knew the meaning of קסם or that of a similar root and supplied an etymological translation that is not quite suited to the context. NETS translates this as "the instruments of divination." Dorival notes that Origen, Rabbah Numbers, and some targumim also understand the Greek word in this way (1994, 421).

ἐν ταῖς χερσὶν αὐτῶν. The MT employs the singular form of יד with ב, a common, idiomatic collocation that can denote agency or control without respect to number of agents (or number of hands, for that matter). What explains G's plural ἐν ταῖς χερσίν then? The translator of Genesis does not render ביד + suffix with consistency, but equivocates between singular and plural forms of χεῖρ. That is, he does not appear to distinguish whether singular (Gen 30.35; 32.17) or plural forms of χεῖρ (Gen 16.6; 35.4) are more appropriate, neither does he correlate singular and plural forms with singular and plural agents (see Gen 16.6, 9; 27.17; 30.35). In rare cases, the Hebrew idiom is not represented literally but with an idiomatic Greek phrase that captures the semantic force of the Hebrew; for example, see μετὰ ἑαυτῶν (Gen 43.22) or παρ' ᾧ (Gen 44.17).

The translators of Exodus and Leviticus develop this and are moderately consistent in their distinction between singular and plural agents: ἐν/εἰς + singular χεῖρ is generally used with singular agents (Exod 4.2; 6.1; 7.15, 17; 13.9; 14.8; 15.20; 17.5, 9; 22.3; Leu 26.46; exceptions 4.21; 32.15; 34.29) while ἐν/εἰς + plural χεῖρ is used with plural agents (12.11; 23.31; Leu 26.25). A brief glance at Numbers demonstrates that G reflects this distinction as well: a singular form of χεῖρ with singular agent (about 18x, first in Num 4.28; exception: 21.34) and plural with plural agents (22.7; 31.6 [although a misrendering of a singular pronominal suffix for plural). Thus in this instance, G likely chooses to use ἐν ταῖς χερσίν to reflect the plural agents, though the singular בידם appears in his *Vorlage*.

καὶ εἶπαν αὐτῷ τὰ ῥήματα Βαλάκ. G prefers λαλέω for דבר (110x). The only exceptions are found in Num 14.17, 26; 15.1; 17.1 [MT 16.36]; 22.7, 35 (1°); 23.2; 24.13; 32.27, 31. The aorist of λέγω (i.e., εἶπον) and related forms appear about 120x, rendering forms of אמר in all but a few instances (15.35; 18.20; 26.1; 27.6, 18). Wevers notes: "The equation is so carefully maintained that in each of these cases another parent text [i.e., ויאמר] is probably to be presupposed" (1982, 128).

22.8

ויאמר אליהם לינו פה הלילה והשבתי אתכם דבר כאשר ידבר יהוה
אלי וישבו שרי מואב עם בלעם

καὶ εἶπεν πρὸς αὐτούς Καταλύσατε αὐτοῦ τὴν νύκτα, καὶ ἀποκριθήσομαι
ὑμῖν ῥήματα[a] ἃ ἂν λαλήσῃ κύριος πρός με· καὶ κατέμειναν οἱ ἄρχοντες
Μωὰβ παρὰ Βαλαάμ.

And he said to them, "Lodge here tonight, and I will answer you matters the Lord may speak to me." And the rulers of Moab stayed with Balaam.

[a] We[ed] has ῥήματα; however I will argue below that πράγματα is the better reading, which I will treat as the OG. This is a difficult text critical issue; ῥήματα is attested in primarily later manuscripts: Codex M, 416, 458, 767, a few other minuscules, and in Latin codex 100. This is against the better-attested πραγμα (A, 426, Cyrillus Alexandrinus I, 440) and πραγματα (B, F, V, and the rest). Wevers prefers ῥήματα, arguing "[w]henever ἀποκρίνειν is used to represent השיב and has an object modifier either ῥῆμα or λόγος is used in the LXX for דבר but never πρᾶγμα" (1982, 129). I have examined the following examples confirming Wevers's line of argument: Num 13.27 [MT 26], Ies 14.7; 22.32; 2 Rgns 3.11; 3 Rgns 12.24p, 12.24q; 18.21; 21.12; 4 Rgns 18.36; 1 Suppl 21.12; 2 Suppl 10.6, 9; 2 Esd 5.11; Idt 6.17 (plural ῥήμα); Prov 18.3; 22.21; 24.26; Zech 1.13; Esa 36.21; Ier 51.20 (MT 44.20); see also βουλή in Dan θ 2.14. Wevers also asserts that the lesser-attested plural ῥήματα is preferable to the singular ῥημα as it could lead to the singular reading (1982, 129). The root of the problem is the polyvalence of דבר, which can mean both "word" and "matter," represented by ῥῆμα/λόγος and πρᾶγμα respectively. However, the key text critical judgment is to explain *how* the grammatically smoother ῥήματα could lead to the more awkward (and earlier attested) πράγματα. In my judgment, it seems more likely that a later copyist would correct a translator's infelicitous selection of πράγματα for דבר in this context *than* a copyist substituting the incorrect πράγματα for ῥήματα. In other words, it is likely that a translator working from the (potentially ambiguous) Hebrew *Vorlage* would make the mistake rather than a later copyist. Undoubtedly, ῥήματα is the *grammatically better* reading (as Wevers makes clear) and for this reason is the easier reading; however, πράγματα is, in my view, *preferable* as the earliest attainable.

Καταλύσατε αὐτοῦ τὴν νύκτα. This phrase is evidence of G's grasp not only of his *Vorlage*, but also concern for his target language. On the one hand, his style can be characterized as isomorphic, but it also employs

Greek conventions well. When καταλύω is used intransitively, it takes on the meaning "to lodge." Although first occurring in Gen (19.2; 24.23, 25), κοιμάομαι ("to sleep") is used through the rest of the occurrences of לין (10x). G's rendering here, departing from this tendency, captures the sense of the Hebrew. Although לין appears only here in Numbers, καταλύω is used for ישב in 25.1. Greek αὐτοῦ stands for the Hebrew adverb פה. Although αὐτοῦ derives from the genitive form of αὐτός, it is used as a separate lemma meaning "just here" or "right here" (see LSJ, s.v. "αὐτοῦ"). Elsewhere in Numbers, פה is rendered with αὐτοῦ in 32.6 (also Gen 22.5), but ὧδε in 32.16 (see Gen 19.12). The accusative τὴν νύκτα is an adverbial accusative denoting extent of time (Smyth §1582–83: "the accusative of time implies that the action of the verb covers the *entire* period" [emphasis original]). Thus, Balaam asks the messengers to stay through that night and he would presumably answer them the following morning.

ἀποκριθήσομαι ὑμῖν πράγματα. The future deponent form of ἀποκρίνομαι is used for the *hiphil weqatal* of שוב. It is not unusual that the object to whom the report is brought is marked as an accusative with את, and rendered with a dative (see 3 Rgns 12.6; cf. Gen 37.14, suffixed pronoun instead of את: השבני). The lemma ἀποκρίνομαι without ῥῆμα or λόγος is *semantically* sufficient to carry the collocation דבר + השיב. (see Gen 37.14; 3 Rgns 12.9, 16; Esa 41.28). Nevertheless, G renders דבר with the plural of πράγμα. Two issues must be noted here: first, ῥῆμα or λόγος is not used, although expected (see Wevers 1998, 365; see text critical comment ᵃ above); second, πράγματα is plural whereas דבר is singular. The plural can be explained by attraction to the following phrase ἃ ἄν λαλήσῃ. Attraction to the relative pronoun—in contradistinction to attraction of the relative to the antecedent—places emphasis upon the relative clause (Smyth §2533). However, the choice of πράγμα can only be attributed to a translational misfire, namely, rending a *possible* gloss of דבר but one that is unsuitable to its context. Thus, Wevers's comment that "only ῥήματα is appropriate" is accurate (1998, 365) and in my opinion, it is for this reason that later copyists "corrected" to the appropriate reading.

ἃ ἄν λαλήσῃ κύριος. On the use of ἄν, see comment at 22.6. The collocation ἃ ἄν represents כאשר. The sense of the Hebrew is that of comparison, "just as," or, "in the manner which" rather than "the things which." In fact, G renders כאשר with a variety of phrases to express this idea: καθά (15x), ὃν τρόπον (12x), καθάπερ (3x), καθώς (2x), ὡς καί (2.17), καθὼς ὡσεί

(11.12), διότι (27.14), and καθότι (33.56). This, however, is the only time that G renders it in this manner. Further, כאשר appears circa two hundred times in the Pentateuch and is never rendered with a simple relative pronoun except here; in a few places ἄν is added to denote contingency (e.g., Leu 24.20, 27.14). G's reading makes good contextual sense and conveys Balaam's willingness to present whatever God might say to him; it is, however, somewhat removed from an adequate rendering.

καὶ κατέμειναν οἱ ἄρχοντες Μωάβ. The verb καταμένω is a rare word in the LXX, appearing only three times: Gen 6.3; Num 20.1; and here. In Num 20.1, it also renders ישב and denotes Israel's sojourn in Kadesh Barnea before entering Edom. G's usual gloss, κατοικέω (ca. 20x), is obviously inappropriate to the context since it implies permanent residence rather than delay of a single evening. Later in this account, G selects the cognate ὑπομένω when Balaam requests the elders stay a night on their second journey to him (22.19).

22.9

ויבא אלהים אל בלעם ויאמר מי האנשים האלה עמך

καὶ ἦλθεν ὁ θεὸς πρὸς Βαλααμ καὶ εἶπεν αὐτῷ Τί οἱ ἄνθρωποι οὗτοι παρὰ σοί;

And God came to Balaam and said to him, "Why are these people with you?"

καὶ ἦλθεν ὁ θεὸς πρὸς Βαλααμ. The MT has the Tetragrammaton to refer to the divine in 22.8 but אלהים in verse 9. G seems to distinguish these, rendering them with κύριος and θεός, respectively. In the following narrative, the MT alternates between יהוה (22.8, 12, 13, 18, 22–27 [angel of YHWH], 28, 31, 32, 34, 35) and אלהים (2.9, 10, 11, 12, 18, 20, 22, 38). However, G only uses κύριος at 22.8, 18, 19, 31, 34, preferring θεός in most instances. The following table summarizes the uses of θεός and κύριος in Num 22; bolded verses mark where the OG and MT agree.

Verse	אלהים	יהוה	
8		κύριος	"just as the Lord speaks to me"
9	θεός		"God came to Balaam"
10	θεός		"Balaam said to God"

12		θεός	MT: "YHWH said to Balaam"; G: "God said to Balaam"
13		θεός	MT: "YHWH does not permit"; G: "God does not permit"
18		κύριος	MT: "Lord, my God"; G: "Lord, God"
18	θεός		MT: "Lord, my God"; G: "Lord, God"
19		κύριος	"the Lord will speak"
20	θεός		"God came to Balaam"
22		θεός	MT: "angel of YHWH"; G: "angel of God"
22		θεός	MT: "angel of YHWH"; G: "angel of God"
23		θεός	MT: "angel of YHWH"; G: "angel of God"
24		θεός	MT: "angel of YHWH"; G: "angel of God"
25		θεός	MT: "angel of YHWH"; G: "angel of God"
26		θεός	MT: "angel of YHWH"; G: "angel of God"
27		θεός	MT: "angel of YHWH"; G: "angel of God"
28		θεός	MT: "YHWH opened the mouth"; G: "God opened the mouth"
31		θεός	MT: "angel of YHWH"; G: "angel of God"
32		θεός	MT: "angel of YHWH"; G: "angel of God"
34		κύριος	"angel of the Lord"
35		θεός	MT: "angel of YHWH"; G: "angel of God"
38	θεός		"The word that God puts"

In summation, the OG agrees with the MT in nine of twenty-two instances. In the twelve instances of disagreement, the phrase מלאך יהוה rendered with ὁ ἄγγελος τοῦ θεοῦ accounts for ten of these; indeed the MT and OG only agree on this phrase at 22.34. The other three instances of disagreement are found at 22.12, 13, 28. In this case, although Balaam went to consult with κύριος, θεός comes to him and eventually Balaam states that θεός (for יהוה) refuses to grant the request of the men (v. 13).

καὶ εἶπεν αὐτῷ. The MT does not have an equivalent for αὐτῷ. When the MT has אמר and indicates an interlocutor, it uses אל + pronoun or substantive, which G usually renders with πρός + accusative (ca. 65x) or a bare dative (16x). Less frequently, ל is used and rendered most often with the bare dative (14x), but also rendered with πρός + accusative (4x). In the Balaam episode (chaps. 22–24), the numbers are somewhat different: אל + pronoun = πρός + accusative (15x); אל + pronoun = dative (7x); ל

= dative (6x); לֹ = πρός + accusative (2x). Thus, the appearance of αὐτῷ here could indicate a *Vorlage* of either אליו or לו, with a slightly higher probability of אליו. 4Q27 confirms this reading: ויאמר] אליו מי האנשים האלה. Moreover, it is present in the Pesh but not Tg. Onq. By the time of Origen, it must have been omitted from the Hebrew text and so was placed under the obelus to indicate that it was not present in the proto-MT (as witnessed in the Syro-Hexapla; see We^ed ad loc.). Thus, with reasonable certainty, it can be asserted that אליו was present in G's *Vorlage* (see Wevers 1998, 365 n. 15). Note also that G and Pesh agree against MT and Tg. Onq. at 12.6 in the presence of πρὸς αὐτούς; there are no extant Qumran fragments for this phrase, however.

Τί οἱ ἄνθρωποι οὗτοι παρὰ σοί; Although this rendering nearly retains the structure of the corresponding Hebrew phrase, מי האנשים האלה עמך, G departs from the MT in one important way: Τί in this construction can only mean "what" or "why" and not "who," which would be represented by τίνες. This is a unique rendering in Numbers; in every other instance, מי is rendered with τίς (6x). G perhaps read מה in his *Vorlage*, which is found in SamPent rather than מי of the MT. In support of this reconstruction, G renders מה with τί in 9.8; 11.11 (2x), 20; 14.3, 41; 15.34; 20.4, 5; 22.19, 28, 32, 37; 23.8 (2x), 17, 23; 32.7.

Wevers notes that τί "can mean either 'what' or 'why'" (1998, 365). NETS follows the former, rendering the phrase with "What are these men with you?" (cf. LXX.D: "Was machen diese Menschen bei dir?"; *BdA*: "Qu'est-ce, ces hommes"). According to this interpretation, τί would carry the sense of "what *is the nature* of these men with you?" (see Smyth §310). Accordingly, a plausible answer to such a question might be "ἡ γερουσία Μωάβ." While it is not beyond the realm of possibility, it does not cohere with the context. The better sense is "why are these men with you?" Not only is it grammatically possible, but the answer Balaam gives in the following verses corresponds with this interpretation of the question—that is, they are here because Balak sent them (v. 10).

22.10

ויאמר בלעם אל האלהים בלק בן צפר מלך מואב שלח אלי
καὶ εἶπεν Βαλαὰμ πρὸς τὸν θεὸν Βαλὰκ υἱὸς Σεπφὼρ βασιλεὺς Μωὰβ
ἀπέστειλεν αὐτοὺς πρός με λέγων

And Balaam said to God, "Balak son of Sepphor, king of Moab, sent them to me, saying,

ἀπέστειλεν αὐτοὺς πρός με. The MT has the shorter שלח אלי, and assumes that the men are the objects of Balak's sending. Although the ellipsis is not ambiguous in the MT, it is certainly not a smooth reading. Insofar as Tg. Onq, Tg. Neof., and Pesh do not feel the need to make any similar additions here, it is clear that a literal rendering will do an adequate job.

λέγων. This is most likely a case of an alternative *Vorlage*. The collocation ויאמר/וידבר (or other verbs of speaking) + לאמר appears about seventy-five times in Numbers alone and is usually rendered with a corresponding verb + λέγων or λέγοντες (depending upon the number of speakers). To suppose that G picked up on this pattern and so included λέγων here—although plausible—is belied by two factors. First, it is not used with a verb of speaking but with שלח/ἀποστέλλω. Thus, this instance does not fit the pattern. Second, לאמור is attested in 4Q27. In this instance and 20.14, λέγων is added after verbs of *sending* and not *speaking*. However, at some point in the MT after Origen's Hexapla (since only these are not marked with the obelus), it was omitted from the MT, perhaps because it fell out of vogue to use לאמר with verbs other than אמר and the like and so was omitted in the Masoretic tradition.

22.11

הנה העם היצא ממצרים ויכס את עין הארץ עתה לכה קבה לי אתו
אולי אוכל להלחם בו וגרשתיו

Ἰδοὺ λαὸς ἐξελήλυθεν ἐξ Αἰγύπτου, καὶ ἰδοὺ κεκάλυφεν[a] τὴν ὄψιν τῆς γῆς, καὶ οὗτος ἐγκάθηται ἐχόμενός μου· καὶ νῦν δεῦρο ἄρασαί μοι αὐτόν, εἰ ἄρα δυνήσομαι πατάξαι αὐτὸν καὶ ἐκβαλῶ αὐτὸν ἀπὸ τῆς γῆς.

'Behold, a people has come out of Egypt, and behold, it [a]covered the sight of the earth, and it is lying in wait next to me. And now come, curse it for me, if indeed I shall be able to strike it, and I will cast it out from the land.'"

[a] κεκάλυφεν. Wevers's critical text reads the perfect form witnessed in Vaticanus and 71 (also in 509 with variant orthography = Ra). Unsurprisingly, circa twenty minuscules attest the form κατεκάλυψεν, harmonizing with verse 5. The rest of the manuscripts, however, read ἐκάλυψεν (aorist). Wevers notes that he would now

regard the aorist form as the original and proposed the emendation to the critical text (1998, 366). The perfect tense was probably an early but secondary harmonization with the perfect form of ἐξελήλυθεν preceding. The lemma text commented on here follows his later opinion and emends the text and translation after it.

Apart from a few minor changes, this verse repeats the message Balak sent with the elders to Balaam in verses 5–6. A comparison of the two reveals that the MT has more changes than G; in other words, G's version of verse 11 is harmonized with verses 5–6. In my opinion, however, it is unlikely that G actually did most (or any?) of the harmonization.

22.5b–6a		22.11	
MT	OG	MT	OG
הנה העם היצא ממצרים	ἰδοὺ λαὸς ἐξελήλυθεν ἐξ Αἰγύπτου	הנה העם היצא ממצרים	ἰδοὺ λαὸς ἐξελήλυθεν ἐξ Αἰγύπτου
הנה כסה את עין הארץ	καὶ ἰδοὺ κατεκάλυψεν τὴν ὄψιν τῆς γῆς	ויכס את עין הארץ	ἰδοὺ ἐκάλυψεν τὴν ὄψιν τῆς γῆς
והוא ישב ממלי	καὶ οὗτος ἐγκάθηται ἐχόμενός μου	(omitted)	καὶ οὗτος ἐγκάθηται ἐχόμενός μου
עתה לכה נא ארה לי את העם הזה	καὶ νῦν δεῦρο ἄρασαί μοι τὸν λαὸν τοῦτον	עתה לכה קבה לי אתו	καὶ νῦν δεῦρο ἄρασαί μοι αὐτόν
כי עצום הוא ממני	ὅτι ἰσχύει οὗτος ἢ ἡμεῖς	(omitted)	(omitted)
אולי אוכל נכה בו	ἐὰν δυνώμεθα πατάξαι ἐξ αὐτῶν	אולי אוכל להלחם בו	εἰ ἄρα δυνήσομαι πατάξαι αὐτὸν
ואגרשנו מן הארץ	καὶ ἐκβαλῶ αὐτοὺς ἐκ τῆς γῆς	וגרשתיו (omitted)	καὶ ἐκβαλῶ αὐτὸν ἀπὸ τῆς γῆς

Most of the substantial differences are due to a variance in *Vorlage*. On λαὸς ἐξελήλυθεν and העם היצא, see below in the commentary proper. Whereas MT has three "omissions" in verse 11 when compared to verses 5–6, G and 4Q27 adds in two of them. Although the MT has no counterpart to καὶ οὗτος ἐγκάθηται ἐχόμενός μου, 4Q27 has והואה ישב [ממולי]. Furthermore, there is a good possibility that the final letter of this verse in 4Q27 is a צ, thus probably reading מן הארץ. Here, at least, there is good reason for thinking that G was reading a (harmonized) text akin to 4Q27. All three, however, do omit the phrase ὅτι ἰσχύει οὗτος ἢ ἡμεῖς/כי עצום הוא ממני.

Beyond these differences in *Vorlage*, G uses the same phrase, δεῦρο ἄρασαί μοι, to render both לכה נא ארה לי (v. 6) and לכה קבה לי (v. 11). Conversely, אולי is rendered with ἐάν in verse 6 and εἰ ἄρα in verse 11; 4Q27 clearly attests אולי as well, for which see below.

λαὸς ἐξελήλυθεν. The MT reads "the people *who* came out"; that is, a definite substantive modified by an articular attributive participle. This substantival phrase becomes the subject of the verb כסה, which naturally follows without an intervening conjunction. The presence of καί before ἰδοὺ ἐκάλυψεν alerts us to a change. G's first clause is a full verbal clause, not a subject phrase. Insofar as 4Q27 reads הנה עם יצא (cf. the MT's העם היצא) it is with reasonable certainty that we can propose that G was in fact reading a verbal clause followed by ויכס, another verbal clause. Wevers offers some speculation regarding the origin of these variant Hebrew readings (1998, 366). If it was יצא that he had before him, he rendered it with a perfect, rather than an aorist. See commentary on 22.5 for the significance of the perfect.

καὶ ἰδοὺ ἐκάλυψεν τὴν ὄψιν τῆς γῆς. Given the above explication, ἰδού must have arisen through harmonization with verse 5, either by G himself or his *Vorlage*. G does not sustain the stative aspect of the perfect verb with which he began, but makes use of an aorist (ἐκάλυψεν). If the translator is making an oblique reference to Israel's functional defeat of the land Egypt (see above on v. 5), then the aorist in fact fits the situation better—that is, *they covered*. If, on the other hand, it refers to the covering of the earth as a metaphor of Israel's capability, the perfect would indeed fit the context better—that is, *they are* (or *have been*) *covering*.

καὶ οὗτος ἐγκάθηται ἐχόμενός μου. This phrase is not present in the MT, but as argued above, likely in G's parent text. It also appears in 22.5; see commentary there.

καὶ νῦν δεῦρο ἄρασαί μοι αὐτόν. This phrase appears exactly as it does in 22.6 (see commentary there). However, the MT, which we are taking as G's *Vorlage* for lack of any other witnesses, varies in three ways primarily. First, the often-untranslated particle of entreaty, נא, although present in 22.6, does not appear in the MT here. Second, the verb represented by ἄρασαί is אֹר in 22.6 but קבב here. This is the first occurrence of the latter in Numbers, but it appears ten times in Num 22–24; ἀράομαι renders it only here and 23.8, but καταράομαι or a cognate is preferred (8x). G's phrasing here is likely influenced by the parallel text in 22.6. Third, the third-person pronoun is present in both MT and LXX, whereas the phrase τὸν λαὸν τοῦτον/העם הזה את appears in 22.6; αὐτόν neatly refers to λαός, as well as corresponding to the MT's אתו in gender and number.

εἰ ἄρα δυνήσομαι πατάξαι αὐτόν. Curiously, instead of representing אולי with ἐάν, as he does in verse 6, G uses the collocation εἰ ἄρα, which can carry the sense "perhaps" (see BDAG, s.v. "ἄρα," 3). Smyth states, εἰ ἄρα is "commonly used of that which is improbable or undesirable" (§2790). It appears only four times in the entire LXX tradition: Gen 18.3; Num 22.11; Ps 57[58].12; OG Dan 6.21. An example from Thucydides, *Hist.* 1.27, is instructive: ἐδεήθησαν δὲ καὶ τῶν Μεγαρέων ναυσὶ σφᾶς ξυμπροπέμψαι [συμπροπέμψαι], εἰ ἄρα κωλύοιντο ὑπὸ Κερκυραίων πλεῖν ("But they beseeched also the Megareans to join in escorting them with boats, if perchance [εἰ ἄρα] they might be forbidden to sail by the Corcyraeans"). In Thucydides, the εἰ ἄρα clause states some *undesirable* event; in Num 22.11, it states two improbable outcomes. Thus, the rendering here implies that Balak's desired outcome is quite unlikely, which is working against the narrative context in which Balak is attempting to flatter Balaam. Although G uses four different glosses for the five occurrences of אולי in the Balaam episode (see at 22.6), εἰ ἄρα carries the sense better than the others. *BdA* does not recognize the difference between εἰ ἄρα and ἐάν and renders both "dans l'espoir." NETS is similarly problematic, reading "if" at 22.6 and "if indeed" at 22.11. A better rendering for 22.11 might be, "*perhaps* I shall be able to strike it." LXX.D captures it well: εἰ ἄρα is rendered with *vielleicht* (22.11) and ἐάν with *wenn* (22.6).

The MT here is smoother than the parallel 22.6, using a first person common singular with an infinitive phrase, להלחם, as opposed to the obscure נכה בו. In 22.6, G offered the rendering δυνώμεθα πατάξαι ἐξ αὐτῶν ("we might be able to strike some of them") for this difficult phrase. In 22.11, G uses the same lemmata to render both, δύναμαι and πατάσσω, but does not render the ב with a preposition (see ἐκ in v. 6). He also switches the tense and mood from present subjunctive to future indicative and the number from plural to singular. The future tense coheres well with his use of εἰ ἄρα and with the following future, ἐκβαλῶ—that is, a future possibility.

The four occurrences of לחם *niphal* + ב, a standard Hebrew idiom for "fight against," in OG Numbers are all rendered differently: πολομέω + πρός (21.1), πολομέω + accusative (21.26; see also Exod 1.10; 14.25; Deut 1.30), παρατάσσω + dative (21.23; see also Exod 17.9, 10), and πατάσσω + accusative (here). Nowhere else in the Pentateuch, however, does πατάσσω translate לחם. In the twenty-one other occurrences of πατάσσω in OG Numbers, it always renders a form of נכה. Thus, it is a safe assumption that G rendered it to match 22.6, preferring consistency over what may have been his usual lexical choice in other contexts. A simple accusative is the preferred object of πατάσσω; curiously, this is the case in every instance but 22.6. A combination of preference for rendering two parallel texts similarly and a tendency towards acceptability explains how the present reading might have arisen.

καὶ ἐκβαλῶ αὐτὸν ἀπὸ τῆς γῆς. As mentioned above, whereas MT has only וגרשתיו, it is likely that G's parent had מן הארץ as well, probably witnessed in 4Q27. The MT in 22.6 has a *yiqtol* form with a suffixed third person mascular singular pronoun, but a suffixed *weqatal* in 22.11. G uses the future ἐκβαλῶ in both instances, which suits the context well. However, in 22.6 he renders the pronoun *ad sensum* with a plural and in 22.11, he renders it according to its grammatical number with a singular.

22.12

ויאמר אלהים אל בלעם לא תלך עמהם לא תאר את העם כי ברוך
הוא

καὶ εἶπεν ὁ θεὸς πρὸς Βαλαάμ Οὐ πορεύσῃ μετ' αὐτῶν οὐδὲ καταράσῃ
τὸν λαόν· ἔστιν γὰρ εὐλογημένος.

And God said to Balaam, "You shall not go with them, nor shall you curse the people, for it is blessed."

Οὐ πορεύσῃ μετ' αὐτῶν. The MT represents God's prohibition to Balaam with the normal negative and a *yiqtol*. G follows this closely; οὐ μή can be used to express a dramatic or strong prohibition (Smyth §1919, 2756), but G chooses the simple οὐ—which is attested everywhere in the manuscripts—to express denial of permission (Smyth §1917). Contextually, G's choice is the better of the two. The verb πορεύομαι is G's preferred rendering of הלך, using it about about twenty times throughout the thirty-seven occurrences of הלך in Numbers. In the Balaam episode, it appears thirteen times to designate the simple act of moving between locations. However, if the context warrants a further nuance, G is not hesitant to use ἀποτρέχω ("hurry away"; e.g., 22.13; 24.14), ἀπέρχομαι ("depart"; e.g., 24.25 [2x]), ἀκολουθέω ("follow"; e.g., 22.20) or δεῦρο ("come!"; e.g., 22.6, 11, 16).

οὐδὲ καταράσῃ τὸν λαόν. Instead of breaking the syntax into two parallel clauses as the MT does ("you will not … you will not"), G uses the coordinating compound negative particle, οὐδέ. This may have been influenced by 4Q27's אל … ואל structure, which read אל rather than the MT's לא and a conjunction (ואל) rather than an asyndetic construction. There is a conjunction in SamPent, Pesh, Vulgate, Tg. Neof. and twelve Kennicott manuscripts (see Wevers 1998, 367 n. 20). In all likelihood, G has before him a text with a conjunction. Since there is a negative clause preceding this clause in Greek, οὐδέ is properly rendered with "nor," as NETS has it. Of the twenty-three occurrences of οὐδέ in Numbers, ten of them render ולא. G chooses his preferred rendering of ארר, καταράομαι. Some stylistic coherency is added by using cognates in 22.12 and 13 (ἀράομαι and καταράομαι), whereas the MT has קבב and ארר, respectively.

ἔστιν γὰρ εὐλογημένος. A strictly isomorphic rendering would have lead to something like ὅτι εὐλογημένος οὗτος. G's reading, however, is much less clumsy. The reorganization of the syntax probably developed from the choice to use the postpositive γὰρ rather than ὅτι (see also at 21.26). Then, for stylistic reasons, G moves the copula to the front and makes the participle εὐλογημένος the final element.

22.13

ויקם בלעם בבקר ויאמר אל שרי בלק לכו אל ארצכם כי מאן יהוה
לתתי להלך עמכם

καὶ ἀναστὰς Βαλαὰμ τὸ πρωὶ εἶπεν τοῖς ἄρχουσιν Βαλάκ Ἀποτρέχετε πρὸς τὸν κύριον ὑμῶν· οὐκ ἀφίησίν με ὁ θεὸς πορεύεσθαι μεθ' ὑμῶν. And after Balaam rose in the morning, he said[a] to the rulers of Balak, "Run off to your master; God does not permit me to go with you."

[a] NETS reads "And Balaam rose up in the morning and he said," giving the impression that G employed simple parataxis—which is not the case here. My rendering above understands the participle as temporal. See again at 22.14.

καὶ ἀναστὰς Βαλαὰμ τὸ πρωί. G's concern to produce an acceptable text is clear here, although he leaves the unidiomatic καί, isomorphically rendering the Hebrew ו, which is not needed in the Greek construction. First, he employs the *participium coniunctum* construction, thus making εἶπεν the main verb (see also Gen 24.25 [καὶ ἀναστὰς πρωὶ εἶπεν]; 26.31). This is the first use of ἀνίστημι in the Balaam episode; however, it is used ten times in chapters 22–24 and only six times in the rest of the book. In all but 22.22, it renders a form of קוּם. The adverb πρωί with or without an article is used frequently in the Pentateuch to render בבקר ("in the morning"), beginning at Gen 19.27 (ca. 35x). In Numbers, every occurrence of בבקר is rendered with τὸ πρωί, the only exception is 22.41. Throughout the OG Pentateuch, this phrase is nearly formulaic in its consistency (see Wevers 1998, 367).

Ἀποτρέχετε. G renders the second-person imperative form of הלך with a more semantically specific lemma (see also Num 24.14); ἀποτρέχω appears only rarely in the rest of the LXX, thirty times in total. In the Pentateuch, it translates הלך (Gen 12.19; 24.51; Exod 3.21; 10.24), שוב (Gen 32.10; Leu 25.41), and יצא (Exod 21.5, 7). Whereas שוב and יצא are semantically closer to ἀποτρέχω than הלך, there is a clear precedent for rendering הלך with ἀποτρέχω, particularly in contexts where הלך indicates departure. Indeed, LSJ notes "depart" and "run home" as its definitions. NETS could just as well have had "run home" or "depart" (cf. BdA, "Repartez;" LXX.D, "Kehrt … zurück).

πρὸς τὸν κύριον ὑμῶν. The MT reads "to your land" here, as does Pesh, Tg. Onq., and Tg. Neof. However, G reads πρὸς τὸν κύριον ("to your master"). According to Nathan Jastram, 4Q27 *may* have read עדוניכמה ("to your master"), rightly marking every letter except the two final letters with a hollow dot, מה (Jastram 1994, 232). Thus, it may be that G was reading "to your lord" in his parent text. I disagree, then, with Wevers's assertion that "This is a somewhat free paraphrase of MT, which had ארצכם" (1998, 367). On the reading in 4Q27, Wevers notes, "the first letters of ארציכמה seem to be an equally possible transcription based on the Plate" (1998, 367 n. 22). In the absence of high-resolution photographs to examine the "scant" ink, Jastram's analysis must stand. In my opinion, G's careful and quite literal translation militates against Wevers's assertion that this is "a somewhat free paraphrase" and it is better to see this as present in G's Hebrew text—albeit difficult to discern from 4Q27. G's rendering "to your

master" better suits the context than the MT, "to your land" (אל ארצכם),
since the messengers have been sent from Balak, designated as "the messengers of Balak," and delivered the words of Balak (so also Wevers 1998,
367; cf. Rösel and Schlund 2011, 482).

οὐκ ἀφίησίν με ὁ θεός. G neglects to render the כי, and simply adds this
clause to the previous one asyndetically; We^ed accordingly adds a raised
dot to mark the break in G's syntax. The MT employs the construction
מאן+ infinitive of נתן to convey God's denial of permission (Exod 22.16;
Num 20.21; 22.13). G's construction is not isomorphic, but a rather idiomatic paraphrase, since he uses the phrase οὐ + ἀφίημι to render this
whole construction. Compare with Exod 22.16 (μὴ βούληται ὁ πατὴρ αὐτῆς
δοῦναι) and Num 20.21 (καὶ οὐκ ἠθέλησεν Ἐδὼμ δοῦναι); see also Gen 37.35;
39.8; 48.19; Deut 25.7. Curiously, in Num 22.14, מאן appears again with an
infinitive and G renders it with οὐ θέλει.

Indeed, οὐκ ἀφίημι appears only here in the OG Pentateuch to render
מאן + infinitive of נתן. Yet the other two instances of a negated ἀφίημι in
the Pentateuch render לא נתן, conveying denial of permission (Gen 20.6;
Exod 12.23), which may explain the choice of ἀφίημι by G here to express
the same.

θεός. Finally, G uses θεός for יהוה, as he did in 22.12 and passim following (22.22, 23, 24, 25, 26, 27, 28, 31, 32, 35). For an overview of this
phenomenon, consult the table at verse 9.

22.14

ויקומו שרי מואב ויבאו אל בלק ויאמרו מאן בלעם הלך עמנו
καὶ ἀναστάντες οἱ ἄρχοντες Μωὰβ ἦλθον πρὸς Βαλὰκ καὶ εἶπαν Οὐ
θέλει Βαλαὰμ πορευθῆναι μεθ᾽ ἡμῶν
And when the rulers of Moab arose, they went[a] to Balak and said,
"Balaam does not want to go with us."

[a] NETS again gives the impression that G has retained the parataxis of his source,
rendering "And the rulers of Moab arose and went." My translation here reflects
the adverbial participle followed asyndetically by the finite clause. See also at
22.13.

καὶ ἀναστάντες οἱ ἄρχοντες Μωὰβ ἦλθον. G renders the wayyiqtol form of
קום just as he did in 22.13 with a participium coniunctum. On the καί, see

at 22.14. Similarly, as in 22.13, G again follows the convention of his target language and does not supply καί for the *waw* on ויבא.

Οὐ θέλει Βαλαὰμ πορευθῆναι μεθ᾽ ἡμῶν. As in 22.13, the construction מאן + infinitive appears here. G's rendering in both instances produces readable Greek expressed in two different ways. Compared to the previous instance, G now uses the periphrasis οὐ + θέλω for the single word מאן. His rendering coheres with Genesis's precedent to use a similar construction (Gen 37.35; 39.8; 48.19; see also Exod 10.4; Num 20.21; Deut 25.7), but differs from the translator of Exodus's preferred construction of οὐ/μή + βούλομαι (Exod 4.23; 7.27; 9.2; 10.3; 16.28; 22.17 [MT 16]).

The astute reader of G's text would notice that a slight transformation has taken place. Balaam's response to the rulers of Balak was "God does not permit me to go with you" (22.13). However, the rulers report that, "Balaam *does not want* to go with us" (22.14). This, however, is clearly not the case. The MT does not suffer from a similar problem. The rulers repeat to Balak in 22.14 MT Balaam's words in 22.13 MT: "Balaam refused." On the one hand, G's rendering follows translational equivalents established in the rest of the Pentateuch. On the other, it leads G to a slight, but significant, retelling of the narrative appearing in his *Vorlage*. In light of G's transformation, Balak's response in the following verse makes good sense: he offers rich rewards to entice Balaam. There is a warrant for suggesting that G's transformation is intentional. It is in the fact that he has carefully selected his translational equivalents for מאן in 22.13 and 14, and not allowed one stereotyped rendering to flatten the narrative.

22.15

ויסף עוד בלק שלח שרים רבים ונכבדים מאלה

καὶ προσέθετο ἔτι Βαλὰκ ἀποστεῖλαι ἄρχοντας πλείους καὶ ἐντιμοτέρους τούτων

And Balak added again to send rulers, more numerous and more distinguished than these.

καὶ προσέθετο ἔτι Βαλὰκ ἀποστεῖλαι. The combination προστίθημι + infinitive is well known as an equivalent for יסף + infinitive (ca. 55x in the Pentateuch alone; see Thackeray 52–53). NETS's rendering, "and Balak added again," conveys the stilted nature of the Greek rendering under influence of the Semitic parent (*pace* LXX.D, "Und so sandte Balak noch einmal" and *BdA*, "Et de nouveau encore Balak envoya," but see Dorival 1994, 424,

"Balak ajouta encore d'envoyer"). Only in Gen 8.10 is יסף rendered with πάλιν, followed by a finite verb that represents the Hebrew infinitive; יסף עוד is a common collocation in the MT (e.g., Gen 18.29; 38.5, 26), which is consistently rendered by προστίθημι ἔτι in the OG.

The infinitive ἀποστεῖλαι is the Hebraistic complement to προσέθετο, since προστίθημι prefers to take nouns for objects (see LSJ, s.v. "προστίθημι"). In Numbers, G renders שלח with ἐξαποστέλλω only in 5.2, 3, 4; 13.2. Subsequently, the simpler form ἀποστέλλω is used. Furthermore, G prefers the aorist infinitive (123x) to the present in a ratio slightly over 2:1.

ἄρχοντας πλείους καὶ ἐντιμοτέρους τούτων. Balak responds to Balaam's refusal by sending *more numerous* (πλείους) and *more honorable* (ἐντιμοτέρους) emissaries. Elsewhere, G has used the comparative πλείων to render forms of רב (Num 9.19; 20.15; 26.54; 33.54)—but they are merely intensive and not true comparatives (see Smyth §1067). The near demonstrative τούτων must refer to those who had just returned. Although G does not render מן with a separate word, his rendering is grammatically sufficient on levels of adequacy and acceptability. Since τούτων and the "greater rulers" both refer to emissaries sent from Balak, the bare genitive indicates that the comparison is between the two groups, not two different people who sent emissaries (Smyth §1069a–b: "The genitive is usual if ... two objects have the same verb in common").

The MT uses a participle נכבדים where G uses a comparative adjective, ἐντιμοτέρους; ἐντιμοτέρους appears only here in Numbers and a positive form appears in Deut 25.28, rendering a participial form of כבד (also Ies 3.5). This simple change in grammatical category makes the two comparative adjectives coordinate, and so was probably made for stylistic reasons.

22.16

ויבאו אל בלעם ויאמרו לו כה אמר בלק בן צפור אל נא תמנע מהלך
אלי

καὶ ἦλθον πρὸς Βαλααμ καὶ λέγουσιν αὐτῷ Τάδε λέγει Βαλὰκ ὁ τοῦ Σεπφώρ Ἀξιῶ σε, μὴ ὀκνήσῃς ἐλθεῖν πρός με·

And they came to Balaam and said to him, "This is what Balak son of Sepphor says, 'I beg you, do not hesitate to come to me.

This verse represents a departure from G's normal style, including a present tense for *wayyiqtol* form, ὁ τοῦ Σεπφώρ for בֶּן צִפּוֹר, and translation of the particle נָא. Nevertheless, the translation is quite smooth in Greek.

καὶ ἦλθον πρὸς Βαλαὰμ καὶ λέγουσιν αὐτῷ. Coming and speaking is a common consecution in Numbers. However, G rarely renders the first *wayyiqtol* with an aorist and the second with a present; his usual convention is to render both *wayyiqtol* forms with aorists linked with καὶ (in the immediate context, see Num 22.7, 9, 14, 20; cf. 32.16 where an aorist is followed by an imperfect). Likely, as Wevers points out, the present is a historical present (1998, 368; see also 20.19; 22.28, 30). Smyth notes, "in lively or dramatic narration the present may be used to represent a past action as going on at the moment of speaking or writing" (§1883). G's choice, in other words, is for stylistic and narratological reasons.

Τάδε λέγει. The phrase τάδε λέγει is a stereotypical rendering for כֹּה אָמַר (see Wevers 1998, 368). Apart from the first occurrence of כֹּה אָמַר in Gen 32.5, which is rendered by οὕτως λέγει, τάδε λέγει is found circa 360 times in the OG.

ὁ τοῦ Σεπφώρ. This phrase renders בֶּן צִפּוֹר and is an idiomatic construction, in contradistinction to more-literal υἱὸς Σεπφώρ in 22.2, 4. In Numbers, this idiomatic construction appears thirteen times to render the phrase בֶּן + proper noun. Its more literal counterpart, υἱός, is used with much greater frequency. Since G is not bound by (admittedly contrived) categories of *literal* and *free*, he spontaneously chooses to use ὁ τοῦ Σεπφώρ although it does comport with his idiomatic rendering in the rest of the verse.

Ἀξιῶ σε. G now translates the particle נָא with a verbal clause. Although rarely choosing to render it, he does so in Num 12.13 with δέομαι σου (cf. 12.11; see also Gen 19.18). The verb ἀξιόω itself means "request, ask" (see LSJ, s.v. "ἀξιόω," II.2). Relatively speaking, the lemma itself appears infrequently in the LXX outside of Tobit and 1–4 Makkabees and only rarely with the meaning "to ask" (see, e.g., Esth 4.8; 7.8; Dan OG/θ 1.8; 2.16). According to Wevers, "the translator wants to record the pleading character of this second invitation" (1998, 368; see also Dorival 1994, 424).

The phrase ἀξιῶ σε is, however, quite commonly found in the papyri; for example, P.Enteux. AppB (246–222 BCE, Ghoran), ἀξιῶ οὖν σε, ἐπειδὴ διὰ τὸ ἰσχύειν αὐτὸν ταῦτα συντ[ετέλεσται, μεταπεμψάμενον αὐτὸν ἐπαναγκάσαι ἀποδοῦναί μοι τὴν … εὐτύχει ("I ask you, therefore, since he is stronger, complete these things"). It is frequently followed by an infinitive (see, e.g., BGU 3.1006 [third century BCE, unknown provenance]; BGU 6.1244 [225 BCE, Herakleopolite Nome]). Thus, it is likely that G picked up this formula from the conventional language of his Ptolemaic environs.

μὴ ὀκνήσῃς ἐλθεῖν. The word ὀκνέω is used only here in the Pentateuch and elsewhere only six times (Judg A/S 18.9; Idt 12.13; Tob 12.6, 13; 4 Makk 14.4; Sir 7.35). It renders מנע, which can be used with a direct object to mean "hold back something, deprive." Here, the infinitive construct form is attached to a מ, indicating the action from which he should not hold back (see 1 Sam 25.26; Jer 2.25). The phrase ὀκνέω + infinitive carries the sense of "to hesitate," capturing the sense of the Hebrew well here.

22.17

כי כבד אכבדך מאד וכל אשר תאמר אלי אעשה ולכה נא קבה לי
את העם הזה

ἐντίμως γὰρ τιμήσω σε, καὶ ὅσα ἂν εἴπῃς, ποιήσω σοι· καὶ δεῦρο ἐπικατάρασαί μοι τὸν λαὸν τοῦτον.

For I will honor you honorably, and whatever things you say I will do for you. And come, curse for me this people."'

ἐντίμως γὰρ τιμήσω σε. Elsewhere, G renders the intensifying infinitive absolute with a cognate participle (12.14; 13.30 [1°]; 22.30; 24.10; 30.7, 13, 15, 16), cognate noun in the nominative (13.30 [2°]), dative (14.18; 15.31, 35; 18.15; 23.25; 26.65; 35.16, 17, 18, 21, 26, 31), or accusative (23.11; 27.7; 30.3), or quite freely (22.38). This distribution more or less matches that of the entire LXX's renderings of infinitive absolutes (see Tov 1999, esp. 253). In 24.11, the same Hebrew construction (כבד אכבדך) is not rendered with any representation of the infinitive absolute. Thus, the use of the adverb is unusual for G; in the LXX, Tov counts only eleven (Tov 1999, 253). However, its presence might help explain why G did not render מאד: perhaps a concern for acceptability prohibits overloading a verb with adverbial modifiers. Not only is this construction rare but ἐντίμως itself appears only here and in Tobit in the LXX.

The conjunction γάρ conveys the reason for the preceding command, rather than the direct cause. G often renders כי with ὅτι, leading to some grammatical infelicities, such as the one noted at 22.6 and elsewhere in the LXX (see again Aejmelaeus 1993, 11–30). G's choice of γάρ here suits the context.

καὶ ὅσα ἄν. G neglects כּוֹל, which he also does elsewhere and simply leaves ὅσα as a headless relative (see also 4.26 [2°], 6.3; 16.33). Headless ὅσος clauses are also found at 23.12; 24.13; 32.31, making a total of six in Numbers. In compositional Greek, ὅσος can take on the meaning of πᾶς (see Mayser §§2.3.95; 2.1.345, and the examples cited there). Consider, for example, the following occurrence of ὅσος in P. Grenf 1.21 (126 BCE): ἐκαταλείπω καὶ [δίδωμι τὰ ὑπάρχοντά μοι ἔγγαι]ά τε καὶ ἔπιπλα καὶ κτήνη καὶ ὅσα ἂν προσεπικτήσωμαι ("I bequeath and give my property in land and movable objects and cattle and whatever else [= everything] I may have acquired"; trans. Hunt and Edgar, LCL) Accordingly, G's rendering captures the quantitative sense of אֲשֶׁר כּוֹל (see *HALOT*, s.v. "כּוֹל," 10) neatly in his idiomatic phrasing.

In addition, G uses a subjunctive verb with ἄν, marking conditionality. Thus, G's *whatever* things you [might] say I will do *for you*" (NETS, emphasis added) makes the contingency of what Balaam is permitted to say explicit—there are no limits!—while at the same time making implicit whom Balaam is to speak to by omitting the MT's "to me." For a point of comparison, Balak's promise to Balaam in the MT is, "all that you should say *to me*, I will do."

εἴπῃς, ποιήσω σοι. G does not render אֵלַי in the MT (תֹּאמַר אֵלַי). The effect of this is to leave Balak's statement as open-ended as possible. However, G has σοι in agreement with 4Q27—which reads אֶעֱשֶׂ[ה לְכָה—against MT. Unfortunately, 4Q27 is lost at אֵלַי. Reading "I will do for you" (OG, 4Q27, Pesh MS 7a1), makes good sense in the present context; otherwise, it is only implied that Balak's words denote his eagerness to reward Balaam in whichever way he pleased.

καὶ δεῦρο ἐπικατάρασαί μοι τὸν λαὸν τοῦτον. As G has done previously (e.g., 22.6, 11), he renders לְכָה with δεῦρο and does not represent נָא. The verb ἐπικατάραομαι is used only rarely in the LXX and primarily in Numbers (elsewhere, Ps 151.6; Mal 2.2). It renders forms of אָרַר in Num 5 (7x) and is not used again until this occurrence. On other cursing language, see at verse 6; ἐπικατάραομαι translates קָבַב; however, in 23.7 it translates אָרַר. G does not seem to make a distinction between the Greek lexemes he chooses or the Hebrew words he renders; *pace* Wevers, who notes that the change to ἐπικαταράομαι "was intended to reflect the change from ארה in v[erse] 6 to קבה here" (1998, 369; note that קבב also appears in verse 11 and is rendered with ἀράομαι). However, the compound form does seem to match the heightened emphasis of Balak's second request to Balaam.

22.18

ויען בלעם ויאמר אל עבדי בלק אם יתן לי בלק מלא ביתו כסף וזהב
לא אוכל לעבר את פי יהוה אלהי לעשות קטנה או גדולה

καὶ ἀπεκρίθη Βαλαὰμ καὶ εἶπεν τοῖς ἄρχουσιν Βαλάκ Ἐὰν δῷ μοι Βαλὰκ πλήρη τὸν οἶκον αὐτοῦ ἀργυρίου καὶ χρυσίου, οὐ δυνήσομαι παραβῆναι τὸ ῥῆμα κυρίου τοῦ θεοῦ ποιῆσαι αὐτὸ μικρὸν ἢ μέγα ἐν τῇ διανοίᾳ μου·

And Balaam answered and said to the rulers of Balak, "If Balak gives me his house full of silver and gold, I shall not be able to transgress the word of the Lord God to do it, whether small or great in my mind.

τοῖς ἄρχουσιν Βαλάκ. In every other instance of either "rulers of Balak" or "rulers of Moab" in the Balaam episode, the MT uses a plural construct form of שר. Here, however, the MT has עבדי בלק. G does not depart from his normal strategy and renders with the formulaic τοῖς ἄρχουσιν Βαλάκ (e.g., 22.8, 13, 14, 35). Unfortunately, neither 4Q23 nor 4Q27 are extant at this phrase. Moreover, Tg. Neof., Tg. Onq., and Pesh all witness to "his servants." We[ed] does not note any telling differences in the manuscript tradition. Thus, it is probably best to conclude that G rendered עבדי בלק with ἄρχουσιν Βαλάκ according to his established pattern (also Dorival 1994, 424; Rösel and Schlund 2011, 483). Therefore, this could count as inner-Greek harmonization (see Tov 1985, 20).

Ἐὰν δῷ μοι Βαλάκ. This phrase serves as the protasis of a conditional sentence. G selects ἐάν + aorist subjunctive (δῷ) to render אם + yiqtol rather than εἰ + future indicative. Interpretations of what the commonly used ἐάν + subjunctive means are many (see Tjen 2010, 56–67), but I follow Tjen in affirming that it "expresses various ranges of possibility" (Tjen 2010, 67) but not a "vivid future condition" (contra Smyth §2323). The future in the apodosis (δυνήσομαι) is usual in these constructions (see Smyth §2326). Therefore, the Greek protasis suggests that *whatever* Balak chooses to do will not change Balaam's response.

πλήρη τὸν οἶκον αὐτοῦ ἀργυρίου καὶ χρυσίου. The expression מלא ביתו כסף
וזהב and its rendering, πλήρη τὸν οἶκον ἀργυρίου καὶ χρυσίου, are difficult
(see also Num 24.13); מלא is the head noun ("fullness," "full amount"; see
HALOT), followed by a genitive phrase ביתו, which could be analyzed as
a attributive genitive (see Joüon §129.c.1) or partitive (Joüon §129.c.8). I
prefer the latter. In this interpretation of the MT, he is giving the fullness
of the gold and silver in his house (i.e., not his house itself). However, G
uses an idiomatic expression that uses the adjective πλήρης with a noun in
the same case (as opposed to with a genitive noun, see LSJ, s.v. "πλήρης,"
I). When πλήρης is used with a noun of the same case, the fullness or completeness of the noun itself is expressed (see LSJ, s.v. "πλήρης," III.2). For
example, see Xenophon, *Anab.* 7.5.5: εἰ γὰρ ἐκήδου, ἧκες ἂν φέρων πλήρη
τὸν μισθόν ("For if you cared, you would have come bringing the full
wage"); also, P. Rev. Laws 17.2–3 (258 BCE): καὶ ἀπέ[χ]ηι ὁ [ο]ἰκονό[μος]
πλῆρες τὸ ἀδιέγγυον μέρο[ς τῆς] ὠνῆς ("and the steward received the full
portion of the price not covered by security"). In this way, it comes close
to meaning "entire" or "totality of." Here then, G has Balaam saying that
if Balak will give his entire house, and so on. Of importance is the genitive
following the head noun; it functions as a standard genitive of content (see
Smyth §1323). Putting it all together, G's Greek construction, according
to the rules of idiomatic Greek, could be paraphrased as "the entire house
containing silver and gold," *not* "the house full of silver and gold."

οὐ δυνήσομαι παραβῆναι τὸ ῥῆμα κυρίου τοῦ θεοῦ. Tjen notes that a protasis
of ἐάν + subjunctive—as is found here—is frequently followed by a future
indicative (2010, 39, 43). The effect here is to say that no bribe or reward
that Balak can give will alter Balaam's inability to transgress the word of
God. Wevers notes that παραβαίνω, although rendering עבר only eleven
times, is a contextually sensitive rendering conveying the moral connota-
tion (1998, 370–71).

The MT employs an idiom to convey what Balaam was not willing to
transgress, namely, "the mouth of the Lord my God." There are two possible explanations for why G might have used τὸ ῥῆμα κυρίου rather than
τὸ στόμα κυρίου or the like. First, G was motivated by an antianthropomor-
phizing exegetical tradition. Second, G is rendering a Hebrew idiom with
an idiom in Greek while retaining quantitative equivalence. If the former
were the case, we would expect to find a *consistent* tendency away from
anthropomorphisms, which we do not. For comparison, it is instructive
to look at Pesh here. Pesh seems to take the second alternative, but using a

different strategy: "the word of the mouth of the Lord." In other words, the Hebrew idiom, "to transgress the mouth" was not an acceptable idiom in Syriac and so he inserted "the word" to increase acceptability in his target language. However, G sticks close to a goal of quantitative equivalence while disallowing the interference of a Hebrew idiom. The second is the better interpretation of G's action here. Elsewhere, G renders על פי יהוה with διὰ φωνῆς κυρίου (4.37, 41, 45, 49).

κυρίου τοῦ θεοῦ. Here the question is why the translator might have neglected to render the suffixed first-person common singular pronoun in the phrase יהוה אלהי ("YHWH, my God"). Again, this is potentially theologically loaded—did G not want to concede that Balaam was actually a worshiper of YHWH? Textual tradition suggests the omission of the pronoun is original until Origen added it. SamPent and Pesh both contain it, and unfortunately, the suffix falls in a lacuna in 4Q27. In Numbers, the consecution of יהוה followed by אלהים + suffix appears six times, and only once with a first person common singular suffix. At 10.9, 10, and 15.41 (2x), the MT reads יהוה אלהיכם, where the second person masculine plural suffix refers to the Israelites. For this phrase, G only has κυρίου at 10.9, but κύριος ὁ θεὸς ὑμῶν at 10.10 and 15.41 (2x). At 23.21, Balaam states יהוה אלהיו עמו and G renders κύριος ὁ θεὸς αὐτοῦ μετ' αὐτοῦ. The suffix on אלהים alone (i.e., without יהוה)—which in all but 25.2 refers to the Israelites and their God—is also consistently rendered by G (see 6.7; 15.40, 41 [2x]; 25.13; 33.4). At 25.2, G is careful to render אלהיהן, referencing to the Moabites' gods, by εἰδώλων αὐτῶν ("their idols"). In the rest of the Pentateuch, the possessive suffix is avoided infrequently. The second person masculine singular suffix is omitted at Gen 27.20; Deut 17.15; 18.5; 19.2; 21.5; 30.1, 3 (2x), 6; a first person common plural is omitted in Exod 8.10 [MT 8.6] and a first person common singular in Deut 4.5. Added to this is the absence of evidence to suggest an alternative *Vorlage*. I tentatively conclude that the omission is best explained from a theological perspective. Rösel and Schlund find that G achieved a distancing of the deity from Balaam: "Die LXX gibt das Suffix des hebr. יהוה אלהי nicht wieder und erreicht damit eine Distanzierung: Balaam wird nicht als JHWH-Verehrer gekennzeichnet" (2011, 483). The solution proposed by Rösel and Schlund makes the best sense: G is distancing the deity from Balaam.

On this rendering's effect on the narrative, Wevers states, "the omission neutralizes the reason for Balak's invitation. After all, as a diviner or prophet who worshipped Yahweh as his God, Balaam's blessing or curse would be more powerful or effective against Israel, the people of Yahweh" (1998, 370). Wevers assumes, according to the MT's account, that Balak was summoning Balaam because he was a prophet of Yahweh himself. *Neutralizes* is perhaps too strong a term here; the omission may weaken the impetus to summon Balaam but does not entirely negate his status as prophet (see 22.6).

ποιῆσαι αὐτὸ μιχρὸν ἢ μέγα. How this infinitive phrase relates to the preceding is difficult to decide; that is, is it epexegetical to παραβῆναι τὸ ῥῆμα κτλ.? Or, a second, asyndetic, infinitive complement to δυνήσομαι? G is not concerned with this, however, since he renders his Hebrew *Vorlage* without making any changes. The word αὐτό, however, is a plus. It could refer to ῥῆμα—the nearest neuter substantive (so Dorival 1994, 425)—but this would make little contextual sense. It seems, rather, that the neuter refers to the entire idea of "transgressing the word of the Lord," or perhaps the act that would have amounted to a transgression (see Wevers 1998, 371). In 24.13, where Balaam repeats his words here, the same addition appears (but with πονηρὸν ἢ καλόν, instead of μιχρὸν ἢ μέγα). Perhaps G feels that "to do a small or great thing" is not actually a transgression, and so he adds "to do it [i.e., a transgression], either small or large." In effect then, Balaam is stating that he cannot transgress God's word in any way for any amount of money that Balak might be able to provide. NETS reads here "to do it, whether small or great." "Whether" has no basis in the OG text, but does accurately capture the sense. It could be translated literally as "to do a small or great thing [i.e., transgressing the word of the Lord God]."

ἐν τῇ διανοίᾳ μου. This, also, is a plus in the OG vis-à-vis MT. The often-harmonizing SamPent, similarly, does not witness this phrase. Prima facie, this addition appears to be harmonized in line with מלבי of 24.13 as Rösel and Schlund suggest: "möglicherweise orientierte sich die LXX auch an מלבי in 24.13" (2011, 483). The Hebrew idiom used at 24.13 is מלבי, meaning "from my own volition" and not "in my thoughts." G apparently understands this and translates it with a nonidiomatic, nonliteral rendering παρ' ἐμαυτοῦ. However, since G uses παρ' ἐμαυτοῦ at 24.13, it is unlikely that G did the harmonizing (see Tov 1985, 20: "Harmonizations which presuppose different Hebrew readings should not be made the center [of an investigation of harmonizations]"). Furthermore, 4Q27 has been reconstructed by Jastram to read בלבי, although the only extant letter is the *lamed*, which is marked as uncertain. Curiously, Wevers does not note this and attributes the change to translation technique (1998, 370–71). On the basis of 4Q27, I submit that there is a good chance that G was indeed reading בלבי in his *Vorlage*.

Since I am arguing that בלבי was in his *Vorlage*, little comment is required beyond noting that G rendered his text well. בלבו, or similar phrases, are rendered with ἐν τῇ διανοίᾳ αὐτοῦ (Gen 17.17; 27.41; 35.34; see also Gen 24.45; cf. Exod 4.14; but ἐν τῇ καρδίᾳ at Exod 36.2). Although this precise phrase does not appear anywhere else in Numbers, לב is rendered with διανοία at 32.7, but καρδία at 32.9. In the Pentateuch, both of these serve as equivalents, with καρδία the more common (ca. 30x) followed by διανοία (ca. 15x; cf. διανοέομαι at Gen 6.6; 8.21 [1°]), but also νοῦς (1x, Exod 7.23) and στῆθος (1x, Exod 28.30).

22.19

ועתה שבו נא בזה גם אתם הלילה ואדעה מה יסף יהוה דבר עמי

καὶ νῦν ὑπομείνατε αὐτοῦ καὶ ὑμεῖς τὴν νύκτα ταύτην, καὶ γνώσομαι,
τί προσθήσει κύριος λαλῆσαι πρός με.

And now remain here, you too, this night, and I will know what the Lord will add to speak to me."

καὶ νῦν ὑπομείνατε αὐτοῦ. On equivalents for ישׁב, see at 22.8. The verb ὑπομένω appears only here in the Pentateuch; previously, a cognate, καταμένω, was used of the rulers of Moab staying the night (22.8); ὑπομένω can mean "wait for," and is often used with an accusative, denoting the object of the waiting. Here, what they are to wait for is implied in the following clause. On αὐτοῦ, see at 22.8. Unlike at 22.8, αὐτοῦ renders the idiomatic prepositional phrase, בזה, similarly meaning "here" (also at Exod 24.14).

τὴν νύκτα ταύτην. On the temporal accusative, see at 22.8. G adds the near demonstrative pronoun here, slightly clarifying the definite nature of the Hebrew.

καὶ γνώσομαι, τί προσθήσει κύριος λαλῆσαι πρός με. G's rendering is isomorphic. The indefinite pronoun τίς often stands in place of the indeclinable מה (e.g., Num 13.19 [MT 13.18]; 15.34; 23.17). For προστίθημι see comments at verse 15. The preposition עם appears twenty times in Numbers and is rendered variously by G, depending on contextual constraints: for example, μετά (10.32; 22.12, 13, 14), ἐν (14.24, 43), παρά (22.8, 9), and πρός

(20.3; 22.19). The verb λαλέω normally appears with πρός (ca. 100x), which has influenced the translation of עם with πρός in these instances. According to G, Balaam expects the Lord (κύριος) to speak *to him*, whereas in the MT he speaks *with* YHWH.

Curiously, G apparently has no problem rendering both דבר עם (22.19) and דבר אל (22.20) with λαλέω πρός. For G, contextual sensitivity and Greek idiom frequently overrides what might be called "consistency."

22.20

ויבא אלהים אל בלעם לילה ויאמר לו אם לקרא לך באו האנשים קום
לך אתם ואך את הדבר אשר אדבר אליך אתו תעשה

καὶ ἦλθεν ὁ θεὸς πρὸς Βαλαὰμ νυκτὸς καὶ εἶπεν αὐτῷ Εἰ καλέσαι σε πάρεισιν οἱ ἄνθρωποι οὗτοι, ἀναστὰς ἀκολούθησον αὐτοῖς· ἀλλὰ τὸ ῥῆμα, ὃ ἂν λαλήσω πρὸς σέ, τοῦτο ποιήσεις.

And God came to Balaam by night and said to him, "If these people are here to call you, rise up, and follow them, but the word that I speak to you—this you shall do."

καὶ ἦλθεν ὁ θεὸς πρὸς Βαλαὰμ νυκτὸς καὶ εἶπεν αὐτῷ. Despite the fact that Balaam states that יהוה/κύριος will speak to him (22.19), אלהים/θεός comes to him. Here, at least, G does not feel the need to make any changes to the divine name. The temporal adverbial accusative לילה is rendered well with a genitive of time (νυκτός), indicating the period of time in which something takes place rather than a point in time or duration of time (see Smyth §1444).

Εἰ καλέσαι σε πάρεισιν οἱ ἄνθρωποι οὗτοι. This is the fourth conditional in the chapter. The following table summarizes the structural elements of the conditionals in Num 22.1–20:

Verse	OG/MT	Protasis	Apodosis
22.6	OG	ἐάν + present subjunctive	καί + future indicative
	MT	אולי + *yiqtol*	*wayyiqtol*
22.11	OG	εἰ (+ἄρα) + future indicative	καί + future indicative
	MT	אולי + *yiqtol*	*weqatal*
22.18	OG	ἐάν + aorist subjunctive	future indicative
	MT	אם + *yiqtol*	*yiqtol*

| 22.20 | OG | εἰ + present indicative | aorist imperative |
| | MT | אִם + *qatal* | imperative |

Tjen identifies aorist subjunctives as the most common renderings of the *qatal* form in Numbers, followed by aorist indicatives and then perfect indicatives. He counts six instances where אִם + *qatal* is rendered with εἰ + present indicative (2010, 139–48). The condition here is not whether or not the men are present (πάρεισιν), but rather whether they intend to call Balaam or not. In contradistinction to the conditionals in 22.6 and 18, G's use of the simple condition here does not suggest that its fulfillment is unlikely or improbable.

Whereas the MT has the men *coming* (בוא) to summon Balaam, G using πάρειμι focuses on the *presence* of the men rather than their action of coming. As Wevers notes, "of course, if someone has come, he is then present" (1998, 371). Logically, the tense must be present for such a change in focus to make sense in the narrative context. This translation effectively reverses the cause (their coming) and effect (their arrival). For reversal as a translational strategy, see van der Louw 2007, 66. A second possible motivation may have been to avoid repeating an aorist of ἔρχομαι (= ἦλθεν) for בוא a second time in the sentence.

On καλέω and cognates, see at 22.5. G follows his *Vorlage* in fronting the complementary infinitive. The periphrastic direct object phrase using the preposition לְ, is well rendered by a simple accusative.

ἀναστὰς ἀκολούθησον αὐτοῖς. Hebrew often places the imperative form of קום (as well as הלך) next to another imperative, indicating an action subordinate to the following imperative. G represents this with the *participium coniunctum* instead of stacking two imperatives next to each other (see also on δεῦρο in 22.6), but as Aejmelaeus remarks, such pleonastic employment of two verbs of motion is unidiomatic (1993, 6). The use of ἀκολουθέω is both idiomatic and semantically more specific than the MT's "go with them" (לך אתם). It represents a slight transformation: the rulers of Balak are not simply Balaam's traveling companions, but they will lead him back to Balak.

ἀλλά. The phrase וְאַךְ is rendered with ἀλλά, apparently neglecting to translate the conjunction וְ and (correctly) interpreting אַךְ as adversative; וְאַךְ is relatively rare in the Pentateuch, appearing only here and Gen 9.5, where it is rendered by καὶ γάρ. In Num 14.19, אך (without the ו) is rendered with ἀλλά; in 18.15 and 31.23, it is rendered with ἀλλ' ἤ. Elsewhere, it is appropriately rendered with πλήν (18.3, 17; 31.22; 36.6). In all likelihood, G regarded the disjunctive sense of אך to be adequately rendered by ἀλλά and ignored the ו conjunction since καὶ ἀλλά is quite awkward in Greek.

τὸ ῥῆμα, ὃ ἂν λαλήσω πρὸς σέ, τοῦτο ποιήσεις. This clause represents a good example where G has followed the word order of his *Vorlage*, but it none-theless produces idiomatic Greek. Syntactically, τὸ ῥῆμα, ὃ ἂν λαλήσω πρὸς σέ is a fronted direct object phrase of the verb ποιήσεις. Thus, the appear-ance of τοῦτο is resumptive. However, resumption in the main clause after a fronted relative clause is idiomatic in Greek, as is found in Xenophon's *Mem.* 2.1.25, οἷς ἂν οἱ ἄλλοι ἐργάζωνται, τούτοις σὺ χρήσῃ ("whatever others acquire by labour, that you shall enjoy"; example and trans. from Smyth §2565). Additionally, Smyth finds that "conditional relative clauses that vividly anticipate the realization of a future event take the subjunctive with ἄν" (§2565). Thus, G's addition of ἄν adds some emphasis or vividness in the Greek that is not present in his *Vorlage*.

22.21

ויקם בלעם בבקר ויחבש את אתנו וילך עם שרי מואב

καὶ ἀναστὰς Βαλαὰμ τὸ πρωὶ ἐπέσαξεν τὴν ὄνον αὐτοῦ, καὶ ἐπορεύθη μετὰ τῶν ἀρχόντων Μωάβ.

And after Balaam rose up in the morning, he saddled[a] his donkey and went with the rulers of Moab.

[a] NETS's translation again suggests that G has retained the parataxis present in the Hebrew: "And Balaam rose up in the morning and saddled his donkey." My translation here reflects the *participium coniunctum* attached asyndetically to the main verb, ἐπέσαξεν (also 22.13, 14).

καὶ ἀναστὰς Βαλαὰμ τὸ πρωί. On this phrase, see at 22.13.

ἐπέσαξεν τὴν ὄνον αὐτοῦ. The Hebrew verb חבש only occurs in one other instance in the Pentateuch meaning "to saddle" (Gen 22.3), elsewhere it means "bind" or "tie up" (Exod 29.9; Leu 8.13). The phrasing in Gen 22.3 OG is very similar to G's phrasing here, despite the fact that their *Vorlagen* differ:

Gen 22.3	Num 22.21
וישכם אברהם בבקר ויחבש את חמרו	ויקם בלעם בבקר ויחבש את אתנו
ἀναστὰς δὲ Ἀβραὰμ τὸ πρωὶ ἐπέσαξεν τὴν ὄνον αὐτοῦ	καὶ ἀναστὰς Βαλαὰμ τὸ πρωὶ ἐπέσαξεν τὴν ὄνον αὐτοῦ

The curious similarity between the Greek of Gen 22.3 and Num 22.21 suggests that perhaps G relied on it to produce his translation here or wanted the reader to recollect Abraham's action, but this lies outside the realm of certainty. Employing the noun ὄνος with the feminine article is a creative way to render the feminine gendered Hebrew word אתון ("she-donkey"), a rendering he uses fourteen times in Num 22.

καὶ ἐπορεύθη μετὰ τῶν ἀρχόντων Μωάβ. In the Greek of verse 20, Balaam was commanded to *follow* (ἀκολουθέω) the men, but now he simply *goes with them* (v. 21). G does not seem concerned with pressing the idea of following here; πορεύομαι + μετά is the expected rendering for עם + הלך (see e.g., 10.32; 22.12). This illustrates well the tendency of G: he alternates between serial fidelity to his *Vorlage*, relying upon established equivalences, and minor modifications that enhance or downplay contextual elements. In other words, consistency is not a characteristic of G's translation technique.

Summary

In this pericope, Balaam is summoned twice by delegates from Balak, the king of Moab, to curse the Israelites. After the second, God allows Balaam to go on the condition that Balaam speaks only what κύριος puts in his mouth. G's translation technique generally adheres closely to his *Vorlage*, but makes minor departures to improve the Greek style or subtly interpret the narrative.

A Tale of Two Eunuchs:
A Commentary on Greek Esther 2.19–23 and A.12–17

Cameron Boyd-Taylor

The Septuagint version of Esther (OG) poses significant challenges to the SBLCS commentator. Not only is the Greek narrative substantially longer than that of the Masoretic text (MT), but where it does parallel the Hebrew the relationship between the two is not always transparent. There is moreover some likelihood that OG underwent redaction subsequent to its translation from the Hebrew. Complicating matters further is the existence of the so-called L text (Alpha text = AT), preserved in only four manuscripts, which was once thought to be Lucianic. While the textual history underlying OG and AT is far from obvious, the current consensus denies that one is a straightforward recension of the other. If one's aim is to comment on the text-as-produced, Esther proves resistant. One way of proceeding is to distinguish between the text that comes down to us, the received text, a heterogeneous entity with a complex history, and the material shared by OG and MT, where there is sufficient transparency to delineate the methods of a translator (G) working with a source text. The focus of the commentary would be the latter. While the overall design of the text-as-received would not be lost sight of, it would not be the primary object of analysis. Rather one would begin with the parallel material and proceed inductively, speaking to the question put by the Guidelines: what has the translator done, and why. Issues in the history of the text would thus be bracketed. In the following commentary I employ this methodology. The pericope I have chosen—the discovery by Mardochaios of a plot against the Persian king by two eunuchs—exemplifies the problems raised by a composite text. In OG the pericope is mirrored in two episodes, Esth 2.19–23 (plot[1]) and A.12–17 (plot[2]), a doublet unique to the LXX version, as the former lacks a parallel in AT and the latter a parallel in MT, Josephus, and the Old Latin (OL). While almost identical structurally, each text arguably functions as a distinct scene within the narrative in its final form. Yet only the translation of plot[1] may be securely attributed to G. For the purposes of the present commentary plot[2] is therefore treated as part of the text-as-received. It will be the subject of §2. I shall begin with plot[1].

Literature

♦ **Aeschines**. 1919. *Speeches*. Translated by C. D. Adams. LCL 106. Cambridge: Harvard University Press. ♦ **Aristophanes**. 1998. *Clouds; Wasps; Peace*. Translated by Jeffrey Henderson. LCL 488. Cambridge: Harvard University Press. ♦ **Aristotle**. 1926. *Nicomachean Ethics*. Translated by H. Rackham. LCL 73. Cambridge: Harvard University Press. ♦ **Bingen**, Jean. 2007. *Hellenistic Egypt: Monarchy, Society, Economy, Culture*. HCS 49. Berkeley: University of California. ♦ **Brosius**, Mara. 2007. "New Out of Old? Court and Court Ceremonies in Achaemenid Persia." Pages 17–57 in *The Court and Court Society in Ancient Monarchies*. Edited by A. J. S. Spawforth. Cambridge: Cambridge University Press. ♦ **Bush**, Frederic. 1996. *Ruth/Esther*. WBC 9. Dallas: Word. ♦ **Cavalier**, Claudine. 2012. *La Bible d'Alexandrie 12: Esther*. Paris: Cerf. ♦ **Clines**, David J. A. 1984. *The Esther Scroll: The Story of the Story*. JSOTSup 30. Sheffield: Sheffield Academic. ♦ **Dandamayev**, Muhammad A. 1993. "Courts and Courtiers in the Median and Achaemenid Periods." *EIr* 6:356–59. ♦ **Diogenes Laertius**. 1925. *Lives of Eminent Philosophers, Volume I: Books 1–5*. Translated by R. D. Hicks. LCL 184. Cambridge: Harvard University Press. ♦ **Dorothy**, Charles V. 1997. *The Books of Esther: Structure, Genre and Textual Integrity*. JSOTSup 187. Sheffield: Sheffield Academic. ♦ **Dover**, Kenneth. 1980. *Plato: Symposium*. CGLC. Cambridge: Cambridge University Press. ♦ **Ehrenberg**, Victor. 2010. *The Greek State*. Routledge Library Editions: Political Science 23. London: Routledge. ♦ **Fox**, Michael V. 1991. *Character and Ideology in the Book of Esther*. Columbia: University of South Carolina Press. ♦ **Frye**, Northrop. 1976. *The Secular Scripture: A Study of the Structure of Romance*. Harvard: Harvard University Press. ♦ **Glickman**, Elaine Rose. 1999. *Haman and the Jews: A Portrait from Rabbinic Literature*. Northvale, NJ: Aronson. ♦ **Hacham**, Noah. 2007. "3 Maccabees and Esther: Parallels, Intertextuality and Diaspora Identity." *JBL* 126:765–85. ♦ **Harvey**, Charles D. 2003. *Finding Morality in the Diaspora: Moral Ambiguity and Transformed Morality in the Book of Esther*. BZAW 128. Berlin: de Gruyter. ♦ **Herodotus**. 1920–1925. *The Persian Wars*. Translated by A. D. Godley. 4

vols. LCL 117–20. Cambridge: Harvard University Press. ♦ **Hengel**, Martin. 2004. *The Septuagint as Christian Scripture: Its Prehistory and the Problem of its Canon.* Translated by M. E. Biddle. Grand Rapids: Baker Academic. ♦ **Isocrates**. 1928. *To Demonicus; To Nicocles; Nicocles or the Cyprians; Panegyricus; To Philip; Archidamus.* Translated by George Norlin. LCL 209. Cambridge: Harvard University Press. ♦ **Josephus**. 1937. *Jewish Antiquities, Volume IV: Books 9–11.* Translated by Ralph Marcus. LCL 326. Cambridge: Harvard University Press. ♦ **Josephus**. 1943. *Jewish Antiquities, Volume V: Books 12–13.* Translated by Ralph Marcus. LCL 365. Cambridge: Harvard University Press. ♦ **Lenfant**, Dominique. 2012. "Ctesias and his Eunuchs: A Challenge for Modern Historians." *Histos* 6:257–97. ♦ **Levinsohn**, Stephen H. 1992. *Discourse Features of New Testament Greek.* Dallas: Summer Institute of Linguistics. ♦ **Llewellyn-Jones**, Lloyd, and James **Robson**. 2010. *Ctesias' History of Persia: Tales of the Orient.* Routledge Classical Translations. London: Routledge. ♦ **Lysias**. 1930. *Lysias.* Translated by W. R. M. Lamb. LCL 244. Cambridge: Harvard University Press. ♦ **Moore**, Carey A. 1971. *Esther: A New Translation with Introduction and Commentary.* AB 7b. Garden City, NY: Doubleday. ♦ **Moore**. 1977. *Daniel, Esther and Jeremiah: The Additions; A New Translation with Introduction and Commentary.* AB 44. Garden City, NY: Doubleday. ♦ **Paton**, Lewis Bayles. 1908. *A Critical and Exegetical Commentary on the Book of Esther.* ICC. Edinburgh: T&T Clark. ♦ **Plato**. 1925. *Statesman; Philebus; Ion.* Translated by Harold North Fowler and W. R. M. Lamb. LCL 164. Cambridge: Harvard University Press♦ **Pausanias**. 1935. *Description of Greece, Volume IV: Books 8.22–10 (Arcadia, Boeotia, Phocis and Ozolian Locri).* Translated by W. H. S. Jones. LCL 297. Cambridge: Harvard University Press. ♦ **Plutarch**. 1914. *Lives, Volume II: Themistocles and Camillus; Aristides and Cato Major; Cimon and Lucullus.* Translated by Bernadotte Perrin. LCL 47. Cambridge: Harvard University Press. ♦ **Plutarch**. 1919. *Lives, Volume VII: Demosthenes and Cicero; Alexander and Caesar.* Translated by Bernadotte Perrin. LCL 99. Cambridge: Harvard University Press. ♦ **Plutarch**. 1926. *Lives, Volume XI: Aratus; Artaxerxes; Galba; Otho; General Index.* Translated by Bernadotte Perrin. LCL 103. Cambridge: Harvard University Press. ♦ **Plutarch**. 1928. *Moralia, Volume II: How to Profit by One's Enemies; On Having Many Friends; Chance; Virtue and Vice; Letter of Condolence to Apollonius; Advice About Keeping Well; Advice to Bride and Groom; The Dinner of the Seven Wise Men; Superstition.* Translated by Frank Cole Babbitt. LCL 222. Cambridge: Harvard University Press. ♦ **Polybius**. 2010. *The Histories, Volume II: Books 3–4.* Translated by W. R. Paton. Revised by F. W. Walbank and Christian

Habicht. LCL 137. Cambridge: Harvard University Press. ◆ **Polybius**. 2011.
The Histories, Volume IV: Books 9–15. Translated by W. R. Paton. Revised
by F. W. Walbank and Christian Habicht. LCL 159. Cambridge: Harvard
University Press. ◆ **Polybius**. 2012. *The Histories, Volume V: Books 16–27*.
Translated by W. R. Paton. Revised by F. W. Walbank and Christian Habicht. LCL 160. Cambridge: Harvard University Press. ◆ **Pseudo-Aristotle**.
1837. *De Rhetorica ad Alexandrum*. Edited by Immanuel Bekker. Aristo-
telis Opera Volume 11. Oxford: Oxford University Press ◆ **Spicq**, Ceslas.
1994. *Theological Lexicon of the New Testament*. Translated by James Ernest.
3 vols. Peabody, MA: Hendrickson. ◆ **Strabo**. 1917. *Geography, Volume I:
Books 1–2*. Translated by Horace Leonard Jones. LCL 49. Cambridge: Har-
vard University Press. ◆ **Stronk**, Jan P. 2010. *Ctesias' Persian History. Part I:
Introduction, Text and Translation*. Reihe Geschichte 2. Dusseldorf: Wellem.
◆ **Tov**, Emanuel. 2008. "Three Strange Books of the LXX: 1 Kings, Esther and
Daniel Compared with Similar Rewritten Compositions from Qumran and
Elsewhere." Pages 369–93 in *Die Septuaginta: Texte, Kontexte, Lebenswelten*.
Edited by Martin Karrer and Wolfgang Kraus. WUNT 219. Tübingen: Mohr
Siebeck. ◆ **Xenophon**. 1998. *Anabasis*. Translated by Carleton L. Brown-
son. Revised by John Dillery. LCL 90. Cambridge: Harvard University Press.
◆ **Xenophon**. 1914. *Cyropaedia, Volume II: Books 5–8*. Translated by Walter
Miller. LCL 52. Cambridge: Harvard University Press.

§1. Greek Esther 2.19–23

Outline
This pericope is made up of three parts: (1) it presents Mardochaios serving at court (v. 19), where, as a result of his advancement, two eunuchs plot
to assassinate the king (v. 21); (2) the matter becomes known to Mardochaios, who alerts Esther, who in turn informs the king (v. 22); the king acts
on the information (v. 23a); and (3) orders that Mardochaios's loyalty be
recorded (v. 23b). Verse 20 is an aside noting Esther's adherence to Mardochaios's instructions.

Commentary

2.19

ובהקבץ בתולות שנית ומרדכי ישב בשער המלך
ὁ δὲ Μαρδοχαῖος ἐθεράπευεν ἐν τῇ αὐλῇ.
And Mardochaios was serving in the court.

This verse marks a new section with the introduction of Mardochaios and the setting of the court. The pericope is generically a report, defined here as a third-person presentation of actions involving two or more parties without the development of dramatic tension (Dorothy 1997, 51). There is no direct counterpart to the scene in AT, leading Michael Fox (1991, 40) to suggest that it was absent in proto-AT (an early stratum within the Hebrew tradition), and added by the redactor of MT. It was, however, almost certainly present in the Hebrew source of OG, which renders a text similar to MT and reflects its structure. The intrigue has nevertheless undergone various thematic modifications that have an impact on the structure of the Greek narrative (Cavalier 2012, 104).

MT begins with a temporal reference, ובהקבץ בתולות שנית ("When the virgins were being gathered together," NRSV) (strictly speaking, *a second time*: note שנית, a crux for the Hebrew). This reference serves to establish the time frame of the ensuing events, and is thus parallel to בימים ההם in verse 21, which resumes the narrative following a parenthetical remark in verse 20 (Paton 1908, 188). G has recast the opening of the pericope, dropping the temporal reference, moving ahead the introduction of Mardochaios, and setting the scene at court.

ὁ δὲ Μαρδοχαῖος ἐθεράπευεν. The textual linguistic features of this clause combine to establish the beginning of a distinct incident. The order of the Greek subject and verb (S-V), which follows the Hebrew order ומרדכי ישב, marks the clause as a point of departure for what follows (see Levinsohn 1992, 31). At the same time G uses the marked equivalent δέ rather than the default equivalent καί to render the Hebrew conjunction ו. Stephen Levinsohn (1992, 31) classifies δέ as a developmental particle. In this context it signals a progression in the narrative. In accordance with Greek linguistic convention G renders the Hebrew participle by a past indicative form, ἐθεράπευεν, the imperfect aspect of which indicates an ongoing activity.

Μαρδοχαῖος. The proper name of the protagonist has been assimilated to Greek morphology. AT and Josephus use the same form. The consonantal form of the name in MT is מרדכי, pointed מָרְדֳּכַי.

ἐθεράπευεν ἐν τῇ αὐλῇ. The reference to Mardochaios serving as an attendant of some sort is distinctive to OG. It locates Mardochaios both with respect to occupation and to setting. Compare MT, ישב בשער המלך

("[he] was sitting at the King's Gate," NRSV). See also 6.10 (MT), where
the king refers to Mordecai as מרדכי היהודי היושב בשער המלך ("the
Jew Mordecai who sits at the king's gate," NRSV), which G renders τῷ
Ἰουδαίῳ τῷ θεραπεύοντι ἐν τῇ αὐλῇ ("the Judean who serves in the court,"
NETS). The phrase ἐν τῇ αὐλῇ might simply refer to a physical location,
"in the courtyard," but given that G replaces ישב by ἐθεράπευεν (LSJ, s.v.
"θεραπεύω," I. "to be an attendant, do service"), it likely carries the sense
"at court" (LSJ, s.v. "αὐλή," IV. "the Court"), indicating that Mardochaios
is a courtier. Compare Polybius, *Hist.* 26.1 (from Athenaeus 5.193d), in
reference to Antiochus Epiphanes, ὡς ἀποδιδράσκων ἐκ τῆς αὐλῆς ἐνίοτε
τοὺς θεραπεύοντας ("escaping from his attendants at court" [Paton, LCL]).
It is conceivable that G inferred that Mardochaios was a courtier from the
Hebrew reference to his presence at the gates (see below, ἐν τῇ αὐλῇ).

Reference to Mardochaios's service at court carries special thematic
resonance in the text-as-received. In A.1 Mardochaios is described as
ἄνθρωπος μέγας θεραπεύων ἐν τῇ αὐλῇ τοῦ βασιλέως ("a great man serving
in the court of the king," NETS), and is thus unambiguously identified
as a courtier at the outset of the narrative. As such, he is a direct rival
to both the eunuchs and to his antagonist Haman. While present in the
extant Hebrew text, the theme of court rivalry has heightened significance
in OG. Since it is unlikely that G was responsible for the composition of
Addition A, this transformation cannot be located within the production
of the translation. Yet whatever its origin it impacts significantly on the
received text.

ἐν τῇ αὐλῇ. Compare MT בשער המלך, "at the king's gate." In a more isomorphic translation we might expect ἐν τῇ πύλῃ τοῦ βασιλέως (see, e.g.,
1 Suppl 9.18). The expression שער המלך occurs eleven times in MT (Esth
2.19, 21; 3.2, 3; 4.2 [2x]; 4.6; 5.9, 13; 6.10, 12) and is consistently matched
by the single word αὐλή in OG (at 2.21 there is no match). Carey Moore
(1977, 175) suggests that the rendering arose from a copying error in the
transmission of the Greek text. On his view a copyist read αὐλή instead of
πυλή (the uncials A and Π being easily confused). This hypothesis has little
to commend it, as it does not explain why the word מלך is not represented
in OG.

In every instance in MT the phrase שער המלך is used to locate a scene
in which Mardochaios figures. Recent scholarship has tended to interpret
the Hebrew expression in reference to the royal court. Fox (1991, 38–39)
argues that it refers to the court in its entirety, thus implying that Morde-

cai holds a government office in the palace compound. This, however, is speculative. Lewis Paton (1908, 188) notes that at this point in the Hebrew narrative Mordecai is not obviously an official. The king's gate was a place of congregation, and Mordecai could simply be there to pick up news about Esther. While servants of the king are found at the gate (3.2, 3), Mordecai is not explicitly identified as one of them in MT. How G understood the Hebrew, however, is uncertain. He may have read the phrase שער המלך in reference to the royal court and rendered it idiomatically. On the other hand, his work may represent a transformation, such that Mardochaios has been deliberately relocated from his position at the gates, the threshold of the palace establishment, to a position within the court.

2.20

אין אסתר מגדת מולדתה ואת עמה כאשר צוה עליה מרדכי ואת
מאמר מרדכי אסתר עשה כאשר היתה באמנה אתו

ἡ δὲ Εσθηρ οὐχ ὑπέδειξεν τὴν πατρίδα αὐτῆς· οὕτως γὰρ ἐνετείλατο αὐτῇ Μαρδοχαῖος φοβεῖσθαι τὸν θεὸν καὶ ποιεῖν τὰ προστάγματα αὐτοῦ, καθὼς ἦν μετ' αὐτοῦ, καὶ Εσθηρ οὐ μετήλλαξεν τὴν ἀγωγὴν αὐτῆς.

But Esther did not reveal her ancestry. For so Mardochaios had commanded her: to fear God and to do his ordinances, just as when she was with him. So Esther did not change her way of life.

ἡ δὲ Εσθηρ ... Μαρδοχαῖος. The first two clauses of the Greek text have counterparts in MT and adhere to the form of the Hebrew fairly closely. The particle δέ, which has been introduced without warrant by the translator, here marks a parenthetical remark (see Levinsohn 1992, 31). The parenthesis expresses the secrecy motif and characterizes Esther's relationship to Mordechai as one of filial obedience. It reiterates a similarly phrased remark at 2.10, which was rendered by G without elaboration.

Εσθηρ. The proper name of the female protagonist is rendered by an uninflected transliteration. AT and Josephus use the same form. The corresponding Hebrew form אסתר is pointed אֶסְתֵּר in MT.

τὴν πατρίδα αὐτῆς. G uses the single phrase πατρίδα αὐτῆς to replace two Hebrew phrases, מולדתה (HALOT, s.v. "מוֹלֶדֶת," 2. "relations, the relatives"), and עמה (HALOT, s.v. "עַם," C. 1. "people," with an emphasis on connections of kinship and religious ceremonial: the race to which one belongs). G may simply have regarded the two Hebrew terms as redundant. Yet at Esth 2.10 both members of the pair are rendered: עַם by the word γένος (LSJ, s.v. "γένος," I. "race, stock, kin"), and מוֹלֶדֶת by πατρίς; and again at 8.6, where G renders עַם by the word λαός (LSJ, s.v. "λαός," II. "a people"), and מוֹלֶדֶת by πατρίς. The translator twice matches the words מוֹלֶדֶת and πατρίς, and it is therefore not unlikely that the former cued the latter in the present context as well. In Greek compositional literature the substantive πατρίς generally refers to a place, not a kinship group, and it is probable that G intended it thus (LSJ, s.v. "πατρίς," II. Subst., = "πάτρα," I. "fatherland, native land"). See 2 and 4 Makkabees where the word consistently means "[one's] country," often in reference to Judea. Of the four further occurrences of πατρίς in the translation literature of the LXX, the word is used as a match for מוֹלֶדֶת three times (all within the phrase אֶרֶץ מוֹלֶדֶת): at Ier 22.10 and Iezek 23.15 it is used adjectivally to modify γῆ in the phrase "native land" (NETS), while at Ier 26.16 (=MT 46.16) it occurs as a substantive and may be glossed "fatherland" (NETS). That the use of πατρίς in these contexts is a marked translation equivalent (rather than a mere default) becomes evident when one surveys the rendering of מוֹלֶדֶת in the LXX. The Greek matches fall into roughly three distinct semantic categories: (1) *people related by ties of descent, kin*: Gen 12.1 συγγένεια; Gen 31.3; 43.7; and Num 10.30 γενεά; (2) *offspring*: Gen 48.6 ἔκγονα; and (3) *birth,* for which two subcategories may be distinguished, (3a) *nativity, birth*: Iezek 16.3, 4 γένεσις; compare Leu 18.9 (מוֹלֶדֶת בַּיִת) ἐνδογενοῦς; and (3b) (place of) *origin* or *birth*, where the source text reads some form of אֶרֶץ מוֹלֶדֶת, Gen 11.28 ἧ ἐγενήθη; Gen 24.4 οὗ ἐγενόμην; Gen 24:7 ἧς ἐγενήθην; Gen 31.13 and Routh 2.11 γενέσεως; Ier 22.10 and Iezek 23.15 πατρίδος; Ier 26:16 [=MT 46:16] τὴν πατρίδα. As it is reasonable to assume that G distinguished these three senses of מוֹלֶדֶת, we would expect (*ceteris paribus*) to find in the present verse a rendering such as συγγένεια (LSJ, s.v., II. "one's kin, kinsfolk"; cf. Gen 12.1) or γενεά (LSJ, s.v., I. of the persons in a family, 1. "race, family"; cf. Gen 31.3; 43.7; Num 10.30), that is, a rendering within the first category above. That G replaces מוֹלֶדֶת by πατρίς is suggestive of a subtle but deliberate transformation from the first to the third category. Compare Leu 25.10 where πατρίς renders מִשְׁפָּחָה (HALOT, s.v. "מִשְׁפָּחָה," 1. "extended family, clan," group in which the sense of blood relationship is still felt). There the context is the return to one's family during the Jubilee Year. For both Esther and Leviticus the Greek translator appears to have assumed the perspective of the Hellenistic diaspora. Since the time of Ptolemy II subjects of Ptolemaic Egypt were obliged by law to identify themselves by their πατρίς; failure to do so was punishable by death (Bingen 2007, 61). An individual's legal and fiscal identities were thus defined as Macedonian, Thracian, Persian, or Judean, as the case may be (an Egyptian would indicate the nome from which they came).

φοβεῖσθαι … αὐτοῦ. In these two clauses, which are not paralleled in MT, G elaborates upon Mardochaios's instructions to Esther. In the Hebrew version the clause כאשר צוה עליה מרדכי ("as Mordecai had charged her," NRSV), refers back to Mordecai's orders that Esther conceal her ethnic identity. The Greek rendering of this clause, οὕτως γὰρ ἐνετείλατο αὐτῇ Μαρδοχαῖος, instead points forward to the further injunction that she continue "to fear God and to do his ordinances" (NETS). G's elaboration, ideologically freighted as it is, threatens the coherence of the narrative, since it would presumably be impossible for Esther to both conceal her ethnic identity at court and observe the practices enjoined upon her by Mardochaios. The translator could evidently rely on the suspension of disbelief by his target audience.

The theme of piety is a salient feature of OG in its received form. It is greatly developed in the prayers of Addition C, which, as David Clines (1984, 171) observes, serve to refashion the story as a form of exemplary tale, in which Mardochaios and Esther become models of Jewish piety. Such piety, it is implied, is pivotal in delivering the people of Israel from crisis (Fox 1991, 271).

φοβεῖσθαι τὸν θεόν. The phrase "to fear God" would have been intelligible to any Greek speaker; the sentiment it expresses was traditional. See for instance Isocrates, 1.16, τοὺς μὲν θεοὺς φοβοῦ, τοὺς δὲ γονεῖς τίμα, τοὺς δὲ φίλους αἰσχύνου, τοῖς δὲ νόμοις πείθου ("Fear the gods, honour your parents, respect your friends, obey the laws" [Norlin, LCL]). (Yet compare Plutarch, *Superst.*, 2, who articulates the philosophical response of a later time, associating fear of the gods with ignorance.) Notwithstanding its universality, the expression had a Jewish literary background that is undoubtedly in play here. In the LXX θεός frequently renders אל ("god"), but can also stand for יהוה, that is, the God of Israel, who in Hellenistic Judaism is identified inter alia as the creator and ruler of all things. In the present context, where θεός is introduced without qualification and in reference to a Jewish point of view, it arguably refers to YHWH thus conceived. The Hebrew expression יראת יהוה ("the fear of YHWH") and the variant יראת אלהים ("the fear of God"), is a conventional motif in the Hebrew Bible.

In certain instances (Gen 20.11; Iob 28.28; Esa 11.2; 33.6) the expression is rendered by the word θεοσέβεια (LSJ, s.v. "θεοσέβεια," "service or fear of God"), but elsewhere it is translated more literally as ὁ φόβος κυρίου (e.g., Pss 19[18].10; 34[33].12; 111[110].10; Esa 11.3). The motif figures significantly in the book of Proverbs, where it is associated with the pursuit of enlightenment, as for example in Prov 1.7: יראת יהוה ראשית דעת חכמה ומוסר אוילים בזו ("The fear of the Lord is the beginning of knowledge; fools despise wisdom and instruction," NRSV). The Hellenistic translator of Proverbs renders the first stich by Ἀρχὴ σοφίας φόβος θεοῦ ("Beginning of wisdom is fear of God"), which is elaborated upon in the third line with, εὐσέβεια δὲ εἰς θεὸν ἀρχὴ αἰσθήσεως ("and piety unto God is the beginning of perception," NETS). It is telling that φόβος θεοῦ is paralleled with εὐσέβεια (LSJ, s.v. 1. "reverence towards the gods or parents, piety or filial respect"). As Ceslas Spicq (1994, 196) notes (citing J. Rudhardt with approval), the word εὐσέβεια enunciates the Greek concept closest to the modern idea of religion.

In contrast to MT, OG in its received form is marked by explicit sacral themes. That this transformation may at least in part be attributable to G is evident in the references to the God of Israel. Whereas the Hebrew version is singular in the Bible for the fact that it makes no such references, OG contains four in verses parallel to MT (2.20 θεός; 4.8 κύριος; 6.1 κύριος; 6.13 θεός). This is no small difference, and various explanations have been offered. On the theory of Clines (1984, 109) MT represents a late recension in which there has been a deliberate excision of all such language. This is an intriguing hypothesis, yet speculative, and it has not won much favor amongst specialists. On balance these passages in OG look like the elaboration of a shorter text by G, for in most instances we find together with the reference to God motifs peculiar to the Greek translation. The first two references (2.20 and 4.8) occur within injunctions to piety by Mardochaios to Esther; the third is a statement by the narrator attributing Artaxerxes's sleeplessness to the Lord's intervention (6.1); and the fourth is placed on the lips of Haman's wife, who acknowledges that God is with Mardochaios (6.13). These elaborations, significant as they are, may simply represent ad hoc interventions on the part of G, rather than moves within a larger redactive strategy. Yet together they actualize the theme of divine providence latent in MT, and carry an ideological force. In a useful discussion, Fox (1991, 270) emphasizes their impact upon the understanding of history conveyed by the text-as-received: they foreground the sacral dimension of events, in which the true meaning of crisis and deliverance is found.

ποιεῖν τὰ προστάγματα αὐτοῦ. This refers to Pentateuchal legislation, the observance of which had become central to the piety of certain circles within Hellenistic Judaism. Reference to this legislation (absent in MT) is also introduced by G at 8.11, where the king's decree permits the Judeans of every city to assemble and defend themselves. In the Greek they are ordered χρῆσθαι τοῖς νόμοις αὐτῶν ἐν πάσῃ πόλει ("to live in accordance with their laws in every city," NETS). This theme is further amplified in the text-as-received. See Addition C, which, as Clines (1984, 169) has noted, assimilates the narrative to the "scriptural norm" defined by the Penta-teuchal law.

The word πρόσταγμα is associated with Ptolemaic institutions, and is well attested in the papyri in reference to royal ordinances (Cavalier 2012, 69). The chief implement of Hellenistic government was the royal edict, published either as law or directed as instructions to specific recipients; in Egypt the most common form was the πρόσταγμα, which was also used in administrative measures and judicial decisions (one should not, how-ever, seek too much precision here, as there was no single nomenclature) (Ehrenberg, 2010). In the Greek Pentateuch the word πρόσταγμα (typi-cally the plural form) matches various Hebrew terms that (in context) refer to divinely authorized ordinances. Examples include: Exod 18.16 חקי האלהים (BDB, s.v. "חֹק," 7. pl. *enactments, statutes* of a law; see also Exod 18.20; Deut 11.32; 12.1); Lev 4.2 מצות יהוה (BDB, s.v. "מִצְוָה," 2. b. pl. *commands* of D and later codes; see also Exod 20.6; Lev 26.3, 14); Lev 18.5 חקתי (BDB, s.v. "חֻקָּה," 2. pl. *statutes*: d. of the prescriptions of the codes of D, H, P; see also Lev 20.22; 26.43); Lev 19.37 משפטי (*DCH*, s.v. "מִשְׁפָּט," 3. *ordinance*; see also Lev 20.22); Lev 24.12 פי יהוה (*DCH*, s.v. "פֶּה," 3. mouth as equivalent of *speech*, a. *command, declaration*; see also Num 9.18 [2x]; 9.20; 9.23 [2x]; 33.38; 36.5); Lev 18.30 משמרתי (BDB, s.v. "מִשְׁמֶרֶת," 3. *charge, injunction* of יהוה; see also Gen 26.5). Given this background, it is not surprising that during the Hellenistic period certain Greek-speaking Jewish authors came to use τὰ προστάγματα as a short-hand for the pentateuchal laws, especially as they pertained to individual piety (see, e.g., 3 Makk 7.11; and 1 Esd 8.7). It is likely that in using this term G has in mind interdictions surrounding marriage and diet, as well as prescriptions regarding cultic practices such as libations, but also prac-tices not prohibited de jure, such as commensality.

G's reference to Pentateuchal law raises the question of intertextual-ity. Certainly the expression ποιεῖν τὰ προστάγματα is reminiscent of the language of the Greek Pentateuch (e.g., Leu 26.14; Deut 11.32). Yet it does not obviously reference a particular text or group of texts. In this regard it should be noted that πρόσταγμα collocates more strongly with the verb φυλάσσω (rendering שמר) than with ποιέω in the Pentateuch. Both verbs are frequently used in the same context (see also Leu 18.4, 5, 26, 30; 19.37; 20.8, 22), and in certain instances both are construed with πρόσταγμα (see, e.g., Leu 20.8, καὶ φυλάξεσθε τὰ προστάγματά μου καὶ ποιήσετε αὐτά). But if the phrasing of Mardochaios's injunction was not modeled on specific Pentateuchal passages, it undoubtedly echoes its language, and one could make the case that this was deliberately so. Verbal echoing suggests that the translator assumed some degree of familiarity with the Greek Pentateuch on the part of his implied reader.

Apart from the present context and 8.11, G uses πρόσταγμα in a strictly secular sense (cf. Gen 47.26). Thus at 8.14 it renders the Hebrew word דת (BDB, s.v. "דָּת," 1. *decree, edict, commission* of Persian king) in reference to the second royal edict concerning the Judeans; at 8.17 it refers to the same edict, but here the Greek word evidently renders דבר המלך (BDB, s.v. "דָּבָר," I.1.b, *word of command*), though דת occurs in the same context and may have primed the match; at 9.4 it is introduced by G without a Hebrew warrant, again in reference to the second edict. In Hellenistic Egypt the form of a letter (ἐπιστολή) could serve any purpose, including relations between the monarch and local governors (Ehrenberg, 2010). Hence the use of the word πρόσταγμα for the royal edict (8.14, 17), a letter addressed by the king to his rulers, is altogether conventional. In the received text πρόσταγμα occurs a further time at D.10 in reference to a decree concerning the protocol of the throne room.

καθὼς ἦν μετ' αὐτοῦ. Here OG rejoins MT, rendering כאשר היתה באמנה אתו ("just as when she was brought up by him," NRSV). Yet the function of the clause differs in each version. In the Hebrew text it modifies the third clause, which is not represented in the Greek, ואת מאמר מרדכי אסתר עשה ("for Esther obeyed Mordecai," NRSV). In OG, on the other hand, it modifies the reference to Esther's piety: she is expected to continue as she did when she was with living with Mardochaios. G does not provide a match for the phrase באמנה, consisting of the preposition ב and the noun אמנה, a *hapax legomenon* (DCH, s.v. "אָמְנָה," II. *fosterage*; or אָמְנָה, *her fostering*), which in this context refers back to Mordecai's guardianship of Esther. It is possible that G was not familiar with the Hebrew word; conversely he may have sought a more economical phrasing. Just possibly the rendering involves a subtle shift away from an explicit reference to fosterage. Compare 2.7, where such a reference is recast by G: ויהי אמן את הדסה ("Mordecai had brought up Hadassah," NRSV), is replaced by καὶ ἦν τούτῳ παῖς θρεπτή ("And this man had a foster child," NETS); and later in the verse the clause, לקחה מרדכי לו לבת ("Mordecai adopted her as his own daughter," NRSV), is rendered ἐπαίδευσεν αὐτὴν ἑαυτῷ εἰς γυναῖκα ("he trained her for himself as a wife," NETS).

οὐ μετήλλαξεν ... αὐτῆς. This clause, which represents a further elaboration of the piety theme, has no counterpart in MT. The translator stresses that Esther continued to adhere to the ritual practices of her people when she entered the royal palace. The tension with the secrecy motif of the opening of this verse is evident. Taking up the theme of filial obedience from the Hebrew source, G confirms that Esther adhered to Mardochaios's instructions. This theme is further developed in the text-as-received. In Esther's prayer (Addition C) she asserts that she neither dined at Haman's table, nor drank the wine of libation.

μετήλλαξεν. The word occurs in three books of the LXX: Esth 2.7, 20; 1 Esd 1.29; and 2 Makk 4.7, 37; 5.5; 6.31; 7.7, 13, 14, 40; 14.46 (an original Greek composition), yet this is the only example of its unmarked sense (LSJ, s.v. "μεταλλάσσω," I. change, alter); elsewhere it bears the idiomatic sense "to die" (LSJ, s.v. II. 2. quit [τὸν βίον]).

ἀγωγήν. In compositional literature outside the LXX the word may denote either a system of education or the form of life shaped by such a system (LSJ, s.v. "ἀγωγή," II. 2. direction, training. 4. way of life, conduct). See for example Aristotle, Eth. nic., 1179b: ἐκ νέου δ' ἀγωγῆς ὀρθῆς τυχεῖν πρὸς ἀρετὴν χαλεπὸν μὴ ὑπὸ τοιούτοις τραφέντα νόμοις ("And it is difficult to obtain a right education in virtue from youth up without being brought up under right laws" [Rackham, LCL]). The word occurs in three books of the LXX, of which only Esther is a translation: Esth 2.20; 10.3; 2 Makk 4.16; 6.8; 11.24; and 3 Makk 4.10. At 2 Makk 11.24, it is used in reference to Jewish νόμιμα ("customs"), as opposed to Ἑλληνικά (i.e., "Greek [customs]"). The νόμιμα are in turn referred to as τὰ ἐπὶ τῶν προγόνων αὐτῶν ἔθη (2 Makk 11.25) ("the customs of their ancestors," NETS). In the present context the term likely refers to the repertoire of traditional practices and observances which would be part of the acculturation of a Jewish girl in the Greek-speaking diaspora and would mark her social identity (such customs would be coextensive with τὰ προστάγματα above).

2.21

בימים ההם ומרדכי ישב בשער המלך קצף בגתן ותרש שני סריסי
המלך משמרי הסף ויבקשו לשלח יד במלך אחשורש

καὶ ἐλυπήθησαν οἱ δύο εὐνοῦχοι τοῦ βασιλέως οἱ ἀρχισωματοφύλακες
ὅτι προήχθη Μαρδοχαῖος, καὶ ἐζήτουν ἀποκτεῖναι Ἀρταξέρξην τὸν
βασιλέα.

The two eunuchs who were the king's chief bodyguards were irri-
tated because Mardochaios was promoted, and they sought to kill
Artaxerxes the king.

Compare MT which begins with a circumstantial clause, comprising a temporal reference, בימים ההם ("in those days"), and a notice regarding Mordecai, ומרדכי ישב בשער המלך ("he was sitting at the king's gate," NRSV),
that repeats an identical notice made at verse 19. The Hebrew verse is a
resumption of verse 19, which was interrupted by the parenthesis of verse
20; thus בימים ההם likely corresponds in time to when the virgins were
gathered (Paton 1908, 189). The temporal reference at verse 19 was not
rendered by G, hence there is no match for the phrase בימים ההם in verse
21 (since it now lacks an antecedent). Although the present verse might
conceivably derive from a Semitic *Vorlage* different from MT, a prima facie
case can be made for Greek elaboration of a source text similar to MT.

ἐλυπήθησαν. For the aorist indicative passive form of the verb (LSJ, s.v.
"λυπέω," II. passive, *to be grieved, distressed*) see, for example Plato, *Phileb.*,
52b, ὅταν τις στερηθεὶς λυπηθῇ διὰ τὴν χρείαν ("when a man who has lost
[knowledge] is pained by the lack of it" [Fowler and Lamb, LCL]). In the
present context it renders the Hebrew verb קצף (HALOT, s.v. *qal* "קָצַף," to
be angry, to be furious. 1. A. a person's anger towards one or more other
people). For the Hebrew-Greek match, see also 1 Rgns 29.4 and 4 Rgns
13.19. The equivalency also occurs at Esth 1.12 in reference to king Artaxerxes. In the present context the passive form of the Greek verb connotes
deep disquietude. Compare Lysias, 9.20, where the form is used contras-
tively with ἀγανακτέω (LSJ, s.v. II. metaphorical, *to be displeased, vexed*):
τούτων μὲν οὖν ἀδικούντων μετρίως [ἄν] ἠγανάκτουν, ἡγούμενος τετάχθαι
τοὺς μὲν ἐχθροὺς κακῶς ποιεῖν, τοὺς δὲ φίλους εὖ· παρ' ὑμῶν δὲ τοῦ δικαίου
στερηθεὶς πολὺ ἄν μᾶλλον λυπηθείην ("The injustice of these men only
caused me a moderate annoyance, as I considered it ordained that one
should harm one's enemies and serve one's friends; but to be deprived of
justice at your hands would cause me a far deeper distress" [Lamb, LCL]).

εὐνοῦχοι. The denotation of the Hebrew word סריס (*HALOT*, s.v. "סָרִיס," [> Akkadian *ša rēši* "the one at the head."] 1. *high official*, political or military. 2. *eunuch*) remains somewhat uncertain, with some philologists maintaining that it refers exclusively to castrated men, and others arguing that it may designate a noncastrated dignitary or official. Hebrew סריס occurs without qualification thirty-five times in the Hebrew Bible (excluding the book of Esther), and is typically rendered by εὐνοῦχος in the LXX (Gen 39.1; 40.2, 7; 1 Rgns 8.15; 3 Rgns 22.9; 4 Rgns 8.6; 9.32; 20.18; 24.12, 15; 25.19; 2 Suppl 18.8; Esa 56.3, 4; Ier 29[36].2; 41[48].16; 52.25), but also by σπάδων (LSJ, s.v., "eunuch") (Gen 37.36; Esa 39.7) and δυνάστης (BDAG, s.v., 2. "court official") (1 Suppl 28.1; Ier 34[41].19); at Ier 38[45].7 the word is not rendered. The expression רב סריס, which occurs four times, is rendered by ἀρχιευνοῦχος (LSJ, s.v., "chief of the eunuchs") once (Dan 1.3 in both Greek versions), and by personal names twice (4 Rgns 18.17; and Ier 39[46].3); Ier 39.13 is a LXX minus. The expression שר סריס, occurring six times in the first chapter of the book of Daniel, is consistently rendered by ἀρχιευνοῦχος in both Greek versions (1.7, 8, 9, 10, 11, 18). Hebrew Esther has a dozen occurrences of סריס (1.10, 12, 15; 2.3, 14, 15, 21; 4.4, 5; 6.2, 14; 7.9) all rendered by εὐνοῦχος (at 2.23 εὐνοῦχος is evidently introduced by G). Etymologically the Greek word εὐνοῦχος denotes a functionary: "one who keeps (-ουχος) the bed (εὐνή)." Early attestation of the word is found especially among Asiatic Greeks in contact with Lydia and Persia, including Hipponax in the late sixth century BCE, and Herodotus and Hellanicus in the fifth century BCE (Lenfant 2012, 268). Dominique Lenfant (2012, 285) concludes that in the Greek sources that come down to us the word unequivocally designates a castrated male.

G does not name the eunuchs here. Compare MT, which identifies them as בגתן and תרש (2.21) (בִּגְתָן וָתֶרֶשׁ; "Bigthan and Teresh," NRSV). In plot[2] G refers to the two eunuchs as Γαβαθα καὶ Θαρρα, forms that may ultimately derive from transliterations of the Hebrew. Josephus's version, which parallels plot[1], refers to them as Βαγαθῶος and Θεοδέστης.

ἀρχισωματοφύλακες. Compare MT which describes the eunuchs as שמרי הסף, the ones "who guarded the threshold" (NRSV), possibly referring to the men who guarded the king's private apartment (Moore 1971, 31). The use of ἀρχισωματοφύλαξ (LSJ, s.v., "chief of the body guard") by G arguably marks a transformation. Claudine Cavalier (2012, 157) notes that the title is associated with the Ptolemaic court and designates a high functionary. Josephus, *A.J.*, 12.2.5, uses it in reference to the official of

Ptolemy Philadelphus entrusted to serve as an emissary to Eleazar the high priest of Jerusalem, ἀπέσταλκα δέ σοι περὶ τούτων διαλεξομένους Ἀνδρέαν τὸν ἀρχισωματοφύλακα καὶ Ἀρισταῖον ἐμοὶ τιμιωτάτους ("And I have sent Andreas, the commander of the bodyguard, and Aristaeus—men whom I hold in the greatest honour" [Marcus, LCL]). Within the LXX the word occurs at 1 Rgns 28.2 where Anchous, son of Ammach, king of Geth, offers to make Dauid chief of the bodyguard, rendering Hebrew, שמר לראשי ("bodyguard," NRSV). In the present context it was likely intended by G to underscore the high status of these eunuchs. There are numerous references to eunuchs serving as royal guards in Greek literature. Herodotus, *Hist.* 1.113, refers to bodyguards (δορυφόροι), who are subsequently identified as eunuchs, serving Harpagos under Median rule (1.117). According to Xenophon, *Cyr.*, 7.5.59–65, Cyrus the Great chose to employ eunuchs on account of their reputed loyalty to their masters, ταῦτα δὴ γιγνώσκων ἀρξάμενος ἀπὸ τῶν θυρωρῶν πάντας τοὺς περὶ τὸ ἑαυτοῦ σῶμα θεραπευτῆρας ἐποιήσατο εὐνούχους ("Recognizing these facts, he selected eunuchs for every post of personal service to him, from the door-keepers up" [Miller, LCL]).

The two unnamed eunuchs of plot[1] may be distinguished from those of plot[2] (Gabatha and Tharra) by their status. While the latter merely guard the courtyard (A.12), the former are significant functionaries of the court. In the received text the term ἀρχισωματοφύλακες thus marks plot[1] as a distinct episode (Cavalier 2012, 157).

ὅτι προήχθη Μαρδοχαῖος. The narrator indicates that the motive of the two conspirators was anger over Mardochaios's advancement at court. Compare MT which does not provide a motive for the eunuchs' plot. This elaboration by G operates at a literary level: it both contributes psychological complexity to the narrative and underscores the related themes of court rivalry and palace intrigue present in the Hebrew text. Within the Greek text-as-received the reference to Mardochaios's advancement takes on further significance, inviting a reading of plot[1] in light of the events of plot[2], where Mardochaios's service to the king is acknowledged by his promotion.

καὶ ἐζήτουν. From this point onward G adheres to a source very similar in form to MT.

ἀποκτεῖναι. A single verb replaces the idiom שלח יד ב ("lay hands on") and specifies the intended action as one of killing. The Hebrew idiom occurs four times in Esther. At 3.6 it is not represented in OG. A more isomorphic rendering occurs at 6.2, ἐπιβαλεῖν τὰς χεῖρας. At 9.2, however, G again uses a single verb (ἀπόλλυμι) to replace the idiom, recasting the clause in the passive voice. Point-to-point rendering of the source language is not a constraint for the translator. In the present instance G has evidently aimed at clarity and succinctness.

2.22

ויודע הדבר למרדכי ויגד לאסתר המלכה ותאמר אסתר למלך בשם
מרדכי

καὶ ἐδηλώθη Μαρδοχαίῳ ὁ λόγος, καὶ ἐσήμανεν Εσθηρ, καὶ αὐτὴ ἐνεφάνισεν τῷ βασιλεῖ τὰ τῆς ἐπιβουλῆς.

But the matter became known to Mardochaios, and he alerted Esther, and she explained to the king the details of the plot.

ἐδηλώθη Μαρδοχαίῳ ὁ λόγος. The structure of this clause adheres to that of the Hebrew closely (V^{pass}-S-IO). G has, however, switched the order of the two substantives so that S (λόγος) is last, likely due to the fact that the thematic participant of the narrative will switch from the eunuchs to Mardochaios. The match of דבר and λόγος is common, yet works well in this context. Compare the parallel in plot[2] (A.13) where Mardochaios personally overhears the plot. In the present context, as in MT, he learns of it from an unnamed informant. Josephus, A.J., 11.207, identifies this individual as a Judean named Barnabazos: Βαρνάβαζος τῶν εὐνούχων οἰκέτης τοῦ ἑτέρου, τὸ γένος ὢν Ἰουδαῖος, συνεὶς τὴν ἐπιβουλὴν τῷ θείῳ κατεμήνυσε τῆς γυναικὸς τοῦ βασιλέως Μαρδοχαίῳ ("Barnabazos, the servant of one of these eunuchs, who was a Jew by race, discovered their plot and revealed it to Mordecai, the uncle of the king's wife" [Marcus, LCL]).

Εσθηρ. Compare MT where Esther is identified as the queen (אסתר המלכה).

καὶ αὐτὴ ἐνεφάνισεν. G avoids repeating the name Esther, using instead a pronoun, which he moves into the first position (S-V), since Esther is now the thematic participant. Compare MT, ותאמר אסתר. G does not render ותאמר, "and she told," by a common match (for example καὶ εἶπεν), perhaps because there is no reported speech. The Greek phrase ἐνεφάνισεν τινὶ τινά here carries the nontechnical sense, "she informed somebody of something" (BDAG, s.v. "ἐμφανίζω," 2. "make known, explain, inform"). Compare Acts

23.22, μηδενὶ ἐκλαλῆσαι ὅτι ταῦτα ἐνεφάνισας πρός με ("Tell no one that you have informed me of this," NRSV). The Hebrew phrase בשם מרדכי, "in the name of Mordechai," is not rendered, which is surprising given that it is a crucial detail. This may reflect a tendency toward the abbreviation of Hebrew phrasing. In verse 23 the Greek text clearly indicates that the king was made aware of Mardochaios's role in reporting the plot.

τὰ τῆς ἐπιβουλῆς. This phrase represents an elaboration by G. In the Hebrew clause, ותאמר אסתר למלך ("and Esther told the king," NRSV), the verb has no direct object (though one is implied). The Greek phrasing, which uses the neuter plural article with an arthrous noun in the genitive to convey the sense "that pertaining to something," is idiomatic. The noun is widely attested in the sense required here (LSJ, s.v. "ἐπιβουλή," *plan formed against* another, *plot, scheme*). Compare 3 Makk 1.2, 6, where a plot (ἐπιβουλή) to murder Ptolemy Philopator is foiled by a Judean named Dositheus.

2.23

ויבקש הדבר וימצא ויתלו שניהם על עץ ויכתב בספר דברי הימים
לפני המלך

ὁ δὲ βασιλεὺς ἤτασεν τοὺς δύο εὐνούχους καὶ ἐκρέμασεν αὐτούς· καὶ προσέταξεν ὁ βασιλεὺς καταχωρίσαι εἰς μνημόσυνον ἐν τῇ βασιλικῇ βιβλιοθήκῃ ὑπὲρ τῆς εὐνοίας Μαρδοχαίου ἐν ἐγκωμίῳ.

So the king interrogated the two eunuchs and hanged them. Then the king ordered to make an entry as a memorial in the royal archive in commendation of Mardochaios's loyalty.

ὁ δὲ βασιλεύς. Over against the Hebrew, the subject of the clause is made explicit by G, and brought forward, as the king is now the thematic participant. The use of the particle δέ rather than καί may be intended to mark a thematic development (see Levinsohn 1992, 31).

ἤτασεν τοὺς δύο εὐνούχους. The eunuchs are reintroduced at this point by G, which neatly anticipates the next clause. Compare MT, ויבקש הדבר וימצא ("When the affair was investigated and found to be so," NRSV). G has avoided mimicking the Hebrew idiom, replacing the passive construction with an active one, and elaborating the reference to an investigation.

καὶ ἐκρέμασεν αὐτούς. The Greek verb likely refers to crucifixion in this context (LSJ, s.v. "κρεμάννυμι," I. 2. *to hang*, τινα; *crucify*). See Plutarch,

Caes. 2.2, καὶ σὺν γέλωτι πολλάκις ἠπείλησε κρεμᾶν αὐτούς ("and often laughingly threatened to hang them all" [Perrin, LCL]), where κρεμᾶν is picked up at 2.4 by ἄπαντας ἀνεσταύρωσεν ("crucified them all"). Compare MT, ויתלו שניהם על עץ ("both the men were hanged on the gallows," NRSV). G avoids a formal rendering of the Hebrew prepositional phrase in favor of a more idiomatic and economical expression. There is some uncertainty as to what manner of execution is intended in the Hebrew text (BDB, s.v. "עֵץ," 2. b. of *pole* on which bodies of slain were exposed; late [in Persia] used for executing criminals [? by hanging = *gallows*]). According to Herodotus, *Hist.* 3.159, Darius I impaled (ἀνεσκολόπισε) the leading men of Babylon on stakes after capturing the city. Yet, as Moore (1971, 31) notes, the height of Haman's pole argues against impaling. The reference may thus be to the practice of exposing bodies following execution (Bush 1996, 373). See for example Herodotus, *Hist.* 3.125, where Polycrates is murdered by Oroetes in some undisclosed manner and then later crucified (ἀνεσταύρωσε): hanged aloft (ἀνακρεμάμενος), "he was washed by Zeus when it rained" (Godley, LCL). Whether G's rendering represents the current understanding of the Hebrew idiom or an historical actualization is impossible to say. Bush (1996, 373) observes that the translation reflects the prevalence of crucifixion in the Roman era.

καὶ προσέταξεν ... ἐγκωμίῳ. G recasts this clause somewhat. Cavalier (2012, 157) suggests that the translator accords political importance to the episode by purposely echoing vocabulary designating the official status of a benefactor of the king in the Persian court.

καὶ προσέταξεν ὁ βασιλεύς. In OG the king takes the initiative. Note that the thematic subject is explicitly identified by G, which underscores his agency. Compare the impersonal use of the passive form in MT, ויכתב ("it was written"), which does not specify the agent (though reference is made to the presence of the king: לפני המלך).

καταχωρίσαι. The Greek verb carries the precise sense required for this context (LSJ, s.v. "καταχωρίζω," III. "set down in a book, place on record"). See, for example, Strabo, *Geogr.*, 1.2.3, Ὅμηρον γοῦν ὑπέρ τε τῶν Αἰθιόπων ὅσα ἐπύθετο καταχωρίσαι εἰς τὴν ποίησιν καὶ περὶ τῶν κατ᾿ Αἴγυπτον καὶ Λιβύην ("Homer, for instance, made a place in his poems for everything that he had learned about the Ethiopians and the inhabitants of Egypt and Libya" [Jones, LCL]). The verb occurs only twice elsewhere in the LXX (1 Suppl

27.24 and 3 Makk 2.29). It is introduced into a context similar to the present one at 1 Suppl 27.24 (where it renders עלה), καὶ οὐ κατεχωρίσθη ὁ ἀριθμὸς ἐν βιβλίῳ λόγων τῶν ἡμερῶν τοῦ βασιλέως Δαυιδ ("and the number was not entered in the Book of Histories of the Days of King Dauid," NETS).

εἰς μνημόσυνον. G introduces this phrase without warrant from the Hebrew not only here but at 9.32 and 10.2 as well. (In the received text it also occurs in Addition A.) Literally it means "as a memorial" (Moore 1977, 178). The phrase occurs elsewhere in the LXX (Exod 17.14; Ps 112[111].6; Sir 45.9, 11, 16; 45.16; 50.16; Esa 66.3), and was taken up by certain early Christian authors (Mark 14.9 = Matt 26.13 and Acts 10.4). At Exod 17.14 it renders זכרון (BDB, s.v. "זִכָּרוֹן," 1. d. *memorial-record*; in a book), and at Ps 112(111).6 it matches לזכר (BDB, s.v. "זֵכֶר," 1. *remembrance, memory*: a. of persons). While it is conceivable that the phrase was warranted by G's source, it seems rather that it had special resonance for the translator and was introduced independently. Its use in the present scene is echoed at 9.32, where, following the demise of Mardochaios's antagonist Haman and the deliverance of the Judeans, Esther records the establishment of Purim εἰς μνημόσυνον, and then again at 10.2 where, the kingdom being secured, the king records its wealth and glory εἰς μνημόσυνον. Within the received text the occurrence of the phrase εἰς μνημόσυνον here in plot[1] echoes the outcome of plot[2] (A.15), καὶ ἔγραψεν ὁ βασιλεὺς τοὺς λόγους τούτους εἰς μνημόσυνον ("And the king wrote these things in the record," NETS).

In the phrase εἰς μνημόσυνον it is possible to read an intertextual reference to the figure of Amalek. At Exod 17.14 the Lord declares his intention to blot out את זכר עמלק ("the remembrance of Amalek," NRSV), which the Greek translator renders τὸ μνημόσυνον Ἀμαλήκ ("the memorial of Amalek," NETS). Moreover Moses is commanded by the Lord to record this divine resolution: כתב זאת זכרון בספר ("write this as a reminder in a book," NRSV), rendered κατάγραψον τοῦτο εἰς μνημόσυνον ἐν βιβλίῳ in OG. Compare Deut 25.19 where a second such reference is made to the erasure of Amalek's memory: תמחה את זכר עמלק ("you will blot out the remembrance of Amalek," NRSV). (Here the Greek version renders זכר by ὄνομα.) In rabbinic tradition the figure of Amalek is identified both genealogically and typologically with Haman as a paradigm of evil, such that in Haman the sages saw "the remembrance of Amalek" whom God had sworn to blot out (Glickman 1999, 24). That in introducing the phrase εἰς μνημόσυνον G intended to echo the narrative of Amalek is, however, speculative.

μνημόσυνον. Outside of Hebrew-Greek translation, the word μνημόσυνον typically carries the sense "memorial," that is, "that which evokes a memory" (Spicq 1994, 500). In Herodotus's *Historiae* it refers to edifices that perpetuate the memory of a person: at 1.185 and 186 to building works; at 2.100 to the gateway of a temple; and at 2.148 to a labyrinth. Diogenes Laertius, *Lives of Eminent Philosophers* 3.1.40, uses it by extension in reference to the preservation of Plato's memory in both his writings and his friends: ἀλλὰ καὶ ἠξίου μνημόσυνον αὐτοῦ λείπεσθαι ἢ ἐν φίλοις ἢ ἐν βιβλίοις ("His wish always was to leave a memorial of himself behind, either in the hearts of his friends or in his books" [Hicks, LCL]); and Pausanias, *Descr.* 10.5.3, in reference to places and geographical features associated with the memory of Oedipus, ἔδει δὲ ἄρα παθημάτων τῶν Οἰδίποδος ἀνὰ πᾶσαν τὴν Ἑλλάδα ὑπολειφθῆναι μνημόσυνα ("Fate would have it that memorials of the sufferings of Oedipus should be left throughout the length and breadth of Greece" [Jones, LCL]). It is used similarly by the author of Wis 10.7, in reference to the signs of physical devastation that serve as lasting reminders of the wickedness of the Pentapolis, the five cities of the plain (see Gen 14.1–12). Less frequently μνημόσυνον is used in reference to written reminders, for example by Aristophanes, *Vesp.* 538, καὶ μὴν ὅσ' ἂν λέξῃ γ' ἁπλῶς μνημόσυνα γράψομαι 'γώ ("That I shall, and I'm going to jot down every single point he makes" [Henderson, LCL]).

In the Greek Pentateuch μνημόσυνον is used to render זכרון (Exod 12.14; 13.9; 17.14; 28.12 [2x]; 28.23[29]; 30.16; 39.7 [36.14]; Leu 23.24; Num 5.15, 18; 17.5; 31.54), and זכר (Exod 3.15; 17.14; Deut 32.26), both in the sense "memorial *or* remembrance," but also אזכרה (BDB, s.v. "אַזְכָּרָה," "memorial offering") (Leu 2.2, 9, 16; 5.12; 6.8; Num 5.26). The equivalencies are not, in themselves, lexicographically remarkable. For Greek-speaking Jews, however, it is not implausible to suppose that the word μνημόσυνον acquired a certain resonance over time due its use as a translation equivalent, especially in light of its liturgical associations, which are unparalleled outside of the LXX. Spicq (1994, 501) observes that μνημόσυνον is variously used in reference to the Passover in the Feast of Unleavened Bread (Exod 12.14; 13.9), the stones in the ephod (Exod 28.12; 39.7), and the breastplate (Exod 28.29; 30.6): all are calls to remembrance for Israel (especially for their offenses); at the same time, the use of μνημόσυνον in reference to burnt offerings (Leu 2.2, 9, 16; 5.12; 6.8; Num 5.26) identified it with the Jerusalem temple cult. In view of this background, it is quite possible, as Spicq suggests, that the author of 2 Makk 6.31, in using μνημόσυνον in reference to the death of Eleazar, as "a memorial of courage," intended it to carry liturgical connotations. Whether such connotations underlay the use of the word by G cannot be ascertained with any confidence, but it is not unlikely.

The singular form of the word μνημόσυνον is introduced by G a total of five times (2.23; 9.27, 28; 9.32; 10.2) and represents an important motif within the translation. In the present context it refers to the memorialization of Mardochaios through chronicling. It is used in a very similar context at Mark 14.9. At Esth 9.27–28 it occurs twice in reference to Israel's remembrance of the days of Purim; there it is perhaps cued by the parallel Hebrew context in which the word זכר occurs once. Remembrance is of course central to the Esther scroll: the plot turns on acts of recording and remembering, which in turn are memorialized in the Feast of Purim. G appears to have deliberately emphasized this theme. It is in turn echoed in the received text, where the word μνημόσυνον occurs a further two times (A.15; and E.22). At E.22, the second decree of the king (an original Greek composition), the Feast of Purim is identified as a μνημόσυνον τῆς ἀπωλείας ("a memorial of destruction," NETS).

The plural form of μνημόσυνον occurs at Esth 6.1 in the phrase γράμματα μνημόσυνα τῶν ἡμερῶν ("written daily annals," NETS), which renders ספר הזכרנות דברי הימים ("the book of records, the annals," NRSV), in reference to the record of Mardochaios's service at 2.23. Here μνημόσυνον was perhaps cued by the Hebrew word זכרון. Whether the resulting Greek phrase was a conventional way of denoting such records is uncertain.

ἐν τῇ βασιλικῇ βιβλιοθήκῃ. Compare MT, which refers to a record entered בספר דברי הימים ("in the book of the annals," NRSV; literally, "the book of the words of days"). For a formal rendering of the Hebrew expression, see 1 Suppl 27.24, ἐν βιβλίῳ λόγων τῶν ἡμερῶν. G replaces the phrase with a reference to a library (LSJ, s.v. "βιβλιοθήκη," 2. "library, collection of books"). For this sense of the word, see Polybius, *Hist.* 12.27.4, ὅτι τὰ μὲν ἐκ τῶν βυβλίων δύναται πολυπραγμονεῖσθαι χωρὶς κινδύνου καὶ κακοπαθείας, ἐάν τις αὐτὸ τοῦτο προνοηθῇ μόνον ὥστε λαβεῖν ἢ πόλιν ἔχουσαν ὑπομνημάτων πλῆθος ἢ βιβλιοθήκην που γειτνιῶσαν ("Inquiries from books may be made without any danger or hardship, provided only that one takes care to have access to a town rich in documents or to have a library near at hand" [Paton, LCL]). Ezra 6.1 refers to בית ספריא, or "archives" (NRSV) (literally, "the house of books") at the time of Darius I (522–486 BCE), and the Aramaic phrase is rendered ταῖς βιβλιοθήκαις by the Hellenistic translator of 2 Esdras. The author of 2 Makkabees makes reference to an archive (βιβλιοθήκη) created by Nehemiah (2.13). There, as in the present context, the existence of a royal library provides a guarantee for the knowledge of Jewish traditions independent of the Pentateuch, in particular those regarding the festivals. The Greek historian Ctesias likewise claimed to have used Persian royal archives as a source, though some scholars have denied their existence (Llewellyn-Jones and Robson 2010, 58).

ἐν ἐγκωμίῳ. The matter is recorded in the form of an encomium. This detail has no counterpart in MT and represents an elaboration by G. The Greek word ἐγκώμιον denotes a specific literary genre. Originally it seems to have denoted a song of welcome addressed by a festive crowd (κῶμος), but by the fourth century BCE it was applied to speeches composed in praise of any kind of person or thing (Dover 1980, 11-12). Thus it is used interchangeably with ἔπαινος (LSJ, s.v. 2. "complimentary address, panegyric"). Rules for the genre are articulated in Pseudo-Aristotle, *Rhet. Alex.* 35, a late fourth-century BCE work mistakenly attributed to Aristotle in late antiquity. Included in an ἐγκώμιον are: (1) the blessings enjoyed by the addressee, that is, τὰ ἔξω τῆς ἀρετῆς ἀγαθά ("the goods which fall outside of virtue"); (2) a description of his virtues, specifically, εἰς σοφίαν καὶ δικαιοσύνην καὶ ἀνδρείαν καὶ ἐπιτηδεύματα ἔνδοξα ("wisdom, justice, courage and notable habits of life"); (3) reference to his forebears; and (4) notable achievements (see Dover 1980, 12).

The word ἐγκώμιον is used only once elsewhere in the LXX, at Prov 10.7, where it marks a transformation, μετ' ἐγκωμίων replacing the Hebrew phrase לברכה (BDB, s.v. "בְּרָכָה," 2. "source of blessing"). The sentiment expressed by the Greek proverb is apposite to the present context: μνήμη δικαίων μετ' ἐγκωμίων, ὄνομα δὲ ἀσεβοῦς σβέννυται ("The memory of the righteous comes with eulogies, but the name of the impious is extinguished," NETS). In using the term ἐγκώμιον in this key passage G is perhaps inviting a reading of the book of Esther as a eulogy in memory of the righteous. Martin Hengel (2004, 80–81) suggests that translations directed at Greek-speaking Jews became an important instrument of religious propaganda particularly after the attainment of Judean independence (see the spurious letter of the Jerusalemites to Jews in Egypt, 2 Makk 1.10b–2.18).

ὑπὲρ τῆς εὐνοίας Μαρδοχαίου. A further elaboration of the source by G, describing the theme of the ἐγκώμιον. The virtues are of primary importance in encomia (Dover 1980, 12). Pseudo-Aristotle, *Rhet. Alex.* 35, writes, τὰ μὲν τῆς ἀρετῆς δικαίως ἐγκωμιάζεται, τὰ δ' ἔξω κλέπται ("The qualities which pertain to virtue are the proper subjects of eulogy; those which fall outside are smuggled in"). In Hellenistic royal propaganda of this period εὔνοια represents the signal virtue of a loyal subject. Within the LXX the word is found primarily in nontranslational literature, but the exception is telling. At 1 Makk 11.33 it is used in a putative copy of a letter of Demetrius II Nicator (king of Syria 145–139 and 129–125 BCE) in reference to the loyalty of the Judean nation, which he intends to repay (cf. 1 Makk 11.53 where the narrator notes the failure of Demetrius to return the favors he received). The word is used in the same sense in 3 Makkabees, an original Hellenistic Greek composition which deals inter alia with a theme central to the book of Esther: the pious Jew as loyal subject of the king. At 3 Makk 3.3, as the Judean population of Egypt faces persecution on the false charge of sedition, the narrator assures the reader that they maintained their εὔνοιαν καὶ πίστιν ἀδιάστροφον ("good will and unswerving loyalty," NETS), towards the royal house. At 3 Makk 6.26 when, as a result of divine intervention, the king (Ptolemy Philopator) comes to his senses and accuses his advisors of treason, he describes his Judean subjects as, "those who from the beginning have exceeded all nations in their good will [εὔνοια] towards us" (NETS). At 3 Makk 7.7 it occurs in the context of a royal letter, again in reference to the loyalty of the Jews (also 2 Makk 9.21, 26 in a letter of King Antiochus to his Judean citizens, and 2 Makk 11.19 in a letter of Lysias to the Judeans).

The word εὔνοια is twice introduced by G without warrant from the Hebrew: in the present context, where the king orders that Mardochaios's loyalty be recorded, and at 6.4 where the king is reminded of that loyalty. Charles Harvey (2003, 226) concludes that the conscientious loyalty of Mardochaios to the king is deliberately underscored. The motif finds further expression in the received text, specifically through Additions B and E (the letters of the king). Noah Hacham (2007, 784) has suggested that the author of these additions, perhaps taking his cue from 3 Makkabees, speaks to the anxieties of diaspora Jews living in uncertain times, encouraging them to place their hope in royal recognition of Judean loyalty and service. The Greek version of Prov 24.1 counsels, φοβοῦ τὸν θεόν, υἱέ, καὶ βασιλέα καὶ μηθετέρῳ αὐτῶν ἀπειθήσῃς ("My son, fear God and the king, and disobey neither of them," NETS). This ethos is vividly realized in the Greek text-as-received, which characterizes Mardochaios and Esther as both loyal subjects and devout Jews. Compare B.3, where the word εὔνοια is used ironically of the traitor Haman.

Summary
The plot against the king (plot¹) occurs as a result of Mardochaios's advancement at court and concludes with the king ordering that an encomium be written in his honor. In an aside, G introduces a distinct motif: Esther's piety. In the text-as-received the action refers back to Mardochaios's discovery of an earlier intrigue (plot²) at A.12–17.

§2. Greek Esther A.12–17

Outline
The pericope is made up of two reports. The first (vv. 12–16) falls into three parts: (1) it presents Mardochaios resting in a courtyard (v. 12), where (2) he uncovers a plot of regicide (vv. 13–14); and as a result (3) is rewarded by the king (vv. 15–16). In the second two-part report (v. 17), (1) Haman is introduced as an antagonist, (2) plotting revenge against Mardochaios.

Commentary

A.12
καὶ ἡσύχασεν Μαρδοχαῖος ἐν τῇ αὐλῇ μετὰ Γαβαθα καὶ Θαρρα τῶν δύο εὐνούχων τοῦ βασιλέως τῶν φυλασσόντων τὴν αὐλήν,
And Mardochaios took his rest in the courtyard with Gabatha and Tharra, the two eunuchs of the king who guarded the courtyard.

This verse constitutes the introduction to a report that extends over A.12–16 (Dorothy 1997, 51). In the incident reported, Mardochaios foils a plot against the king, and is honored accordingly. While the present episode (plot²) has no direct counterpart in MT, it parallels an incident in the Hebrew narrative (MT 2.19–23, see above) translated by G (plot¹), the threefold structure of which it mirrors. Plot² has a direct counterpart in AT (A.10–18), but is not represented in either OL or Josephus. AT lacks a parallel to plot¹. The tradition history of the doublet thus remains uncertain, and it is difficult to determine whether it arises from two stories reporting distinct plots or from a single underlying prototype (Cavalier 2012, 104). The balance of probability favors the latter. It is altogether likely that plot² was not an original part of the Esther scroll (see Moore 1977, 179–180), but adapted from plot¹. Moore (1977, 180) regards the absence of plot² in OL as external evidence that it was not originally part of Addition A, and, as such, introduced as late as the second century CE. This remains speculative.

For the purposes of a historical-critical commentary, a key issue is whether plot² had a Semitic *Vorlage* (and thus a source external to the Greek tradition). At present there is a lack of consensus on this matter, though a growing number of scholars are inclined to view the pericope as a translation. OG and AT appear to have a common source for plot², from which they diverge in their choice of vocabulary and syntax (Cavalier 2012, 140). On the hypothesis that plot² is a translation one may speculate regarding its textual relationship to the material translated by G. It is possible, for instance, that the pericope was present in G's source (along with so-called Additions A, C, D and F), as Emanuel Tov (2008, 382) has argued. In the absence of decisive evidence, however, it seems prudent to treat the introduction of plot² as part of the received text, that is, as a secondary elaboration of the translation produced by G. The want of an extant source obviously precludes an analysis of translation technique.

Within a literary analysis of the text-as-received the question arises as to whether the doublet represents two reports of the same incident or two distinct episodes. Moore (1977, 179), who assumes the former, enumerates various contradictions and inconsistencies between the two accounts that he attributes to later editors, since the original translator (he assumes) would have reconciled any differences. But there are indications that plot² and plot¹ function as distinct incidents within the temporal progression of the narrative, each with an important place in its economy (Cavalier 2012, 139). On this view the thematic mirroring of the two episodes is intentional and not a mere by-product of translation and redaction. Whatever its tradition history, plot² represents an integral part of OG as it comes down to us.

καὶ ἡσύχασεν Μαρδοχαῖος. There is no transition from A.11, where Mardochaios ponders the meaning of his dream, rather the two scenes are simply juxtaposed. Such juxtaposition is characteristic of popular narrative (see Frye 1976). Nevertheless a day-night sequence is implied in the text-as-received, suggesting that the following episode is at some level a fulfillment of the dream (Dorothy 1997, 51). The pericope is at the same time metaphorically linked to the motif of the two dragons (Cavalier 2012, 105).

Compare AT, which provides an explicit thematic connection with what has preceded, the narrator stating that the meaning of the dream was made clear to Mardochaios on the day he slept in the courtyard: ἐπίκρισις αὐτοῦ [i.e., τὸ ἐνύπνιον] διασαφηθήσεται αὐτῷ ἕως τῆς ἡμέρας ἧς ὕπνωσε Μαρδοχαῖος ἐν τῇ αὐλῇ ("Its interpretation would become clear to him on the day on which Mardochaios napped in the court," NETS). It is possible that AT represents an elaboration of the narrative sequence of OG.

Assuming that there is less than twenty-four hours separating the dream from the business in the courtyard, the uncovering of the conspiracy occurs in the second year of Artaxerxes. Moore (1977, 177) sees a contradiction here with plot¹ in which the incident occurs in the seventh year of the king, subsequent to the coronation of Esther (2.21). Yet if one reads the doublet as two distinct episodes there is no contradiction.

ἐν τῇ αὐλῇ. One may ask what location is signified by this phrase, and what the presence of Mardochaios there implies about his status. The Greek word αὐλή can refer to either a courtyard or a royal court (see commentary above on 2.19). Where the setting is a royal palace, the two meanings are obviously not exclusive, which seems to be the case here. Mardochaios is located within a palace courtyard—that is where the action takes place—at the same time, he is a functionary at court in the company of royal officials. In the received text he is described in A.2 as ἄνθρωπος μέγας θεραπεύων ἐν τῇ αὐλῇ τοῦ βασιλέως ("a great man serving in the court of the king," NRSV). Compare plot¹ from which the setting of the present scene may have taken its cue. In that context G makes reference to Mardochaios serving in the court (2.19), replacing a reference in the Hebrew to his presence at the king's gate.

Within the narrative world of the text-as-received Mardochaios apparently resides in the royal court at the outset of the action, and is thus an active participant in palace intrigues, and a peer of the courtier Haman. Muhammad Dandamayev (1993) notes that Greek literary sources refer to various foreign dignitaries, ambassadors, and rulers dependent on the Achaemenids who were to be found in residence at the imperial court. According to Herodotus, *Hist.* 3.129–33, Democedes of Croton, personal physician to Darius I, was included among the royal table companions. Plutarch, *Them.* 29, relates that the eponymous Athenian of his narrative became influential at the Persian court and participated in the king's domestic entertainments. Other examples could be enumerated.

Mardochaios is placed in Susa on the first of Nisa (A.1). The present episode thus occurs in the springtime. This is consistent with Greek sources, according to which the imperial court was located in Susa during the spring, and relocated seasonally, spending the summer in Ecbatana, and autumn and winter in Babylon (Xenophon, *Cyr.* 8.6.22; *Anab.* 3.5.15). The coronation palace was at Pasargadae (Plutarch, *Art.*, 3).

Γαβαθα καὶ Θαρρα. These appear to be transliterations of Semitic names. Whether the Greek forms underwent corruption in the course of transmission is uncertain. In the Hebrew counterpart to plot[1] (2.21, see above), the two eunuchs are referred to as בגתן and תרש (בִּגְתָן וָתֶרֶשׁ). Compare the reference in AT's version of plot[2], μετὰ Ἀστάου καὶ Θεδεύτου, which uses Greek forms (Ἀστα[γ]ής and Θεδευτός) (Dorothy 1997, 54). Josephus's Θεοδέστης is perhaps based on Θεδευτός of AT, which as Ralph Marcus (Josephus 1937, 414) observes, may in turn be a corruption of Hebrew תרש, since ר and ד are easily confused in Hebrew script. H. Willrich reportedly connected Θεδευτός with Theodotos, an Egyptian deserter who according to 3 Makk 1.2 attempted to kill King Ptolemy IV, but the similarity is likely coincidental (Josephus 1937, 414).

τῶν δύο εὐνούχων τοῦ βασιλέως. Compare the reference in plot[1] to οἱ δύο εὐνοῦχοι τοῦ βασιλέως (2.21), which is a rendering of שני סריסי המלך (MT). The match of εὐνοῦχος with סריס is conventional in the LXX (see commentary on 2.21). While the motif of the two eunuchs is present in the Hebrew, the doubling of the motif in the Greek text-as-received gives it further literary significance. The figure of the εὐνοῦχος had become a stock character in Greek stories about the Persian court. In classical Greek literature the εὐνοῦχος serves both as a literary cliché and as a component of ethnic prejudice against the Persian Empire (Lenfant 2012, 297).

In Herodotus eunuchs appear as personal attendants serving the Persian king or his dignitaries (Lenfant 2012, 271). They do not, however, figure prominently in his depiction of the court. It is in the *Persica* of Ctesias of Cnidus, a Greek physician in the Persian court at the end of the fifth century BCE, that they take on a more significant role. (The *Persica*, an extensive history of the Persian Empire, is extant only in fragments; for text and translation, see Stronk 2010.) In Ctesias's narrative, eunuchs serve as prominent attendants of the royal family, and are especially notable for their involvement in palace intrigues (Lenfant 2012, 269). The difference between Herodotus and Ctesias in their depiction of eunuchs can be interpreted in two ways: it may reflect an actual historical development, suggesting that eunuchs did in fact become more influential during the reign of Xerxes; on the other hand, it may be part of the larger trend in

Greek historiography toward using clichés to emphasize the decadence of the Persian Empire (Lenfant 2012, 272–3). The prominent role given to eunuchs in the received text of Greek Esther possibly reflects this trend, though it should be emphasized that in this respect it is picking up and extending a feature of the Hebrew narrative. The motif of plotting eunuchs may well have had wide circulation in the Hellenistic Near East, independent of its use by Greek authors.

τῶν φυλασσόντων τὴν αὐλήν. The eunuchs serve as palace guards. Compare the Hebrew version of plot[1] (2.21), where the eunuchs (סריסי המלך) are referred to as שמרי הסף ("[those] who guarded the threshold," NRSV). OG is more detailed in describing the conspirators than AT, which simply calls them eunuchs. In the text-as-received the two eunuchs involved in plot[2] evidently have a lower status within the court hierarchy than those involved in plot[1], who are described as ἀρχισωματοφύλακες ("chief body-guards"; see the commentary above on 2.21).

A.13

> ἤκουσέν τε αὐτῶν τοὺς λογισμοὺς καὶ τὰς μερίμνας αὐτῶν ἐξηραύνησεν καὶ ἔμαθεν ὅτι ἑτοιμάζουσιν τὰς χεῖρας ἐπιβαλεῖν ’Αρταξέρξῃ τῷ βασιλεῖ, καὶ ὑπέδειξεν τῷ βασιλεῖ περὶ αὐτῶν.
>
> He both overheard their deliberations and inquired into their ambitions, and learned that they were preparing to lay hands on Artaxerxes the king, and told the king about them.

This verse marks the beginning of the body of the report (vv. 13–14), which is comprised of (1) a description of Mardochaios's actions (v. 13), and (2) those of the king (v. 14). Compare the body of the report in plot[1] (2.22–23), which the present episode mirrors structurally.

ἤκουσέν … λογισμοὺς … μερίμνας … ἐξηραύνησεν. The first two clauses have a pleasing chiasmic structure. This stylistic feature is consistent with the hypothesis of a relatively free adaptation of the source. Moore (1977, 180) suggests that A.11–17 is composed in better Greek than that of the previous pericope A.4–10, but this may simply reflect the generic differences between a dream sequence and a narrative.

αὐτῶν τοὺς λογισμούς. In this reference to the eunuchs' machinations, one notes that the genitival (αὐτῶν) precedes the noun it modifies, which is the preferred order in Greek prose composition; compare AT A.12 τοὺς λόγους αὐτῶν ("their words," NETS). The Greek word λογισμός denotes a process of careful thought and planning, with connotations of moral duplicity (LSJ, s.v. "λογισμός," II. without reference to number, *calculation, reasoning*). See for example Aeschines, *Tim.* 1.84, ἀλλ᾽ οὕτως ἰσχυρόν ἐστιν ἡ ἀλήθεια, ὥστε πάντων ἐπικρατεῖν τῶν ἀνθρωπίνων λογισμῶν ("but so strong is the truth that it prevails—over all the calculations of men" [Adams, LCL]). If there was a Semitic source for plot[2], the underlying form would likely have been מחשבות (BDB, s.v. "מַחֲשָׁבָה," 1. "thought." 2. "device, plan, purpose"); see, for example, Ps 33(32).10, 11; Prov 6.18; 12.5; 15.22, 26; 19.21; Ier 27:45.

τὰς μερίμνας. Although the plural form typically carries the sense "cares *or* anxieties" (cf. Prov 17.12), in the present context the word likely refers to the eunuchs' "ambitions" (LSJ, s.v. "μέριμνα," 3. *pursuit, ambition,* esp. in plural). Compare AT A.12 τὰς διαβολὰς αὐτῶν ("their schemes," NETS). The word μέριμνα occurs infrequently in the LXX (1 Makk 6:10; Ps 55[54].23; Prov 17.12; Iob 11.18; Sir 30.24; 31.1; 38.29; 42.9; Dan 11.26). Where a Hebrew source text is extant (Ps 55[54].23; Prov 17.12; Job 11.18) there is no straightforward equivalency upon which to base a retroversion.

ἐξηρεύνησεν. In OG Mardochaios not only overhears the conspiracy but investigates it (LSJ, s.v. "ἐξερευνάω," "search out, examine"), and thus has a more active role than in AT where he simply hears of it (Dorothy 1997, 54). Compare plot[1] where the matter is brought to his attention (2.22), καὶ ἐδηλώθη Μαρδοχαίῳ ("But the matter became known to Mardoch-aios," NETS).

Here Mardochaios's role is similar to that of the court functionary referred to by Herodotus, *Hist.* 1.114 (in a story about Cyrus's childhood), as ὀφθαλμὸς βασιλέος, "the king's eye." The young Cyrus, playing the king's part in a make-believe court, appoints the other children to their respective roles: ὁ δὲ αὐτῶν διέταξε τοὺς μὲν οἰκίας οἰκοδομέειν, τοὺς δὲ δορυφόρους εἶναι, τὸν δέ κου τινὰ αὐτῶν ὀφθαλμὸν βασιλέος εἶναι, τῷ δὲ τινὶ τὰς ἀγγελίας φέρειν ἐδίδου γέρας, ὡς ἑκάστῳ ἔργον προστάσσων ("Then he set them severally to their tasks, some to the building of houses, some to be his bodyguard, one [as I suppose] to be the King's Eye; to another he gave the right of bringing him messages; to each he gave his proper work" [Godley, LCL]). Dandamayev (1993) notes that according to Greek sources the entire court was under the constant surveillance of the so-called "ears and eyes" of the king, agents who were independent of other authorities and reported any suspicion of sedition directly to the king. See Xenophon, *Cyr.*, 8.2.10, τοὺς γὰρ ἀπαγγείλαντας ὅσα καιρὸς αὐτῷ εἴη πεπύσθαι μεγάλως εὐεργετῶν πολλοὺς ἐποίησεν ἀνθρώπους καὶ ὠτακουστεῖν καὶ διοπτεύειν τί ἄν ἀγγείλαντες ὠφελήσειαν βασιλέα ("for by rewarding liberally those who reported to him whatever it was to his interest to hear, he prompted many men to make it their business to use their eyes and ears to spy out what they could report to the king to his advantage" [Miller, LCL]).

τὰς χεῖρας ἐπιβαλεῖν Ἀρταξέρξῃ. The construction resembles the Hebrew idiom ב יד לשלח ("to lay hands on"). Thus at 6.2 G renders לשלח יד במלך by ἐπιβαλεῖν τὰς χεῖρας Ἀρταξέρξῃ. Compare AT A.12 τοῦ ἐπιθέσθαι Ασσυήρῳ τῷ βασιλεῖ ("to assault Assyeros the king," NETS) (LSJ, s.v. "ἐπιτίθημι," B. med. III. 2. "make an attempt upon, attack"). A common Hebrew source is thus possible. Yet the phrasing of OG is not unidiomatic and thus cannot be enlisted in support of the hypothesis of interference from a Hebrew parent. See, for example, Polybius, *Hist.* 3.2.8, καὶ τὰς χεῖρας ἐπιβάλλειν Φίλιππος μὲν τοῖς κατ' Αἴγυπτον καὶ Καρίαν καὶ Σάμον, Ἀντίοχος δὲ τοῖς κατὰ Κοίλην Συρίαν καὶ Φοινίκην ("Philip laying hands on Egypt and on Caria and Samos, while Antiochus seized on Coele-Syria and Phoenicia" [Paton, LCL]).

In Ctesias's depiction of the Persian court there are many references to eunuchs taking part in plots or assassination attempts against the king (see Lenfant 2012, 270). These occur under Semiramis, Cyrus, the Magus, Xerxes II, and Darius II. In later *Persica* (the sources of the final chapters of Plutarch's *Artaxerxes*) and the historians of Alexander the Great, eunuchs are notable for their involvement in court plots (Lenfant 2012, 274). The motif became quite popular in Hellenistic historiography, which might in turn have influenced the adaptation of plot[2] within the received text.

καὶ ὑπέδειξεν τῷ βασιλεῖ. The Greek verb may simply mean "warn" (compare Matt 3.7), but more likely refers to the passing on of information (LSJ, s.v. "ὑποδείκνυμι," I. 3. "report"). Moore (1977, 178) renders it "he informed the king." At Tob 1.19 (both texts) the verb carries this sense in a similar context: πορευθεὶς δὲ εἷς τῶν ἐν Νινευη καὶ ὑπέδειξεν τῷ βασιλεῖ περὶ ἐμοῦ ("But one of the people of Nineue went and informed the king about me," NETS). There is no reference to an intermediary, and whether Mardochaios reported directly to the king is uncertain. Compare plot[1] (2.22) where in both OG and MT Esther acts as an intermediary. The absence of any reference to Esther in plot[2] differentiates it from plot[1] in the received text. Dorothy (1997, 49) observes that in this section the reader is asked to focus on Mordecai and the king as main characters.

A.14

Καὶ ἐξήτασεν ὁ βασιλεὺς τοὺς δύο εὐνούχους, καὶ ὁμολογήσαντες ἀπήχθησαν.

Then the king interrogated the two eunuchs, and when they confessed, they were led away.

ἐξήτασεν ὁ βασιλεύς. This parallels the Greek version of plot[1], ὁ δὲ βασιλεὺς ἤτασεν τοὺς δύο εὐνούχους (2.23), where emphasis is likewise placed on the king's agency. Compare the Hebrew version of plot[1], which uses an impersonal construction, ויבקש הדבר וימצא ("When the affair was investigated and found to be so," NRSV). (The Hebrew verbs are pointed as passive forms in the MT.) At A.14 AT elaborates upon the king's actions (καὶ ἤτασεν ὁ βασιλεὺς τοὺς δύο εὐνούχους) with a further reference to Mardochaios, καὶ εὗρε τοὺς λόγους Μαρδοχαίου ("and found Mardochaios's words true," NETS), thus underscoring his role in the affair (Dorothy 1997, 54).

καὶ ὁμολογήσαντες. Compare plot[1] (2.23) where in both OG and MT there is no reference to the eunuchs' confession. AT, however, agrees with OG plot[2] (καὶ ὁμολογήσαντες οἱ εὐνοῦχοι ἀπήχθησαν).

ἀπήχθησαν. Moore (1977, 178) suggests that execution is here implied. The Greek verb (also used by AT in this context) is well attested in reference to arrest and imprisonment (LSJ, s.v. "ἀπάγω," IV. 3. "carry off to prison"). See Lysias, 25.15, ὑπ' ἐμοῦ γὰρ ἐν τῇ ὀλιγαρχίᾳ οὔτε ἀπαχθεὶς οὐδεὶς φανήσεται, οὔτε τῶν ἐχθρῶν οὐδεὶς τετιμωρημένος, οὔτε τῶν φίλων εὖ πεπονθώς ("I had no hand during the oligarchy, you will find, either in the arrest of anybody, or in taking vengeance upon any of my enemies, or in conferring a favour on any of my friends" [Lamb, LCL]).

A.15

Καὶ ἔγραψεν ὁ βασιλεὺς τοὺς λόγους τούτους εἰς μνημόσυνον, καὶ Μαρδοχαῖος ἔγραψεν περὶ τῶν λόγων τούτων·

And the king wrote these things in the record, and Mardochaios wrote concerning these things.

ἔγραψεν ὁ βασιλεύς. The matter is officially recorded. This detail is likely derived from plot[1] where it represents an important plot device. It is interesting that here the king is the subject of the verb "to write," emphasizing his agency (though it is possible that this is not meant literally). AT agrees with OG in this regard. Compare plot[1] (2.23) where the Hebrew version uses an impersonal construction (implying the king's oversight), ויכתב בספר דברי הימים לפני המלך ("It was recorded in the book of the annals in the presence of the king," NRSV). In that passage G evidently recast the Hebrew so as to make explicit the king's initiative in recording Mardochaios's service.

According to Herodotus, *Hist.* 8.85.3, a person who had rendered important service to the Persian king was styled a εὐεργέτης βασιλέος ("benefactor of the king"): Φύλακος δὲ εὐεργέτης βασιλέος ἀνεγράφη καὶ χώρη ἐδωρήθη πολλῇ. οἱ δ᾽ εὐεργέται βασιλέος ὀροσάγγαι καλέονται περσιστί ("and Phylacus was recorded among the king's benefactors and given much land. These benefactors of the king are called in the Persian language, orosangae" [Godley, LCL]). The official recording of the benefactor's name was evidently conventional. See, for instance, Herodotus, *Hist.* 8.90.4, ὅκως γάρ τινα ἴδοι Ξέρξης τῶν ἑωυτοῦ ἔργον τι ἀποδεικνύμενον ἐν τῇ ναυμαχίῃ, κατήμενος ὑπὸ τῷ ὄρεϊ τῷ ἀντίον Σαλαμῖνος τὸ καλέεται Αἰγάλεως, ἀνεπυνθάνετο τὸν ποιήσαντα, καὶ οἱ γραμματισταὶ ἀνέγραφον πατρόθεν τὸν τριήραρχον καὶ τὴν πόλιν ("For whenever Xerxes, from his seat under the hill over against Salamis called Aegaleos, saw any feat achieved by his own men in the battle, he inquired who was the doer of it, and his scribes wrote down the names of the ship's captain and his father and his city" [Godley, LCL]). Herodotus, *Hist.* 3.140, knows of official lists of the king's benefactors in royal archives, and it is not unlikely that there was a body of tales in circulation concerning these individuals (for Histiaeus of Miletus and Coes the Mytilenaean see 5.11; for Xenagoras see 9.107). A feature of such stories was evidently the granting of a request. See for instance Herodotus, *Hist.* 3.139–141, which tells the story of a Greek benefactor (εὐεργέτης) of Darius. While campaigning in Egypt with Cambyses, Darius approached Syloson, an exile from Samos, to purchase a cloak he much admired. Syloson refused to sell the cloak, but rather gave it to him. Later when Darius assumed the throne, Syloson appeared at court claiming to be a benefactor of the king, and, upon relating the story of the cloak, was granted his request that his native Samos be restored. The story, the basis of a proverb, was undoubtedly a popular tale. (For the granting of requests, see also Herodotus, *Hist.* 5.11.)

εἰς μνημόσυνον. The phrase means literally "for a memorial." In the present context it refers to the memorialization of a person through chronicling. (Presumably Mardochaios's Judean ethnicity was recorded in the present instance.) See plot[1] (2.23), where the same phrase is introduced by G without warrant from the Hebrew. Memorialization functions as a key motif in the Greek text-as-received. The phrase εἰς μνημόσυνον does not occur in AT.

καὶ Μαρδοχαῖος ἔγραψεν. This detail is absent in plot[1] and does not figure in the larger narrative. In the text-as-received it has the effect of further underscoring Mardochaios's agency. Moreover it relates to the theme of memory and memorialization, as it establishes the existence of a specifically Jewish record of the events reported in plot[2]. Compare the parallel in AT (A.15) where the verb is passive. There Mardochaios does not write "concerning these things" but is written about, thus anticipating the events of chapter 6 in the received text (Cavalier 2012, 139): καὶ ἐγράφη Μαρδοχαῖος ἐν τῷ βιβλίῳ τοῦ βασιλέως περὶ τοῦ μνημονεύειν τῶν λόγων τούτων ("and Mardochaios was written about in the book of the king so that these things would be remembered," NETS). AT's reference to "the book of the king" is reminiscent of the Hebrew version of plot[1] (בספר דברי הימים).

A.16

> Καὶ ἐπέταξεν ὁ βασιλεὺς Μαρδοχαίῳ θεραπεύειν ἐν τῇ αὐλῇ καὶ ἔδωκεν αὐτῷ δόματα περὶ τούτων.
> And the king ordered Mardochaios to serve in the court and gave to him gifts for these things.

Mardochaios is rewarded by the king immediately. This is an important element, further differentiating plot[2] from plot[1] (Cavalier 2012, 139). In plot[1] such recognition is inexplicably delayed until a later point in the narrative, when the king is reminded of the omission (6.2). Here a relationship is established between Mardochaios and the king at the outset, one with important implications for the theme of court rivalry in the text-as-received. In this respect it is in sharp contrast to MT.

θεραπεύειν ἐν τῇ αὐλῇ. In the text-as-received, this development is in tension with A.2, where Mardochaios is already identified as serving in the court; A.2 may be read as a proleptic reference, anticipating the present scene.

On the other hand, Mardochaios's role in plot² does seem to imply that he holds a position at court from the outset. Thus, the present verse may be understood in reference to a new appointment or promotion. (Compare AT where he is specifically appointed to serve the king: he will guard the doors.) In the received text of OG the king's public acknowledgement of Mardochaios as a benefactor in the opening scene bears on the interpretation of plot¹, where, over-against the Hebrew, G attributes the conspiracy of the eunuchs to their dissatisfaction with Mardochaios's advancement (2.21). On one reading, which is admittedly quite persuasive, the outcome of plot² provides the dramatic motivation for plot¹, transforming the place of the latter in the overall design of the narrative. That this was perhaps due to fortuity in the transmission of the text, rather than a conscious literary strategy on the part of a redactor, does not lessen its significance for the text-as-received.

Mara Brosius (2007, 55) observes that the key to the working of the Achaemenid court was personal recognition by the king and his bestowal of gifts to reward service. This is emphasized by Xenophon, *Cyr.*, 8.1.39, who credits Cyrus II with initiating the practice of inspiring loyalty through rewarding his subjects with gifts, preferment, and positions of authority: Πρὸς δὲ τούτῳ καὶ τῶν ἄλλων οὕστινας μάλιστα ὁρῴη τὰ καλὰ διώκοντας, τούτους καὶ δώροις καὶ ἀρχαῖς καὶ ἕδραις καὶ πάσαις τιμαῖς ἐγέραιρεν· ὥστε πολλὴν πᾶσι φιλοτιμίαν ἐνέβαλεν ὅπως ἕκαστος ὅτι ἄριστος φανήσοιτο Κύρῳ ("And besides this, he used to reward with gifts and positions of authority and seats of honour and all sorts of preferment others whom he saw devoting themselves most eagerly to the attainment of excellence; and thus he inspired in all an earnest ambition, each striving to appear as deserving as he could in the eyes of Cyrus" [Miller, LCL]). A system of royal favor and patronage—a service aristocracy—developed in which royal acknowledgement of individual courtiers provided them with the opportunity to increase their wealth and to enhance their status (Brosius 2007, 55). The system thus encouraged intense rivalries. This facet of Persian court culture was well known to Hellenistic authors, and became an established literary motif. While present in the Hebrew narrative, it is further developed in the Greek text-as-received, where rivalry and intrigue within the court is established early on as a central theme.

καὶ ἔδωκεν αὐτῷ δόματα. Mardochaios is rewarded not only with a promotion within the hierarchy of the court, but with gifts as well. According to Xenophon, *Anab.* 1.2.27, a Persian king showed favor through bestowing specific gifts, that is, δῶρα ἃ νοίζεται παρὰ βασιλεῖ τίμια, ἵππον χρυσοχάλινον καὶ στρεπτὸν χρυσοῦν καὶ ψέλια καὶ ἀκινάκην χρυσοῦν καὶ στολὴν Περσικήν ("gifts which are regarded at court as tokens of honour—a horse with a gold-mounted bridle, a gold necklace and bracelets, a gold dagger and a Persian robe" [Brownson, LCL]).

A.17

Καὶ ἦν Αμαν Αμαδαθου Βουγαῖος ἔνδοξος ἐνώπιον τοῦ βασιλέως· καὶ ἐξήτησεν κακοποιῆσαι τὸν Μαρδοχαῖον καὶ τὸν λαὸν αὐτοῦ ὑπὲρ τῶν δύο εὐνούχων τοῦ βασιλέως.

But Haman son of Hamadathos, a Bougean, was highly esteemed by the king, and he sought to harm Mardochaios and his people because of the two eunuchs of the king.

The introduction of Haman marks the beginning of the second report (A.17), which has no counterpart in MT (compare the introduction of Haman at 3.1). Here he is identified from the outset as the antagonist of Mardochaios, and his motivation is established. His appearance is thematically linked to the palace intrigue, a transformation that has important implications for the text-as-received.

Αμαν Αμαδαθου Βουγαῖος. The proper-name designation (PN) of Haman favored by G (3.1; 9.10). In the Hebrew text the PN המן בן המדתא האגגי ("Haman son of Hammedatha the Agagite," NRSV), occurs four times (3.1, 10; 8.5; 9.24); and there are two variants, המן האגגי (8.3) and המן בן המדתא (9.10). Elsewhere the character is simply referred to as המן. At 3.1 G renders the Hebrew PN Αμαν Αμαδαθου Βουγαῖος. Αμαν is an uninflected transliteration of Hebrew המן, and Αμαδαθου, represents a partial assimilation of בן המדתא to Greek convention: בן ("son of") is picked up by the genitive case of the transliteration. With the third item, however, OG diverges markedly from the Hebrew. While Haman is identified in MT as an Agagite (perhaps Amalekite, so later Jewish tradition), OG identifies him as a Bougean. The origin and meaning of the Greek term remains unknown (Moore 1977, 178). The designation appears again at 9.10, where המן בן המדתא is rendered Αμαν Αμαδαθου Βουγαῖος. G simply uses Αμαν at 3.10, 8.3, and 8.5. At 9.24, however, where MT reads המן בן המדתא האגגי, OG reads Αμαν Αμαδαθου ὁ Μακεδών. Dorothy (1997, 55) sees contemporizing exegesis in the change of PN designation. The substitution suggests to Moore (1977, 178) that Bougean (like Macedonian) was an updated term of reproach: just as the Hebrew narrative uses Agagite to represent the implacable enemy of the Israelites, so G supplies contemporary terms for Hellenistic readers, the once opprobrious term "Bougean" giving way to "Macedonian." (Compare the parallel to plot[2] in AT where Haman is likewise identified as Μακεδών.) This might suggest that the Greek form of the PN used at 9.24 is later (tradition historically) than that of A.17.

ἐνώπιον τοῦ βασιλέως. Moore (1977, 178) considers this a Hebraism, with ἐνώπιον matching Hebrew לִפְנֵי. Compare AT κατὰ πρόσωπον τοῦ βασιλέως, also a Hebraism, and thus suggestive of a common source.

ἐξήτησεν κακοποιῆσαι τὸν Μαρδοχαῖον. Given the thematic link between the introduction of the character Haman and plot[2], and the juxtaposition of this section with the dream sequence, it is implied that Haman's determination to harm Mardochaios is in fulfillment of the dream. As Dorothy (1997, 51) observes, this has major implications for the rest of the book's structure: the main plot is in effect a second complete fulfillment of the present episode.

ὑπὲρ τῶν δύο εὐνούχων. In the received text of OG Haman's hostility is a direct result of the fact that Mardochaios has informed on the conspirators with whom Haman was presumably in league (Moore 1977, 178). Cavalier (2012, 140) observes that this alters the sense of the book entirely. Compare MT in which Haman's hatred arises from Mordecai's refusal to prostrate himself. Moore (1977, 178) sees this as another inconsistency between OG and the Hebrew narrative, but it apparently represents a deliberate transformation. The implication that Haman was complicit in plot[2] is echoed in the text-as-received at Addition E.14, where Artaxerxes reveals Haman's scheme to transfer the Persian Empire to the Macedonians. His intention in persecuting Mardochaios, we learn at E.13, was to isolate the king by destroying his σωτῆρα ("savior") and διὰ παντὸς εὐεργέτην ("constant benefactor," NETS). Plot[2] may thus be read as part of a larger conspiracy against the empire (Cavalier 2012, 106). This suggests further that, for the narrative world of the text-as-received, Haman is also complicit in plot[1]. In this respect the abrupt juxtaposition of Haman's promotion with the conclusion of plot[1] at 3.1 takes on added significance for the Greek reader.

Compare AT A.17 where, as part of his reward from the king, Mardochaios receives Haman as his servant, which in turn motivates Haman's hatred. That the two texts are here genetically related is, however, relatively certain. The two read almost identically, with the exception of three minuses in AT relative to OG.

OG καὶ ἔδωκεν αὐτῷ <u>δόματα</u> περὶ τούτων <u>καὶ ἦν</u> Αμαν Αμαδαθου Βουγαῖος <u>ἔνδοξος</u> ἐνώπιον τοῦ βασιλέως·

AT καὶ ἔδωκεν αὐτῷ _____ περὶ τούτων _____ Αμαν Αμαδάθου Μακεδόνα _____ κατὰ πρόσωπον τοῦ βασιλέως

Summary
This pericope presents an initial fulfilment of Mardochaios's dream (with specific reference to the motif of the two dragons at A.5). Mardochaios is established as a benefactor of the king (A.16), with Haman as his implacable enemy (A.17). Whereas in MT Haman's antagonism stems from Mordecai's refusal to prostrate himself (3.5–6), in the received text of OG it results from his role in thwarting a plot against the king (plot[2]) in which Haman is evidently implicated. In this way the story of Esther and Mardochaios unfolds against the background of an intrigue at court in which Mardochaios figures as a key player.

It's a Question of Intelligence: Iob 34

Claude E. Cox

Literature

Beer, Georg. 1897. *Der Text des Buches Hiob*. Marburg: Elwertsche.
♦ **Bratsiotis**, N. P. 1975. בשׂר. *TDOT* 2:317–32. ♦ **Cadell**, Hélène.
1995."Vocabulaire de la Législation ptolémaïque: Problème du sens de
dikaiôma dans le Pentateuque." Pages 207–21 in Κατὰ τοὺς ό: *Selon les
Septante; Trent études sur la Bible grecque des Septante; en hommage à
Marguerite Harl*. Edited by Gilles Dorival and Olivier Munnich. Paris:
Cerf. ♦ **Clines**, David J. A. 2006. *Job 21–37*. WBC 18A. Nashville: Nelson.
♦ **Davidson**, A. B. 1918. *The Book of Job*. CBSC. Cambridge: Cambridge
University Press. ♦ **Dhorme**, Édouard. 1967 [French 1926]. *A Com-
mentary on the Book of Job*. Translated by H. Knight. Nashville: Nelson.
♦ **Fabry**, H.-J. 1978. דל. *TDOT* 3:208–30. ♦ **Fohrer**, Georg. 1963. *Das Buch
Job*. KAT 16. Gütersloh: Mohn. ♦ **Fox**, Michael V. 2005. "LXX-Proverbs
as a Text-Critical Resource." *Textus* 22:95–128. ♦ **Gordis**, Robert. 1978.
The Book of God and Man: A Study of Job. Chicago: University of Chicago
Press. ♦ **Gorea**, Maria. 2007. *Job Repensé ou Trahi? Omissions et raccourcis
de la Septante*. Études Bibliques NS 56. Paris: Gabalda. ♦ **Heater**, Homer.
1982. *A Septuagint Translation Technique in the Book of Job*. CBQMS 11.
Washington, DC: Catholic Biblical Association of America. ♦ **Homer**.
1924. *The Iliad with an English Translation*. Translated by A. T. Murray.
LCL 170–71. London: Heinemann. ♦ **Homer**. 1950. *The Iliad*. Translated
by E. V. Rieu. Penguin Classics. Harmondsworth: Penguin. ♦ **Orlinsky**,
Harry M. 1959. "Studies in the Septuagint of the Book of Job." *HUCA*
29:229–71; 30:153–67. ♦ **Pietersma**, Albert. 1985. Review of *Iob*, edited by
Joseph Ziegler. *JBL* 104:305–11. ♦ **Plutarch**. 1868. *Phocion*. In vol. 4 of *Plutarch's Lives: The Translation called Dryden's corrected from the Greek and
Revised*. Edited by A. H. Clough. Boston: Little, Brown. ♦ **Pope**, Marvin

H. 1965. *Job*. AB 15. Garden City, NY: Doubleday. ◆ **Pseudo-Justin**. 1996. *Cohortatio ad Graecos*. In vol. 4 of *Orphica: Fragments from Hellenistic Jewish Authors*. Edited by Carl R. Holladay. SBLTT 40; SBLPS 14. Chico, CA: Scholars Press. ◆ **Tjen**, Anwar. 2010. *On Conditionals in the Greek Pentateuch: A Study of Translation Syntax*. LHBOTS 515. New York: T&T Clark. ◆ **Xenophon**. 1914. *Cyropaedia*. Translated by Walter Miller. 2 vols. LCL 51–52. London: Heinemann.

Outline

The speech in chapter 34 is part of the Elious speeches (chs. 32–37). G retains the basic structure of the source text in chapter 34, while subjecting it to substantial changes. The asterisk tradition indicates that G omitted verses 3–4, 6b–7, 11b, 18b, 23a, 25b and one extended passage, 28–33. Like the source text, the OG has five sections: the narrator introduces the speaker (1); Elious invites "the wise" to listen and cites several of Iob's claims (2–9). Third and fourth, Elious defends the Lord against these claims in two parts (10–20 and 21–27). Finally, Elious addresses Iob directly and tells him that he should quit his foolish talk (34–37). Notably G preserves the conclusion intact.

Commentary

34.1: Introducing the speaker

וַיַּעַן אֱלִיהוּא וַיֹּאמַר

Ὑπολαβὼν δὲ Ἐλιοῦς λέγει

Now Elious says in reply:

G renders the formulaic introduction in the typical way: a participle + finite verb represents the two, coordinated finite verbs of the source text. The participle ὑπολαβών + λέγω means "answer and say" or simply "reply" (LSJ, s.v. "ὑπολαμβάνω" 3.a; BDAG, s.v., 1.d). It appears with this meaning several times in Plato's dialogues (e.g., *Phaed.* 69.e.6; *Leg.* 705.d.6) and in numerous other classical writers (e.g., Thucydides, Plutarch, Herodotus, Xenophon).

34.2–9: Elious cites Iob's claims

34.2, 4b (source text 2–4)

 וידעים האזינו לי || מלי שמעו חכמים   2
וחך יטעם לאכל || [כי אזן מלין תבחן   3
[משפט נבחרה לנו || נדעה בינינו מה טוב]   4

2a Ἀκούσατέ μου, σοφοί·
2b, 4b ἐπιστάμενοι ἐνωτίζεσθε τὸ καλόν·

"Hear me, you wise men;
Know and give ear to what is good—

Ziegler does not include τὸ καλόν ("what is good") as part of his text. On this issue see Pietersma 1985, 308. Ziegler's citation of the evidence is: (2b) fin B′-S* O 534] + το (> 523 Syn) καλον rel: cf. 4b fin. The choice of the shorter text reflects an overreliance on MSS B-S, in reality one witness. Ziegler points us to the end of θ′ 4b as the source of τὸ καλόν (= מה טוב ["what is good," NRSV]). Note that Theodotion uses ὅ τι καλόν to translate מה טוב, not τὸ καλόν. For his part, Édouard Dhorme (1967) thinks the shorter text is the result of homoioteleuton, (2b) האזינו to (4b) בינינו ("among ourselves") but Dhorme too often clarifies omissions in the OG with this explanation. Rather, G is responsible for skipping from (almost) the end of verse 2 to the end of verse 4.

Ἀκούσατέ μου. G represents מלי ("my words") with μου ("me") in the genitive after ἀκούω. Hexaplaric witnesses (O II) replace μου with τα ρηματα μου ("my words") (= MT); see also 33.31. The verb ἀκούω is G's default rendering of שמע ("hear"), as is the case throughout the LXX.

ἐπιστάμενοι. The participle ידעים is usually read as a vocative (e.g., "You learned" NJPS), parallel to חכמים = σοφοί (so Zi, note the comma following ἐπιστάμενοι in his text; Brenton; NJPS). However, at 7.20b ἐπιστάμενοι is arthrous when used as a vocative and the same is true at 6.19b, where οἱ διορῶντες is vocative. Therefore ἐπιστάμενοι should be regarded as a circumstantial participle, so that both lines of the OG begin with a second-person plural imperative (see NETS). On the articulated participle used as a vocative, see BDF §§147; 412(5).

ἐνωτίζεσθε. G uses ἐνωτίζομαι to render אזן hiphil ("give ear") in five of the six occurrences of אזן in Job (32.11; 33.1; 34.2, 16; 37.14; the exception is at 9.16) and this corresponds to the choice of OG translators generally (27x out of 41x). The first extant use of ἐνωτίζομαι is in Gen 4.23, so it appears to be a LXX neologism derived from ὠτίον, diminuative of οὖς ("ear"). All instances of its use in Iob involve the imperative and an accusative direct object, as in verse 2.

τὸ καλόν. G's omission means that ἐνωτίζεσθε has τὸ καλόν as a direct object. The expression τὸ καλόν does not occur elsewhere in Iob, but it occurs elsewhere in the LXX, including five times in Deuteronomy, where in each case it appears with τὸ ἀρεστόν ("what is pleasing") (6.18; 12.25, 28; 13.18; 21.9). Following as it does σοφοί, it is possible that τὸ καλόν is to be understood in the light of Greek philosophy, where it is a concept that appears from the fifth century BCE onward. There its opposite is τὸ αἰσχρόν ("the shameful, base; vice"; LSJ, s.v. "καλός" [III.2]; "αἰσχρός"). But, since G is less likely to borrow from Greek philosophy than from the law, there may well be an allusion to OG Deuteronomy. The fact that τὸ καλόν resonates with Greek philosophy is a plus for intellectuals among the intended audience.

In the OG, Elious alone is going to tell the other four "what is good," whereas in the source text they are to determine this together (4: נדעה ["Let us"]). What he is going to say is "the good," as the wise will recognize.

34.5, 6a, bβ (source text 5–7)

5   ואל הסיר משפטי || כי אמר איוב צדקתי

6   אנוש חצי בלי פשע || על משפטי אכזב

7   [ישתה לעג כמים || מי גבר כאיוב]

5   ὅτι εἴρηκεν Ἰώβ Δίκαιός εἰμι,
    ὁ κύριος ἀπήλλαξέν μου τὸ κρίμα,
6a ἐψεύσατο δὲ τῷ κρίματί μου,

    because Iob has said, 'I am righteous;
    the Lord dismissed my case,
    but he lied with respect to my case,

In verses 5–9 Elious quotes Job's complaints against the Lord. G omits 6b (actually 6bα: see 8a), 7, apparently because their subject matter is a digression, what with their talk of Iob's wound (6b) and his drinking up scoffing like water (7); note that verse 3 with its simile about food is also omitted.

ὅτι εἴρηκεν. Usually G employs γάρ ("for") to represent causative כִּי, so NETS marks the choice of ὅτι with its translation "because." The perfect εἴρηκεν renders אָמַר qal perfect. Greek has more choices to represent "tenses" than does Hebrew and the perfect carries the nuance that Iob's claim has endured to the present moment. Compare G's use of the imperfect (1.5), aorist (3.3), and present tense (7.4) to render אָמַר perfect in other contexts.

Δίκαιός εἰμι. G uses the predicate adjective and verb "to be" to render צָדֵק qal (stative), as generally (ca. 10x; e.g., 9.2, 15, 20; 10.15; 11.2).

ὁ κύριος ἀπήλλαξέν. G omits waw and uses (ὁ) κύριος to render אֵל ("God") as elsewhere in Iob (5.8). ἀπαλλάσσω ("remove") translates סוּר hiphil ("remove, take away") as at 9.34; 27.5. The use of ἀπαλλάσσω with κρίμα does not occur elsewhere and appears to be G's innovation.

μου τὸ κρίμα. "My case," or "my suit, lawsuit." The Lord has dismissed Iob's right to a trial. Here κρίμα ("judgment") is used in the sense of "dispute, lawsuit" (see GELS), as in the NT at 1 Cor 6.7 (cited in BDAG).

ἐψεύσατο δὲ τῷ κρίματί μου. G adds δέ ("but") to indicate that verse 6a involves a slight shift from 5b: not only will there be no trial but the Lord has acted deceitfully. Brenton translates 6a, "And he has erred (mg: Gr. lied) in my judgment"; Harry Orlinsky (1959, 29:268): "He has lied in my justice"; Homer Heater (1982, 108): "He acted falsely in condemning me." All three translations appear to presume that Iob's case has made it to trial.

The MT vocalizes אֲכַזֵּב as a piel ("lie"), but often it is vocalized as a niphal ("prove oneself a liar," HALOT) as, apparently, in the NRSV; similarly, Tg. Job: "In spite of my right I am counted as a liar." Sometimes the verb is emended, for example, to יְכַזֵּב, the third-person singular ("he lies") on the basis of the LXX (so Pope 1965, 256), almost certainly a mistaken approach. It seems more likely to me that G has changed "I am counted a liar" to "he lied" in order to continue with the third-person singular. This is a change that G often makes for the sake of coherence and readabilty.

There is no manuscript evidence for יכזב, though it could have emerged from the dittography of the final *yod* of משפטי.

G renders על משפטי with τῷ κρίματί μου, a dative of respect (see BDF §197, including Hellenistic examples). Iob has been unable to get the Lord to address his suit. The Lord's "lie, deceit" consists in his refusal to accept that Iob is in the right.

34.8

וללכת עם אנשי רשע || וארח לחברה עם פעלי און

οὐχ ἁμαρτὼν οὐδὲ ἀσεβήσας
ἢ ὁδοῦ κοινωνήσας μετὰ ποιούντων τὰ ἄνομα
τοῦ πορευθῆναι μετὰ ἀσεβῶν.

seeing that I have not sinned or acted impiously
or shared a way with doers of lawless acts,
to walk with the impious.'

G omits verse 7. This and the change from third-person to first-person in verse 8 means that in the OG all of verses 5–6a, 8 becomes a citation by Elious of what Iob said. The OG 8a is marked with an obelus in MSS 706 740 Syh, indicating that Origen found it in his LXX text and that it was without an equivalent in the Hebrew. In fact, as Beer (1897, 215) recognizes—followed by Dhorme (1967, 511) and Heater (1982, 108)—OG 8a renders בלי פשע ("without transgression") (6bβ). Zi puts a question mark after ἀσεβῶν because he has punctuated the ecclesiastical text as one text, where verse 7 initiates a question. NETS places a period at the end of verse 8.

οὐχ ἁμαρτὼν οὐδὲ ἀσεβήσας. G uses first the negated participle οὐχ ἁμαρτὼν to render בלי פשע (6bβ). See 33.9 where G employs the same unusual equivalence; there too Elious is quoting Iob. Note that ἁμαρτάνω does not elsewhere render פשע ("transgression") in the LXX apart from Iob 33.9; Prov 28.24; 29.6. Indeed ἁμαρτία, the noun, rarely renders פשע (7x in Psalms; 3x LXX Daniel). The circumstantial participle expresses concession, "though I have not sinned," perhaps even cause, "because …" (see "since I have done no wrong" [33.9a]; Smyth §§2060, 2064, 2066).

Dhorme (1967, 511) followed by Heater (1982, 108) suggests that οὐδὲ ἀσεβήσας ("and did not act impiously") represents a second translation of בלי פשע but read as בלי רשע ("without wickedness"). In favor of this suggestion is the fact that ἀσεβέω and its cognates usually render רשע and its cognates in Iob (e.g., 10.7). Perhaps G saw a certain wordplay in פשע – רשע. At any rate, G has represented בלי פשע with two participial constructions that together serve to emphasize Iob's denial of wrongdoing by including the general sense of פשע (ἁμαρτάνω) and a narrower sense, that is, with respect to religion (ἀσεβέω). G's use of ἀσεβέω in verse 8a anticipates verse 8c. The repetition can only be intentional: Iob definitely avoided acts of impiety.

ἢ ὁδοῦ κοινωνήσας. G chooses the disjunctive ἢ ("or") rather than translate *waw* literally with "and" (δέ or καί). The OG continues with the first-person, whereas the source text shifts to the third-person. As a result G sets up a contrast between Iob's activities as an individual and those undertaken with others.

G paraphrases ארח לחברה ("journey for company") (see *DCH*, s.v. "ארח," "way") with κοινωνέω ("have *or* do in common with, share, take part in *a thing* with *another*" LSJ) + genitive ὁδοῦ so "share a way, road." HRCS connect ὁδός with ארח (?)—their question mark is not really needed—and κοινωνέω with חברה. The verb κοινωνέω and its cognates occur seldom in the LXX where there is a clear source text—about a dozen times—but in most of these the κοινωνέω – חבר equation obtains. Therefore G is using an equivalence employed elsewhere in the LXX. That being said, while G captures the meaning of the source text in verse 8b, the idiom is changed, from share company to share a road or way. With verse 8bc compare Ps 1.1.

τοῦ πορευθῆναι μετὰ ἀσεβῶν. G passes over *waw* ("and [walks]"). In the source text the preposition ל expresses purpose, both with the noun חברה and with the infinitive לכת (הלך), so literally, "(a path) *for* company ... and *to* walk, and so on." G subordinates the infinitive to the first member of the parallel, so the *waw* ([וללכת]) must be passed over. In the OG verse 8b and 8c are not parallel, as in the source text, but one statement. Iob says that he did not share a way or street with the lawless in order to have dealings with the impious. G reduces אנשי רשע (lit. "people of wickedness") to (οἱ) ἀσεβεῖς ("the impious," those who act irreligiously). Not only did Iob do no wrong himself (8a), but he did not associate with those who did (8bc).

34.9

ברצתו עם אלהים || כי אמר לא יסכן גבר

μὴ γὰρ εἴπῃς ὅτι Οὐκ ἔσται ἐπισκοπὴ ἀνδρός·
καὶ ἐπισκοπὴ αὐτῷ παρὰ κυρίου.

For do not say, 'There will be no visitation of a man'—
and there is visitation to him from the Lord!

μὴ γὰρ εἴπῃς ὅτι. G changes the verb from third-person singular to second-
person singular, and changes the introduction to the quotation into an
admonition by adding the particle μή ("[do] not [say]"). In the OG Elious
chides Iob directly. The change in person leaves verse 9 with its causative γάρ
("for") slightly awkward: it opens an address to Iob alone ("you" [sg.]) as one
of "you wise men" (2a). The particle ὅτι marks the opening of direct speech,
as at 7.13; 11.4; 32.7. Its use is a mark of familiar style (Smyth §2590a).

Οὐκ ἔσται ἐπισκοπὴ ἀνδρός. HRCS cite as the equivalents of (9a) εἶναι
ἐπισκοπή and (9b) ἐπισκοπή the verbs סכן ("benefit, profit" BDB) and רצה
("be pleased with, favorable to" BDB), respectively. *DCH* glosses 9aβ as "it
does not profit a man." Certainly the meaning of סכן is the subject of some
speculation; see Clines 2006, 747–48. Nonetheless, at a glance one can see
that G at best paraphrases verse 9a and constructs 9b in relation to 9a.

Since verse 9a cites Iob's own words, G must use the Greek of the passage cited, likely 6.14: ἀπείτατό με ἔλεος, ἐπισκοπὴ δὲ κυρίου ὑπερεῖδέν με
("Mercy has renounced me, and the visitation of the Lord has disregarded
me"). There was a time when this was not true (29.4), but now the Lord has
abandoned Iob. "Man" (ἀνδρός) is generic; it includes Iob.

καὶ ἐπισκοπὴ αὐτῷ. G adds καί. It is not simply a conjunction: Brenton
renders it "whereas"; NETS with "when" (see Smyth §2871). Somehow
ἐπισκοπὴ αὐτῷ represents בִּרְצֹתוֹ—an infinitive construct of רצה with third
singular masculine possessive suffix and prefixed preposition ב, so "that he
should delight himself with God" (ASV). The preposition is replaced by
καί and the suffixed *waw* ("his") becomes αὐτῷ ("to him"), likely a reference to Iob. G then replaces the infinitive construct with a noun that has a
different meaning. It can be no accident that G repeats ἐπισκοπή.

In verse 9a ἐπισκοπή has a positive meaning, if the Lord's attention is a
positive thing. With its repetition in 9b Elious fully, precisely, and exactly
refutes Iob's claim that the Lord does not "visit." The Lord does "visit," but
not in the way Iob expected. If we ask *how* the Lord has "visited" Iob, the
answer may lie in 33.19–22.

παρὰ κυρίου. G changes עם ("with") to "from" (παρά + genitive) to suit the interpretation placed upon verse 9b.

34.10–20: Elious's theodicy, first part

34.10

לכן אנשי לבב שמעו לי

חללה לאל מרשע || ושדי מעול

διό, συνετοὶ καρδίας, ἀκούσατέ μου
Μή μοι εἴη ἔναντι κυρίου ἀσεβῆσαι
καὶ ἔναντι παντοκράτορος ταράξαι τὸ δίκαιον·

Therefore, you intelligent of heart, hear me:
far be it from me to act impiously before the Lord
and before the Almighty, to pervert what is right.

συνετοὶ καρδίας. That is, "intelligent (in matters) of the heart," an interpretation of אנשי לבב, literally "people of heart," "you who have sense" (NRSV); Tg. Job: "you men who are wise of heart." The phrase σύνετος + genitive means "*intelligent in* a thing" (LSJ). In Greek συνετοί is a sufficient rendering of the source text, for in Greek the heart is not the locus of intelligence. Nevertheless G adds καρδίας, following the Hebrew, where the heart is the center of thinking processes. The adjective συνετός is plural, like the underlying Hebrew, and presumably includes Iob if Iob comes around to Elious's point of view.

Μή μοι εἴη ἔναντι κυρίου. G renders the negative interjection, חלילה ל ("far be it from," *HALOT*) with μὴ μοι εἴη (lit. "may it not be to me"), the optative with negative particle μή + dative μοι. That is, G adds לי ("to me") to the source text; the same construction appears at 27.5. The addition permits G to render לָאֵל ("with respect to God") as ἔναντι κυρίου. In OG Iob κύριος is the default translation of אל. So it is that OG 10bc refers to Elious rather than to the Lord (see NRSV). His self-promotion is at the Lord's expense! Elious asserts his piety to gain a hearing (10a) and to lend credence to his opinion, which follows (11).

ἀσεβῆσαι ... ταράξαι. G appears to vocalize מרשע as מֵרְשֹׁעַ, qal infinitive with preposition מן prefixed rather than as a noun with the preposition, as in the MT; see *HALOT*, s.vv. "חָלִיל" and "רשע" *qal*. The same is true of מְעוּל: G has vocalized it as מְעַוֵּל ("to act unjustly"), the *piel* infinitive of עול I; see Fohrer (1963, 464, citing Hölscher et al.) and *HALOT*.

καὶ ἔναντι παντοκράτορος. G repeats the preposition, because שדי ("Shaddai") is parallel to (10b) אֵל ("God"). The word παντοκράτωρ ("almighty") represents שדי as generally in Iob; however, it is an equivalence unique to Iob in the LXX corpus.

ταράξαι τὸ δίκαιον. G interprets מְעוּל ("[far be it from ...] to do iniquity") with ταράσσω ("trouble; throw into disorder") and τὸ δίκαιον ("what is right"), which is a good choice for the immediate and larger context; in the opening lines of the book, G has used the adjective δίκαιος of Iob (1.1). In the OG ἀσεβῆσαι and ταράξαι τὸ δίκαιον are parallel: religious life (θεοσέβεια ["piety"]) embraces ethics. The source text is about the Lord, but G turns it into a pledge by Elious about himself. Finally, G's translation anticipates ταράξει κρίσιν ("pervert justice") (v. 12). The Lord will not pervert justice and Elious shares that virtue.

34.11

כי פעל אדם ישלם לו || [וכארח איש ימצאנו]

ἀλλὰ ἀποδιδοῖ ἀνθρώπῳ καθὰ ποιεῖ ἕκαστος αὐτῶν.

Rather, he repays a person according to what each of them does.

G uses the strong adversative ἀλλά ("rather, but") to represent כי ("for," NRSV). Because G changed the subject in verse 10 to Elious ("far be it from *me*"), the connection with verse 10 in the source text ("far be it from *God*") is severed. In verse 11 G preserves the content of the source text with its assertion of retributive justice, but collapses verses 11a and 11b together to avoid repetition.

ἀποδιδοῖ ... αὐτῶν. So also OG 24.20c. Origen, working in a mechanical fashion, placed verse 11b under the asterisk, but it seems clear that G has incorporated parts of both 11a and 11b in one line, albeit one long line. G uses ἀποδιδοῖ ἀνθρώπῳ ("he repays a person") to render אדם ישלם לו (lit. "of a *person* he will repay *him*"); ποιεῖ = פעל (11a); καθά = (כ)ארח (11b, so Beer 1897, 216); ἕκαστος = איש (11b) as at 2.11, 12; 42.11. G does not represent the words אֹרַח ("path") (v. 11b) or the impersonal יַמְצִאֶנּוּ ("he will make it befall him") (v. 11b), which is now redundant. Gerleman's suggestion (BHS^app) that perhaps we should read כְּפֹעַל (rather than כִּי פֹעַל) in verse 11a—surely based on the OG—can be set aside if καθά renders בְּ (11b).

34.12

אַף אָמְנָם אֵל לֹא יַרְשִׁיעַ ‖ וְשַׁדַּי לֹא יְעַוֵּת מִשְׁפָּט

οἴη δὲ τὸν κύριον ἄτοπα ποιήσειν;
ἢ ὁ παντοκράτωρ ταράξει κρίσιν;

Now, do you think the Lord will do what is amiss?
Or will the Almighty pervert justice?

οἴη ... ἄτοπα ποιήσειν. G changes verse 12 from an assertion of two parallel lines into two rhetorical questions addressed to Iob. G replaces אַף אָמְנָם ("really and truly" HALOT s.v. "אַף"; "of a truth," NRSV), with δέ to indicate a slight shift in Elious's remarks (Smyth §2834, 2836). G has Elious direct his questions to Iob, as is clear from the addition of the second singular οἴη ("[do] you think"). Its use is a rhetorical device to summon the hearer's attention. The verb οἴομαι occurs six times in Iob, not once with an equivalent in the source text (11.2; 34.12; 37.23; 38.2; 40.8; 42.3); it is a verb G likes.

G uses the compound verb (noun + verb) ἄτοπα ποιέω ("do things that are amiss") to render רשע hiphil ("make oneself guilty" HALOT). This rendering is unique in Iob, where ἀσεβέω ("act impiously") usually translates רשע, as in verse 10b. It is likely that G does not use ἀσεβέω a second time because of an interest in variety of expression. The subject of the future infinitive ποιήσειν is in the accusative case, so τὸν κύριον ποιήσειν (Smyth §936). The use of the future infinitive signifies that Elious's claim on behalf of the Lord specifically includes the future (Smyth §1866).

The adjective ἄτοπος means "out of place" and, depending on the context, "absurd; strange; monstrous," as well as "bad, harmful," thus "wrong" at Iob 11.11; 35.13; 36.21a. Elious says that the Lord acts according to what we expect of the divine. The Lord does not act inappropriately; the Lord does not get it wrong.

ἢ ὁ παντοκράτωρ ταράξει κρίσιν. G connects verse 12b to 12a with the disjunctive particle ἤ ("or") as at verses 8b and 8a rather than καί or δέ. The result is that 12a and 12b no longer present two parallel thoughts but two alternatives that say much the same thing. On παντοκράτωρ see 10c. G uses ταράξει κρίσιν to represent יעות משפט (lit. "make justice crooked," i.e., pervert justice; *DCH*, s.v. "משפט" 2.) and thus repeats the source text at 10c. The repetition lends emphasis to Elious's question.

34.13

ומי שם תבל כלה || מי פקד עליו ארצה

ὃς ἐποίησεν τὴν γῆν·
τίς δέ ἐστιν ὁ ποιῶν τὴν ὑπ᾽ οὐρανὸν καὶ τὰ ἐνόντα πάντα;

He it is who made the earth.
And who is it that sustains what is under heaven and all it contains?

ὃς ἐποίησεν τὴν γῆν. G represents both lines of verse 13 in a way that has each refer to creation, in the past (ἐποίησεν [aorist] 13a) and as a continuing event (13b). The Greek ὃς is used as a demonstrative, rather than as a relative pronoun, so NETS "He it is who." Other instances of this usage occur at 22.18; 24.12; 34.19. For 13a, compare Tg. Job "Who entrusted to him to make the earth?" which likewise introduces creation.

G read מי ... ארצה ("who ... the earth") and filled it in with "made" on the basis of Gen 1.1 and similar texts (Ps 113.23; 120.2; 123.8; 133.3; 145.6; Ier 10.12—all "who ..."; Esa 37.16; Ier 39.17). Most of these use "sky and earth," but not all: Esa 45.12; Ier 34.5 have only "earth." The source text in verse 13a has only "earth" and 13b concerns the earth alone. At any rate, G introduces an explicit reference to creation. We need not enter into the problematic issue of the ה- on ארץ ("earth"): is MT אַרְצָה ("to the earth") a misvocalization for אַרְצוֹ = אַרְצֹה ("his earth") (see *BHS*ᵃᵖᵖ; Clines 2006, 749)? The OG provides no help with that question.

ὁ ποιῶν τὴν ὑπ᾽ οὐρανόν. Dhorme (1967, 514) thinks that G was inspired by Ps 23[24].1. This is unlikely since there is only the most general contact. Rather, G draws on verse 13a for ἐστιν ὁ ποιῶν, and τὴν ὑπ᾽ οὐρανόν, and τὰ ἐνόντα πάντα are translations of תבל ("world" BDB) and כֻּלָּהּ ("its whole, all of it"), respectively. G introduces creation as a continuing activity with the use of the present participle ὁ ποῖων, so NETS "that sustains." In verse 13b it is parallel to τὴν γῆν "the earth."

καὶ τὰ ἐνόντα πάντα. G separates תבל כלה, whereas they stand in apposition, "the world, all of it" (*HALOT*, s.v. "כל" 3.) in the source text; compare the NRSV's, "the whole world." Indeed, this is reminiscent of Ps 23[24].1, where ἡ γῆ καὶ τὸ πλήρωμα αὐτῆς renders הארץ ומלואה ("the earth and its fullness"). Human beings are included in OG "all it contains." Implicitly the point seems to be that the Lord who made and sustains all things does not act contrary to this interest by perverting the rules.

34.14–15

14 רוחו ונשמתו אליו יאסף ‖ אם ישים אליו לבו
15 יגוע כל בשר יחד ‖ ואדם על עפר ישוב

14   εἰ γὰρ βούλοιτο συνέχειν
καὶ τὸ πνεῦμα παρ' αὐτῷ κατασχεῖν,
15   τελευτήσει πᾶσα σὰρξ ὁμοθυμαδόν,
πᾶς δὲ βροτὸς εἰς γῆν ἀπελεύσεται, ὅθεν καὶ ἐπλάσθη.

14   For if he should wish to confine
and to keep his spirit with himself,
15   all flesh will die together,
and every mortal return to dust, whence too he was formed.

εἰ … συνέχειν. G paraphrases verse 14 as a whole. Notably G attaches verses 14–15 to the rhetorical questions of verses 12–13 with γάρ, so that they become an example of the Lord's sustaining interest in the world. The particle εἰ ("if") (14a) marks the opening of the protasis of the conditional sentence.

G seems to attest ישיב ("should return, take back") instead of ישים ("set [his mind to himself]") in agreement with two Hebrew manuscripts, the *ketiv* of five oriental manuscripts and the Peshitta (Beer 1897, 216; see Clines 2006, 749). The former reading is widely preferred (so NRSV; Dhorme 1967, 515; Gordis 1978, 388; but not NJPS; Davidson 1918, 272–73; Fohrer 1963, 464; Clines 2006, 749); Tg. Job supports the MT text tradition. The expression שים לב אל means "regard, pay attention to" (*HALOT*, s.v. "שים" 14; see vv. 1.8; 2.3).

G adds βούλοιτο, optative third-person singular. The verb βούλομαι appears nine times in Iob: four times HRCS mark it with a dagger † (30.14; 35.13; 36.12; 37.10); two or three times it renders חפץ ("desire; delight in"

HALOT) (9.3; 13.3[?]; 21.14); once G uses it for אבה ("want") (39.9); once they mark the suggested equivalence with a question mark (34.14 [שים לב?]). That is, apart from three instances where there is a clear equivalent, G's use of βούλομαι in Iob is problematic. At 34.14 it appears G has added it rather than that it represents the use of שים לב. With βούλοιτο G introduces the nuance of choice and desire. The use of the optative in the protasis indicates a low level of possibility, while the use of the future indicative in the apodosis indicates a high level of certainty: it is unlikely that the Lord would so act (14) but if he did, the result stated would be highly likely (15).

So εἰ βούλοιτο συνέχειν represents אם ישיב ("if he should take back"). Note that G uses a synonym of συνέχειν in 14b and that semantically both infinitives are tied to βούλοιτο. G passes over לבו ("his heart") as do the NRSV and other translations and commentators on MT.

καὶ … κατασχεῖν. G adds the conjunction καί to join verse 14b to 14a and passes over ונשמתו ("and his breath"). The Greek τὸ πνεῦμα ("[his] spirit") renders רוח. G uses παρ᾽ αὐτῷ κατασχεῖν ("[if he should wish] with him to keep") to render אליו יאסף ("to himself [should] gather"). The choice of κατέχω ("hold back, withhold") to render אסף is unique, but stands out as a fine, contextual translation. LSJ cite a variety of related meanings for κατέχω that are suggestive: "place under arrest; sequestrate; confine" (of the grave).

G has rendered verse 14 at the sentence level, passing over לבו in 14a and נשמתו in 14b, and adding βούλοιτο to govern the two synonymous infinitives that represent the two finite verbs in the parent text. With G's reduction of "heart," "spirit," and "breath" to "spirit" alone the focus is placed on the Lord's spirit, necessary for all life (so Gen 6.17).

G renders the apodosis of the conditional sentence (15) more or less literally, but adds the adverbial clause at the end of 15b.

τελευτήσει. G uses τελευτάω ("come to an end, die"; see τέλος ["end"]) to render גוע ("perish"). Elsewhere in Iob, except at 27.15 (HRCS †), τελευτάω translates מות ("die") (9x), as throughout the LXX corpus. G's choice of τελευτάω emphasizes the blunt finality of the Lord's decision to withhold his spirit. Tjen (2010, 55) thinks the use of the future indicative in the apodosis after the optative in the protasis betrays interference from the *yiqtol* יגוע.

πᾶσα σάρξ. This is a Hebraism that refers to all living things (Gen 7.21) or all human beings (e.g., Ps 64.3; Esa 40.5). It occurs only here in Iob but would be immediately familiar to readers of the LXX.

πᾶς δὲ βροτὸς εἰς γῆν ἀπελεύσεται. βροτός ("mortal") is a word of the Greek poets that G uses—uniquely in the LXX—seventeen times. G adds πᾶς ("every") to emphasize the inescapability of the will of the deity. The NRSV adds "all," but compare "mankind" (NJPS) and "humanity" (Clines 2006, 744). The verb ἀπέρχομαι εἰς ("go away to") renders על שוב ("return to"). The same equivalence occurs at 1.21, but without prepositions. In the context, "go away to" means "return to" (NETS). Iob's fear is that he will "go away to" the earth (7.21), that is, die.

ὅθεν καὶ ἐπλάσθη. That is, implicitly, formed *by the Lord*. This is an addition to the text by G and Origen placed it under an obelus (÷) to indicate it had no equivalent in the Hebrew text. As Dhorme (1967; followed by Heater 1982) recognizes, it is an allusion to Gen 3.19, (εἰς τὴν γῆν) ἐξ ἧς ἐλήμφθης ("[to the earth] from which you were taken"). Genesis 2.7, 8, 15, use πλάσσω so that the allusion seems to include 2.7 (Bratsiotis 1977, 325). In that case, the allusion is conflated.

34.16

האזינה לקול מלי || ואם בינה שמעה זאת

εἰ δὲ μὴ νουθετῇ, ἄκουε ταῦτα,
ἐνωτίζου φωνὴν ῥημάτων.

But lest he rebuke you, hear these things;
give ear to a sound of words.

εἰ δὲ μὴ νουθετῇ. NRSV, NJPS, TNIV, and others disregard the *waw* that begins verse 16. G renders it with the adversative conjunction δέ ("but") to indicate a slight shift. It seems that the contrast is with verse 13: the Lord sustains all things but he can also be a source of rebuke.

G changes the protasis of the conditional clause ("If …) into a caution ("[But] lest …") by adding the negative particle μή. Gerleman, among others, suggests emending בִּינָה ("understanding") to בִּינֹתָה ("you understand") (BHS[app]), but the OG, Tg. Job, and other versions may well be loosely rendering "And if (there is) understanding (on your part)" (see

Dhorme 1967, 515; Clines 2006, 749–50). G uses νουθετέω for the cognate verb בין in the *hithpael* at 37.14; 38.18.

ταῦτα. G regularly uses the plural for the singular demonstrative pronouns הז and זאת ("this"), depending on the context (e.g., 1.22; 2.10; 5.27; 19.26; 37.14).

φωνὴν ῥημάτων. In Greek the possessive pronoun "my" may be implicit, "(the sound of) of *my* words" (so NETS 2006)—see "hear *me*" (10); this is explicit in the source text.

34.17

ואם צדיק כביר תרשיע || האף משפט שונא יחבוש

ἴδε σὺ τὸν μισοῦντα ἄνομα
καὶ τὸν ὀλλύντα τοὺς πονηρούς ὄντα αἰώνιον δίκαιον.

Look then at him that hates lawless acts
and destroys the wicked, since he is forever just.

Zi sets out the OG in three lines, so that "since he is forever just" becomes 17c. NETS treats verse 17 as two lines. This simplifies discussion of the relationship of the OG to its parent text. G rewrites verse 17; see Beer 1897, 217: *phantasiert* ("fancifies"). The OG has only two points of contact with the parent text: τὸν μισοῦντα and שונא; δίκαιον and צדיק. G takes יחבוש ("Shall one … govern") (17a) with 17b; and the last word of 17b, תרשיע ("will you condemn"), with verse 18.

ἴδε σύ. The translation is "Look then at (him)" or "Look for yourself at (the one)." Elious has just said, "Give ear," that is, use one's ears, and now G has Iob *look at*, use his eyes, in this addition that introduces OG verse 17. G changes 17 from two rhetorical questions that expect a negative answer (see *HALOT*, s.v. "אף" 5.) to an admonition.

τὸν μισοῦντα ἄνομα. G uses ἄνομα to replace משפט. A change of some kind was required after the introduction of ἴδε σύ: now "the one who hates" is the object, not subject as in the source text, of יחבוש ("govern," NRSV). G could not have the Lord hating justice; an opposite was required, such as ἄνομα. That G was motivated by theological reasons in this change (so

Dhorme 1967, 516) is debatable, given the freedom with which the entire verse is treated. It is notable that G chooses ἄνομα—it derives from the translator's own ideas—because the choice reveals the translator's preferred vocabulary for wrongdoing.

καὶ τὸν ὀλλύντα τοὺς πονηρούς. G interprets חבש ("fetter, imprison"; see 40.13 and *HALOT*, s.v. "חבש" *qal* 5.) with ὄλλυμι ("destroy"), and nicely coordinates it with τὸν μισοῦντα by adding καί and by turning the finite verb of the parent text into a participle. G adds the direct object τοὺς πονηρούς ("the wicked"), thus constructing with verse 17b a parallel for 17a. It is the wicked, such as Iob (v. 8), who perform lawless acts.

ὄντα αἰώνιον δίκαιον. G passes over ואם, that is, the connector *waw* and the אם that marks the beginning of a disjunctive question, and uses a participial construction to represent the adjective) צדיק "righteous"). The adjective αἰώνιον ("eternal") is an interpretation of כביר ("mighty"). G preserves the asyndeton of the parent text: αἰώνιον δίκαιον = צדיק כביר. NETS understands the circumstantial participle as expressing cause, so "since he is forever just" (Smyth §§2054, 2056, 2064). The Lord's treatment of the wicked stems from a just character. "Forever" means "always," including Iob's time and place.

34.18a–19

18   [רשע אל נדיבים] || האמר למלך בליעל
19   אשר לא נשא פני שרים || ולא נכר שוע לפני דל
       כי מעשה ידיו כלם

18a   ἀσεβὴς ὁ λέγων βασιλεῖ Παρανομεῖς,
19   ὃς οὐκ ἐπῃσχύνθη πρόσωπον ἐντίμου
οὐδὲ οἶδεν τιμὴν θέσθαι ἁδροῖς
θαυμασθῆναι πρόσωπα αὐτῶν.

18a   Impious is he who says to a king, 'You are acting lawlessly,'—
19   he who felt no reticence before a person of worth
nor knows how to accord honor to the prominent
so that their persons be respected.

ἀσεβὴς ὁ λέγων. G vocalizes האמר as הָאֹמֵר, the masculine participle with an article, "the one who says," rather than MT's infinitive construct אמר

("to say") with the interrogative ה prefixed, so "Is it fit to say ?" (ASVmg)
The OG reading of the Hebrew, shared with the Peshitta and Vulgate, is
widely accepted (BHSapp; NRSV). G takes תרשיע ("you are guilty [who
says]") (v. 17b) with verse 18a. Gerleman (BHSapp) notes two manuscripts
read the third singular ירשיע so it is possible, if remotely, that G is following a text that read יַרְשִׁיעַ הָאֹמֵר ("the one is guilty who says"). Elious has
in mind Iob as that unspecified person.

βασιλεῖ Παρανομεῖς. "To a king" repeats the parent text. I see no "sympathy
for the monarchy" in G's treatment of 18 (contra Gorea 2007, 176). G uses
παρανομέω ("transgress")—it occurs only here in Iob—to interpret בליעל,
a word whose meaning is disputed: HALOT offers "good for nothing" for
the adjective and for 34.18 the more colloquial "ne'er do well." G's rendering is contextual: in verse 17, the Lord hates lawless acts and now this is
the precise accusation made against the deity (by Iob implicitly, according
to Elious). Iob the accuser is surely impious.

In the source text it is clear that verse 19 concerns the Lord, the king
(18a), who shows no partiality. In the OG, however, it is the impious (18a),
in ad hominem language, who have no respect for those deserving of it,
including the Lord. G replaces 19c in its entirety because it has no place
after the changes made to 19ab. Those changes were made to keep Iob the
focus of attention. G is smoothing out the source text for Greek readers.
At the same time G appears to have some interest in retaining the length
of the verse.

ὃς οὐκ ἐπῃσχύνθη πρόσωπον ἐντίμου. Literally, "who was not ashamed at
the face of an honored person." On ὅς see verse 13. G uses ἐπαισχύνομαι
to represent the Hebrew idiom נשא פנים ("lift the face of," i.e., show
respect to; DCH, s.v. "נשא" qal 1b). G employs the same approach, but
with the simplex αἰσχύνω, at 32.21. This lexical choice is unique in the
LXX, where αἰσχύνω generally renders בוש, as at Iob 19.3. Apart from
Il. 18.24—where αἰσχύνω (active mood) πρόσωπον means "soil the face"
and "face" is understood literally—and patristic commentators (Basil,
Chrysostom), this collocation does not occur in Classical Greek, so it
should be regarded as a LXX neologism, indeed, one for which G may
be responsible. In that case, "face" might be retained in the translation
(so Brenton; LXX.D). Note that G is going to use a synonymous LXX
neologism in verse 19c.

G uses ἔντιμος in the singular to render שרים, a plural. The word שר has a variety of meanings, including "royal official, commander" or, more generally, a person of note (see *HALOT*; NRSV: "noble"). The translation ἔντιμος understands שר in a most general way. Plato uses ἔντιμος of people held in honor (*Euthyd.* 281c) and Xenophon of people of high rank (*Cyr.* 8.1.8: ἐφοίτων ... ἐπὶ τὰς θύρας Κύρου οἱ ἔντιμοι σὺν τοῖς ἵπποις, ["the nobles came to Cyrus's court with their horses" (Miller, LCL)]). The change from plural to singular is significant; the single "person of worth" is almost certainly Elious, so Elious intends, "a person of worth, *like me*." The impious's impudent mistreatment of a king (18) is repeated in Iob's behavior.

οὐδὲ οἶδεν τιμὴν θέσθαι ἀδροῖς. G adds the verb οἶδεν ("[nor] knows"). With it G introduces the idea of ignorance: the impious person (Iob) does not know any better!

G treats נכר as a *hiphil*, "recognize," and renders it with the compound verb τίθημι τιμήν ("accord honor"), a few examples of which are extant in classical authors such as Homer, Plato, Libanius, and Plutarch. In the *Iliad* the goddess Hera addresses Apollo on behalf of Achilles, εἰ δὴ ὁμὴν Ἀχιλῆϊ Ἕκτορι θήσετε τιμήν ("if indeed ye gods will vouchsafe like honour to Achilles and to Hector" [24.57; Murray, LCL]). Rieu renders the expression with "had it in mind to value" (Homer 1950, 438). J. Dryden uses "show respect" in his translation of Plutarch's *Phoc.* (17.9.2), a good English equivalent, if less literary than NETS.

The word ἀδρός, literally meaning "stout, thick," is used metaphorically with the meaning "fine, well-grown" (LSJ). NETS uniformly renders it as "prominent," "the prominent (ones)" in the plural (2 Rgns 15.18; 3 Rgns 1.9; 4 Rgns 10.6, 11; Iob 29.9; 34.19; Esa 34.7; Ier 5.5). HRCS cite דל ("[the] poor") as the equivalent of ἀδρός in the parent text; Dhorme (1967, 517) and H.-J. Fabry (1978, 216) think G has read גדול ("great") instead of דל. Rather, it is more likely that G uses ἀδρός to render שוע ("[the] noble, eminent"; *HALOT*, s.v. "שוע" I B.) and changes the number from singular to plural; see σ′ πλουσίοις ("to the rich"). If the "person of worth" is Elious, "the prominent (ones)" are likely Elious and the three friends; OG 19b forms a nice parallel for 19a. G passes over לפני דל ("than the poor," NRSV).

θαυμασθῆναι πρόσωπα αὐτῶν. G replaces verse 19c of the source text with this retake on 19a, altered to suit its relationship with 19b. G apparently wants to emphasize that certain people—let alone the Lord!—should be respected. For this restatement G uses θαυμάζω πρόσωπον (lit. "admire the face"), presumably to be understood metaphorically, a collocation that first appears in Greek literature at Gen 19.21 as a translation of נשא פנים. A *TLG* search locates only one occurrence of θαυμάζω πρόσωπον outside the LXX and related materials, and in that case it is used literally of admiring someone's face (Chariton, *Callihroe*, 2.2 [second century CE]). It should therefore be regarded as a LXX neologism. G has used it already at 13.10; 22.8; 32.22.

G's use of familiar Semitic expressions ἐπαισχύνομαι πρόσωπον and θαυμάζω πρόσωπον preserves something of the source text for Jewish readers in a translation that usually aspires to meet the literary expectations of a Greek environment. That the two expressions occur in such close proximity is striking.

34.20

יגעשו עם ויעברו || רגע ימתו וחצות לילה
ויסירו אביר לא ביד

κενὰ δὲ αὐτοῖς ἀποβήσεται τὸ κεκραγέναι καὶ δεῖσθαι ἀνδρός·
ἐχρήσαντο γὰρ παρανόμως
ἐκκλινομένων ἀδυνάτων.

But the crying out and begging of a man will prove to be
of no use to them;
for they treated them contrary to the law
when the powerless were being turned aside.

NETS sets up its translation in three lines and the Greek above follows that arrangement. This is appropriate because elements of OG verse 20b and 20c reflect the Hebrew of 20b and 20c, respectively. Zi joins 20c (above) to 20b so that the OG in his edition has two long lines.

κενὰ … ἀνδρός. G again rewrites the source text. G seems to be offering an expansive interpretation of verse 20a and possibly (20bα) יגעשו עם ("the people are shaken," NRSV), read as a reversal of fortune for the impious (v. 18; the disrespectful of v. 19) as a group and for Iob in particular: "in a moment they die, in the middle of the night," that is, God takes the impious suddenly in the night and there is no one to help them. G adds the adversative δέ so that verse 20 marks a slight shift. Most notably ἀνδρός ("of a man"), masculine singular, represents עַם and without doubt refers to Iob! A person like Iob will cry out and beg the Lord but it will be of no use.

The parallel infinitival constructions τὸ κεκραγέναι καὶ [τὸ] δεῖσθαι ἀνδρός stand in apposition to κενά (lit. "empty"), a predicate nominative and subject of ἀποβήσεται (Smyth §1987). The indirect object αὐτοῖς ("to them") appears to refer to the impious. The verb ἀποβαίνω, used impersonally in the sense of "turn out to be" is a favorite for G. Once humbled, the impious should expect no mercy from those they have held in disrespect, including the Lord (see v. 21).

ἐχρήσαντο γὰρ παρανόμως. Or, "for they acted lawlessly." G connects verse 20b to 20a with γάρ so that 20bc provides the reason for the merciless treatment that will come upon the impious. Verse 20b represents G's interpretation of יַעֲבֹרוּ: G understands עבר not as "pass away" (NRSV) but as "overstep, contravene" (HALOT, "עבר" I qal 7), hence "transgress (the law)." The verb χράομαι ("use [someone or somehow], treat") is another verb G likes to employ (also 16.9). NETS adds "them"—it refers to the powerless of 20c, which is required for the rendering of χράομαι into English.

παρανόμως. "Lawlessly, contrary to the law" (of Moses) is an echo of 18a, where the impious make the accusation against the king that he is breaking the law.

ἐκκλινομένων ἀδυνάτων. There is an echo here of OG 24.4. G paraphrases verse 20c with this circumstantial participle construction in the genitive absolute that explains *how* the impious acted lawlessly (Smyth §2058, 2060). The passive participle ἐκκλινομένων ("turned aside") represents יָסִירוּ ("they remove"), סור hiphil, which, indeed, can be understood to have an indefinite subject and be rendered with a passive verb (GKC §144g; so NRSV).

G seems to read אַבִּיר ("the mighty," NRSV) as the participle אֹבֵד ("one perishing"; so Dhorme 1967, 519) and uses ἀδύνατος ("powerless") to render it. Further, G may have read לֹא בְיָד as "nothing in (his) hand"; Beer says ἀδυνάτους represents לֹא בְיָד (1897, 218). In Iob the powerless are the poor, but not just the poor, and they are the opposite of the ἀσεβεῖς ("the impious") (20.19; 24.4, 22). Iob claims he was a "father of the powerless" (29.16), a claim Elious implicity refutes.

34.21–27: Elious's theodicy, second part

34.21–22

21 וכל צעדיו יראה || כי עיניו על דרכי איש

22 להסתר שם פעלי און || אין חשד ואין צלמות

21 αὐτὸς γὰρ ὁρατής ἐστιν ἔργων ἀνθρώπων,
λέληθεν δὲ αὐτὸν οὐδὲν ὧν πράσσουσιν·
22 οὐδὲ ἔσται τόπος
τοῦ κρυβῆναι τοὺς ποιοῦντας τὰ ἄνομα·

21   For he is an eyewitness of human deeds,
and nothing of what they do has escaped him,
22   nor will there be a place
to hide for those that do lawless acts.

αὐτὸς … ἀνθρώπων. G follows the source text with its causative particle: γάρ ("for") renders כי, so that verses 21–22 serve to explain why the impious should not expect mercy (20a).

The expression "his eyes (are) upon" is rendered using the following elements: the pronoun αὐτός ("he"), the verb "to be" (ἐστιν), a predicate noun, ὁρατής ("viewer, eyewitness"), and the genitive case. Only G Iob uses ὁρατής among LXX translators, here and at 35.13. Its cognate verb is used in an Alexandrian poem that predates OG Iob. Pseudo-Justin (third–fourth cemtury CE) cites Pseudo-Orpheus, οὐδέ τις αὐτὸν εἰσορᾷ θνητῶν, αὐτὸς δέ γε πάντες ὁρᾶται ("and no one among mortals sees Him, though He indeed sees everyone" [trans. Holladay; Pseudo-Justin 1996, 104–5; see also 66–68]). In Eusebius the poem is attributed to Aristobulus (second century BCE; see Eusebius, *Praep. ev.*, 13.12, and Pseudo-Justin 1996, 66; 129 n. 37).

According to Dhorme (1967, 519), G avoids the anthropomorphism of "his *eyes*," but note that G uses the same elevated language with respect to wisdom at 28.21 (Orlinsky, 1959, 30:165; 29:237–38). G interprets דרכים ("ways") with ἔργοι ("works, actions, deeds"), a contextual rendering that has in mind verse 20bc.

λέληθεν δὲ αὐτὸν οὐδὲν ὧν πράσσουσιν. This, too, is a paraphrase, wherein the positive assertion of the source text, parallel to 21a, is restated as a contrastive parallel. This translation technique, whereby a positive statement is turned into a negative that means the same thing, is called "converse translation"; it is also known from the targumim; see Orlinsky 1959, 29:231–38, cited in Fox 2005, 116 n. 35; Fox refers to articles on this technique by M. Klein and R. P. Gordon.

G's treatment of verse 21b represents an interest in stylistic variation. G paraphrases כל צעדיו ("all his steps") with οὐδὲν ὧν πράσσουσιν ("nothing of what they do"), a fitting parallel for ἔργοι ("deeds") (v. 21a). If anything, the OG is more comprehensive than the source text: "he sees everything," a truism, becomes "nothing, not a thing" escapes the Lord. The verb πράσσω carries the nuance of not simply "doing" but of practicing (see LSJ, s.v. "πράσσω," II.4 and 5; IV.).

οὐδὲ ἔσται τόπος. Zi prints verse 22 as one long line and NETS 2006 follows suit. However, the Greek divides nicely into two lines, like *BHS*; OG 22a is a paraphrase, as is clear from a comparison of the OG and MT and their respective translations. G connects verse 22 to 21 with δέ and supplies the verb "to be," notably in the future tense (ἔσται). G makes 22a more inclusive than the source text, since "no place" is a larger domain than "gloom and darkness."

τοὺς ποιοῦντας τὰ ἄνομα. This is a Hebraism; see verse 8. The plural participle is in the accusative case as the subject of the (purposive) infinitive τοῦ κρυβῆναι (see Smyth §§936 and 2008). G used ἄνομα ("lawless acts") at verse 17. Elious and the friends believe Iob is such a person in spite of the disclaimer Elious cites (v. 8). This is true also of the source text.

34.23b–24, 25a (source text 23–25)

23 [להלך אל אל במשפט || [איש ישים עוד כי לא על]
24 ירע כבירים לא חקר || ויעמד אחרים תחתם
25 לכן יכיר מעבדיהם || [והפך לילה וידכאו]

23b ὁ γὰρ κύριος πάντας ἐφορᾷ,
24   ὁ καταλαμβάνων ἀνεξιχνίαστα,
ἔνδοξά τε καὶ ἐξαίσια, ὧν οὐκ ἔστιν ἀριθμός·
25a ὁ γνωρίζων αὐτῶν τὰ ἔργα

23b For the Lord observes all people—
24   he who comprehends inscrutable things,
things both glorious and extraordinary, without number,

25a   he who discloses their workings.

Origen worked mechanically in preparing the Hexapla. The OG of verse 23 is a line shorter in the OG than the Hebrew, so he marked 23a as lacking a translation in the OG, but he might as well have so marked 23b instead, for the OG is a translation of neither line. Yet we may note that γάρ represents כי (23a); πάντας likely represents איש ("anyone") (23a); the prefix ἐπί- ("upon") of ἐφοράω represents the preposition על (23a); and κύριος renders אל ("God") (23b). G uses these elements, perhaps triggered by כי—which also begins verse 21—to construct a line parallel to verse 21 so that OG 23b now serves not simply as a restatement of verse 21 but also as an introduction to the liturgical "he who …," with its articulated participles, in verses 24–25.

   G's treatment of verse 23 makes emphatic Elious's claim that the Lord sees all humans and their deeds. G uses ἐφοράω at 21.16; 22.12; 28.24, each of which is similar to verse 23b.

   G read ידע ("knows") instead of ירע ("shatters"; see Beer 1897, 218). *Resh* and *daleth* are easily confused. Since they look alike, G had the option of reading one or the other. Dhorme (1967, 521) is right that לא חקר ("no inquiry, investigation") (v. 24a)—combined with reading ידע—leads G to 9.10a, where ἀνεξιχνίαστα ("inscrutable things") renders אין חקר ("beyond understanding," NRSV). Indeed, G *replaces* a translation of (Hebrew) verse 24b with OG 9.10b (so Beer 1897, 218; Dhorme 1967 ["an exact quotation"]; Heater 1982, 115). Further, G models OG 24–25 on 9.5–10 with its articular participles. In turn, at 9.10 G replicated 5.9! G likes this characterization of the deity that incorporates a doxological formula.

   Elious in OG 24 repeats what had earlier been said by Eliphaz and Iob, respectively. That is, he confirms what Eliphaz had said and throws back at Iob what Iob had earlier affirmed. The repetition serves to recall the glorious wisdom of the Lord, surely beyond human understanding. G omitted 24b because its content in the source text made no sense after OG 24a. The same is true of 25b in the source text, now completely out of place.

ὁ γνωρίζων. G passes over לכן ("thus," NRSV) and represents the finite verb יכיר ("he knows") with the articulated participle, "the one who reveals," to form a parallel with verse 24 ὁ καταλαμβάνων. The use of γνωρίζω ("make known") to translate נכר, here as commonly in the *hiphil*, "know," is unique in the LXX. G omits 25bα and reads 25bβ (וידכאו) with verse 26a.

αὐτῶν τὰ ἔργα. G used ἔργα for "deeds" in verse 21 and one might be tempted to see αὐτῶν τὰ ἔργα as referring to human actions, specifically those of the impious, as in NETS 2006. Certainly that is the referent in the source text. However, G replaced verse 24 with a quotation of OG 5.9; 9.10. Both those passages involve cosmological phenomena. "Their" now refers to the glorious (cosmological) activities of OG verse 24. The same Lord who comprehends the workings of the universe surely brings that same level of scrutiny and understanding to the observation of human life. If we ask where the "workings" of the universe are revealed, perhaps G has in mind the creation stories and creation text in Esaiah.

34.26

תחת רשעים ספקם || במקום ראים [וידכאו 25bβ]

ἔσβεσεν δὲ ἀσεβεῖς, ὁρατοὶ δὲ ἐναντίον αὐτοῦ,

Now, he extinguished the impious—
but they are visible before him,

The translation of 26b is that of the 2014 NETS revision, with the addition of the copula verb "are" and its subject "they."

ἔσβεσεν δὲ ἀσεβεῖς. OG verse 26a represents רשעים וידכאו. The Syriac also takes וידכאו with verse 26. In Iob ἀσεβής and cognates in 90 percent of their occurrences represent the root רשע; see also 34.8. G shares this understanding of wickedness as impiety with other LXX translators, especially in Psalms and elsewhere in the wisdom literature. Note the coincidental homophony in ἔσβεσεν (δὲ) ἀσεβεῖς.

The use of δέ for *waw* marks a shift in the narrative. G continues with the third-person singular, that is, with the Lord as subject, representing וידכאו ("they are crushed"), third plural passive, with the third singular active, ἔσβεσεν ("he [the Lord] extinguished"). Beer 1897, 218, followed by Dhorme 1967, 521, thinks that σβέννυμι renders דעך ("be extinguished"), since the former translates the latter at 18.5, 6; 21.17.

This need not be the case. HRCS mark four of the eight occurrences of σβέννυμι with † (4.10; 16.15; 34.26; 40.12), which indicates that G uses this verb freely with respect to the source text. At 4.10; 30.8; and 40.12, G uses it metaphorically, as in verse 26. It seems most likely to me that G has used σβέννυμι to render דכא ("crush"), a verb that is used in Job in parallel with בצע piel ("cut off," "destroy" [6.9]) and יגה hiphil ("torment") (19.2).

G passes over both תחת ("for," NRSV, but meaning uncertain) and ספקם ("he strikes them," NRSV). ספק means "slap, chastise" (BDB) and ספקם, in spite of being third-person singular, is not likely a candidate for the source of ἔσβεσεν. Finally, it should be noted that ἔσβεσεν means much the same as "he handed them over to darkness" at OG 24.14.

ὁρατοὶ δὲ ἐναντίον αὐτοῦ. This is G's paraphrase of ובמקום ראים, literally, "in a place of seeing ones," glossed as "while others look on" (NRSV). In the Hebrew God punishes the wicked while others look on. However, ὁρατοί ("visible") represents ראים ("seeing"), but understood in a passive sense, "seen"; its antecedent is ἀσεβεῖς ("[the] impious"). The word ὁρατοί recalls its obverse, ὁρατής ("one that views") (21a): the Lord "views, witnesses" while humans are "the viewed, the visible." Their misdeeds do not escape his observation. The phrase ἐναντίον αὐτοῦ seems to represent במקום ("in a place") but as seen strictly from the deity's point of view, "before him." In Iob everything takes place before the Lord. Nothing is hidden from his sight.

How ὁρατοὶ δὲ ἐναντίον αὐτοῦ is to be understood depends in part on how δέ is taken. Does it retain an adversative nuance? If so, then we can render this verbless clause as "but (they are) visible before him," that is, "but they remain visible," which may be taken to mean that the Lord "extinguished" the impious but, nevertheless, they remain visible before him in the realm of the dead—he is the Lord, after all, and even sees what lies in death, beyond our view. This understanding of the OG may be shared by LXX.D, which translates, "und sichtbar sind sie vor ihm" adding the copulative verb, present tense, "(they) are." Rather than "und" (LXX.D), δέ usually indicates some kind of slight shift, in this case between 26b and 26a. There is some type of contrast between the two lines: the impious are extinguished *but even then* do not escape from the Lord's examining eye; see Ps 138.8.

NETS 2006 rendered 26b with, "yes, they were in plain view before him." This understands 26b to have a connection with 21b–22. This connection need not require the past tense ("were") rather than the present ("are"), if 26b states a general truth, but the former intimates that their punishment followed the Lord's clear observation of the wrongdoings of the impious. This interpretation of 26b seems to be what we have in Brenton's "for they are seen before him," which carries both the notion of general truth and the Lord's observation of the behavior of the impious as the explicit reason ("for") why the Lord extinguished them.

The difficulty of making sense of verse 26b is apparent in the various textual corruptions that later took place. The O and L groups add "enemies" to the line and Lucianic witnesses L lII Arm add a verb, εγενοντο. The result is "but visible before enemies"; "and they became visible before their enemies"; and "but enemies visible before him." See Ziegler's apparatus. These corruptions represent early attempts at clarification.

34.27

וכל דרכיו לא השכילו || אשר על כן סרו מאחריו

ὅτι ἐξέκλιναν ἐκ νόμου θεοῦ,
δικαιώματα δὲ αὐτοῦ οὐκ ἐπέγνωσαν

because they turned aside from God's law
and his requirements they did not recognize.

ὅτι. G renders the phrase אשר על כן ("because") simply, with the causative ὅτι, a saving of two words.

ἐκ νόμου θεοῦ. This is a notable interpretation of מאחריו ("from after him"). For G to "turn aside from following him" means to turn aside "from God's law," that is, from the law of Moses, the benchmark of all wrongdoing in Hellenistic Judaism, G's audience. See the references to law in OG 8b, 17b, 18a, 20b, 22, 37. G makes clear the reason God "extinguished" the impious in the past (26a).

δικαιώματα ... οὐκ ἐπέγνωσαν. G uses δικαιώματα ("requirements," "ordinances," Brenton; "règles du droit" Cadell 1995, 220) to interpret כל דרכיו ("all his [the Lord's] ways"). The word δικαίωμα occurs only here in Iob, and only here in the LXX does it represent דרך ("way"). The lines are synonymously parallel as in the source text, so "his requirements" = "the requirements of God's law." G narrows the focus from the general in the source text ("from following him"; "his ways") to the specific in both lines of the translation. G uses ἐπιγινώσκω ("recognize" LSJ) to render שכל hiphil ("understand, comprehend" HALOT). This equivalence too is unique in the LXX. With it G clarifies the source text for readers. It was not that the impious failed to understand the law; rather, they refused to take it to heart.

[34.28–33]

28 [וצעקת עניים ישמע || להביא עליו צעקת דל
29 ויסתר פנים ומי ישורנו || והוא ישקט ומי ירשע
ועל גוי ועל אדם יחד
30 ממלך אדם חנף ממקשי עם
31 נשאתי לא אחבל || כי אל אל האמר
32 אם עול פעלתי לא אסיף || בלעדי אחזה אתה הרני
33 כי אתה תבחר ולא אני || המעמך ישלמנה כי מאסת
ומה ידעת דבר]

34.34–37: Conclusion

34.34

שמע ליוגבר חכם || אנשי לבב יאמרו לי

διὸ συνετοὶ καρδίας ἐροῦσιν ταῦτα,
ἀνὴρ δὲ σοφὸς ἀκήκοέν μου τὸ ῥῆμα.

So, the intelligent of heart will say these things,
and a wise man will have grasped what I said.

Pope characterizes the Hebrew text of verses 28–33 as "replete with difficulties" (1965, 259). G omits these verses—in the source text they continue
Elious's defense of God—and skips to the conclusion of Elious's speech,
neatly joining verse 34 to verse 27 with the addition of διό ("so"), thus
recalling the opening of Elious's address at verse 10, where διό (συνετοὶ
καρδίας) renders לכן ("therefore"). In verse 34 the OG looks back, whereas
the source text looks ahead, to verse 35.

συνετοὶ καρδίας ... ταῦτα. G repeats the translation made at verse 10: see
the discussion there. Though not explicitly stated either here or in verse
10, Elious is one of the "intelligent of heart." G replaces לי ("to me") with
"these things," that is, the things that Elious has said, thus changing entirely
the focus of the text.

ἀνὴρ ... μου τὸ ῥῆμα. G reads שמע as qal third-person masculine singular—
MT vocalizes it as a participle (שֹׁמֵעַ)—and represents it with the perfect
ἀκήκοεν, so NETS "will have grasped" (see Smyth §1950). This translation takes the reader back to what Elious has said to this point. Again לי

is replaced, with τὸ ῥῆμα μου ("what I said"), a parallel for ταῦτα ("these things"). Like "these things," τὸ ῥῆμα μου refers to what Elious has said about the Lord's justness and the impiety of a person who accuses the Lord of acting lawlessly (18). "A wise man" will have grasped the truth of Elious's remarks. If Iob is such a person, he will acquiesce.

34.35

ודבריו לא בהשכיל || איוב לא בדעת ידבר

Ἰὼβ δὲ οὐκ ἐν συνέσει ἐλάλησεν,
τὰ δὲ ῥήματα αὐτοῦ οὐκ ἐν ἐπιστήμη.

But Iob did not speak with intelligence,
and his words were without knowledge.

Ἰὼβ δὲ οὐκ ... ἐλάλησεν. G adds δέ ("but"). This little word sets up a contrast between what the "intelligent of heart" and "a wise man" would say (34)—represented by Elious—and what Iob has said. In the OG verse 35 is no longer a direct quotation of Job's remarks, as in the source text (see NRSV). Rather, it is Elious's negative assessment of what Iob has said.

G uses σύνεσις ("intelligence") to render דעת ("knowledge"), as at 15.2; 21.22; 33.3. Note the cognate adjective συνετοί at verse 34: Iob is doubly unintelligent for he neither belongs to the group of the intelligent nor does he speak with intelligence! G either reads ידבר as a preterit or deliberately chooses the aorist for the imperfective aspect, so that ἐλάλησεν ("did [not] speak") looks back to Iob's speeches.

ἐν ἐπιστήμη. G follows the source text in rendering 35b as a verbless clause. NETS supplies "were"; the NRSV supplies "are." G represents השכיל, the hiphil infinitive construct of שכל, so "insight, cleverness" (HALOT), with the noun ἐπιστήμη ("knowledge") a synonym of σύνεσις (35a). It is the Lord who teaches σύνεσιν καὶ ἐπιστήμην ("understanding and knowledge") (21.22). According to Elious, Iob does not possess such knowledge.

34.36–37

36 על תשבת באנשי און || אבי יבחן איוב עד נצח
37 || יספוק בינינו || עשף כי יסיף על חטאתו
וירב אמריו לאל

36   οὐ μὴν δὲ ἀλλὰ μάθε, Ἰώβ,
μὴ δῷς ἔτι ἀνταπόκρισιν ὥσπερ οἱ ἄφρονες,
37   ἵνα μὴ προσθῶμεν ἐφ᾽ ἁμαρτίαις ἡμῶν,
ἀνομία δὲ ἐφ᾽ ἡμῖν λογισθήσεται
πολλὰ λαλούντων ῥήματα ἐναντίον κυρίου.

36   Nonetheless, learn O Iob!
No longer give a response as fools do,
37   lest we add to our sins
and lawlessness be reckoned against us,
while speaking many words before the Lord."

G makes major changes to the content of the source text. Rather than speaking of Job in the third-person, Elious admonishes Iob directly, maintaining the focus on the interaction between the two of them. At the same time, G has Elious include the other friends as possible objects of divine displeasure, given Iob's determination to speak as a fool.

οὐ ... Ἰώβ. G replaces the wish אבי יבחן איוב ("would that Job were tried [or tested]") in the parent text with μάθε Ἰώβ ("learn, O Iob"), an imperative and a vocative of address. Has G interpreted the source text to mean that Job should learn from his testing? No, presumably the point is that Iob is to learn from Elious.

Dhorme conjectures that οὐ μὴν δὲ ἀλλά ("nonetheless") indicates the parent text had אבל (1967, 527), which means "but, however" in later books like Daniel; it does not, however, occur in Job. G likes the heavy collocation of particles οὐ μὴν δὲ ἀλλά and adds it to the text of Iob several times (12.6a; 21.17a; 27.7a; see 2.5). Dhorme weakens an already weak case by supposing that G read בין ("understand") instead of יבחן (1967, 527). What about the omission of עד נצח ("to the limit") and G's treatment of verse 36b in the source text? Contra Dhorme, G is recasting the text, as is often the case.

μὴ δῷς ἔτι ἀνταπόκρισιν. G changes the subordinate clause of the source text, על תשבת, into a prohibition addressed to Iob, a parallel for 36a but in the negative. This is another example of G's use of the stylistic device called "converse translation"; see verse 21. With the addition of ἔτι, G has Elious accuse Iob of speaking like a fool up until now. Dhorme (1967, 527) suggests that G read אל תשיב ("do not answer" see HALOT, s.v. "שוב," hiphil 5.) rather than עַל תְּשֻׁבֹת (literally "against the answers," i.e., "because he responds," *HALOT* s.v. "תְּשׁוּבָה"); and this makes sense: the two look and sound similar. The suggestion does not require that the source text had such a reading.

G uses the compound verb δίδωμι ἀνταπόκρισιν ("give an answer"; see LSJ, s.v. "δίδωμι" I.5) to represent the elliptical (דְּבָר) תָּשִׁיב, as at 13.22. *What* was Iob responding to? Elious likely has in mind the traditional teaching about suffering as espoused by the friends.

ὥσπερ οἱ ἄφρονες. Gerleman notes that a few Hebrew manuscripts have the particle -כְּ instead of the prepostion (בְּ)אַנְשֵׁי אָוֶן ("among [people of iniquity]"; *BHS*ᵃᵖᵖ). G may be following such a witness, but one cannot be certain. The phrase οἱ ἄφρονες ("the fools") is an interpretation of אַנְשֵׁי אָוֶן suitable for the context: "the fools" is the opposite of the σοφοί ("wise") (v. 2) and συνετοὶ καρδίας ("wise of heart") (vv. 10, 34). G used τὰ ἄνομα ("lawless acts") for אָוֶן ("evil") at verses 8, 22 (cf. NRSV), but in 36b the translation must relate to G's μάθε ("learn") in the previous line.

ἵνα μὴ προσθῶμεν ἐφ' ἁμαρτίαις ἡμῶν. In verse 37 G continues with Elious's direct speech to Iob, changing the meaning completely, as Dhorme notes (1967, 528). G disregards כִּי ("for"), which, in the source text, subordinates verse 37 to 36b. Since in 36 Elious addresses Iob in the second-person, we might expect G to change the third-person of the parent text to second again but, no, in 37 Elious speaks in the first-person plural, "we … *our* … *us*." G may have made this adjustment on the basis of בֵּינֵינוּ ("among *us*"). G uses προστίθημι to render יסף *hiphil* as generally in Iob (e.g., 20.9; 27.1) and elsewhere in the LXX.

The OG is ambiguous: By "we," does G mean Elious and Iob, or does G intend to include all five of the disputants? It seems likely that "we … our" includes all of them, but surely Elious is speaking diplomatically or, more accurately, tongue-in-cheek because it is not the understanding of Elious and the three friends that is on trial. In their view, it is only Iob who is a sinner; only Iob is guilty of lawlessness.

ἀνομία δὲ ἐφ' ἡμῖν λογισθήσεται. G (and Pesh) reads פֶּשַׁע ("rebellion," NRSV) with verse 37b. This sets in motion dramatic changes to the reading of the source text. The word ἀνομία renders פֶּשַׁע, as at 7.21; 8.4; 13.23 (probably); 14.17. In Iob transgression is lawlessness; in fact, all wrongdoing qualifies as lawlessness.

G seems to read ספוקי as ספק V ("abound, be abundant; multiply," *DCH*; see the by-form שפק II in *HALOT*). It may be that G intends an echo of 31.28 with the choice of λογίζομαι. There Iob says, if he has been guilty of narcissism, ἀνομία ἡ μεγίστη λογισθείη ("may (this too) be reckoned to me as the greatest lawlessness"). These are the only two occurrences of λογίζομαι in Iob. This verb and its cognates belong to the world of financial services, accounting and such like. Elious warns Iob about continuing along the course he has taken so far, a foolish choice (36).

G represents בינינו ("among us") with ἐφ᾽ ἡμῖν ("against us"). This understanding of the preposition –ב in the source text is almost required following the use of λογίζομαι. "Against us" may be facetious but, at the same time, Elious is pressuring Iob with a caution that Iob's "position" may adversely affect all of them. If this suggestion is correct, the OG is a free translation of יספוק that recalls an earlier passage.

πολλὰ λαλούντων ῥήματα. G paraphrases verse 37cα with this circumstantial participle and its direct object πολλὰ ῥήματα ("many words"). Notably the OG includes "us" among the too talkative; compare the source text ירב אמריו ("he [Job] multiplies *his* words"). The offense takes place *in the course of* or *while* speaking too many words (Smyth §2070): see, for example, verse 18. Elious's point seems to be that too much talk can result in careless talk (see 6.4). In wisdom literature proper speech occupies an important place.

ἐναντίον τοῦ κυρίου. G uses this phrase to represent לאל ("toward God"), usually understood in a hostile sense, "against God" (BDB s.v. "ל"1.d; so NRSV and NJPS; JB: "heaping abuse on God"). The same translation of the preposition ל is used at 8.4. κύριος renders אל, as throughout Iob. The OG can be rendered the same as the source text, so "against the Lord" (9.4; 15.25, 26), but this seems the less likely because the friends have not, in Elious's view, been speaking in opposition to the Lord.

Summary

G's treatment of chapter 34 is remarkable for the extent of the editing of the parent text by abbreviation, intratextual replacements, interpretation, and basic changes of meaning. These characteristics of its treatment by G mean that the summary for 34 is far more extensive than is usually true in the commentary. As translation, OG Iob reflects a flexible approach (see

Fox 2005, 95–96) to the source text in verse after verse. The result of G's work is a seamless whole that reflects an over-all approach to the speech, intended to keep the focus on Elious and Iob.

The source text is abbreviated by omitting verses 3–4, 6b–7—both pieces because their subject matter differs from the context; 18b, 23a, 25b and, in their entirety, verses 28–33. In fact, the situation is more complicated than the asterisk tradition indicates: G joins 6bβ to 8, so not all of 6b is omitted; the two lines of 11 are collapsed into one (Origen marked 11b with an asterisk); G replaces verse 23 with a one-line restatement of 21. G's abbreviation represents 32 percent of the source text, more than that of chapter 33 (19 percent), but less than that of chapters 36–37 (49 percent).

On the other hand, there are many small additions, often only a word, that consistently change the meaning and direction of the source text. Here is a list: + ἕκαστος (v. 11a) makes explicit the application to Iob; + οἴη (v. 12a) is a rhetorical device that directs the question to Iob; + γάρ makes verses 14–15 examples of the Lord's sustaining; + πᾶς (v. 15a) emphasizes inclusivity; + ὅθεν καὶ ἐπλάσθη (v. 15b) provides an allusion to the creation story in Genesis (3.19); + μή (v. 16a) changes the clause from a protasis to a caution; + ἰδὲ σύ (v. 17a), another rhetorical device, solicits Iob's attention; + τοὺς πονηρούς (v. 17b) provides a parallel for "lawless acts" (v. 17a); + οἶδεν ("[nor] knows") (19b) introduces the idea of ignorance; + γάρ (v. 20b) makes verse 20b the cause of the assertion in 20a; + διό turns verse 34 into a conclusion whereas the source text looks ahead; + ὅτι (v. 36b) limits the chiding of Iob to what he has said so far; Iob can change. Perhaps here is the place to mention the use of ἤ ("or") in place of "and" or "but" at verses 8b and 12b so that each verse in the OG sets forth alternatives.

G replaces a translation of the parent text at verses 23 and 24: G omits all of 23 and, as just noted, puts in its place a summary of 21 to introduce what follows; G replaces a translation of verse 24b with the OG of 9.10b and models verses 24–25 on the participial constructions in 9.5–10. G rewrites the content of verse 17 almost entirely.

Elious's speech is interpreted by G. Nowhere is this clearer than in verse 27a, where the impious like Iob are said to be guilty of turning aside from "God's law," the law of Moses. But there are numerous other examples of G's placing an interpretation upon the source text. In verse 6a it is not now a question of Iob being "counted a liar" (NRSV) but of the Lord who has lied to Iob; OG 10bc refers to Elious, not the Lord; verse 11a now contains Elious's contradiction of Iob's claim; verse 13 refers to creation, past *and* present; G brings divine displeasure to bear on Iob in verse 16a;

verse 19a and 19bc now appear to refer to Elious and the three friends, respectively; verse 20a is a clever interpretation that understands Iob as one of the impious.

G smoothens the text for the target readers by continuing rather than changing persons of verbs or by making such changes to suit an understanding placed upon the text as a whole: third-person to first (v. 8); third singular to second (v. 9a); third plural to third singular (v. 25bβ); third singular to first plural (v. 37a). G divides the source text differently than *BHS*: see 17 || 18; 37a || 37b.

G's treatment of verses 34–37 is especially notable. The addition of διό turns verse 34 into a retrospective conclusion and nicely attaches verse 37 to 27. G then makes verse 35 into Elious's own assessment of what Iob has said so far rather than that of "the wise" in the source text (34). Next, verse 36 is changed into a direct address to Iob; in the same verse "people of iniquity" is interpreted as "fools." Finally, G has verse 37 continue Elious's direct address to Iob. All this strikes the reader as the work of a skillful editor, who comes to the text with an understanding of what the text *should* say for its audience.

There are several examples of Hebraisms and neologisms in chapter 34; for example, μετὰ ποιούντων τὰ ἄνομα (v. 8b = MT 8a; 22); πᾶσα σάρξ (v. 15a); οὐκ ἐπαισχύνθη (v. 19a); θαυμασθῆναι πρόσωπα (v. 19c). While introducing a strangeness of expression for readers of good Greek, this same strangeness preserves a certain familiarity for Semitic readers who knew the LXX generally and the phraseology of its underlying source language.

God, Judges, Snakes, and Sinners:
A Commentary on the Old Greek Text
of Psalm 57 (MT 58)

Jannes Smith

Literature

♦ **Ausloos**, Hans. 2006. "למנצח in the Psalm Headings and Its Equivalent in LXX." Pages 131–39 in *XII Congress of the International Organization for Septuagint and Cognate Studies: Leiden 2004*. Edited by Melvin K. H. Peters. SCS 54. Atlanta: Society of Biblical Literature. ♦ **Austermann**, Frank. 2003. *Von der Tora zum Nomos: Untersuchungen zur Übersetzungsweise und Interpretation im Septuaginta-Psalter*. MSU 27. Göttingen: Vandenhoeck & Ruprecht. ♦ **Barthélemy**, Dominique. 2005. *Critique textuelle de l'Ancien Testament*. OBO 50/4. Fribourg: Presses Universitaires; Göttingen: Vandenhoeck & Ruprecht. ♦ **Cox**, Claude. 1981. "Εἰσακούω and Ἐπακούω in the Greek Psalter." *Bib* 62:251–58. ♦ **Dahood**, Mitchell. 1955. "The Etymology of *Malta'ôt* (Ps 58,7)." *CBQ* 17:300–303. ♦ **Dahood**. 1968. *Psalms II*. AB 17. Garden City, NY: Doubleday. ♦ **Day**, John N. 2002. "The Imprecatory Psalms and Christian Ethics." *BSac* 159:166–86; ♦ **Field**, Frederick. 1964. *Origenis Hexaplorum quae supersunt*. Hildesheim: Olms. · **Flashar**, Martin. 1912. "Exegetische Studien zum Septuagintapsalter." *ZAW* 32:81–116, 161–89, 241–68. ♦ **Goldingay**, John. 2007. *Psalms, Volume 2: Psalms 42–89*. BCOTWP. Grand Rapids: Baker Academic. ♦ **Hartley**, Vivian. 2001. *The Psalter According to the Seventy*. Westport, ON: WORDSmith. ♦ **Hossfeld**, Frank Lothar, and Erich **Zenger**. 2005. *Psalms 2: A Commentary on Psalms 51–100*. Translated by Linda M. Maloney. Hermeneia. Minneapolis: Fortress. ♦ **Kasser**, Rodolphe, and Michel **Testuz**, eds. 1967. *Papyrus Bodmer XXIV: Psaumes*

XVII–CXVIII. Geneva: Bibliotheca Bodmeriana. ◆ **Kraus**, Hans-Joachim.
1972. *Psalmen.* BKAT 15. Neukirchener-Vluyn: Neukirchener Verlag.
◆ **Mozley**, F. 1905. *The Psalter of the Church: The Septuagint Psalms Com-
pared with the Hebrew, with Various Notes.* London: Cambridge University
Press. ◆ **Munnich**, Olivier. 1983. "La Septante des Psaumes et le Groupe
Kaige." *VT* 33:75–89. ◆ **Olofsson**, Staffan. 1997. "The Kaige Group and the
Septuagint Book of Psalms." Pages 189–230 in *IX Congress of the Interna-
tional Organization for Septuagint and Cognate Studies: Cambridge, 1995.*
Edited by Bernard A. Taylor. SCS 45. Atlanta: Scholars Press. ◆ **Olofsson**.
2001. "Law and Lawbreaking in the LXX Psalms: A Case of Theologi-
cal Exegesis." Pages 291–330 in *Der Septuaginta-Psalter: Sprachliche und
theologische Aspekte.* Edited by Erich Zenger. HBS 32. Freiburg: Herder.
◆ **Pietersma**, Albert. 1980. "David in the Greek Psalms." *VT* 30:213–26.
◆ **Pietersma**. 1990. "Ra 2110 (P. Bodmer XXIV) and the Text of the Greek
Psalter." Pages 262–86 in *Studien zur Septuaginta Robert Hanhart zu
Ehren.* Edited by Detlef Fränkel, Udo Quast, and John W. Wevers. MSU
20. Göttingen: Vandenhoeck & Ruprecht. ◆ **Pietersma**. 2001. "Exegesis
and Liturgy in the Superscripts of the Greek Psalter." Pages 99–138 in
*X Congress of the International Organization for Septuagint and Cognate
Studies: Oslo 1998.* Edited by Bernard A. Taylor. SCS 51. Atlanta: Scholars Press. ◆ **Pietersma**. 2008. "Translating a Translation, with Examples
from the Greek Psalter." Pages 169–82 in *Translating a Translation: The
LXX and Its Modern Translations in the Context of Early Judaism.* Edited
by Hans Ausloos, J. Cook, F. García Martínez, B. Lemmelijn, and M.
Vervenne. BETL 213. Leuven: Peeters. ◆ **Pietersma**. 2010. "A Commentary on Psalm 15 in Greek: Text-Production and Text-Reception." Pages
523–42 in *Die Septuaginta: Texte Theologien, Einflüsse.* Edited by Wolf-
gang Kraus and Martin Karrer. WUNT 252. Tübingen: Mohr Siebeck.
◆ **Ridderbos**, Jan. 1958. *De Psalmen: 2, Psalm 42–106.* COut. Kampen:
Kok. ◆ **Rösel**, Martin. 2001. "Die Psalmüberschriften des Septuaginta-
Psalters." Pages 125–48 in *Der Septuaginta-Psalter: Sprachliche und
theologische Aspekte.* Edited by Erich Zenger. HBS 32. Freiburg: Herder.
◆ **Tate**, Marvin E. 1990. *Psalms 51–100.* WBC 20. Waco, TX: Word.
◆ **Venetz**, Hermann-J. 1974. *Die Quinta des Psalteriums: Ein Beitrag zur
Septuaginta- und Hexaplaforschung.* Collection Massorah. Hildesheim:
Gerstenberg. ◆ **Wesselschmidt**, Quentin F. 2007. *Psalms 51–150.* ACCS
8. Downers Grove, IL: InterVarsity Press.

Outline

Humans are asked whether they speak uprightly, in light of evidence to the contrary (2–3). Sinners are aliens and liars (4), unable and unwilling to listen (5–6). But divine vengeance has disarmed them (7, 9b) so that, weakened before God's bow, they disappear like ebbing water (8) and melting wax (9a). The righteous will prosper (11). Therefore God exists (12).

Commentary

57.1

למנצח אל תשחת לדוד מכתם

Εἰς τὸ τέλος· μὴ διαφθείρῃς· τῷ Δαυιδ εἰς στηλογραφίαν.

Regarding completion. Do Not Destroy. Pertaining to Dauid. For a stele inscription.

Εἰς τὸ τέλος. The placement of למנצח at the start of a superscription, as well as its association with supervision of temple activities in Ezra and Chronicles, suggest the translation "to the leader." G, however, associated consonantal למנצח with לנצח ("forever"). If τέλος means "end, outcome, completion," and εἰς τέλος "in the end, in the long run" (LSJ), then one might be led to suppose that εἰς τὸ τέλος refers to a specified end, but of what is not clear, nor will it have been of concern to the translator. G consistently wrote εἰς τέλος for לנצח (14x), and εἰς τὸ τέλος for למנצח (55x, all in superscriptions). Hence the מ morpheme appears to have triggered the Greek article. One might wonder whether G read למנצח as למו נצח; לְמֹו, a fuller form of the inseparable preposition לְ, does not occur in Psalms, so one cannot check how G handled this item elsewhere (unlike לָמֹו which G readily recognized as alternative for לָהֶם ["for them"]). By analogy, בְּמֹו (11[10].2) and כְּמֹו (29[28].6; 58[57].5, 8, 9, 10; 61[60].7, etc.) do occur in the Psalter, and G recognized them as alternatives for בְּ and כְּ respectively, but did not mark them as such by articulating the objects of their Greek equivalents. One suspects, then, that G read למנצח and produced what Flashar called a *Verlegenheitsübersetzung* (1912, 94), writing τέλος for נצח, εἰς for לְ, and τό to account quantitatively for the מ morpheme. If so, G's equivalent reflects an item-for-item modus operandi rather than, for example, an eschatological interpretation of the psalm (contra Rösel 2001, 138; for a full treatment see Ausloos 2006).

τῷ Δαυιδ. NRSV's vague "Of David" does not specify whether the Hebrew preposition indicates authorship ("by": e.g., Hab 3.1; Ezek 27.3; 30.3) or topic ("regarding": e.g., MT Jer 23.9; 46.2, 13; 48.1; 49.17, 23, 28). Had G wanted to express the former, he could have written τοῦ Δαυιδ, as did Aquila (Field 1964, 184). The genitive also appears in the transmission history of the Greek Psalter, but G consistently used the dative (so Pietersma, who argues that the six occurrences of τοῦ Δαυιδ in Rahlfs's text are secondary [1980, 213–26; 2001, 103–4]). Given that the dative's is his default rendering, its occurrence here need not imply that G had a specific episode from David's life in mind.

εἰς στηλογραφίαν. Like its Hebrew counterpart, στηλογραφία occurs only in the titles of six psalms (15, 55–59). The *Supplement* to LSJ cites what otherwise appears to be the oldest attestation of the word, in a Greek inscription (*IG* 9[2].13.4, 14a3) from the first century AD. One need not conclude, however, that G was the first to use the word, since the noun στηλογραφός ("inscriber") is known from an inscription dated to the fourth century BCE and the verb στηλογραφέω ("inscribe") from inscriptions of the third and second centuries BCE, and στηλογραφία is easily formed from these. More difficult to answer is the question why G so interpreted מכתם, the meaning of which was already unknown to Aquila and Symmachus and remains obscure to this day. Pietersma (2010, 524–25) has suggested that G's determination to translate a word he did not understand led him to construe כתם as כתב ("write"), hence γραφία ("writing"), to which he added στηλο- to account quantitatively for the preformative מ, on the analogy of εἰς τὸ τέλος for לנצח. Evidence for such "etymologizing" is not hard to find elsewhere in Psalms (e.g., ἐν τοῖς περιλοίποις σου for במיתריך in 20.13). One wonders, however, why G would opt for στηλο- to fill the slot. Since διαφθείρω is found in a Greek inscription (dated 175–171 BCE) with reference to "the 'breaking' of a stone—ἐάν τινα ὑγιῆ λίθον διαφθείρηι κατὰ τὴν ἐργασίαν ὁ τῆς θέσεως ἐργώνης" (MM, 157), one might speculate that G's interpretation of מכתם was informed by the adjacent "Do not destroy," which he may then have construed as a warning not to corrupt the text, or possibly not to break the stele on which he supposed it was once written. Such speculation yields little fruit, however, because it cannot be demonstrated that G *intended* μὴ διαφθείρῃς to be interpreted in such a manner, since διαφθείρω is his standard equivalent for שחת. Nor can such an interpretation explain the first occurrence of στηλογραφία, in the superscription of Ps 15, which lacks μὴ διαφθείρῃς.

57.2

האמנם אלם צדק תדברון || מישרים תשפטו בני אדם

Εἰ ἀληθῶς ἄρα δικαιοσύνην λαλεῖτε;
εὐθεῖα κρίνετε, οἱ υἱοὶ τῶν ἀνθρώπων;

Do you then truly speak righteousness?
Do you judge fairly, O sons of men?

Εἰ ἀληθῶς. G frequently handled the ה-interrogative contextually; where a question expects the answer "No," he wrote μή, whether or not the Hebrew had a corresponding negative particle (29.10; 49.13; 76.8; 77.19, 20; 84.6; 87.11, 12, 13; 93.20). The resulting nuance would have suited the current context rather well: "Surely you do not speak righteousness, (do you)?" Instead G opted for εἰ, leading all the daughter versions to translate the first clause as a protasis to the second. Hartley (2001, 99) has done the same ("If you truly speak righteousness, judge rightly, O you sons of Men"), and Hossfeld and Zenger (2005, 83), too, construe the Greek as a condition. It is not surprising that the Greek text should so be read in its reception history, but it is a mistake to suppose that G would have intended such a reading: Rahlfs supplied a note to clarify, first, that εἰ translates not the conditional particle אם, but the interrogative particle ה, and second, that κρίνετε is not imperative but indicative, since it translates a Hebrew *yiqtol*. Rahlfs ends the line with a question mark, thus assuming that εἰ can mark a direct question in Greek. A similar instance of εἰ to introduce a direct question is found in 72.11, there not for ה but for יֵשׁ: "Is there knowledge in the Most High?" (NETS). It is perhaps an extension of the use of εἰ to introduce indirect questions ("Tell me whether ..."; see Smyth §2671). Third Reigns 8.27 and its parallel, 2 Suppl 6.18, likewise have εἰ ἀληθῶς for האמנם. Like its Hebrew counterpart, ἀληθῶς occurs only here in the Psalter. G's default use of ἀλήθεια for אמונה (21x out of 22) likely triggered his choice of ἀληθῶς for האמנם here.

ἄρα ... οἱ υἱοι τῶν ἀνθρώπων. MT's אֵלֶם is generally associated with אלם I ("to be dumb," *HALOT*; hence Aquila's ἀλαλία), but how does one speak (תדברון) mutely? Commentators typically emend to אֵלִים ("gods") construed as a vocative and referring either to human judges (Ridderbos 1958, 2:126; Day 2002, 169–71) or to heavenly beings responsible for justice on earth (Goldingay 2007, 2:202–4). G's choice of inferential ἄρα (not to be

Smith

confused with interrogative ἆρα) suggests that he read אֻלָם ("on the other hand"). Both אֻלָם and ἆρα are grammatical particles which one would not expect to appear in an opening verse since they presuppose preceding discourse. If אלם is not a vocative, then to whom is the verse addressed? As a consequence of G's choice, בני אדם is the only candidate. The effect is to alter the profile of the psalm from a complaint against judicial authorities to a litany against humanity.

57.3

אף בלב עולת תפעלון || בארץ חמס ידיכם תפלסון

καὶ γὰρ ἐν καρδίᾳ ἀνομίας ἐργάζεσθε ἐν τῇ γῇ,
ἀδικίαν αἱ χεῖρες ὑμῶν συμπλέκουσιν.

Indeed, in the heart you devise acts of lawlessness on the earth;
injustice your hands braid.

καὶ γάρ. In the Hebrew psalm אף ("in fact") marks what follows as the answer to the question of verse 2; καὶ γάρ ("indeed") translates eight of twenty-three occurrences of אף and fourteen of thirty-five instances of גם ("also") in Psalms. Following a suggestion made by his teacher Barthélemy, Venetz (1974, 80–84) has touted the latter equation as evidence for recensional activity analogous to *kaige*, but unconvincingly (see Munnich 1983, 77–78; Olofsson 1997, 204). The phrase καὶ γάρ had become a formula well before the LXX was produced, attested, for example, in Xenophon (Smyth, §2813–15).

ἀνομίας. G's use of ἀνομία ("lawlessness") to translate a variety of words for sinful activity (עולה, עון, בליעל, זמה, רשע, and שקר) levels the diversity of the Hebrew and more generally reflects the prevalence of νομ- (law-related) words in the Greek Psalter (for which see especially Olofsson 2001; Austermann 2003). A number of manuscripts have the singular ἀνομίαν, doubtless a secondary adjustment (since one would not expect a plural abstract "lawlessnesses"). The plural matches the Hebrew and may be read as distributive (so NETS). According to Hossfeld and Zenger the Greek "emphasizes not so much the voluntary acts of the heart as the active doing of lawlessness" (2005, 83). But since G uses his standard equivalent, such an argument cannot be made for the text-as-produced.

ἀδικίαν αἱ χεῖρες ὑμῶν συμπλέκουσιν. MT points חמס as construct and תפלסון as second-person masculine plural: "you clear a way for the violence of your hands." But G read חמס as absolute and construed the verb as third-person feminine plural (i.e., תְּפַלֵּסְן, according to Mozley 1905, 95), with ידיכם as subject. That G understood the meaning of the Hebrew verb is clear from his choice of ὁδοποιέω in 77.50: "He made a path for his wrath." But here, needing an activity of the hands, he opted for συμπλέκω ("twist together, braid"), which occurs only here in the Psalter (cf. περιπλέκω in 49.19; 118.61). Its metaphorical sense is also attested in nontranslation Greek literature (LSJ). By construing ידיכם as subject rather than object, and the verb as third-person rather than second-person plural, G stopped short of producing a Greek idiom for intimacy (συμπλέκω τινὶ τὰς χεῖρας ["join hands with someone"]), and instead conceived injustice as a handicraft.

57.4

זרו רשעים מרחם ‖ תעו מבטן דברי כזב

ἀπηλλοτριώθησαν οἱ ἁμαρτωλοὶ ἀπὸ μήτρας,
ἐπλανήθησαν ἀπὸ γαστρός, ἐλάλησαν ψεύδη.

Sinners were estranged from the womb;
they erred from the belly; they spoke lies.

ἀπηλλοτριώθησαν ... ἀπὸ μήτρας. The passive voice may indicate that G read the niphal (נזרו, by dittography of preceding נ) rather than the qal (MT) of זור. To the Greek reader the passive verbal phrase ἀπηλλοτριώθησαν ἀπό might suggest (surgical) removal from the womb (if ἀπό were construed spatially; see LSJ), or abandonment since birth (if ἀπό were understood temporally). It is unlikely that G intended either interpretation, however, since the semantic component which ἀπαλλοτριόω shares with זור is that of estrangement or alienation, with a nuance of hostility.

ἐλάλησαν ψεύδη. MT has two parallel clauses, but, reading דברו rather than MT's דברי, G produced a third indicative clause. As Rahlfs notes, ψεύδη ("lies") could be accented as the neuter plural form of either the adjective ψευδής (ψευδῆ) or the noun ψεῦδος (ψεύδη). Both the adjective and the noun in Psalms as equivalents for כזב ("falsehood, lies").

57.5–6

חמת למו כדמות חמת נחש ‖ כמו פתן חרש יאטם אזנו
אשר לא ישמע לקול מלחשים ‖ חובר חברים מחכם

θυμὸς αὐτοῖς κατὰ τὴν ὁμοίωσιν τοῦ ὄφεως,
ὡσεὶ ἀσπίδος κωφῆς καὶ βυούσης τὰ ὦτα αὐτῆς,
ἥτις οὐκ εἰσακούσεται φωνὴν ἐπᾳδόντων
φαρμάκου τε φαρμακευομένου παρὰ σοφοῦ.

They have wrath in the likeness of the snake,
like an adder, deaf and plugging its ears,
which will not listen to a voice of enchanters,
nor of a charm being administered by a wise man.

θυμός. Hebrew חמה can mean either "heat," or "poison, venom" of animals,
or "wrath." In 139.4 G opted for "venom" in the phrase ἰὸς ἀσπίδων ("venom
of vipers"), aided no doubt by the accompanying phrase "under their lips."
Here one might have expected him to do the same, but he opted for the
meaning "wrath" and chose θυμός, perhaps because it refers in the first
instance to the sinners (αὐτοῖς). G was not the first to make such a choice.
A similar passage in Deut 32.33 has θυμός twice, once for חמה ("venom")
and once for ראש ("poison"): "their wine is the wrath of dragons, and the
wrath of asps beyond cure" (NETS). MT's חמת 2° is not represented in
LXX, due perhaps to haplography of ‑מת.

κωφῆς καὶ βυούσης. In the Hebrew the wicked are compared to "the deaf
adder that stops its ear." If one presumes that his *Vorlage* was consonantally identical to MT, G may have inserted καί to clarify that a comparison
is being made to a snake that is not only unable (κωφῆς) but also unwilling (βυούσης τὰ ὦτα αὐτῆς) to hear. Certainly verse 6 suggests unwilling-
ness, since G opted for εἰσακούω, which has the nuance of heeding and
responding to what is heard (L&N §24.60; Cox 1981, 251–58). A simpler
explanation, however, is that G was operating from a parent text slightly
different from MT: reading ואטם in place of יאטם and construing it as a
participle functioning as an additional attributive adjective, he wrote καὶ
βυούσης.

τὰ ὦτα αὐτῆς. G opted for the plural despite the singular of the Hebrew. In
fact only here out of twenty-two occurrences of אזן did he deviate from the

number of the source text, possibly because of the indirect plural referent with which the verse begins.

φαρμάκου τε φαρμακευομένου παρὰ σοφοῦ. G understood the Hebrew phrase to function as an additional genitive of קוֹל and thus cast it as a genitive, inserting τε to mark it as coordinate to ἐπᾳδόντων. However, where MT has a *pual* participle ("skilled, expert"), G read מחכם as a מִן prepositional phrase, מֵחָכָם, and wrote παρὰ σοφοῦ ("by a wise man"). Reading חֶבֶר ("charm") for MT's חוֹבֵר ("enchanter"), he opted for φαρμάκου. Then, at pains to preserve the repetition of the Hebrew, and needing a passive verbal form for its agent παρὰ σοφοῦ, he turned חברים into φαρμακευομένου.

57.7

אלהים הרס שנימו בפימו מלתעות כפירים נתץ יהוה

ὁ θεὸς συνέτριψεν τοὺς ὀδόντας αὐτῶν ἐν τῷ στόματι αὐτῶν,
τὰς μύλας τῶν λεόντων συνέθλασεν κύριος.

God crushed their teeth in their mouth;
the molars of lions the Lord shattered!

ὁ θεὸς συνέτριψεν ... συνέθλασεν κύριος. In MT verse 7 begins a modal sequence that extends at least to the end of verse 9 and possibly to the end of the psalm. The vocatives אלהים and יהוה are, however, unmarked, and the imperatives are consonantally indistinguishable from perfects. G therefore stayed in the indicative, invariably using aorists for what he read as perfects, and futures for what he read as imperfects. The effect is to recast the divine response from a plea for action to reported action. Aquila, however, has the imperative: ἐκρίζωσον, κύριε ("Root out, Lord"; Field 1964, 185). G handled הרס ("break down, destroy") contextually, using καθαιρέω ("take down") in 10.3 and 27.5, but συντρίβω ("crush"—more appropriate for removing teeth) here. The verb συντρίβω is his default equivalent for the Hebrew שבר ("break") and translates הרס only here in Psalms. The result is a Greek text identical to 3.8: ὀδόντας ἁμαρτωλῶν συνέτριψας ("the teeth of sinners you shattered"). G uses συνθλάω ("shatter") to translate נתץ ("tear down, smash") only here in Psalms; he used καθαιρέω in 51.7 and again for its by-form נתש in 9.7.

τοὺς ὀδόντας αὐτῶν ... τὰς μύλας τῶν λεόντων. Hebrew כְּפִיר refers specifically to the young lion able to hunt food for himself and distinguishable
by his mane (HALOT). In 16.12 (of young lions in hiding) and 103.21
(of dependent young lions) G translated it with σκύμνος ("whelp"), but
here, as in 34.17 and 90.13, he opted for the general label λέων. Hebrew
מַלְתְּעוֹת refers properly to the jawbone (HALOT), though Dahood suggested "fangs" (1955, 300–303). Here, perhaps guessing its meaning from
the parallel ὀδόντας ("teeth"), G chose μύλας ("molars"), which also shares
the first two consonants of its Hebrew counterpart. The semantic distinction between the two Greek nouns is clear from Pss. Sol. 13.3: "Evil wild
animals rushed upon them; with their teeth [ὀδοῦσιν] they tore their flesh,
and with their molars [μύλαις] they crushed their bones" (NETS). While
breaking their "fangs" (NRSV) would render lions unable to capture their
prey, crushing their molars would leave them unable to eat it; either way
they would soon perish of starvation.

57.8

ימאסו כמו מים יתהלכו למו || ידרך חצו כמו יתמללו

ἐξουδενωθήσονται ὡς ὕδωρ διαπορευόμενον·
ἐντενεῖ τὸ τόξον αὐτοῦ, ἕως οὗ ἀσθενήσουσιν.

They shall vanish like water that flows through;
he will bend his bow until they become weak.

ὡς ὕδωρ διαπορευόμενον. Evidently reading יתהלכו as a relative clause
(with gapped relative particle), G rendered it, aptly enough, with an
attributive participle. For similar examples in which gapped relative +
yiqtol is translated with a present participle functioning attributively,
see ἀθετῶν in 14.4; ἱστῶν in 17.34; ἐρχομενή in 21.31; συσσείοντος in 28.8;
καταρτιζομένου in 28.9; περιεχούσης in 31.7; διανεύοντες in 34.19; ἀνοίγων
in 37.14, passim. In 57.9 (below), however, G opted for an aorist participle (ταχείς).

ἐντενεῖ τὸ τόξον αὐτοῦ. The verb דרך can mean "to bend the bow by firmly
planting the foot in the middle of it" (HALOT), but in MT the arrow is
said to be trodden rather than the bow. Barthélemy (2005, 4:366) calls the
use of "arrow" for "bow" an example of catachresis (applying a term to an
object which it does not properly denote). G for his part solved the prob-

lem by supplying a bow: τόξον is his standard equivalent for קשת ("bow"), but here and in 63.3, it translates חץ ("arrow"). It is of some interest that LSJ's entry includes the meaning "bow and arrows" for the plural τόξα. G at any rate wrote the singular, presumably to mimic the singular of חצו (so MT's *ketiv*, but *qere* חציו). Both here and in 63.3 G opted for a Greek idiom: ἐντείνω τόξον ("bend the bow") is attested in Aeschylus, *Ag.* 364, and an Aeschylus fragment (*Frag.* 83; LSJ).

ἕως οὗ ἀσθενήσουσιν. Though it sometimes translates עד אשר (see 111.8), ἕως οὗ is not a Hebraism (it occurs, e.g., in Herodotus *Hist.* 2.143), and need not be taken to attest to a different *Vorlage* here. Still in interpretive mode, G chose ἕως ("until") for כמו ("as") as better suited to the imminent demise of the victims of God's bow (Mozley 1905, 98). The verb ἀσθενέω is G's default equivalent for כשל *qal* ("stumble") (9.4; 26.2; 30.11; 104.37; 106.12; 108.24; cf. ἐξασθενέω for כשל *hiphil* in 63.9). It similarly translates מעד ("slip") in 17.37 and 25.1, but more accurately stands for לאה ("be weary") in 67.10 and דאב ("become faint") in 87.10. Here it stands in for מלל ("wither"), which occurs twice elsewhere, in 36.2 and 89.6, both times of grass, and is appropriately translated as ἀποξηραίνω ("dry up") and σκληρύνω ("harden") respectively. Here the reference is to humans, so G opted for ἀσθενέω ("become weak, sick"), perhaps associating it with the adjective אמלל ("feeble"), which he translated as ἀσθενής in 6.3 (cf. Mozley 1905, 95). The sense of the Greek may be that the sinners grow faint at the sight of God's bow aimed at them.

57.9

כמו שבלול תמס יהלך || נפל אשת בל חזו שמש

ὡσεὶ κηρὸς ὁ τακεὶς ἀνταναιρεθήσονται·
ἐπέπεσε πῦρ, καὶ οὐκ εἶδον τὸν ἥλιον.

Like wax that melts they will be removed;
fire fell, and they did not see the sun.

ὡσεὶ κηρὸς ὁ τακείς. Hebrew שבלול means "snail," which makes its way in תמס ("slime"), used adverbially, hence "slimily," that is, with a slimy trail (GKC §118q). G, however, having read תמס as the *niphal* imperfect third-person feminine singular of מסס ("melt"), which he translated with τήκω ("melt"), guessed the meaning of שבלול from the subject of the other three occurrences of מסס in Psalms, namely, דונג ("wax") = κηρός (21.15; 67.3; 96.5). For ταχείς see verse 8 above.

ἀνταναιρεθήσονται. If the Hebrew metaphor is about a snail that dissolves as it goes (יהלך) (so Kraus 1972, 533; Tate 1990, 82), it is equally clear that the changes forced upon G demanded a new role for יהלך. Thus, since the figurative language in the preceding verses is about the "sinners," it makes sense that the verb in 9a be made to refer to them as well, the more so since 9b already has a plural verb in the source text. Twice in the LXX is ἀνταναιρέω paired with הלך, here and in 108.23.

ἐπέπεσε πῦρ. The Hebrew next compares the destiny of the wicked to that of נפל אשת ("a woman's stillborn child," i.e., they do not see the sun). But G read נפל as the homographic verb נפל ("fall"), and interpreted אשת as אֵשׁ ("fire"), guided perhaps by the melting wax of the first stich. The resulting Greek describes the fate of sinners as death by fire from above.

57.10

בטרם יבינו סירתיכם אטד || כמו חי כמו חרון ישערנו

πρὸ τοῦ συνεῖναι τὰς ἀκάνθας ὑμῶν τὴν ῥάμνον,
ὡσεὶ ζῶντας ὡσεὶ ἐν ὀργῇ καταιγιεῖταιᵇ ὑμᾶς.

ᵃBefore your thistles take note of the thorn-shrub, as if in anger it will bestormᵇ you, as if aliveᵃ.

ᵃ Greek uncertain; ᵇ καταπίεται ("devour") = Rahlfs

τὰς ἀκάνθας ὑμῶν. The Hebrew סירות can be the plural for either סיר ("cooking pot") or סירה ("thorn"); NRSV opted for the former, and G the latter. That G knew the meaning of סיר is clear from 59.10 = 107.10, where he translated it as λέβης ("cauldron"). Here the context gives little direction, unlike in Eccl 7.6: "the crackling of thorns [סירים] under the pot [סיר]" (NIV). The verb בין ("understand, sense") will not have helped to tip the balance either, since one would not readily attribute perception to either pots or thorns. The nearby occurrence of אטד ("bramble"), which G glossed as ῥάμνος ("thorn-shrub"), may well have triggered his choice for a similar plant, ἀκάνθα ("thorn"), which he otherwise reserved for קוץ ("thorn") (31.4 [cf. MT קיץ ("summer")]; 117.12). The Greek term is general (BDAG, MM), whereas Hebrew סירה refers specifically to the thorny burnet (*Poterium spinosum*; see *NIDOTTE* 3:246 and the literature cited there).

ὡσεὶ ζῶντας ὡσεὶ ἐν ὀργῇ. The meaning of the Hebrew is obscure, and G makes no effort to enlighten the reader but simply translates item for item. The preposition כ (here כמו) is often prefixed to both members of a comparison, which here would mean something like "alive and burning alike." Thus NRSV has "whether green or ablaze," referring evidently to the thorns heating the pots. G opted for ὡσεί ("as if"), which can also be used of comparisons to mean "like, just as" (LSJ). Unlike the Hebrew preposition, comparisons in nontranslational Greek do not repeat ὡσεί. Hence G's isomorphic approach has produced two comparisons. The Greek follows the word order of the Hebrew; ὡσεὶ ζῶντας precedes ὡσεὶ ἐν ὀργῇ, but NETS has reversed the order to reflect the fact that ζῶντας is cast as an accusative plural modifying ὑμᾶς.

καταιγιεῖται ὑμᾶς. Rahlfs has καταπίεται ὑμᾶς uncontested, which would be an odd translation choice given that it is G's default for בלע ("to swallow") and does not overlap with the semantic range of its Hebrew counterpart שער (also spelled סער) ("to storm"). Papyrus Bodmer XXIV (2110) has since provided the variant καταιγιεῖται (from καταιγίζω ["rush down like a storm"]; Kasser and Testuz 1967, 114, l. 22), which correlates with G's choice of the noun καταιγίς ("squall, hurricane") for the same Hebrew root in 49.3; 54.9; 82.16; 106.25, 29; and 148.8. Indeed, καταιγίς appears to have been something of a favorite for G: ten of its twenty-nine occurrences in LXX are found in Psalms, for a variety of Hebrew nouns. Pietersma has adopted this reading in NETS (see also Pietersma 1990, 266–67). Its subject is either πῦρ ("fire") from verse 9 (so NETS's "it," though one wonders whether G even thought that far), or God (i.e., "he"). NETS's barely intelligible translation deliberately reflects the fact that G was more interested in formal correspondence to the Hebrew than coherence in Greek. The sole antecedent for ὑμᾶς in the Greek psalm is the "sons of men" of verse 2. Since the Hebrew verb has a third-person singular suffix with energic *nun*, Mozley deems ὑμᾶς a Greek corruption for ἡμᾶς or αὐτούς (1905, 95), but the former lacks manuscript support and the latter has hexaplaric support, suggesting that it was a secondary correction toward the Hebrew. Hence either the *Vorlage* had a second-person plural suffix, or, if it was the same as MT, G adjusted the pronoun to clarify the antecedent (see Pietersma 2008, 174).

57.11–12

ישמח צדיק כי חזה נקם || פעמיו ירחץ בדם הרשע

ויאמר אדם אך פרי לצדיק || אך יש אלהים שפטים בארץ

εὐφρανθήσεται δίκαιος, ὅταν ἴδῃ ἐκδίκησιν ^{c}·
τὰς χεῖρας αὐτοῦ νίψεται ἐν τῷ αἵματι τοῦ ἁμαρτωλοῦ.
καὶ ἐρεῖ ἄνθρωπος Εἰ ἄρα ἔστιν καρπὸς τῷ δικαίῳ,
ἄρα ἐστὶν ὁ θεὸς κρίνων αὐτοὺς ἐν τῇ γῇ.

A righteous one will be glad when he sees vengeance done[c];
he will wash his hands in the blood of the sinner.
And a person will say, "If then there is a return for the righteous,
then God exists, judging them on the earth."

[c] + ἀσεβῶν ("to impious ones") = Rahlfs

ὅταν ἴδῃ ἐκδίκησιν. The Greek has a temporal clause referring indefi-
nitely to the future ("whenever that might be"), as it typically does when
G understood כי to introduce a temporal clause (2.12; 36.24; 48.10, 16,
19; 70.23, 24, 74.3; 101.1; 118.32, 171; 119.7; 126.5). Rahlfs has ἐκδίκησιν
ἀσεβῶν ("vengeance of [i.e., "for," an objective genitive] impious ones"),
judging the omission of ἀσεβῶν to be a hexaplaric adjustment toward the
Hebrew. But 2110 (not available to Rahlfs), an important witness to the
prehexaplaric text of the Psalter, also leaves it out, suggesting that its omission in agreement with the Hebrew is not hexaplaric but original.

τὰς χεῖρας αὐτοῦ νίψεται. G followed normal Greek usage of λούω for washing the body, νίπτω (earlier νίζω) for washing hands and feet, and πλύνω
for washing clothing. G predictably rendered פעם ("footstep, instance")
with διάβημα ("step") in 16.5; 84.14; 118.133; 139.5, and with πούς ("foot")
in 56.7. Here (and in 73.3) he opted for χείρ ("hand"), however, producing
Greek resembling that of 25.6 and 72.13 (νίπτομαι ἐν ἀθῴοις τὰς χεῖράς μου
["I wash my hands in innocence"]), though there the Hebrew noun is כף,
which unlike פעם can refer to either the sole or the palm. One wonders,
then, what might have prompted the shift from "feet" to "hands." To associate the shift with G's choice of ἐντείνω ("stretch") for דרך ("tread"; i.e.,
bending a bow with the hand rather than the foot) in verse 8 is scarcely
credible. It is possible that the *Vorlage* had כפיו ("his hands"), as at 25.6
and 72.13 (so *BHS*), though no Hebrew evidence for such a variant sur-

vives. The fact that 73.3 likewise has χείρ for פעם diminishes the like-lihood that the difference is due to the parent text. At 73.3 the choice may be contextual, that is, a more suitable object for the Hebrew impera-tive הרימה ("lift up"). Here context may likewise have played a role: the Hebrew image of wading in the blood of sinners suggests participating in (or at least enjoying) the vengeance carried out on them. G may have written "hands" in order to avoid such a distasteful notion (since ven-geance belongs to the Lord), suggesting that in the Greek the righteous disavows participation. On the basis of a Ugaritic parallel, Dahood (1968, 63) translates the Hebrew clause as "wash his hands *of* blood," but had G so interpreted it, he could have written ἀπὸ τῶν χειρῶν αὐτοῦ νίψεται τὸ αἷμα ("he will wash the blood from his hands"; see LSJ, s.v. "νίζω" II. "wash off"). Rather G may have understood the clause to mean washing one's hands (in the blood of the sinner) for the purpose of making them clean. That is to say, the bloody end of the sinner serves to cleanse the hands of the righteous one, perhaps by impelling him to avoid a similar fate. One in fact finds such an interpretation in the psalm's reception his-tory: "For hear the prophet saying, 'The righteous shall rejoice when he sees the vengeance on the ungodly; he shall wash his hands in the blood of the sinner.' Not rejoicing on account of it, God forbid, but fearing that he might suffer the same things, he will render his own life more pure" (Chrysostom, *Hom. Phlm.* 3, quoted in Wesselschmidt 2007, 36). At any rate, the resulting translation contrasts the hands of the righteous with the hands of sinners in verse 3.

Εἰ ἄρα ... ἄρα ἐστὶν ὁ θεός. The repetition of εἰ and ἄρα from verse 2 creates the illusion that G has produced an *inclusio* not present in the Hebrew psalm. But here the choice of inferential ἄρα ("then") for emphatic אך ("surely" [2x]) indicates that εἰ does not introduce a question. In fact, the occurrence of εἰ without formal warrant from the Hebrew suggests an interpretive move on the part of the translator. Perhaps he construed the second inference as deduced from the first ("then ... so then") and thus cast it as an apodosis to the first ("if ... then"). Of some interest is the inclusion of the article, making ὁ θεός the subject rather than the predicate of ἐστίν. That is to say, G did not write, "then there is a God" (cf. 13.1: οὐκ ἔστιν θεός "there is no God"), but "then God exists." The article with θεός is standard, doubtless to distinguish between Israel's God and any god, and thus its omission is noteworthy. The effect of the whole is that the return for the righteous proves God's existence. G cast the condition as real, in keeping

with the gladness of the righteous one in verse 11: if then there is a return
for the righteous (and there is), then God exists.

κρίνων αὐτούς. MT has a plural participle (שפטים ["judging"]) attributed to אלהים, an honorific with plural agreement. But G evidently read
שפטם, that is, singular participle with third masculine plural suffix, writing κρίνων αὐτούς ("judging them"). But who is "them"? The omission of
ἀσεβῶν ("impious ones") (above) leaves the pronoun without an explicit
antecedent, and the reader of NETS might be forgiven for thinking that it
refers to "the righteous," though mistakenly, since the latter is singular. G
simply rendered the pronominal suffix with its Greek equivalent, evidently
more concerned with formal equivalence than clarity of reference.

Summary

Whereas the Hebrew psalm is usually read as addressed to "gods," the Greek
addresses "sons of men." Further, G's translation of Hebrew imperatives
with Greek indicatives in verse 7 makes the psalm slightly less "imprecatory" than its *Vorlage*. Finally, standard equivalents at times have different
meanings than their Hebrew counterparts.

Appendix
Preamble to the Guidelines for the Contributors
to the SBL Commentary on the Septuagint

The objective of the Society of Biblical Literature Commentary on the Septuagint (SBLCS) is to elucidate the meaning of *the text-as-produced* in distinction from *the text-as-received*. Meaning, however, is neither to be presupposed nor to be superimposed from either the source text or the text-as-received (cf. Prospectus [2]). Inherent in this goal statement are four fundamental principles.

1.1. **The commentary is *genetic*, in the sense that it seeks to trace the translation *process* that results in the *product*, i.e., the so-called original text of the Old Greek** (cf. Prospectus [1]).

   1.1.1. The text-as-produced is conceptualized as a *dependent* entity, derived from its source text. That is to say, it is perceived to be *compositionally* dependent on its source, though not *semantically* dependent (see Prospectus [3]).

   1.1.2. The aim is to uncover the strategies and norms by means of which the text came into being. Therefore, the commentator will analyze the relationship between the target text and the source text, attempting to account for the *process* underlying the derivation of the Greek version from its Semitic parent. It is from this analysis that the commentator will formulate his or her principles of interpretation and procedural methodology.

1.2. **The primary focus of the commentary is the *verbal make-up* of the translation, understood in terms of *conventional* linguistic usage (i.e., the grammar and lexicon of the target language) rather than in terms of what may be encountered in translation Greek** (see Prospectus [5]).

1.2.1. The text-as-produced can be said to have semantic autonomy because it means what it means in terms of the grammar and lexicon of the Greek language at the time of the Septuagint's production.

1.2.2. The "reader" of the text-as-produced is conceptualized as the *prospective* or *implied* reader, a construct based on the text itself, in distinction from any reader, actual or hypothetical, exterior to the text. The prospective reader is to be inferred from those features of the text's make-up that are indicative of a specific linguistic, literary, or cultural aim (e.g., transcriptions and Hebraisms).

1.3. **The text-as-produced represents *a historical event* and should be described with reference to the relevant features of its historical context.**

1.3.1. The translation is to be viewed as a fact of the culture that produced it inasmuch as it is a specimen of discourse within that culture.

1.3.2. The verbal make-up of the translation should be understood in relation to the cultural system in which it was produced, that is to say, the sort of text it is as a Greek document.

1.3.3. Since unintelligibility is one of the inherent characteristics of the text-as-produced, it should not always be assumed to make sense (see §1.2.1 above).

1.4. **The text-as-produced is *the act of a historical agent*—the translator—and should be described with reference to the translator's intentions, to the extent that these are evident** (see Prospectus [4]).

1.4.1. The meaning of the text is best understood as encompassing both *what* the translator did and *why*.

1.4.2. The commentator's task thus includes the following: (a) to search out the intention of the translator insofar as this may be inferred from the transformation of the source text and the verbal make-up of the target text; (b) to describe the possibilities *deliberately* marked out by the language of the text (see §3.2.3.1 and 3.2.5.1 below).

1.4.3. It should not be presupposed in any given instance that the translator's primary intention was to produce an intelligible text.

Contributors

Cameron Boyd-Taylor
Trinity Western University

Dirk Büchner
Trinity Western University

Claude E. Cox
McMaster Divinity College

Robert J. V. Hiebert
Trinity Western Seminary/ACTS

Spencer A. Jones
Trinity Western University

Larry Perkins
Northwestern Baptist Seminary/ACTS

Albert Pietersma
University of Toronto, emeritus

Jannes Smith
Canadian Reformed Theological Seminary

CPSIA information can be obtained
at www.ICGtesting.com
Printed in the USA
BVOW08s2322031117
499518BV00001B/63/P